U.S.-Korean Relations from Liberation to Self-Reliance

U.S.-Korean Relations from Liberation to Self-Reliance

The Twenty-Year Record

Donald Stone Macdonald

An interpretative summary of the archives
of the U.S. Department of State
for the period 1945 to 1965

Westview Press

BOULDER • SAN FRANCISCO • OXFORD

Copyright © 1992 by Westview Press, Inc.

Published in 1992 in the United States of America by Westview Press, Inc., 5500 Central Avenue, Boulder, Colorado 80301-2847, and in the United Kingdom by Westview Press, 36 Lonsdale Road, Summertown, Oxford OX2 7EW

Library of Congress Cataloging-in-Publication Data
Macdonald, Donald Stone.
    U.S.-Korean relations from liberation to self-
reliance : the twenty-year record / Donald Stone Macdonald
        p.   cm.
    Includes bibliographical references and index.
    ISBN 0-8133-8193-2
    1. United States—Foreign relations—Korea.   2.
Korea—Foreign relations—United States.   3. United
States—Foreign relations—Korea (South).   4. Korea
(South)—Foreign relations—United States.   5. United
States—Foreign relations—1945-   .   6. United
States—Foreign relations—1961–1963.   I. Title.
II. Title: US-Korean relations from liberation to self-
reliance.
E183.8.K7M23   1992
327.730619—dc20   90-28786
                                                                              CIP

Printed and bound in the United States of America

The paper used in this publication meets the requirements
of the American National Standard for Permanence of Paper
for Printed Library Materials Z39.48-1984.

10   9   8   7   6   5   4   3   2   1

Contents

Preface

In recent years, relations between the United States and Korea, and U.S. policies toward Korea, have been extensively questioned and sometimes harshly criticized. Some of the criticism is justified, but much of it is based on ignorance or misunderstanding of the factual record. This book is intended as a modest contribution toward better understanding. It covers the critical twenty-year period from 1945, when a desperately poor Korea was liberated from Japanese colonial rule, to 1965, when south Korea's capacity for self-reliant rapid economic growth was internationally recognized.

The 1960s marked a major watershed in relations between the United States and Korea. Up to 1960, a powerful patron of varying generosity dealt with a dependent client of great poverty but rising expectations. The following year, 1961, saw both a new administration and a new philosophy of international relations in the United States, and a new and tough regime in Korea, determined to achieve self-reliance and economic progress.

By 1965, the economy of the Republic of Korea had passed the take-off stage and begun its amazingly rapid growth. The U.S.-Korean relationship became far more businesslike, far more hard-headed on both sides. A new breed of diplomats and administrators managed these relations in both countries, with less sentiment and talk of elder brother-younger brother obligation or anti-Communist solidarity, and more quid-pro-quo bargaining, in which diminishing U.S. military and economic assistance was conditioned on results.

The record of those twenty important years in the national life of Korea is an intrinsically interesting one. It challenges some of the simplistic theories about U.S. neo-colonialism and imperialism that are currently fashionable. It shows that U.S. policies were written with the long-range benefit of both countries in mind; but that short-run calculations often took precedence--some for mutual benefit and some for unilateral benefit of the United States.

Like most records of human events, this one falls considerably short of what a totally altruistic United States could have done for Korea. Moreover, it displays a truly inexcusable ignorance about Korea on the part of the United States at the start of the relationship. This said, however, it is arguable that as international relations go, those between the two countries show a considerable amount of faith and human concern on both sides--more, perhaps, than has been the norm in this troubled world.

The interaction of Korea and the United States in the formative years after World War II, chronicled in the pages that follow, still affect the relations of the present. It was to furnish a picture of the formative years, warts and all, for the guidance of Department of State officers who had not lived through the earlier period, that this study was commissioned. It was commenced in 1971 and completed in 1975. Its security classification (originally Secret) was removed in 1989, thus making its publication possible. The scope and method of the study are described in its original preface, which follows on page xv.

In revising the original manuscript for publication, modest changes in wording were made to improve readability; some portions were eliminated; and supplementary material of the original document, that either could not be declassified or had been lost, had to be excluded. The first and last original chapters (a summary and a collection of topics of lesser importance) were eliminated; the original chapters 5 (Korean-Japanese relations) and 6 (Korean international relations) were combined into a single international relations chapter (Chapter 4 of this volume); and the original chapters on political and economic matters were each divided into two sections for convenience in reference. Additionally, sections and paragraphs that dealt with materials already in the public domain, such as a discussion of Korean political parties that had very little connection with the larger questions of U.S. policy, were condensed or deleted. With these exceptions, the content of this book is the same as the original secret document.

The romanized spellings of Korean names in this edition are, as nearly as possible, those customarily used by the individuals themselves, except that family names appear first (except for President Syngman Rhee) and given names, usually of two syllables, are hyphenated with a capital initial letter for each syllable. (The original study frequently used the standard McCune-Reischauer spellings used by the Department of State for its biographic files.) I here offer my apology to those, living and dead, whose names may have been misspelled.

The qualifiers "north" and "south" used to identify the two halves of Korea have been deliberately spelled without capital letters throughout this book to highlight the fact that in the hearts of its people Korea remains a single nation, notwithstanding its division at the end of World War II.

The original endnote numbers in the text have been reproduced in this edition (with some renumbering to accommodate rearrangements of text). However, only the endnotes for the original preface and chapters 3 and 5 (Chapter 2 and part of Chapter 4 in the present work) were released by the Department of State. These are presented in the Notes at the back of the book to demonstrate the kind of research that underlies the entire work. Otherwise, the endnotes are largely a collection of numbers leading nowhere. They were retained because, if the remaining footnotes could be made available in future, they would provide detailed citations of many documents in the archives that have not been included in the annual *Foreign Relations of the United States* series. Inquiries concerning the declassification of Department of State documents dated since 1954 can be addressed to the Department's Office of Freedom of Information, Privacy, and Classification Review, Room 1512, Department of State, 2201 C Street, N.W., Washington, DC 20520-1512; for documents of earlier date, requests can be addressed to the National Archives.

Readers of this book need to bear in mind that it is not, and does not pretend to be, an inclusive or definitive analysis of Korean-U.S. relations. As the original preface pointed out, it is based exclusively on materials in the archives of the Department of State. A comprehensive study would take account of the records of the Executive Office of the President, the National Security Council, the Department of Defense, and the U.S. Army as well as the archives of Presidents Truman, Eisenhower, Kennedy, and Johnson, the archives of the Republic of Korea, memoirs of Korean and American political figures, press accounts, oral histories, and the works of individual scholars. The present work can at best serve as an additional and hopefully useful source of information on the evolution of U.S.-Korean relations.

In obtaining the original study and preparing it for publication, I have had invaluable assistance from Ms. Lynn Arts, Mr. James Bjork, Mr. Thomas H.P. Dunlop, Dr. Edward R. Griffin, Mr. Frank M. Machak, Ms. Donna Mazella, Ms. Connie Oehring, Mr. Amos Zubrow, and my wife, Jean; to all I give my deepest thanks.

Preface to the Original Study

The story of America's relationship with Korea is a strange one, with elements of contradiction and paradox that often make the record almost unbelievable. Yet the record is there--evidenced not only by many drawers full of government files, but by the memories of people still active who were observers and participants during the period of America's renewed interest, since World War II, in a nation it had previously charged off as not worthy of respect.

This survey is a modest effort to summarize the records, as contained in the classified archives of the Department of State, of U.S. relations with the Republic of Korea (and its antecedents) during the twenty-year postwar period from 1945 to 1965. The purpose is to provide a background on these relations that will be useful to American officials who deal with Korean affairs now and in the future.

Obviously, no short survey can be comprehensive and all-inclusive. An effort was therefore made to select trends and events that most directly affected broad American policies toward Korea, or were involved in a significant way with the successful or unsuccessful execution of policy, or significantly colored the American-Korean relationship.

This selectivity has required some significant omission and abbreviation. It seemed impractical, for example, to deal fully with the fascinating and often very detailed account of Korean political and economic evolution contained in the archives, or with the events of the Korean war. (For those who are interested in the war period, an excellent study by the Historical Office is available.[1]) The important topic of north Korea, and U.S. policies and actions in the United Nations concerning Korea, are discussed only peripherally, as they relate to U.S.-ROK relations.

The emphasis of this survey is on the political aspects of U.S.-ROK relations, since the details of economic and military relations would require specialized treatment by authorities in those fields in considerable length to do them justice. However, the broad outlines of economic and military relations were included to the extent that they affected the political picture.

In presenting this survey, a choice had to be made between a chronological narrative and a somewhat artificial division into separate topics. The latter course was followed. Following an introduction and summary (Chapter I), separate chapters deal successively with the evolution of official U.S. policy (Chapter II), the problems of unification and North-South relations (Chapter III), politico-military and security issues (Chapter IV), Korean-Japanese relations (Chapter V), Korean international relations (Chapter VI), Korean political evolution (Chapter VIII), and specific areas of U.S. interest (Chapter IX). A separate volume of annexes contains a chronological listing of major developments; a selection of particularly significant documents that are not readily available elsewhere (published treaties and agreements, for example, are not included); and a chronological listing of American and Korean incumbents of key positions from 1945 to 1965.

The research method employed was to examine all classified documents in the Department's archives under relevant file headings during the period 1945 to 1965, and some unclassified files, abstracting onto index cards those that were considered significant. Some documents were photographically copied, in part or in whole. A few of these were included in the volume of annexes. The index cards and copies of documents were turned over to the Bureau of Intelligence and Research for possible future reference.

This procedure left some unavoidable gaps. In the first place, key policy documents for the period 1945 to 1948 are in U.S. Army archives or those of the State-War-Navy Coordinating Committee, and only a few of these are reproduced or referred to in the State archives. Even after 1948, and particularly during the Korean war years (1950-1953), some policy documents referred to in State messages were transmitted in military channels, but were not available in State files. Additionally, considerable useful material on U.S. policy remained in the office files of the Bureau of Far Eastern Affairs, its predecessor and successor agencies, and its subdivisions (such as the Office of Northeast Asian Affairs and the Korea desk), as demonstrated by a sample search through one collection of such materials; but a thorough screening of these comparatively unorganized documents was not practicable. Particularly in the later years of the survey period, some sensitive messages were found to have been retained by the Executive Secretariat, and therefore were not used. However, it was possible to utilize the files of the Executive Secretariat on Korea policy papers, which comprised the principal source of the material in Chapter II.

It must also be noted that very little use was made of non-governmental materials on Korea, and no use whatever of official or unofficial Korean archives (except to the extent that such materials were picked up in Department of State documents). A truly comprehensive analysis of ROK-U.S. relations should take account of such materials. Perhaps future scholars will be able to do so.

Even though the source materials for this study were limited, as above noted, they were very voluminous (totalling an estimated 5,000 documents or more that were actually drawn upon). Accordingly, it seemed impractical to provide specific footnote keys for all data. Instead, one footnote was placed at the end of each paragraph when material in that paragraph was drawn from specific documents. The corresponding source entries (grouped at the end of the study) list all documents drawn upon in the various paragraphs, with the primary purpose of furnishing clues to additional specific material for those whose needs are not met by the summarization in the study itself. (Such material, in the first instance, may be sought in the index cards and document copies from which the study was prepared; or the original documents may be obtained from the archives.) Paragraphs without footnotes are generalizations by the researcher, drawn from materials in the archives, supplemented by his own recollections.

This survey would have been impossible without the help of many people in the Office of Research and Analysis for East Asia and the Pacific; the Historical Office; the Office of External Research; the Records Services Division; and the National Archives. My personal appreciation goes to the directors and staffs of these organizations. In particular, I should like to express my thanks for the cooperation and assistance of Mssrs. Wilmer F. Sparrow and Harold J. Slaughter of the Foreign Affairs Documentation Research Center and Miss Evi Blake and Miss Virginia Sharp of the Bureau of Intelligence and Research.

U.S.-Korean Relations from Liberation to Self-Reliance

1

Evolution of U.S. Policy
on Korea, 1945-1965

Pre-Independence Policies

Early Stages

Prior to the end of World War II in the Pacific, very little planning for Korea was done. To deal with various contending Korean expatriate groups, the Department of State took the somewhat lofty pose that no group would be recognized as speaking for the Koreans with authority until the Korean people themselves had a chance to choose their government. Beyond this position, State Department files reflect little thinking as to Korea's postwar status, although there were a few public indications of quasi-official thinking on the subject.[1]

When Lieutenant General John R. Hodge entered Korea as the commander of American forces (XXIV Corps) in September 1945, he had little policy guidance beyond the Army field manual on military government and General MacArthur's General Order No. 1, which was primarily concerned with Japan. The first policy paper on Korea reached him in October, and gave only general guidelines for what was essentially a holding operation, although calling for removal of Japanese officials and for liberalization of the political structure.[2]

General Hodge refused to recognize any Korean group as anything more than a political party (although encouraging a proliferation of parties). To end certain groups' aspirations to governmental status, the Military Governor, Major General Arnold, stated in October that the U.S. Military Government in Korea (known after January 1946 as USAMGIK) was the only government. In the beginning, an attempt was made to utilize the Japanese administration as an interim measure, but strong Korean opposition necessitated an early end to this device. Priority was then given to a rapid evacuation of all Japanese military

1

and civilian residents. However, formal separation of Korea from Japan was delayed and General Hodge continued to report to Washington through Tokyo for many months.[3]

Trusteeship: The Moscow Agreement

The idea of trusteeship for Korea as a means of attaining national independence and democratic government, originated with President Franklin D. Roosevelt. He at first (probably with the Philippine experience in mind) thought of a 40-year period of international tutelage, but this view overlooked Korea's long history as an autonomous entity within the Chinese world order. It would appear that Stalin and the Soviets originally favored immediate Korean independence, and subsequently acquiesced in the trusteeship proposal. John Carter Vincent, as Director of the Office of Far Eastern Affairs of the Department of State, made the trusteeship idea public in a speech on October 20, 1945. It was vigorously opposed by Koreans of all persuasions.[4]

Nevertheless, a five-year four-power trusteeship for Korea (China, the USSR, the United Kingdom, and the United States) was agreed to at the Moscow Foreign Ministers' Conference and announced in the Declaration of December 27, 1945. To carry out this decision, a Joint Committee constituted by the Soviet and American commanders in the field was to confer on economic and administrative coordination between the two commands, while a Joint Commission, also composed by the two commanders, was to formulate recommendations for a provisional Korean Government and for a trusteeship agreement to guide Korea toward full independence.[5]

The reaction of the Korean public in the southern zone to the Moscow decision was one of vociferous opposition. Only the Communists, after a delay during which they got new instructions, changed their position to support trusteeship. General Hodge, in an endeavor to calm public opinion, indicated (since he had not been informed to the contrary) that trusteeship was a Soviet idea. Soviet propaganda soon put him straight, but American authorities retreated from the earlier endorsement of trusteeship to an acknowledgement that Korean political development might make it unnecessary.

Attempts to Implement the Moscow Agreement

The State-War-Navy Coordinating Committee (SWNCC) formulated a series of documents in 1945 and 1946, which purported to guide the American representatives on the Joint Committee, as well as the American commander in the field in his governmental responsibility. Since primary reliance was being placed in Washington on developing joint plans and arrangements with the Soviets for the government of all Korea, policy for the administration of the American zone was a holding operation pending Soviet-American agreement.

This fact, coupled with the almost total lack of American preparation for the Korean occupation, resulted in failure to respond promptly and aggressively with the needed fundamental steps to make Korea move ahead.[6]

From the outset, U.S. policy on Korea was based on three points, which, as expressed in 1946, were:

--To establish a self-governing Korea, independent of foreign control and eligible for membership in the United Nations.

--To insure that the National Government so established shall be a democratic government fully representative of the freely expressed will of the Korean people.

--To assist the Koreans in establishing the sound economy and adequate educational system necessary for an independent democratic state.[7]

In short, the United States wanted Korean independence and democracy, and recognized the need for economic and educational assistance to the Koreans in order to attain these objectives. In the earlier stages, however, there was scant recognition of the enormous cost and the long time period required for their accomplishment.

U.S. attempts to establish a Korean interim government for all of Korea through negotiation with the Soviets, as envisaged in the Moscow decision, continued until the summer of 1947, when it became evident that differences in position were unbridgeable (see Chapter 3). SWNCC 176/13 of January 5, 1946, called for discussions in the Joint Committee of the two commands, at which the Americans were to discuss only economic and administrative matters, and to seek an integration of the two zones on such matters.

SWNCC 176/18 authorized negotiation with the Soviets and consultation with the Korean people to establish an interim government; it was modified at General Hodge's recommendation, before Joint Commission meetings began, so that the negotiations were to begin with a strong demand for complete political freedom for all Koreans--although the U.S. negotiators were not to allow this issue to halt the conference. By May 1946, however, the conference had adjourned over basic differences between the U.S. and Soviet approaches, which crystallized around the issue of which Korean groups were eligible for consultation by the Joint Commission.[8]

Policy was then altered to call for American initiatives in the southern zone to "reconcile Koreans to the continued division of the country, to give the Koreans of the American zone practice in self-government, and to win popular support for the United States so as to be in a stronger position in future negotiations with the Soviet Union under the Moscow agreement." It also provided for the continuation of the American occupation "so long as it contributes" to "the attainment of basic United States objectives in Korea." General Hodge was to utilize Koreans in governmental positions of responsibility, establish an advisory legislative body, and initiate economic and educational reforms conducive to a lasting democratic system, permitting full freedom of political expression and participation for all political groups.[9]

American policies and actions in south Korea under this revised policy did not prevent Korean pressure from rising. General Hodge in January 1947 reported that there was danger of full-fledged civil war unless an international solution to the Korean problem could be found. As instructed, he had continued attempts to re-establish negotiations with the Soviet commander in Korea through an exchange of correspondence, but with little sign of movement.[10]

Accordingly, a Special Inter-departmental Committee on Korea in February 1947 recommended an approach to the Soviet Union at the governmental level to reconvene the Joint Commission, which "must be aggressive so as not to appear as a sign of U.S. weakness." The Committee also noted the need for a "positive political, cultural, and economic program" both to improve the unsatisfactory condition in Korea and to strengthen the U.S. hand in any future negotiations with the Soviets. "It will be necessary to convince Congress that a strong affirmation of U.S. purposes in Korea, expressed by Congressional approval of a three-year program and separate appropriations for Korea for the fiscal year 1948, is absolutely essential. . . . It is now anticipated that such a program will amount to approximately $600,000,000 for the three years."[11]

Congressional leaders, however, did not go along with any such program at that time. The development effort therefore had to be postponed, even though the Committee found that without it, "the Korean situation will so deteriorate as to seriously impair the U.S. world position." (The Committee had for guidance a set of field recommendations from the staff of the U.S. delegation to the Joint Commission, endorsed by General Hodge. Some of the best American brains were attached to the Commission staff.)[12]

The recommended approach to the Soviet Union was made by Secretary of State George Marshall, concurrently with the April 1947 session of the Council of Foreign Ministers in Moscow. The Joint Commission did reconvene in May, but early hopes of a compromise on the crucial consultation issue were dashed when the Soviets reverted to their original position that only Korean groups supporting the Moscow decision should be consulted.

In August 1947 the Joint Commission adjourned, with the two sides unable to agree even on reporting their differences. The United States then proposed a four-power conference (China, USSR, United Kingdom, U.S.), which the Soviets rejected. As a final resort, the United States referred the problem of Korean unification to the United Nations. There it has been ever since.[13]

Establishment of an Independent South Korea

The uncertainty of American policy-makers about Korea in the face of the impasse with the Soviets is reflected in a memorandum from J.K. Penfield to

Assistant Secretary Walton W. Butterworth in September 1947. The memorandum observes that policy thinking on Korea at the time appeared to be in terms of two alternatives: (1) hold the line, keep the U.S. position indefinitely ("[U.S. Political Adviser to the Commanding General, USAFIK Joseph R.] Jacobs mentions a period of five years"); (2) prepare to withdraw from Korea "as quickly and gracefully as possible."

Both alternatives, Penfield thought, had great disadvantages: the first would make Korea the Greece of the Far East, and more expensive, despite a lesser U.S. strategic interest; the second would have repercussions on relations with the Soviet Union and on the U.S. position in Japan and China. The U.S. weakness in Korea, the memorandum suggested, was due to the ineptness of the administration there. With improvement, the southern zone could be developed politically and economically in a year so it could prevent Communist domination for "a year or two at least."[14]

It had become clear by early 1948 that the original goal of a unified Korea was remote except on Soviet terms, a fact that was underlined by the Soviet refusal to admit a United Nations commission to the northern zone to arrange elections under the UN General Assembly resolution of 1947. One of the first issues confronting the newly established U.S. National Security Council was thus to prepare a Korean policy consistent with the original three points (see page 4 above), which would also take account of the current realities.

These realities were to include "terminating the military commitment of the U.S. in Korea as soon as practicable consistent with the foregoing objectives," since in the face of rapid demobilization and declining defense budgets, the Joint Chiefs of Staff (JCS) believed that "the U.S. has little strategic interest in maintaining its present troops and bases in Korea," numbering about 20,000. Yet simple withdrawal might have serious political consequences for both the United States and the United Nations, unless the south were given the capacity to defend itself against "any but an overt act of aggression." The choice of phrase shows the assessment at the time: that an attack of the sort that actually occurred in 1950 was unlikely.[15]

The National Security Council's policy paper of April 2, 1948 (NSC 8) proposed three possible courses of action: abandon south Korea; support a south Korean government "as a means of facilitating the liquidation of the U.S. commitment of men and money in Korea with the minimum bad effects"; or guarantee south Korea's independence and territorial integrity, by force of arms if necessary.[16]

The second course was favored. It would require that the U.S. provide, before withdrawal, for the training and equipping of "native armed forces capable of protecting the security of south Korea against any but an overt act of aggression by north Korean or other forces." It would also require U.S. economic aid to south Korea to forestall economic breakdown after withdrawal (preferably by December 31, 1948) of U.S. forces. As an essential part of this program, the Korean government should be encouraged "to follow policies which would enhance political and economic stability and retard the growth of Communist influence through political subversion or other non-violent means."

At the same time, the paper continued, "The U.S. should encourage continued UN interest and participation in the Korean problem and should continue to cooperate with the UN in the solution of that problem." (More baldly put, the United States should continue pressure on the UN to take some of the heat off itself.) At the same time, the United States should be prepared for further negotiations with the Soviets on unification, if such should appear useful, while avoiding involvement in the Korean situation such that action "by any faction in Korea or by any other power in Korea could be considered a *casus belli* for the U.S." In retrospect, this language seems remarkable in its remoteness from the realities of the 1950 attack.

Policy Toward the Republic of Korea
Before the Korean War

The general election in South Korea of May 10, 1948, carried out by the U.S. occupation authorities under UN observation, resulted in the establishment of a juridically independent but militarily, economically, and spiritually dependent Republic of Korea (ROK), badly in need of the kind of support envisaged in NSC 8. (The Republic was recognized by the UN General Assembly in its resolution of December 12, 1948, and by the United States on January 1, 1949.)

The Koreans themselves clamored for the retention of U.S. military forces, faced as they were with widespread subversive activity undermining an inexperienced and unprepared government and a faltering economy. The Koreans also clamored for both military and economic aid. But the climate of Congress was not friendly toward the large-scale assistance for Korea which would be required for economic reconstruction. Moreover, the diminution of global U.S. force levels and the worsening situation in Europe brought added pressure for withdrawal of U.S. troops from Korea.

A new examination of U.S. policy in the light of these problems resulted in NSC 8/2 of March 22, 1949. It repeated the over-all policy objectives of NSC 8, but noted that plans to complete the withdrawal of U.S. forces by December 31, 1948, had to be revised. In part this was because the UN General Assembly did not complete its consideration of the Korean question until December 12. Additionally, and of at least equal importance, the U.S. Army presence guaranteed the "minimum Korean external and internal security which is indispensable for any attack on basic policy and economic problems and for successful economic rehabilitation." Concurrently, the ROK Government officially requested retention of a U.S. occupation force "for the time being."[17]

NSC 8/2 noted, without elaboration, "Even with U.S. economic assistance there is no assurance that south Korea can be made economically self-sufficient so long as the peninsula remains truncated." It also noted that the effective maintenance of ROK security forces--65,000 Army, 45,000 police, and 4,000 Coast Guard--"is and will continue for the foreseeable future to be wholly dependent upon military, economic, and technical assistance from the U.S." This pessimistic view of Korean capabilities, logical enough in the circumstances, continued to characterize U.S. policy papers until the Koreans proved in the mid-sixties that it wasn't necessarily so.

Reaffirming the earlier assessment of the Communist threat, NSC 8/2 presented the same three alternative courses of action as NSC 8, and reaffirmed choice of the middle course. In doing so, it noted that no course of action would "entirely eliminate the risk of a serious breakdown in the Korean situation"; yet

> if the significant gains made thus far, in terms both of the welfare and aspirations of the Korean people and of the national interest of the U.S., are to be consolidated, the U.S. must continue to give political support and economic, technical, military, and other assistance to the Government of the Republic of Korea.

Such assistance "need not be dependent upon the further retention of U.S. occupation forces in Korea," provided that (1) current and projected U.S. military assistance programs continued through fiscal year 1950, (2) planned economic and technical assistance continued through that year and "subject to future developments, for the ensuing two years as well," (3) the U.S. "continued its political support of the Government of the Republic of Korea both within and without the framework of the UN."

The language of NSC 8/2 which justified the withdrawal of U.S. occupation forces by June 30, 1949, is significant in the light of the subsequent north Korean invasion:

> Although the possibility is recognized that the withdrawal of U.S. occupation forces from Korea at this time, even with the compensatory measures provided herein, might be followed by a major effort on the part of the Soviet-dominated north Korean regime to overthrow the Republic of Korea through direct military aggression or inspired insurrection, it is believed that this risk will obtain equally at any time in the foreseeable future. It is understood to be the view of the National Military Establishment that the mere further temporary postponement of withdrawal would not serve appreciably to diminish the risk that U.S. occupation forces remaining in Korea might be either destroyed or obliged to abandon Korea in the event of a major hostile attack, with serious damage to U.S. prestige in either case. The Commander-in-Chief, Far East, has reported that the establishment of Korean security forces within the current program is substantially complete and that the state of training and combat readiness of these forces is such as to justify a complete withdrawal of U.S. occu-

pation forces, and has expressed the opinion that troop withdrawal from Korea at this time would not adversely affect the U.S. position in Japan.

On the basis of the foregoing, it is understood to be the judgment of the National Military Establishment and of the responsible military representatives in the field that U.S. occupation forces should be withdrawn from Korea by May 10, 1949.

The specific recommendations of NSC 8/2, in addition to the withdrawal of U.S. occupation forces, included the transfer of a six-month stockpile of maintenance supplies and an emergency reserve, plus necessary basic equipment for the Korean security forces prior to final withdrawal; establishment of a military advisory group (KMAG); legislative authorization for continuing military and economic assistance; a unified American Mission to administer the various American programs; and other activities envisaged in NSC 8. The concluding paragraph of NSC 8/2 read, ironically enough:

In publicly announcing the withdrawal of its remaining occupation forces from Korea, the U.S. should make it unmistakably clear that this step in no way constitutes a lessening of U.S. support of the Government of the Republic of Korea, but constitutes rather another step toward the regularization by the U.S. of its relations with that Government and a fulfillment . . . of the relevant provision of the [UN]GA resolution of December 12, 1948.

Policies During the Korean War

Prior to Chinese Intervention

The surprise north Korean attack of June 25, 1950, set instantly in motion a marathon high-level reconsideration of U.S. policy, which has been described in detail by Glenn Paige in his book, *The Korean Decision.*[18] As a result, the United States obtained from the UN Security Council (the Soviet Union absent) a designation as Executive Agent to establish a Unified Command against the north Korean aggression, under authority of UN Security Council resolutions.[19]

On September 1, 1950, the Executive Secretary of the National Security Council submitted to the Council his draft of a new policy paper on Korea (NSC 81). It dealt principally with the key questions of what to do about military action in and occupation of north Korea, and how to respond to Chinese Communist or Soviet intervention. The Joint Chiefs of Staff (JCS) in a memorandum of September 7, 1950, found the draft "unrealistic" in its approach, "since that approach envisages the stabilization of a front on the 38th parallel."[20]

The JCS paper stated the agreement of "the Joint Chiefs and General [Douglas] MacArthur" that occupation of Korea by UN forces should be limited to the principal cities south of the 38th parallel" and "should be terminated as soon as possible." However,

General MacArthur states that he has reached an understanding with President Rhee that he, Mr. Rhee, upon re-entry into Seoul will immediately grant a general amnesty to all except war criminals and that he will call for a general election to fill the 100 vacant seats in the Korean Parliament [provided in the 1948 ROK Constitution for eventual north Korean representation, at the suggestion of the then Commander of U.S. forces, General Hodge], and thereafter set up a single government for all Korea.

In other words, the political future of a unified Korea was already settled.

Despite the JCS objections, however, the language of NSC 81/1 of September 8, 1950 (approved by the President on September 11, two weeks before the famous amphibious landing at Inch'on, and ordered to be implemented) did not differ substantially from the September 1 draft. The paper specified what the UN Commander should do if the Soviets or Chinese intervened in the north before UN forces crossed the 38th parallel, or if Soviet or Chinese forces intervened below the 38th parallel; but it was silent on what the UN Commander should do if he encountered such forces in the north *after* crossing the parallel, which was what actually happened.[21]

The paper noted that it was "politically improbable" that "no action will be taken by the Soviet Union or by the Chinese Communists to reoccupy Northern Korea or to indicate in any other way an intention to prevent the occupation of Northern Korea by United Nations forces before the latter have reached the 38th parallel." But in the "unlikely contingency" of such inaction--and here lies the basis for the UN Command's march north,

There would be some reason to believe that the Soviet Union had decided to follow a hands-off policy. . . . Only in this contingency could the UN ground forces undertake to operate in or to occupy northern Korea without greatly increasing the risk of general war. . . . If only the ROK forces operate in or occupy Korea north of the 38th parallel, the risk of general hostilities would be reduced, although the possibility of Soviet or Chinese Communist intervention would not be precluded.

The conclusions of NSC 81/1, as approved by the President, were soon overtaken by events; but they involved the ROK Government and its forces, and laid the basis for much that happened later. In broad outline, the lines of action envisaged in these conclusions were:

--military operations by the UN commander to destroy the north Korean forces, if Soviet or Chinese threats did not appear;

--plans for occupation of north Korea, subject to UN and presidential approval (which was obtained);

--a campaign to direct Korean resentments away from the United States and toward the Communists;

--prior discussions with "certain friendly UN members" of terms to be offered the north Koreans, as a means of developing support for operations north of the 38th parallel;

--a leading role for ROK forces in occupying and pacifying the north and in
  disarming north Korean units;
--withdrawal of U.S. and UN forces as soon as practicable;
--recognition of the need for social and economic reforms in the ROK;
--reestablishment of the ROK Government in Seoul and consultation with it
  on unification under UN auspices through free elections;
--U.S. initiatives for involving the UN in solution of the Korean problem,
  including consideration of the "desirability of permanent neutralization of
  Korea" accompanied by appropriate non-aggression guarantees.

After approval of NSC 81/1, a Directive for the Occupation of North Korea
was drafted (apparently in large part by the Department of State, since the text
was reported by Ambassador-at-large Philip Jessup) and transmitted to General
MacArthur on October 28, 1950, after Presidential approval. It envisaged three
phases, beginning with a "temporary substitute for the central North Korean
government." The directive is summarized in Chapter 2, pages 45-46.

Policies After Chinese Communist Entry: Cease-Fire Planning

The successful US/UN military operation under General MacArthur's
command led to the disintegration of north Korean forces, and both UN and
south Korean forces moved rapidly into north Korean territory. The occupation
had barely entered its first phase, however, before the intervention of Chinese
Communist "volunteers" completely changed the picture.

The National Security Council discussed the implications of this intervention
in early November 1950. The Executive Secretary of the NSC then drafted a
revision of the existing policy document (NSC 81/2, November 14, 1950); but
it was withdrawn before all approvals were received, "in view of recent
developments in Korea and in the light of the discussion at the last Council
meeting (NSC Action No. 389)."[22]

The U.S. position regarding a cease-fire in Korea was the next major Korean
policy document. NSC Action No. 390 was approved by the President on
December 11, 1950. It contained the following language:

> We will consider a cease-fire, but must insist upon a cease-fire which does not place UN
> forces at a military disadvantage and which does not involve political concessions. Details
> of a cease-fire should be negotiated in order to protect the security of UN forces before a
> cease-fire is accepted. The Joint Chiefs of Staff will prepare as a matter of urgency the
> military conditions on which a cease-fire would be acceptable.[23]

In response to that document, the Joint Chiefs of Staff stated their views in
a memorandum to the Secretary of Defense on December 12, which was
circulated as NSC 95 of December 13, together with a qualifying memorandum
by the Secretary of Defense. The JCS stated that from the military point of

view, they could not concur in any cease-fire which was not in accordance with their list of terms and conditions; and that any such cease-fire must be agreed to by all governments and authorities concerned, including north Korea and Communist China, before implementation. The terms and conditions foreshadowed much of the substance of the eventual armistice agreement.

The memorandum concluded, ". . . The Joint Chiefs of Staff would point out that execution of any United Nations cease-fire resolution will, in all probability, prevent the attainment of the United Nations objective of a free and united Korea." The Secretary of Defense (George Marshall), in his transmittal memorandum, said he did not think this statement should have been included, but that he was assured that its purpose was not "the possible implication . . . that the Joint Chiefs of Staff felt that a continued fight for the conquest of Korea [was called for] . . ."; rather, the purpose was "to bring to the attention of higher authorities the certain possibility resulting from a cease-fire negotiation."[24]

The Department of State subsequently prepared "a statement of the conditions which the United States Government considers essential to any cease-fire arrangement in Korea." After clearance with the Department of Defense, the statement was transmitted to Ernest Gross, U.S. representative at the UN, for delivery "as the opinion of the United States in its capacity as the Unified Command of UN forces in Korea." Gross and General Crittenberger met on December 15 with the three-man UN group chaired by Ambassador Entezam, President of the UN General Assembly, and delivered the statement, which was favorably received. The Communist Chinese delegation departed before the Entezam committee had any real discussions with it, but the committee telegraphed Peking urging further consideration. (It was not until the following summer, however, that cease-fire negotiations commenced.)[25]

In May 1951 the NSC approved a revision of the regional policy paper for Asia, NSC 48/5. This paper focused on achievement of an acceptable settlement of the Korean conflict and continuation of current objectives in the area, in preference to withdrawal or unification by military decision. Soviet Ambassador Malik's public call for a cease-fire followed in June, after secret informal U.S.-Soviet talks. Armistice negotiations then began.[26]

The same general considerations underlay NSC 118/2, approved by the President on December 20, 1951. This document was a response to State and Defense contingency planning for the failure of the armistice negotiations and specifically to a JCS memorandum of November 3, 1951 (NSC 118). In essence, the JCS paper stated that the achievement of a military decision in Korea would require significant additional U.S. forces and means, and asked that U.S. objectives in Korea be reexamined in the light of this situation. NSC's first response was a draft paper, NSC 118/1, which was then further revised.[27]

As summarized in a memorandum from John Allison to the Secretary of State on December 17, 1951,

The decision taken in NSC 118/1 is to reject as an objective the unification of Korea by force and to continue to seek in Korea the objectives set forth in NSC 48/5, namely, as an ultimate objective, to seek by political means the unification of Korea, and, as a current objective, to seek an acceptable settlement which would include, as a minimum, (1) a satisfactory armistice, (2) establishment of the authority of the ROK over all of Korea south of a determined defensible line, generally north of 38°, (3) development of ROK military power to deter or repel renewed aggression, and (4) withdrawal by appropriate stages of non-Korean armed forces from Korea.

The paper then sets forth certain courses of action to be taken in various contingencies which may arise, including achievement of an armistice, clear failure of armistice negotiations, and protraction of armistice negotiations.

These courses of action follow in general those previously agreed upon by the State and Defense Departments. . . .

According to the paper's provisions, if armistice negotiations failed, restrictions on military advances in Korea would be removed (but large-scale advances would require prior approval by Washington and consultation with the sixteen nations contributing troops), and attacks by U.S. air forces on Chinese Communist air bases would be permitted "whenever the scale of enemy air activity threatens seriously to jeopardize the security of the United States forces in the Korean area, such employment, however, to be specifically authorized by the President."[28]

There were, as usual, differences between State and Defense--on the question of how to invoke economic sanctions against Communist China, among others-- which were uneasily wedded in the final NSC paper, 118/2. Nevertheless, the basic policy remained as summarized above. NSC 118/2 also contained a senior NSC staff study which examined the alternative courses of action open to the United States, and their implications.[29]

As might be supposed, domestic Korean problems received very little attention in NSC 118/2, the primary focus of which was on achieving a settlement of the war. The paper specified that "as an ultimate objective," the United States should continue to seek "by political, as distinguished from military means, a solution of the Korean problem which would provide for a united, independent, and democratic Korea." Meantime, settlement of the Korean conflict should establish the authority of the Republic of Korea south of a defensible boundary "in general, not south of the 38th parallel," and permit "sufficient ROK military power to deter or repel renewed aggression by North Korean forces alone."

NSC 118/2 also called for the U.S. to "continue to seek to develop strong barriers against communist subversion and military aggression in Korea, and to develop political and social conditions in Korea which would facilitate a united, independent and democratic Korea." The U.S. should also, "Working in and through the organs of the UN where feasible, continue to strengthen the government and democratic institutions of the Republic of Korea, and continue to contribute to the United Nations effort for economic recovery and rehabilitation

. . . ." In about four months, this "course of action" would be given a fiery test in the Pusan political crisis of 1952 (see Chapter 5). ROK military units were to be developed and equipped "as rapidly as possible and in sufficient strength, with a view to their assuming eventually responsibility for the defense of Korea."

There was no further change in formal policy for the next eighteen months, while armistice negotiations continued and then were suspended over the issue of prisoner-of-war repatriation. In early 1953, the NSC Planning Board undertook a detailed "analysis of possible courses of action in Korea," which was published on April 2 as NSC 147 for NSC consideration. The rationale was stated in the first paragraph:

> Excluding resort to global war, or complete withdrawal from Korea, or yielding to the communist position on prisoners of war in the armistice negotiations, there appear to be two major alternative courses of action open to the United States in Korea. The first alternative maintains the current restrictions on military operations, the second removes these restrictions. Under each major alternative there are analyzed three possible specific courses of action listed below in order of increasing severity.

The range of these six courses ran from continuation of present policies (Course A) to military defeat of the Communists and reunification of Korea (Course F).[30]

Concurrently with the NSC study, the Department of State's Korea desk proposed to the Bureau of Far Eastern Affairs that military pressure on the Communists be stepped up to cause unacceptable losses, thus pushing them toward political negotiations; and that at the same time the UN forces advance toward the narrow waist of the Korean peninsula, reducing north Korea to essential impotence and realizing much of the benefit of unification for the Republic of Korea, while recapturing much of the Korean population.

In considering this proposal, however, Bureau officers pointed out that the advance to the Yalu had been the only exception to the general U.S. strategy of a worldwide holding operation; that the enemy possessed formidable strength; that the enemy was less likely to endure the strains of a holding operation than the United States; and that to make such an advance possible, military action such as neutralization of forward air bases in Manchuria would be necessary, entailing serious political and military risks.

Subsequently, commenting on press statements (e.g., in *Life* Magazine) that the United States should insist on the Korean waistline as a basis for the peace settlement, the Director of Northeast Asian Affairs (Kenneth Young) noted, "The United States cannot now undo the irrevocable decision made in the spring and summer of 1951 not to press for a territorial or military settlement in Korea by superior force. . . ."[31]

Just as the NSC study was published, the Chinese Communists in a March 30 radio broadcast indicated their willingness to resume the suspended armistice negotiations. Discussion of the pros and cons of the two major alternatives nevertheless continued in the NSC, until progress in the armistice negotiations obviated the necessity for decision on extending the war.[32]   However, NSC Action 794 of May 20, 1953, enumerated measures to be taken in the event of renewal of hostilities.

While these weighty matters were before the NSC, the Council was also asked to consider the problems of reimbursement to the Republic of Korea for local currency advances, and of gaining additional troop contributions from UN member nations for the UN Command.   The latter problem also involved finances: whether, how, and to what extent the United States should reimburse other nations for their contributions. (Concerning currency advances, see Chapter 3.   The troop contribution issue is beyond the scope of this study.)[33]

Armistice and Reconstruction

Post-Armistice Policy

"United States Tactics Immediately Following an Armistice in Korea" was the subject of the next NSC policy paper. A draft by the NSC Planning Board was circulated as NSC 154 on June 15, 1953. "Difficulties with President Rhee" delayed consideration of the paper until July 2. As finally revised, approved by the President on July 3, and circulated on July 7, NSC 154/1 superseded paragraphs 2a and 2d of NSC 118/2 (dealing with action if an armistice was, or was not, achieved).

The paper laid out various interim courses of action designed to maintain economic and political pressures on China and north Korea and to support ROK defense and security, including continuation of covert operations (details not specified); maintenance of UN military strength; continued political, economic, and military support for the ROK government and armed forces; a security commitment to the ROK similar to U.S. treaties with the Philippines, Australia, and New Zealand; and continued activity through the United Nations "to strengthen the government and democratic institutions of the ROK."   ROK representation was to be ensured at the political conference pursuant to the armistice.   A full review was to be undertaken of policy toward Communist China and Korea.[34]

Reconstruction

The damage done by the Korean War, added to Korean technical and administrative deficiencies, created a serious problem of economic reconstruction and development, necessitating even larger resources than those that had boggled the Congress before the war began, and more time.   Moreover, there were Korean nationalist difficulties to be reckoned with, plus the difficulties over payment to the Korean Government for local currency advances to UN forces, and the continuing Korean opposition to the U.S. and UN approach to unification. Additionally, the UN (i.e., the U.S.) military authorities wanted neither to relinquish their wartime control of virtually all aspects of Korean economic activity, nor to grant any priority to civilian economic needs at a time when military requirements strained port and transport facilities to the utmost (see Chapters 2 and 3).

In an effort to cut through these difficulties, and responding to recommendations both from the field and from Washington, Henry J. Tasca was named as a high-level economic adviser to work out a program and modalities for Korean economic assistance. He went to Korea in early 1953 as special representative of the President, and submitted a comprehensive report to the President on June 15, 1953 This report was referred by the NSC to a special inter-agency committee chaired by Norman S. Paul of the Mutual Security Agency.[35]

On July 13, 1953, the inter-agency committee reported to the NSC its general approval of the Tasca report, favoring however a stretchout in the period of the program and suggesting caution in certain investment areas. The committee estimated total requirements over a four-to-five year period at $700 million to $1 billion, in addition to $165 million of funds already appropriated. It pointed out the need for coordination; the shortcomings of the ROK, and the shortage of requisite Korean skills; and the burden of maintaining a 20-division army, which the committee thought should eventually be reduced to 10 divisions (as the Tasca report suggested). The committee also suggested as a planning assumption for the program, the reestablishment of 1949/50 living levels in Korea.[36]

The final NSC policy document on postwar economic and military assistance, NSC 156/1, called for initiating an expanded program of economic assistance for the ROK, with the Tasca report as a basis, since the Korean situation "is now sufficiently clarified [a reference to Assistant Secretary of State Walter Robertson's successful on-the-spot calming of President Rhee, see Chapter 2] so that the U.S. Government is justified in proceeding on the assumption that the Republic of Korea will cooperate in an armistice." Economic aid would be contingent on continuation of such cooperation.

NSC 156/1 specified that when a satisfactory armistice was arranged, aid should be subject to the following conditions: maintenance of ROK armed forces at approved levels (20 army divisions, plus expanded levels of other services) "unless and until a political settlement makes possible a reduction"; contribution toward the goal of a standard of living approximating that of 1949/50; a step-up in the investment component of the program, but with initial investment confined to reconstruction rather than new construction; a limited rate of investment in areas which would be most affected by a renewal of hostilities; and a similarly limited rate of investment in projects which would be subject to reconsideration in the event of unification. The Bureau of the Budget was called upon for an organizational plan for effective administration of economic assistance. A financial appendix dealt with required Congressional funding action and other financial matters, estimating total outlay at $895-1,195 million.[37]

Possible Neutralization of Korea

In mid-1953, probably June, Secretary of State John Foster Dulles suggested that the NSC "should carefully consider what our objective in Korea after an armistice should be." A State Department position paper of June 16, 1953, approved by Secretary Dulles, concluded, "it is in the interests of the U.S., and should be the U.S. objective, to secure a unified and neutralized Korea." This proposal had been foreshadowed in NSC 81/1 in September 1950 (see page 16 above). The paper estimated that the two feasible alternatives were the division of Korea for an indefinite time, with the ROK tied to the United States as a military ally, and a unified, neutralized Korea, under a substantially unchanged ROK. The paper recommended the latter alternative as U.S. objective, on the following grounds:

> An independent and united Korea has been a constant U.S. political objective. This objective can now feasibly be achieved only through the neutralization of Korea. The relinquishment of its military position in Korea which would result from neutralization would not be critical for the U.S. In the event of general war, the desirability of attempting to defend Korea would be problematical. With respect to the danger of local aggression against Korea it would in any case be only the prospect of retaliation by the U.S. forces that would deter such aggression. The danger of internal subversion or indirect aggression in Korea could and should be countered by adequate Korean security forces and economic assistance. On the positive side, the security of Japan would be favored by the withdrawal of Communist military power (including air forces) beyond the Yalu and Tumen rivers. The savings . . . for the U.S. . . . would make possible a strengthening of the military position of the free world in other areas. The unification of Korea would probably be generally regarded as a significant accomplishment by the United Nations, to the enhancement of its prestige. The unification of Korea under the ROK, even on a neutralized basis, would probably also be regarded as a more constructive result of the war and more to the credit of the U.S. than the restitution of the *status quo ante*.

In addition it was argued, as noted in a Bureau of Far Eastern Affairs memorandum to the Secretary, that this course of action "is the most realistic method of attacking the problem of removing Korea as a political and military problem and reducing our commitments there without damage to our strategic or political position." (In retrospect, it is hard to understand how Korean unification, neutral or otherwise, under a "substantially unchanged ROK," could have been considered realistic--but viewpoints were different at the time.)[38]

The Joint Chiefs of Staff opposed neutralization as a goal. In a memorandum for the Secretary of Defense of June 30 (transmitted by the Assistant Secretary of Defense for International Security Affairs) to the NSC,[39] the JCS recommended the basic U.S. objective with respect to Korea would be best achieved

> by the attainment of a unified, independent, and non-Communist Korea. Until this objective is realized, the United States should maintain a strong military posture in the Far East, thus enabling timely and effective support to the Republic of Korea. This posture should include the retention and support of adequate Republic of Korea armed forces.

Further, the JCS maintained, U.S. programs should serve to establish the ROK as "an example, economically and politically, of the advantages of association with the free world" and "create dissatisfaction and unrest in North Korea" to encourage north Korean popular support for a unified and non-Communist Korea.

The JCS objections to the neutralization objective, as summarized by Robert Bowie of the Policy Planning Staff in a memorandum to the Under Secretary of State on July 2, were: (1) the Communists wouldn't accept it; (2) the Communists would not abide by a neutralization agreement; (3) U.S. and UN prestige would suffer; (4) a dangerous precedent would be set for Germany, Austria, or Indochina: (5) it would be to the strategic disadvantage of the U.S.; (6) it would substantially increase U.S. military commitments. Mr. Bowie offered persuasive rebuttals on all these points.

The final policy paper, NSC 157/1 of July 7, 1953, kept the objective of a unified and neutralized Korea, but qualified it somewhat, in the following language:

> It is in the interest of the United States and should be the U.S. objective to secure a unified and neutralized Korea under a substantially unchanged ROK. Such an objective would entail Communist agreement to a unified Korea with U.S. political orientation, in exchange for U.S. agreement to remove U.S. forces and bases from Korea and not to conclude a mutual security pact with Korea. This objective should also involve guarantees for the territorial and political integrity of a unified Korea under the ROK, the admission of the ROK to the UN, and ROK military forces sufficient for internal security and capable of defending Korean territory short of an attack by a major power.[40]

Since the negotiation of a mutual security treaty with the ROK was one of the U.S. concessions for gaining President Rhee's acquiescence in the armistice agreement, the objective of neutralization lost all current relevance almost as soon as it was approved, and thereafter was given diminishing respect as a long-term goal of American policy. Rhee himself rejected neutralization. (See Chapter 2, page 51).

Contingency Planning: Marches North and South

The Korean armistice was achieved on July 27, 1953, over the strenuous objection of President Rhee, who (justifiably) had no confidence of a satisfactory political settlement, wanted to see the Communists militarily defeated and Korea unified by force if necessary (see Chapter 2), and utilized threats of unilateral Korean action--actually executed in the case of Korean prisoners of war--to gain maximum concessions from the United States.

In the bargaining with Assistant Secretary of State Robertson that July, Rhee had set a 90-day deadline for a satisfactory political settlement, and had been making statements threatening to order his forces to attack after that time. Thus there were two major concerns after the armistice: what to do if the ROK marched north, and what to do if the Communists reopened hostilities in violation of the armistice agreement.

The NSC Planning Board responded to these contingencies in a report of October 22, 1953 (NSC 167) on "United States Courses of Action in Korea in the Absence of a Political Settlement." Regarding the possibility of Korean unilateral action, the Planning Board "concluded that all possible courses were so dangerous and difficult that the important task was to make every effort to deter the Republic of Korea from taking such action."

State and Defense agreed on the basic premises, but while State would threaten Rhee with a withdrawal of UN forces if necessary, Defense was not prepared to go that far. Defense would if necessary take Korean leaders into protective custody, but State argued that without the necessary groundwork such action would only rally support for the leaders. The telegram to CINCUNC combined elements of both views. It laid the background for Vice President Richard M. Nixon's visit to Korea in November, which sought to extract written assurances from President Rhee "that he is not going to start the war up again on the gamble that he can get us involved in his effort to unite Korea by force."[41]

Basic differences of views between State and Defense were reflected in two subsequent papers dealing with the second major contingency: action in the event the Communists reopened hostilities. The Joint Chiefs wanted, in such an event, to destroy Communist military power with atomic weapons, large-scale air attacks, and coordinated ground-air-naval follow-up action, to render the enemy incapable of aggression in the area. They would build up Korean forces, and move toward a "unified, independent Korea, allied with the West," thus permitting redeployment of forces from Korea.

State, on the other hand, argued that the final adoption of the "greater sanctions" statement (i.e., the joint declaration of July 27, 1953, by the sixteen contributors to the United Nations forces) had been opposed by British Prime Minister Churchill and his cabinet, and as finally approved was considered to involve no more than possible bombing of airfields on the Manchurian side of the Yalu River plus "hot pursuit" of hostile aircraft. Full military power, including atomic weapons, might in State's view be applied in Korea or on nearby Chinese airbases and troops, China could be blockaded, or certain offshore islands seized, without overt Soviet intervention; but any wider operations would probably bring the Soviets into the war, would not have UN or international sanction, and might cost the United States many of its European bases.[42]

Security Policy, 1953-1960

Policy of 1953-1954

At the same time that the foregoing policy for reacting to renewed hostilities was being developed, the NSC also considered a revised over-all Korea policy paper. This was published as NSC 170/1 on November 20, 1953, and superseded previous policy papers except for NSC 147 (the analysis of alternative U.S. courses of action in Korea).[43]

The long-range objective of the United States on the Korean problem, as stated in NSC 170/1, was essentially the same as for the entire period since World War II. It was reiterated in subsequent documents, with a few modifications, until 1960; but it was a basis for hope, speeches, and propaganda rather than current action. The words were:

> to bring about the unification of Korea with a self-supporting economy and under a free, independent, and representative government, friendly toward the United States, with its political and territorial integrity assured by international agreement and capable of defending Korean territory short of an attack by a major power.

The current objective was the meat of the 1953 paper. "Pending achievement of the above long-range objective," U.S. policy was to maintain a position of strength in Korea (1) in support of the United Nations commitment to oppose aggression, (2) to prevent the area from coming under Communist domination either by subversion or by being overrun, and (3) to ensure the continuance of a free government on the peninsula. Subsequent clauses specified that the United States sought to achieve these objectives through peaceful means, "avoiding or preventing the resumption of fighting in Korea, if possible without compromising our obligations, principles, and military security. (Similar but gradually modified formulations appeared in subsequent policy papers.)

To implement these objectives, the following courses of action were specified:

(1) To prevent or counter resumption of fighting by the ROK. The United States would observe the armistice, and would influence the ROK to do so. President Rhee would be formally told that the United Nations Command (UNC) and United States would not support military operations initiated by the ROK; that if they occurred, U.S. economic aid would stop, and the Commander-in-Chief, United Nations Command (CINCUNC) would keep his forces from being

involved and would provide for their security. Other ROK leaders were to be apprised of these positions. A formal assurance in writing was to be sought from Rhee. The UNC was to make the necessary plans and dispositions for flexibility in meeting any eventuality and for reinforcing statements made to Rhee.

A separate annex (closely held, and given very limited circulation) provided for securing prompt warning of any decision by Rhee to order an attack; for preventing the issue of such an order, or its receipt by field commanders; and for developing "the basis for new South Korean leadership prepared to cooperate in maintaining the armistice," enabling such leadership to assume power if need be, "by means not involving overt U.S. participation," including establishment of UNC martial law if necessary. (The operational responsibilities for carrying out this policy caused some interagency concern.)[44]

If ROK forces actually renewed hostilities unilaterally, actions would be taken along the above lines, plus evacuation of UN civilians, notification to the Communists of continuing UNC adherence to the armistice terms, renewal of hostilities with the Communists only if they attacked in force, and prompt action to win support by other members of the UNC to ensure compliance with the armistice.

(2) Counter resumption of fighting by Communists. If Communist forces renewed hostilities, the Joint Policy Declaration would be invoked; the necessity of expanding the war to China to honor commitments to the UN and the ROK would be made "clear to the world"; "the military and diplomatic measures referred to in NSC Action No. 794 of May 20, 1953, as approved following the urgent review by the Joint Chiefs of Staff and the Department of State" (see above, page 14) would be implemented; and other UN members would be called on for assistance.

(3) Seek satisfactory agreements from the Communists. The search would continue, through negotiations, for a unified and neutral Korea under an independent and representative government. The United States should be prepared *inter alia* to forego U.S. rights under a U.S.-Korea mutual assistance pact, but not precluding U.S. economic and military assistance. (The U.S.-ROK mutual defense treaty had been negotiated but not ratified when NSC 170/1 was issued; the political conference envisaged in the armistice agreement had been postponed.)

Political and economic pressures on Communist China would continue, "including unconventional and covert pressures," until satisfactory settlement "in the areas around Communist China" could be achieved.

(4) Achieve a position of strength in Korea. The mutual defense treaty would be ratified; ROK security would be built up and maintained consistent with the armistice, permitting earliest possible redeployment of the bulk of U.S. armed

forces; a campaign would be conducted for additional armed forces from other UN members.

"Working in and through the organs of the UN where feasible," the United States would "continue to strengthen the government and democratic institutions of the Republic of Korea." The Korean people would be helped through use of UNC facilities so as to evidence the value of U.S. friendship and assistance, "pending a satisfactory understanding with ROK Government with respect to internal measures required to achieve economic stability" (a reference to disputes over economic aid). The economic assistance program would be expanded subject to continued ROK cooperation in maintaining the armistice, toward a goal of reestablishing approximately the 1949-1950 standard of living and establishing an economy requiring a minimum of external aid. The investment component of aid "should be increased as rapidly as is consistent with economic stability," but restricted to projects furthering the goals of the program, with initial emphasis on projects making an immediate contribution to better living conditions and future increased Korean productivity.[45]

In August 1954, during President Rhee's visit to Washington (see Chapter 3, Section F1), the Department of State notified its embassies in Asian capitals, including Seoul, of the policy governing force redeployments in East Asia. The policy was to be communicated to a "small number of appropriate high government officials" of host governments. Briefly, the United States planned gradually to regroup its forces in the Far East, reducing those in Korea to two divisions. Two divisions had already been withdrawn. It was hoped (vainly, as it turned out) that increased Allied units would augment the remaining divisions. Some redeployed U.S. units would be retained in the Pacific area. U.S. support of Allied and ROK forces would continue.[46]

This policy was stated to be in accordance with President Dwight D. Eisenhower's announcement of December 26, 1953, that U.S. ground forces in Korea would be progressively reduced as circumstances warranted. The policy of the December 26 statement was reaffirmed. No prior public announcement would be made of redeployment plans. In justification of the policy, the State message noted that the real deterrent to renewal of hostilities was the Joint Policy Declaration of the Sixteen (countries contributing forces to the United Nations Command) of July 27, 1953. Moreover, U.S. strength in the Western Pacific was at a high level, "since U.S. Far Eastern forces possess enhanced fire power through new weapons," and worldwide American commitments required flexibility in deployment.[47]

Policy of 1955-1956: Attempts at Regional Involvement

In February 1955, a new policy paper was approved as NSC 5514, generally continuing the general line of NSC 170/1 with some rephrasing and shifting of emphasis to take account of changing conditions. For example, the new "current objective" dropped reference to support of the UN commitment and "continuance of a free government"; the new language, putting more emphasis on the ROK role, was as follows:

> (a) to assist the Republic of Korea (ROK) in order to enable it to make a substantial contribution to free world strength in the Pacific area, (b) to prevent more of Korea from coming under Communist domination either by subversion or aggression, and (c) to develop ROK armed forces sufficient for internal security and capable of defending ROK territory short of attack by a major power.[48]

A new section was added dealing with Communist violations of the armistice agreement, including response to unprovoked attack in accordance with paragraph 5g of NSC 5429/5 "even though this may be construed as a violation of the armistice." Provisions regarding military support took account of an ultimate reduction in ROK armed forces, providing for "development of an effective reserve" as well as improvement in effectiveness of active forces.

Attention was given to the need for developing better ROK relations with the free nations of Asia, including Japan, if necessary with "the offer of U.S. good offices to resolve outstanding problems. . . ." The document also called for promoting a "Western Pacific collective defense arrangement, including the Philippines, Japan, the Republic of China, and the ROK, eventually linked with the Manila Pact and ANZUS." In economic matters, an added goal of economic assistance was "to permit the ROK to assume an increasingly greater proportion of the cost of supporting its armed forces." Regarding the search for agreement with the Communists, NSC 5514 embodied the language of the Report of the Sixteen regarding achievement of a unified Korea "established through the holding of genuinely free elections under UN supervision for representation in the National Assembly. . . ."[49]

There were no significant interagency differences in debate on the new paper, and it was readily approved. However, there were problems not reflected in the paper, notably the questions of levels of economic and military aid, modernization of forces, and difficulties occasioned by the continued presence of inspection teams of the Neutral Nations Supervisory Commission (NNSC), established under the armistice agreement, in ROK territory. On the last subject, Defense representatives in NSC meetings were critical of the State Department for failure to achieve the elimination of the NNSC.

Policy of 1957-1959: Issues of Force Reduction and Modernization

The next revision of the over-all Korean policy paper, two years later, focused on the related problems of modernizing U.S. and ROK military forces and reducing the economically burdensome ROK military establishment. Pursuant to direction of the President, the NSC Planning Board prepared an evaluation of four alternative military programs for Korea (NSC 5702, January 14, 1957). The variables in these programs were the ROK force levels; the types of new equipment to be given the ROK military (notably jet aircraft); the modernization of U.S. forces in Korea--specifically the kinds of nuclear-capable weapons to be introduced, and the question of storage of nuclear warheads in Korea; the relative costs involved; and the impact, both internationally and in the ROK.

The study formed the basis for NSC discussions of a revised policy paper. During these discussions--which took six months--the U.S. representative in the Military Armistice Commission made the announcement of June 21, 1957, that in view of Communist violations of sub-paragraph 13d of the armistice agreement (restricting weapon and materiel replacements to the numbers and types existing when the agreement was signed), "the United Nations Command considers that it is entitled to be relieved of corresponding obligations under the provisions of this paragraph until such time as the relative military balance has been restored. . . ."[50]

In the NSC consideration of force level alternatives, Secretary Dulles supported the choice of the Joint Chiefs of Staff, which would transfer four ROK Army divisions from active to reserve status, provide three additional jet squadrons for the ROK Air Force (for a total of six), and provide U.S. forces with dual-capable weapons of types new to Korea. However, the Secretary's agreement was conditioned on provision by Defense of "publishable evidence confirming Communist violations of the armistice sufficient to justify such action to our Allies and before the UN." (Within State, Assistant Secretary Robertson had preferred continuation of then-current force levels, while Robert Bowie at the Policy Planning Staff favored reduction of ten active ROK divisions and compensatory provision of modern weapons to the Koreans, because it would save more money and be less in violation of the armistice.)[51]

Defense did not want to make modernization contingent on the "publishable evidence," preferring to move ahead promptly. President Eisenhower, however, withheld decision until Allied reactions could be obtained. These were generally favorable, although the "publishable evidence" was never satisfactory (see Chapter 3). In June the President directed (1) prompt announcement of modernization, in the light of Communist violations, (2) negotiations with President Rhee for substantial reduction of ROK forces to improve the ROK economy, (3) subsequent modernization of U.S. forces, subject to Presidential decision regarding deployment of nuclear weapons and warheads in Korea. This resolved the State-Defense debate on modernization, and led to the announcement in the Military Armistice Commission noted above.[52]

A revised Korea policy was finally approved as NSC 5702/2 of August 9, 1957. It reflected the above presidential directive, plus a small change of the original draft proposed by State, to allow the possibility of U.S. support for a unilateral ROK military initiative in response to a mass uprising, Hungarian style, in north Korea. However, the envisaged four-division reduction in ROK forces was not fully achieved (see Chapter 3).[53]

The new paper laid down the same long-range objective as its predecessor, but significantly amplified the "current objective" to include "encouraging the ROK in the further development of stable democratic institutions and of cooperative relations with the other free nations in Asia," and "influencing the ROK to conduct its foreign relations in conformity with the purposes and principles of the UN Charter." There was more emphasis on steps to lessen ROK political as well as economic dependence on the United States.

Economic assistance was to "maintain essential consumption at approximately present levels," since the previous target--1949-1950 levels--had been reached. The ROK was to be encouraged *inter alia* to develop "substantially increased numbers of technical, professional, administrative and managerial personnel" to "provide for increased participation by domestic and foreign private investment in Korean economic development," and to "stimulate and develop economic self-help measures, particularly in rural areas."

Regarding north Korea, a section in the new paper called for actions to maximize its non-recognition and non-legitimacy, to discourage political or economic intercourse with it, and to encourage its people to oppose the regime and sympathize with the ROK. The paper continued in effect the restricted annex dealing with actions to prevent unilateral ROK resumption of hostilities. "A minimum of two U.S. infantry divisions and one fighter-bomber wing with necessary support forces" was to remain in Korea through fiscal year 1958.

In the following two years, policy modifications in NSC 5817 of 1958 and NSC 5907 of 1959 were primarily focused on the related problems of ROK military force levels, U.S. force levels in Korea, and weapons modernization. The other major problem at the time was the economic stagnation and political regression in the last years of the Rhee era; but this issue produced little change in already established policy, perhaps because many years of dealing with Rhee had indicated that the range of American capabilities for influence in this area, short of vastly more active intervention in Korean affairs, had been exhausted.

On the problem of forces and weapons, the NSC in 1958 continued the commitment of a minimum of two U.S. divisions, but substituted for the air wing a provision for rotating various U.S. Air Force units of equivalent capability into Korean bases. Modernization of weapons for U.S. forces continued, and deployment of a U.S. Air Force missile unit was to be completed. Regarding ROK forces, the Budget Bureau, with Treasury concurrence, wanted a commitment to further reductions in calendar year 1960, even though President Rhee's opposition was then holding up agreement on the level of 630,000 arrived at under the previous year's policies. State opposed additional reductions, and compromise language was worked out calling for further reductions of ROK forces "as soon as practicable."[54]

By 1959, the problems of force levels and equipment had sharpened: the financial constraints on U.S. aid were growing tighter, yet the equipment of ROK forces was increasingly obsolescent, while their burden on the ROK economy was even more evident. Treasury pushed for drastic further ROK force reductions, but State and Defense (for once on the same side) opposed them. The Department of Defense in an analysis included in the final NSC paper, presented three possible alternative courses of action on ROK force levels, and observed that even the most drastic reduction proposal would not save enough Mutual Assistance Program resources to make possible the degree of modernization and logistic support proposed by the Country Team (the Ambassador and senior U.S. agency representatives in Korea) if continuation of fiscal 1959-60 levels was assumed. Hence, "a decision to reduce force objectives cannot be made on the basis of reducing over-all MAP costs, but only on the basis that with smaller forces a larger proportion . . . could be adequately supported and significantly modernized."[55]

Assistant Secretary Robertson's memoranda to the Secretary and Acting Secretary of State at that time possibly reflected State's position in the NSC debate. He noted that ROK forces played a larger role in East Asian security than simply the defense of the ROK. Further, a second reduction of ROK forces, so soon after the previous hard-fought round, would be exceedingly difficult to impose on President Rhee's government, would pose an unacceptable military risk (in the view of CINCUNC and the Ambassador), would have serious political and economic effect, and would involve atomic-capable weapons and other modern equipment as a *quid pro quo*, which would be "politically unacceptable."[56]

In the end, the usual drafting compromise was worked out, modifying the previous year's policy paper by glorifying a bit the regional role of Korean defense forces, and deleting specific figures for U.S. and ROK force levels in the text, mentioning them only in a footnote.

Regarding the political problems of Korea, there were a number of indications during these two years that U.S. objectives were not being realized. There was, for example, an analytical dispatch on November 21, 1957, from Ambassador Walter Dowling, which called attention to underlying elements of political and social instability and proposed several specific courses of action to deal with them.[57] However, there is no indication of any policy-level reaction to this despatch, and the 1958 policy paper made no changes in the language of the previous year on the subject. In 1959, although concern over the direction of democratic development was more clearly reflected in the annual Operations Coordination Board progress report and in State Department communications, it was the Bureau of the Budget which took the initiative at a Planning Board meeting in June, proposing language that would make continued U.S. support depend upon "a strengthening of the democratic institutions of the ROK."

Reporting this, Assistant Secretary Robertson's memorandum to the Secretary of State on June·23 noted, "We, obviously, could not agree with this proposal."

The new NSC policy paper (5907) simply added to the existing formulation regarding strengthening of ROK institutions the phrase, ". . . make clear to the Government of the ROK the importance with which the United States views the strengthening of democratic institutions." This was very mild language in comparison to the diplomatic pressures which had been applied the previous winter with very qualified success to halt Korea's movement toward a repressive political regime (see Chapter 5).[58]

The Growing Developmental
Emphasis, 1960-1965

The regressive political and economic trends evident during 1958 and 1959 in Korea exploded in the student revolution of April 1960, which overturned the Rhee regime and brought about Korea's brief experiment with parliamentary democracy. After ten months of confused and unaccustomed freedom, the military coup d'état of 1961 returned the country to authoritarian control, stricter and far more efficient than anything the country had experienced since the end of the Japanese regime. These developments dictated a far more thorough reexamination of basic U.S. policy premises on Korea than had been undertaken previously. Moreover, north Korea was laying claim to very rapid economic and social progress, which appeared far greater than the "democratic" ROK had achieved. Additionally, growing U.S. resource constraints argued for a new look at U.S. commitments for economic and military assistance. The inauguration of a Democratic "New Frontier" in 1961 added an incentive for a fresh look; but the process of review was already in motion in the previous year.

A basic and continuing dilemma underlying U.S. policy was how to reduce American costs and involvement in Korea while still maximizing the advantage of a friendly anti-Communist political entity in East Asia. The success of American policies in Korea would contribute both to American security interests and, through democratic Korean political and economic stability and progress, exemplify American ideals and demonstrate their efficacy on the international scene, in competition with Communist developmental models. But the past several years had not brought success, either politically or economically, and the Koreans were clamoring for more aid, not less. A participant in NSC Planning Board meetings of 1960 on Korean policy recalls that only one or two of the score of officials present thought that south Korea, without unification, could ever become economically viable.

One new source of hope was the evolving theory of economic and political development, which suggested new approaches for Korean policy. A few elements of the new thinking, drawn from the same year's report of the Center for International Affairs at the Massachusetts Institute of Technology (directed by Max Millikan) to the Senate Foreign Relations Committee, were built into the 1960 policy paper. This component grew, and emerged as a much larger element of the 1965 National Policy Paper.

At the same time, the Koreans were becoming increasingly sophisticated and competent. The energy and organization of the new Korean military government, faced with the challenge of a tough and more knowledgeable American country team with more sophisticated policy, brought about dramatic economic progress concurrent with declining levels of American support. By 1965, it was clear that Korean economic viability was an attainable goal. This realization had a profound psychological impact on both Koreans and Americans, changing the gloom-and-doom thinking of the 1950s into a spirit of hope and expectation based on perceived accomplishment.[59]

Such optimism was limited, however, by the continuing threat to ROK security and the consequent necessity for maintaining very large ROK armed forces, with the preemptive demands for scarce economic resources from both Korea and the United States. Thus, despite the growing emphasis on Korean internal development in policy papers from 1960 onwards, the security problem continued to overshadow all policy debate.

Policy of 1960: Response to Revolution

The 1960 policy paper, NSC 6018, was the last to be developed within the NSC machinery of the Eisenhower administration. It was approved only days before the President left office, and the Korean military coup profoundly altered the situation four months later. Nevertheless, it reflects the shift in emphasis from the old to the new policy approach.[60]

As in previous years, the point of departure for developing NSC 6018 was the OCB annual progress report. A memorandum of Assistant Secretary Parsons, summarizing the report, noted its unusual length "because of the unusual developments following the March 15 presidential elections. . . ," but stated that while the dramatic developments of the previous six months might "require change in certain details on the Policy in Korea (NSC 5907), the general principles appear to remain valid, and in fact to have been vindicated by the events described in the report."[61]

The 1960 NSC paper redefined the U.S. long-range objective in these terms:

A unified Korea with a self-supporting, growing economy, possessing a free, independent and representative government responding effectively to popular aspirations and dealing effectively with social problems, oriented toward the United States and the Free World, and capable of maintaining internal security and offering strong resistance in the event of external attack.[62]

The "interim objectives," and the courses of action to achieve them, put more emphasis on Korean government responsiveness, freedom, social justice, and control of corruption, as well as strength and stability. They also emphasized economic progress "conducive to political and social stability, to lessened dependence on external military and economic assistance, and to the eventual attainment of a self-supporting economy." Other themes--cooperation with the United States and the Free World, "especially with Japan and other free nations of Asia and Africa," ROK membership in the United Nations, ROK territorial integrity, strong armed forces, and "progress toward Korean unification on terms which are consistent with U.S. security interests"--were more or less the same as in previous policy statements.

NSC 6018 put considerable stress upon cultivating the friendship of ROK military leaders, and impressing U.S. strategic views upon them. An attachment, summarizing the Korean situation as background to the paper, contained the interesting statement, drafted in November, 1960, that "while the possibility of renewed nationwide violence cannot be dismissed, . . . the army is the major potential stabilizing force and a military coup is highly unlikely under present conditions." Unhappily, the military leaders of the May 16, 1961 coup were not among those whose friendship was cultivated; indeed, the cultivation of others may have contributed to the coup leaders' resolution to act.

ROK force reductions were one of the few controversial issues noted in the draft papers for NSC 6018. A JCS proposal would have restricted consideration of reductions to those the ROK Government might make. (The new ROK Government had in fact pledged reductions during its election campaign, and was suggesting a token reduction.) Along somewhat the same lines, the following sentence in the supplementary language of NSC 6018, proposed by the Central Intelligence Agency, was deleted in the final version: "The essential question is whether the military risks of renewed north Korean aggression and the resultant necessity for a very large military establishment continue to overshadow the need for non-military aid to meet the internal threat.[63]

A memorandum from State's Special Assistant for Mutual Security Cooperation (U/MSC) (drafted by Seymour Weiss) expressed the extreme concern of his office over the proposed reliance on nuclear weapons proposed in NSC 6018, which went in some respects beyond the limits established in Basic National Security Policy. Such provisions, taken together with the emphasis of the paper on holding levels of military assistance at current levels and reducing forces (some of which emphasis was reduced in NSC redrafting) would "greatly increase the possibility of a spread of the conflagration. . . ." U/MSC concluded,

. . . the proposed Korean policy is unsound. We believe that it is, at least to some extent, generated by a belief that U.S. funds can be saved by attempting to redress an imbalance on Communist vs. U.S.-ROK power in Korea through use of nuclear weapons rather than through facing the hard and admittedly costly task of building adequate conventional capabilities. . . ."[64]

Despite these objections, however, the language proposed by Defense and JCS was approved in the final paper. At JCS instance, one of the attempts to moderate the policy, by calling for efforts to limit hostilities to the Korean peninsula, was deleted.

The 1961 Task Force

The next Korea policy review was an unusual example of prescience. In the new Kennedy style, an ad hoc presidential task force, headed by Assistant Secretary of State Walter McConaughy (with Deputy Assistant Secretary Avery Peterson as the effective director) was constituted by NSC Action No. 2421 on May 5, 1961, eleven days before the military coup which overturned the Chang Myon administration. The initiative came in response to several indications of troubles in Korea, although the coup itself was not anticipated. Special National Intelligence Estimate SNIE 42-61 of March 16 called attention to weaknesses and dangers. An evaluation report of the Mutual Security Program cited both Korean weaknesses and American program deficiencies. A deputy director of the U.S. Operations Mission in Seoul (Hugh Farley) resigned in order to emphasize and report upon the seriousness of Korean corruption, and to call for reorganization of the U.S. effort in Korea.[65]

A first draft of the task force's report had been completed on the day before the Korean military coup. The event did not change many of the underlying problems studied by the task force, nor the broad outlines of U.S. policy; but extensive revision of the report was necessary to meet the new situation effectively. Ambassador-designate Samuel Berger arrived in Washington on consultation while the report was being drafted, and was therefore able to play an influential role in preparing the policy direction under which he subsequently operated.

There were three categories of recommendations made by the final task force report, mostly in the form of proposed presidential directives. In general, they comprised the strategy and tactics of dealing with the new military regime in such a way as to promote security, stability, economic development, and democracy, giving the Ambassador several negotiating levers. Policy goals were not much altered, but more emphasis was placed on specific areas of priority action, especially in economic development. U.S. assistance was explicitly conditioned on demonstrated Korean willingness to cooperate. Concern for the corruption problem was explicitly included.[66]

The Guidelines Papers, 1962 and 1963

Under the new procedures of the Kennedy administration, the Korea task force recommendations and the 1960 policy paper were replaced in April 1962 by "Guidelines for Policy and Operations: Korea," prepared by the Department of State, and issued by the Secretary of State. This document did not carry the interdepartmental weight of the earlier NSC papers, although it did require interagency coordination and White House review.[67]

In its introductory paragraphs, the guidelines paper reflected the growing American policy emphasis toward economic, political, and social goals, while recognizing the continuing security problem. Noting that Korea was important to the U.S. by contributing materially to the security of Japan and the Western Pacific, the paper added that "U.S. prestige is heavily committed to the preservation of Korea as an independent and non-Communist state and its continued development as an Asian democracy." It continued,

> to keep Korea an asset to us will require significant economic and social progress toward Korean aspirations for individual and national security, human rights and dignity, a better material life, and if possible the ultimate reunification of the peninsula. To this end, the Free World, particularly the United States, must provide the massive assistance required to accelerate economic development, maintain adequate consumption levels, and support the Korean military establishment. We must influence the Korean leaders to work effectively toward meeting their people's needs, both material and non-material, and toward achieving eventual self-support. We must help these leaders to find and achieve their own solutions to these difficult problems.

The paper laid down U.S. objectives for Korea which were essentially similar to those in the 1960 paper, but put more emphasis on self-help, both economically and militarily. Unification was placed with UN membership as "objectives contingent on the general state of East-West relations."

Lines of action placed particular stress on effective Korean planning and programming for prudent allocation of resources to "maximize self-support, stability and development, and reduce dependence upon foreign assistance," listing a series of specific areas and topics for attention, and stressing the assumption of responsibility by the Koreans themselves.

In the economic area, the Guidelines took note of the Korean five-year plan under development, but provided for sanctions such as withholding of aid or of new project starts in the event of poor Korean economic or political performance. Private investment, and purchases with Korean foreign exchange, were to be encouraged. In the political area, emphasis was placed on encouraging effective, moderate, and responsive leadership and return to civilian government through free elections.

In the military field, the guidelines were somewhat more general than the 1960 paper (for example, no reference was made to nuclear warheads). They took note for the first time, however, of the Korean demand for a status of forces agreement (promised by Secretary Dulles in 1953--see Chapter 3) as one manifestation of growing nationalism, and specified that the U.S. should be prepared to enter step-by-step negotiations, subject to the development of acceptable safeguards in Korean law and justice. Mention was made of the need to "seek means to reduce the cost of ROK military forces . . ." but without specifying force reductions. Use of ROK forces for civic action projects was to be encouraged.

In a section on unification, the guidelines stated *inter alia* that the United States, while accepting the current division of Korea, should seek a satisfactory means for peaceful unification; the United States should be prepared to negotiate with the Communists for unification along the lines of established United Nations principles, and to promote ROK support for such negotiations, if it appeared that they would be useful. Emphasis was also placed on promoting the normalization of ROK-Japan relations.

The guidelines were republished in February 1953, with very little change. An added short-range objective called for encouraging the fulfillment of social needs, while recognizing that this was primarily a matter for the Koreans themselves to manage. The economic lines of action were modified to "require" rather than "encourage" the Korean leadership to work for economic development through plans and programs for the allocation of both internal and external resources. Like the 1962 paper, the 1963 guidelines spoke approvingly of the Korean five-year economic plan, but stopped short of blanket endorsement.[68]

National Policy Paper, 1965

The next major policy review was the last within the time frame of this study. One of the new series of national policy papers, it was undertaken in 1964 by the Policy Planning Council of the State Department, assisted by an interagency planning group of about fifteen people, and in consultation with the Ambassador to Korea and country team. Published November 9, 1965, the *National Policy Paper, Republic of Korea* went far beyond previous policy documents in its comprehensiveness and its emphasis on development and self-help. A separate annex discussed policy on nuclear weapons, and a second volume (Part II) contained factual analyses of the various aspects of the Korean situation bearing on U.S. policy.[69]

The paper began with a statement of U.S. interests:

For the present and foreseeable future, the principal U.S. interests in Korea are three: *first*, to maintain the Republic of Korea as a buffer between Japan and Communist Asia and a forward Free World defense position on the Asian mainland; *second*, to prove in Asia through the Korean example, as in Taiwan, that the non-Communist approach to nation-building pays off; *third*, to demonstrate the dependability of U.S. alliance and support.

Additionally, "the eventual reunification of Korea under a free and independent non-Communist government would serve the interests both of Korea and of the U.S." But "the realities of the present day do not admit of the possibility of unification, except on Communist terms." No real progress could be hoped for until the international environment changed and "until the bargaining position of the ROK vis-a-vis the North Korean regime is vastly improved." Yet Korean sentiment for unification was growing, and could not be ignored.

The U.S. objective in Korea was stated in the paper along lines similar to those of 1960, but without reference to the "free . . . representative" form of Korean government. This change reflected the growing American realization that the U.S. could not expect all governments in the world to be molded in its own image:

> The long-range U.S. objective in Korea is to bring about a unified, stable, and independent state with a viable and growing economy, with a government responsive to the needs of its people, with national policies compatible with the needs and objectives of the Free World, and with the ability to maintain internal security and resist limited external attack.

Eight policy goals were postulated for the following five years. They reflected a continuation of the shift in the U.S. approach to Korea away from the earlier patron-client relationship and toward the achievability of real economic, as well as political independence:

(a) *Political stability:* Development of a strong, stable, self-reliant ROK Government responsive to popular needs, with objectives, institutions, and methods compatible with Free World ideals.

(b) *Economic progress:*
   (1) Economic growth averaging at least six percent per year, looking toward ultimate economic self-support and reduction of unemployment.
   (2) As widespread as possible a sharing in the benefits of economic growth.

(c) *External defense:*
   (1) Maintenance of strong and motivated ROK defense forces, capable of assuring internal security, deterring overt aggression by North Korean forces, and defeating attack by North Korean forces should such deterrence fail.
   (2) Organization and equipment of U.S./UN/ROK forces in Korea to deter a combined Chinese Communist-North Korean attack, and with augmentation successfully to defend South Korea against such attack without support by nuclear weapons, should such deterrence fail; but not to foreclose the possibility of using nuclear weapons.

(3) Partial financing by the ROK of internal security forces, to the maximum extent feasible without jeopardizing attainment of economic objectives set forth in this paper.

(d) *Internal security:* Maintenance of ROK internal security forces capable of detecting and controlling subversion and maintaining law and order on a basis of reasonable cooperation with the populace.

(e) *Social evolution:* Development of the attitudes, values, and institutions necessary for a modern free state.

(f) *Progress toward unification:*
    (1) As much progress on the unification issue as is possible and desirable from international and domestic political standpoints.
    (2) Minimization of the influence and prestige of the North Korean regime . . . and whatever weakening of that regime may be feasible. . . .

(g) *International support:*
    (1) Prompt normalization of relations with Japan.
    (2) An active and expanding ROK role on the international scene. . . .
    (3) Maintenance of UN support and a UN role and presence in Korea.
    (4) Formation of an international consultative group with respect to aid to Korea. . . .

  (h) Effective U.S.-ROK relations. . .

In its discussion of U.S. strategy to achieve these eight goals, the paper suggested that priority of effort should go to defense, economic development and political stability; normalization of Korea-Japan relations was also important. Certain key areas and institutions should receive particular developmental emphasis: armed services, civil service, police, educational institutions, labor organizations, youth, communications media, and agencies concerned with finance, social services, and community self-help.

A major aspect of U.S. strategy should be to encourage the Korean leadership to establish national goals and promote their general acceptance . . . formulate realistic action programs . . . exert maximum efforts for self-help in national development . . . develop workable processes of government acceptable to the Korean people and compatible with the development of the economy.

The U.S. should promote sound economic policies, "including whatever appears to be the most effective division between the public and private sectors of the economy." It should "encourage intercommunications between governmental and non-governmental sectors, and foster consensus and persuasion as alternatives to coercion and dictation," while recognizing that only limited success would be likely in Korean circumstances.

In elaboration of these general lines of strategy, the paper specified key issues and directions of development for each of the eight goals. It noted, as a general approach, that "the basic problem in implementing our policies will be to walk the tightrope between giving the Koreans the feeling of long-term security and support which they need, on the one hand, while expecting and enforcing maximum Korean prudence and self-help, on the other." It emphasized the need, shown by past experience, to concentrate U.S. effort in certain selected fields, and firmly to require compliance with agreed programs. It cited the need, at the same time, for American patience and understanding. ". . . Patience and constancy can substitute in some measure for the lack of legitimacy of the new Korean institutions, and must continue to do so until Korean achievements and popular acceptance provide the needed legitimation of these institutions." The paper said that less reliance should be placed on detailed guidance and more on agreed policy and programs, even at the price of "increased opportunity for waste, misappropriation, and error," which in turn would require "continuing investigation and audit, both overt and covert. . . ."

The principal issues in dispute as the policy paper was drafted concerned (1) the allocation of resources, both U.S. and Korean, as between defense and economic development; (2) the extent to which the U.S. should commit itself in advance to the support of Korean economic development programs; (3) the vigor with which the unification objectives should be pursued; (4) the priority to be given to internal security.

On (1), careful economic projections showed that the Koreans were capable of much more rapid development and domestic investment than had previously been thought (a prediction borne out and surpassed in the following years), but emphasized anew that the burden of an oversized military establishment was the chief obstacle to development, in terms of both U.S. and Korean resource availabilities. A key issue was the generation of counterpart funds from the aid program to subsidize the Korean defense budget. U.S. balance-of-payment problems were also involved, particularly in regard to offshore procurement in Korea for Korean forces with U.S. funds. In the end, Defense consented to a reduction in the Korean armed forces from current levels to 500,000 men over a two-to-four-year period, with the proviso that the forces should not be reduced at a time of political sensitivity resulting both from the negotiations with Japan then in progress and from the American request for Korean troops in Vietnam. The reduction was also subject to annual review and assessment of ROK defense needs. (No reduction of forces was ever actually made.)

As for (2), the discussions on the policy paper were in part responsible for the announcement, in the joint communique of Presidents Lyndon B. Johnson and Park Chung Hee in May, 1965, that the U.S. would make $150 million in development loan funds available "for programs and projects to be proposed by the Korean Government and to be agreed to by the United States Government."

On points (3) and (4), the country team in Korea considered in the light of Korean political realities, that earlier drafts of the paper went too far on unification issues and not far enough on internal security. Modifications were made accordingly. The final language on unification called for serious study of possibilities, but otherwise reflected the 1963 position. Provision was made for study and periodic review of "the threats to the internal security of the ROK and appropriate programs to defeat such threats." Such studies were later made, and resulted in vigorous action programs. The appropriateness of this concern was subsequently demonstrated by the peaks of subversion reached, for example, in the nearly-successful attempt by north Korean agents to assassinate President Park in January, 1968.

2

Korean Unification and North-South Relations

Events During the U.S. Occupation

Upon the defeat of Japan in 1945, the primary problem in Korea at first was not unification, for Korea had been a single entity under the Japanese; rather, it was the separation of Korea from Japan and its establishment as an independent state, as promised in the Cairo Declaration.

The State Department archives for 1945 indicate practically nothing about American thinking on this problem--a reflection of the fact that such policy as there was came basically from the Pentagon. However, it seems clear that American officials recognized the need for some kind of international guarantees if true Korean independence and stability were to be achieved. Additionally, the need for political tutelage was recognized. Presumably the four-power trustee-ship proposal, announced pursuant to the Foreign Ministers' Conference in Moscow in December 1945, was a device for meeting these two needs.[1]

The Soviets, on the other hand, expected Korea to be a "friendly democratic state," i.e., a regime receptive to communism perhaps not unlike that of Mongolia. Since the United States would clearly refuse to accept such status, the whole sequence of joint Soviet-American conferences, attempting to implement the Moscow decision, was a charade. The Soviets, despite Stalin's doubts when Roosevelt originally argued for trusteeship, subsequently seized on the issue to ensure a preeminent role for their Korean partisans by directing them to support trusteeship as a tactical device, and demanding that other groups be excluded from consultation by reason of their opposition to trusteeship.[2]

Unification, then, was a problem of competing political ideologies with a territorial dimension. The territorial division aroused Korean nationalism, and thus aggravated the polarization of ideological differences. These differences

37

were not solely born of the occupation; they were rooted in the history of Korea's exposure to the West.[3]

American-Soviet Negotiations, 1946-1947

Implementation of the Moscow decision began in January, 1946, with the establishment of a Joint Committee to work out administrative and economic relationships between the two occupation zones, and a Joint Commission to develop an interim government (see Chapter 1, page 3). The Joint Committee accomplished very little, and never reconvened after February 1946. The Joint Commission met during a two-month period in 1946 from March 20 to May 6, and over five months in 1947 from May 21 to October 18.

Between the two periods, the two commanders corresponded concerning the impasse over which Korean groups should be consulted by the Joint Commission--the Soviets insisting, as already noted, that only those Koreans who supported the Moscow decision on trusteeship should be heard, and the Americans insisting that all shades of opinion should have a voice. (Whether from naivete or deliberation, the Americans had a very large number of political groups, largely non-Communist and anti-trusteeship, in the southern zone, which would clearly outnumber those of the Soviets.)

Another basic issue, which the Americans raised (at General Hodge's insistence) at the very first Joint Commission meeting, was the guarantee of free speech and other political freedoms throughout Korea. The possibility of a compromise formula for consultation appeared briefly, following the Foreign Ministers' Conference in the Spring of 1947; but discussions soon reverted to deadlock.[4]

There was some continuing contact between north and south during this period. The January 1946 conference of the Joint Committee had worked out arrangements for postal exchanges, some movement of persons, transport and communication coordination, and establishment of joint control posts. Electric power supply and interzonal trade were discussed in the conference and in subsequent correspondence between the two commands. The north continued to furnish more than half of south Korea's power until the flow was cut following the 1948 elections; and efforts at barter trade continued under private auspices, but with U.S. and later ROK tacit consent, until the Korean War.

A million or more people moved from north to south Korea in the five years before the war, aggravating still further the differences in political outlook between the two areas. There were numbers of border incidents, including American soldiers wanting to go north.

Each command was represented at the other's capital by liaison officers until 1948. Oddly enough, a Soviet consul had continued to function in Korea after the First World War and during the Second, and remained in his consulate in Seoul during most of the American Military Government period.[5]

The American liaison officer in Pyongyang (the northern headquarters), Lt. Col. Choinsky, reported on the first north Korean general election on November 14, 1946 (concurrent with elections in the south for an interim legislature--see Chapter 7) and on the apparent trend at that time for the Soviet command to retire from governmental functions, "forcing the Provisional People's Committee for North Korea to the front." This marked the Soviet equivalent of the American policy decision (see Chapter 1, page 5) to allow more Korean participation in decision-making and administration, as prospects for unification grew more remote. The Koreanization process in the north was later carefully studied by a team from the State Department's Bureau of Intelligence and Research (led by Richard Scammon), whose report was declassified in 1960. As separate Korean political power groups were built up in north and south, their rival claims to power still further complicated the unification issue.[6]

American administration in south Korea had tended to strengthen the hand of the conservative propertied elements. This conservative strength became an embarrassment in the unification negotiations. For example, General Hodge telegraphed in May 1947 that it appeared that Syngman Rhee, who had already largely consolidated his control of conservative groups, would use every effort to sabotage the work of the Joint Commission.

> In his childish talk he repeatedly refers to alleged promises from General Holdring that we would form a south Korean government and repeated accusations that the coming meeting of the Joint Commission is contrary to U.S. policy and that if I go through with it I am violating orders given me by the U.S. Government.[7]

Although the conservatives wanted a unified Korea, they wanted an anti-Communist government even more, and the collapse of the Joint Commission bothered them not at all. It did bother other south Koreans, however, who attached more importance to unification and less to conservatism--including moderate and liberal leaders around whom the Americans tried to promote a coalition movement. The death rate among such men was suspiciously high.[8]

The Formation of Separate Governments

As envisaged in the policy paper SWNCC 176/30, when the collapse of the Joint Commission negotiations was clear and the Soviets had refused to agree to four-power talks, the U.S. referred the Korean problem to the United Nations General Assembly. The continued Soviet opposition to UN action, and refusal to admit the UN Temporary Commission (UNTCOK) to north Korea, resulted in an election under UN observation in the south only on May 10, 1948, to legitimize a separate south Korean government.

The reason for the Soviet attitude is clear from views expressed by the late Arthur Bunce, then Economic Adviser to the Military Government, in a letter to Edward Martin, Chief of the Division of Japan-Korea Economic Affairs in

State. Writing in July 1947, Bunce said that Soviet policies as evidenced in the Joint Commission and otherwise indicated "their assumption that there will be no true integration, but rather an absorption of the South Korean Interim Government by the People's Committee [the governing authority in the Soviet zone]." He continued:

> . . . Soviet penetration . . . can be effectively countered only by the establishment for all Korea of a provisional government free from direct or indirect Soviet domination. To achieve such a government, we must insure free, democratic elections . . . provide the democratic basis for selection of a government. . . . We believe that the Communists would not gain a majority even in North Korea in elections so conducted. . . . The Soviets, on the other hand, will stubbornly resist every effort to establish a government which they cannot dominate in one way or another. Apart from their long-range objectives, which would appear to be the creation of an actual or quasi-autonomous Korean Soviet republic, the Soviets are finding north Korea strategically useful to their role in the present military operations in Manchuria and North China. . . . They have built up Kim Il Sung enormously. . . . To countenance any other candidate would cause a considerable loss of face for the Soviets; moreover, it would involve the political liquidation of a group they now control absolutely. . . . Even if a provisional government free of Communist domination were established, it could not long survive without specific international guarantees. There unfortunately appear to be no elements in Korean public life comparable in organization, discipline and political potential to the Communists. . . .[9]

Bunce went on to foreshadow what eventually became the aim of U.S. policy:

> . . . I believe that American interests and prestige require us to stay. If we do stay, we must undertake a grant-in-aid program. . . . At the same time we would have to undertake a complete reform of the present government and perfect social and economic reforms based on the likelihood of our being here a long time. We should develop a liberal government of the moderate right and moderate left, and exclude all Communist elements. . . . Under proper direction, South Korea might become an example of democratic, social and economic progress in the Far East. . . . To make it so will be very difficult and very expensive, but it can be done.[10]

A final gasp of the unification-minded moderate Korean leaders was the North-South Conference or "Four Kims Conference" in April 1948, so-called because its principal participants were Kim Il Sung and Kim Tu Bong of north Korea and Kim Koo and Kimm Kiusic of south Korea. American policy appears to have been to discourage it but not overtly obstruct it.[11]

The idea of the conference was conveyed in general terms to USAFIK intelligence officers in October 1947 by an obscure elderly Korean named Chung Young Tyak. The G-2 report commented (in typical jargon), "Purpose of repeating above plan herein is that popularity thereof increasing. No action taken by this Command." In succeeding months, a series of telegrams from the

Political Adviser (Jacobs) reported the uncertainties and shifts of attitude of southern moderates.[12]

In April 1948, Jacobs reported that the success of the Military Government's registration campaign for the forthcoming UN observed elections, despite moderates' calls for their supporters to boycott a separate election in the south, had cooled Kimm Kiu Sic's enthusiasm, and that he was thinking of posing additional conditions for his attendance at the Pyongyang conference:

> While General Hodge and I naturally are most reluctant to see Kim Koo and Kimm Kiusic go to Pyongyang because of immense propaganda value it would give Soviets, we feel we cannot do anything to influence them (we are doing all we can through indirect channels) for reasons that in true oriental style the two Kims would expect something in return and our intervention, becoming public as it must, would give rise to outbursts from Rhee and Kim Seung Soo, another conservative leader, and probably make them forget their differences and thus destroy the healthy rivalry which now exists among rightists. . . .[13]

When a lesser member of the moderate camp (Lyuh Woon Hyung's brother, Lyuh Woon Hong) asked for credentials and assistance in getting a liaison group to Pyongyang on one of the American military supply trains, General Hodge told him

> it was policy of Command neither to assist nor to obstruct departure and travel of representatives invited to attend proposed conference of North-South Korea leaders at Pyongyang. . . . invitees were free to leave South Korea at any time if they travelled by ordinary public facilities. . . . If he were advised in advance . . . he would give instructions to our military and to South Korean police that they should interpose no obstacles.[14]

In the end, the Conference of the Four Kims was held, but was dominated throughout by the north, as General Hodge had indicated in public statements. The conference produced a letter of April 23, addressed to the governments of the USSR and the United States, signed by fifty-six representatives of political and social organizations but with the signatures of Kim Koo and Kimm Kiusic conspicuously absent. The letter blamed the Americans for Korea's political dilemma and called for the UN Commission and foreign troops to withdraw so that Koreans could hold their own free elections. The southern leaders issued a face-saving statement, but the northern "commitments" to them--particularly the continuation of electric power--were promptly invalidated by events.[15]

The United Nations Temporary Commission on Korea (UNTCOK) observed the successful south Korean elections of May 10, 1948, various ensuing steps in the formation of the Republic of Korea, the inauguration of President Rhee and his government on August 15, and the transfer of sovereignty by agreement with the United States on September 9 (see Chapter 5). The UNTCOK report was considered in the 1948 session of the UN General Assembly. In its resolution of December 12, in carefully chosen words, the Assembly declared that

> there has been established a lawful government (the Government of the Republic of Korea) having effective control and jurisdiction over that part of Korea where the Temporary Commission was able to observe and consult and in which the great majority of the people of all Korea reside; that this government is based on elections which were a valid expression of the free will of the electorate of that part of Korea and which were observed by the Temporary Commission; and that this is the only such Government in [not of] Korea. . . .[16]

During the same period the Soviets moved, without UN blessing, to establish a separate government in the North. The Democratic People's Republic of Korea (DPRK) was proclaimed on July 10. Their version of an election was held in August, the Soviets claiming with an eye to propaganda that 77 percent of the *south* Korean people had participated in it.[17]

Despite the careful delimitation of sovereignty of the ROK in the UN resolution, both rival regimes claimed sovereignty over the entire national territory, with the ROK (at General Hodge's suggestion) reserving 100 legislative seats to be filled by subsequent elections in the north, while the DPRK purported to include representatives of the south in its People's Assembly, and declared Seoul to be its capital. Both governments continued to call for national reunification in separate ways: the ROK by calling for UN and international support; the DPRK by calling for withdrawal of all foreign troops so that the Korean people could settle their own problems without foreign interference.

Early Years of ROK
Independence, 1948-1950

The United Nations Role

From the time of their establishment, the two rival Korean regimes engaged in international competition for legitimacy and support, backed by their respective sponsors. In the case of the ROK and the United States, great importance was attached to the United Nations and its role in Korea, beginning with the recognition of the ROK by the General Assembly in December 1948. President Rhee, in off-the-record remarks at a November, 1949 press conference, expressed his view that "the United Nations was a potent moral force, and was doing a great deal to mobilize righteous world opinion" for the Korean cause, although he felt that the UN Commission, with moral power alone, would not make much progress toward unification. Rather, "the Korean problem will be solved before long through general solution of international problems. Anyway, war will come in time. . . ."

be solved before long through general solution of international problems. Anyway, war will come in time. . . ."

Apart from the relatively impotent Commission, the annual debates and resolutions on the Korea question in the General Assembly focused world attention on the problem and gave the ROK a clear edge in legitimacy over the northern regime. Despite aggressive propaganda, north Korea had gained scant recognition outside the Communist orbit by 1950.[18] A UN commission was more or less continuously present in Korea under one name or another (UNTCOK, UNCOK I, UNCOK II from late 1947 until the outbreak of the Korean War, and thereafter, as UNCURK, until its dissolution in 1973) under successive General Assembly resolutions, with the dual mission of working for unification and promoting democratic development. After establishment of the ROK, UNCOK sent requests to the north Korean regime for admission to north Korea, which were heeded only indirectly by abusive propaganda (one UNCOK letter to Kim Il Sung in March 1949 was returned unopened). Just before the outbreak of the Korean War, however, in response to a north Korean invitation, UNCOK Deputy Principal Secretary Gaillard (an American) went to a railroad station just north of the 38th parallel and was handed a bundle of propaganda. UNCOK observed and certified to the withdrawal of American forces in 1949 and offered--without response--to observe the withdrawal of Soviet soldiers from the north. Pursuant to the UN General Assembly resolution of October 21, 1949, it provided UN military observers and could thus more credibly certify to the fact and the responsibility for the north Korean attack of June 25, 1950.[19]

ROK Policies

The United States and the ROK Government (meaning, in effect, President Syngman Rhee) were not in total agreement on unification policy in the prewar period, despite vigorous U.S. support for the south Korean cause. The ROK formula called for elections in north Korea only under UNCOK observation to fill 100 empty seats in the ROK National Assembly, whereas the United States wanted nationwide elections for representatives to determine an all-Korean government. This difference was muted insofar as possible.

The United States was apprehensive that Rhee might launch an attack on the north, once he considered his forces strong enough, possibly calculating that the Americans would have no choice but to support him. At a press conference on August 10, 1949, responding to a request to comment on the change of official slogan, "unification of north and south," to "recovery of lost territory," Rhee said:

> We are waiting for a peaceful solution through the international situation. But we cannot sit safely just waiting for the North Korea's attack. If some intolerable situation develops, we should take some positive action.[20]

Until an upturn in the Spring of 1950, the performance of the new ROK Government was not such as to inspire popular confidence, and north Korea had the reluctant respect of some south Koreans. Such feelings reinforced the desire for unification, and several Koreans proposed unification schemes to UNCOK, despite ROK Government efforts to deny access to anyone who did not have Government permission. In the tense atmosphere of the south, with a serious problem of subversion and guerrilla activity, such attitudes appeared treasonous. The unification issue was therefore entangled in domestic political rivalries and security measures, and it has remained so ever since.

It was natural that the ROK Government should consider itself the legitimate government of all Korea, and take action to support this position. On the domestic front, the principal such action (apart from propaganda) was the appointment of provincial governors for the five north Korean provinces. There was also discussion of separate National Assembly electoral districts for north Korean refugees, but no such districts were actually established.

As described in Chapter 3, the ROK faced a serious challenge to its existence from the day of its establishment, both across the 38th parallel and from internal subversion, insurrection, and disaffection. In retrospect, it is evident that the north Koreans had determined on unifying Korea by any necessary means, although they may at first have expected to do it by low-intensity conflict rather than by the full-scale attack they eventually mounted. As it turned out, the ROK had a better appreciation of the north Korean military buildup and its purpose than did the Americans, who tended to discount Korean reports as propaganda to get more aid, or as inspired by fear and exaggeration. As mentioned above, the United States was apprehensive about possible ROK military unification action, and was therefore reluctant to supply more than the necessary minimum of weapons and supplies.[21]

Resultant south Korean military weakness and unpreparedness, coupled with the withdrawal of U.S. forces and signals from Washington that Korea was not within the American defense perimeter, doubtless were major factors in the north Korean decision. The northern regime certainly recognized, as did the ROK and all other parties, that unification through political negotiation and peaceful means was an exceedingly remote possibility. Had it not been for the American reevaluation of its interests in Korea following the attack, the north unquestionably would have achieved its objective very quickly, although it would then have been faced with a major internal security problem of its own.[22]

The Occupation of North Korea

The north Korean attack of June 25, 1950 brought an American decision first, to support the ROK; second, to do so through United Nations collective action, thus establishing the truth of Secretary of State Dean Acheson's assertion before the National Press Club the previous January that the United Nations would not prove a weak reed in maintaining the security of nations in Asia, even though they were not within the defined American defense perimeter. By September, UN military successes not only opened the possibility of a United Nations occupation of north Korea, but even argued the necessity of it. Moreover, it would have been virtually impossible to prevent the reconstituted ROK forces from moving in on their own.

The U.S. policy considerations underlying the operation were outlined in Chapter 1 (pages 8-10). It was necessary to obtain United Nations support, which was readily forthcoming in the General Assembly resolution of October 7, 1950 (the Security Council having returned to its usual paralysis on security matters when the Soviet Union resumed its seat).

In deference to the obvious danger of Soviet intervention, and the less obvious danger of Chinese intervention, U.S. policy called for using only Korean troops in "the northeastern province bordering the Soviet Union or in the area along the Manchurian border." (In the headlong rush to consolidate control of north Korea, however, the restriction regarding the Manchurian border was disregarded.) The ROK Government was to be reestablished in Seoul, and while recognized as the only lawful government in (not of) Korea, was to be consulted on unification problems. "The unification of Korea should be arranged by representatives of the Korean people chosen in free secret-ballot elections on the basis of universal adult suffrage, the elections to be held under the auspices of the United Nations."

Plans were to be drawn up by the Commander-in-Chief, United Nations Command (i.e., General MacArthur), in consultation with the UN Commander in Korea, for the north Korean occupation, subject to Presidential approval. This language may have been an attempt to encompass the view of the Joint Chiefs of Staff, as expressed in a memorandum to the Secretary of Defense on September 7, 1950 (quoted in Chapter 1, page 14).[23]

The Occupation Directive

A "Directive for the Occupation of North Korea" was prepared, apparently by the Department of State, in implementation of the approved policy, and circulated on October 28. It was approved by the Joint Chiefs of Staff, the Secretaries of State and Defense, and by the President, and transmitted to General MacArthur.[24] It envisaged three phases of gradually diminishing CINCUNC responsibility. The "civil affairs directive" in Part II of the Directive stated that ROK authority north of the 38th parallel had not been recognized, but that "in matters of national scope you should . . . consult with the government of the Republic of Korea through the United States Ambassador to facilitate eventual reunification." A political adviser for north Korea was to be designated by the Department of State. The UN Commander (CINCUNC) was to change the existing political and economic structure in north Korea as little as possible, although he was empowered to appoint and dismiss officials; he was to dissolve the Democratic People's Republic of Korea, but not to create a central government.

The directive, which was marked, "Restricted--U.S. Officials Only," was given in confidence by U. Alexis Johnson to Counselor Greenhill of the British Embassy in Washington on November 8, 1950, with the comment that it was to be released at a suitable future time after hostilities ceased; that the principles had been discussed with a UN Interim Committee on Korea and with the ROK Government, but the text had not been made available to them.[25]

The Civil Affairs Experience in North Korea

United Nations troops, together with Korean forces, moved into north Korea in October 1950, pursuing the shattered north Korean army. Civil assistance got off to rather a slow start. Neither the necessary directives nor the personnel were ready at the time of the seizure of the Pyongyang and Wonsan areas; and the directives, when issued, had to be changed to match the realities encountered.

In mid-November, the Civil Assistance program was "just getting under way," particularly in the main occupied cities, with Embassy advice and assistance. A few Koreans of north Korean origin with special qualifications were sent north to assist in security and public utilities. Provincial governors, deputy provincial governors, mayors were selected locally by UN officers and installed in office; generally they performed well. Local security forces were organized in some cases, but UN and ROK military police played an important role. In general, the population was enthusiastic at the UN entry and caused few security problems. When the UN forces retreated before the Chinese Communist "volunteers" in late November and December, they evacuated many north Koreans who had cooperated with them, and great numbers of others fled south by any means they could.[26]

ROK forces and individuals also moved into north Korea. Their impact was greatest in the X Corps area on the east, where they arrived before the UN troops and in some cases established governments which were subsequently confirmed by the X Corps commander. ROK authorities covertly undertook to expand ROK influence and authority in the Eighth Army area on the west. There was some carpetbagging and staking out of claims, especially by ROK officials of north Korean origin, and a certain amount of anti-Communist witchhunting. The ROK National Assembly on November 6 unanimously adopted a "Message of the National Assembly to the People of North Korea," referring among other things to an election soon for north Korean seats in the ROK legislature.

Territory North of the 38th Parallel
Below the Demilitarized Zone

The United Nations counterattack in the Spring of 1951 drove the battle line north of the 38th parallel once more, leaving an area of several thousand square miles of north Korean territory under UN control. As the lines stabilized, the ROK exhibited interest in taking jurisdiction over this area, as well as sensitivity about territory (including the historic city of Kaesong) that it had lost below the parallel. On December 21, 1952, the ROK National Assembly resolved that the territory north of the parallel should be brought under ROK jurisdiction, provided this did not hinder military operations. The State Department (Johnson), approached by the Australians (who opposed the transfer), told them that the United States continued to be guided by the occupation authority conferred by the October 12, 1950 resolution of the Interim Committee on Korea, but that exercise of limited *de facto* jurisdiction in the area by ROK armed forces as part of their military mission did not affect this position.[27]

After the Armistice of 1953, the United States moved to give the ROK administrative control over the former north Korean territory. On July 3, 1954, Secretary Dulles wrote Senator Wiley, Chairman of the Senate Foreign Relations Committee, that it was intended to recognize coverage of the area by the Mutual Defense Treaty. "The turnover is of an *ad hoc* and *de facto* character and does not imply the *de jure* extension of ROK authority over the area." The turnover was to be timed with President Rhee's return from his visit to the United States. The "sixteen" (contributors to UN forces) concurred in a Washington meeting on July 6.

State then instructed the American Ambassador in Seoul to ask the blessing of the United Nations Commission (UNCURK) for this action. UNCURK, however, was resentful of being faced with a *fait accompli*. It asserted its own authority under the October 12, 1950, resolution of the UN Interim Committee on Korea, and demanded the legal basis for the action, which the State Department derived from the UN Security Council resolution of July 7, 1950. UNCURK eventually did as it was asked, by a resolution, but the incident marred relations with the American authorities thereafter. The UNCURK resolution was considered "helpful in building support for transfer of administrative authority and preventing harmful discussion in the UN General Assembly."[28]

ROK Obstruction of the Armistice

ROK Opposition to Cease-Fire

President Rhee, from the day of his return to Korea in 1945, was a consistent, unswerving, hard-line anti-Communist. Reference has been made (page 43) to his 1949 comment that the Korean problem would eventually be solved because war would come. When it came, once assured of American support, Rhee wanted to crush the north Korean regime by force, and continued in this view forever afterwards, the Chinese Communist intervention notwithstanding. He therefore strongly opposed a cease-fire when the possibility was raised by the Soviet delegate to the United Nations in June 1951; and in general south Koreans supported their President. The National Assembly passed an anti-truce resolution. The U.S. Embassy (then at Pusan, where the UN retreat had forced it the previous January) reported:

> . . . if the position of articulate Koreans is to be taken into consideration in deciding upon the manner of terminating this war, that position must be regarded as one of solid opposition to negotiations which contemplate anything short of the unification of Korea up to the Manchurian border and to a ceasefire which would endanger this objective.[29]

A campaign ensued throughout south Korea with speeches, newspaper articles, mass rallies, and the publication of a public opinion poll showing that virtually everyone opposed a ceasefire.[30] The Embassy in July, however, pointed to an emerging distinction in Korean minds between the 38th parallel and some other temporary demarcation line, quoting an Assembly member to this effect. On July 3, Rhee was quoted as saying, "We want to cease fighting as soon as possible, but the 38th parallel is something we cannot accept." The Embassy concluded, "it would appear that the negotiation of a ceasefire presents no insuperable difficulties in relations with the ROK if the ROK is represented and if reference to the 38th parallel is avoided."

Koreans, however, drew parallels with the previous failure of the U.S.-USSR Joint Commission. Mindful of the American disengagement from Korean defense prior to 1950, they were apprehensive of their future security, and felt that the fate of their country was being settled without their participation, let alone their consent. A statement by the Secretary of State on July 19, ruling out the withdrawal of UN forces, was reassuring to the Koreans, as was the arrival of Kingsley, the Agent General of the United Nations Korea Reconstruction Agency, and the invitation of ROK Ambassador Yang Yu Chan to participate in Washington meetings of the Sixteen.[31]

On July 28, 1951, Rhee wrote President Truman, indicating reluctant agreement to a "temporary military line if the United States will guarantee that no such line will be accepted as part of the political settlement" to be discussed after the ceasefire arrangements.[32] The Embassy commented that the letter gave Rhee a chance to blow off steam, but was only a temporary solution to the difference between the ROK and U.S. viewpoints. Agreement on the ceasefire agenda with a ROK Army general present implied ROK acceptance, while Rhee felt he could not publicly do anything indicating acceptance of partition. Hence he was furious, and Ambassador John J. Muccio and General John Coulter (for CINCUNC) had difficulty in dissuading Rhee from withdrawing the general. Ambassador Muccio prophetically commented, "It is going to be most difficult in the course of negotiations to keep him mollified and to keep him from publicly dissociating himself from negotiations or from indicating he is being forced to go along."[33]

The displacement of the truce talks from Kaesong to Panmunjom, with seeming loss of face for the UN side, and the acceptance by UN negotiators of north Korean control of the Kaesong area south of the 38th parallel, greatly concerned the Koreans. Kaesong seems to have had a disproportionate importance in Rhee's mind--perhaps partly because it was the ancient capital of the Koryo Dynasty (A.D. 936-1392), partly because it was a center of the profitable ginseng industry. Moreover, the closer an actual armistice appeared, the less pleased Rhee became. The Ambassador reported from Seoul in December,

> Since day agreement reached on Armistice agenda item 2, Rhee and govt resumed campaign of last summer against every phase of armistice. Never any doubt Rhee sparked this campaign. . . . Nevertheless campaign has not caught public imagination; most people war weary, ready for armistice. Among Rhee's motives is attempt to improve his prospects for reelection by National Assembly next year.[34]

Rhee's Confrontation of the United States

In an effort to restrain Rhee from his anti-armistice efforts, President Truman on March 4, 1952, referred to Rhee's letter of the previous July. Taking note of increasing open ROK opposition to armistice efforts of the UN Command, the President commented that "only the most serious consequences can ensue" from divergence from UN policies and objectives, and observed that the degree of assistance to the ROK "will inevitably be influenced by the sense of responsibility demonstrated by your government, its ability to maintain the unity of the Korean people, and its devotion to democratic ideals."[35]

Rhee in turn wrote Truman March 21, expressing regret that the ceasefire talks had "dampened the morale and high spirit you so inspiringly and effectively aroused" and had permitted the Communists to build up their strength. "I counted upon a final positive direction coming from the United States at the last moment." Rhee felt he must acquiesce if Truman believed an armistice was necessary; but he could not do so without the support of his people. For this purpose he wanted a mutual security pact, and a speedup in the ROK army expansion program (with the possibility of using ROK troops as "a

UN police force anywhere in the world").[36] These two items were his price for cooperation, and in the end it was paid, with interest.

Truce negotiations had bogged down over the issue of voluntary repatriation of prisoners of war; but as this issue approached a solution in 1953, the old Korean president again endeavored to prevent an armistice and stirred up a full-blown diplomatic crisis with the United States. Despite President Dwight D. Eisenhower's commitment to achieve peace in Korea, Rhee wrote him on April 9, 1953, affirming his intention to fight single-handed, if necessary, to achieve unification. Eisenhower replied on the 23d, cautioning him not to try it.[37] Rhee tried other tactics; he insisted on the withdrawal of Chinese troops from north Korea as a precondition of the armistice, or of a political settlement; and he unilaterally ordered the release of Korean prisoners of war held by ROK troops--an order obeyed by several Korean commanders, in contravention of CINCUNC's operational control.

To underline again Rhee's price for cooperation, on which repeated signals had been sent out, ROK Foreign Minister Pyun Yung Tai raised the subject of a bilateral defense pact with Ambassador Ellis O. Briggs (who had replaced Ambassador Muccio the previous year), and a letter from Rhee to CINCUNC (General Mark Clark) conveyed the same point.[38]

On May 25, 1953, Ambassador Briggs and General Clark called on Rhee, on Presidential instruction, to affirm U.S. support for Korean security, provided the ROK refrained from opposition to the armistice and cooperated in implementing the agreement. As incentive for Korean acceptance, they proposed the "greater sanctions" statement by the Sixteen, U.S. equipment and training of 20 ROK army divisions plus a Marine brigade, and negotiation of a comprehensive military assistance agreement following the armistice. (However, a mutual defense treaty was ruled out.) If the ROK refused to provide the requested assurances of its cooperation, "the United States may be compelled to take all necessary measures to ensure the security of the United States and other United Nations forces in the event of unilateral action on the part of the Republic of Korea." The ROK was also assured that the U.S. would not support a political settlement which permanently divided Korea. This demarche was the first step in implementing policy worked out in Washington.[39]

The boiling crisis threatened to torpedo the armistice negotiations. Assistant Secretary of State Walter Robertson accordingly went to Korea for discussion with Rhee, aimed at reaching a *modus vivendi* on the armistice, ROK security, and U.S. economic and military assistance. These discussions were assessed by the Ambassador to Japan, Robert Murphy, in a closely-held message to the Acting Secretary.[40]

Murphy's assessment of Rhee and his objectives is a revealing one, which the historical record fully substantiates. In his view, Rhee aimed to defeat the armistice by posing conditions the United States could not fulfill, and by seeming to settle all differences except one--a different one in each meeting. He appeared convinced that he had the United States over a barrel: that the United States did not dare quit Korea, and had not moved to weaken Rhee's political position in Korea; thus he was doing what he could to consolidate it. "As I analyze it," Murphy's cable said,

> Rhee's attitude toward us is disdainful because he feels we have made mistakes in the past, are making grave one now, but he is cynically confident his ability manipulate U.S. representatives. . . . His attitude apparently had developed over long time during which he has become overconfident US support and it has been bolstered by individuals. . . . My conclusion is that best now obtainable from Rhee is position where he will reserve his freedom of action and will only passively oppose armistice agreement.

Murphy concluded that Robertson was doing a "first class job of gentle persuasion" on a difficult subject. In the end, Robertson did achieve a substantial measure of agreement, by giving in (as previously planned) to Rhee's demand for a mutual defense treaty, plus a promise that the Secretary of State would visit Korea after signature of an armistice; and Rhee wrote to President Eisenhower and to Secretary Dulles on July 11 that he had "decided not to obstruct in any manner the implementation of the terms" of the armistice.[41]

Yet Rhee, devious to the end, engaged in an exchange of correspondence with Robertson after his departure, and cabled Secretary Dulles on July 24, endeavoring to tighten the screws and get further American concessions-- a tighter treaty, and a promise of American support for military operations after failure of a political conference. Dulles, in his reply of the same day, politely refused, and commented, "Never in all its history has the U.S. offered any other country as much as is offered to you."[42]

Dulles Visit

Following conclusion of the Armistice Agreement on July 27, 1953, Secretary Dulles came to Korea as agreed. The talks with President Rhee on August 5 and 6 covered the political conference, the mutual defense treaty (which was agreed and initialled), U.S. economic assistance, Korea-Japan relations, the United Nations Commander's operational control of ROK forces, and the future of Korea, including possible ROK military initiatives. Rhee rejected the proposal for neutralization of Korea (see Chapter 1, pages 16-17) "until the situation in the Far East was settled." He continued to press for American support of Korean military action if the political conference failed, but the Secretary told him "he could not commit the United States to go to war again along with the Republic of Korea at the end of six months." One of Rhee's many counter-arguments was that "he wanted the United States to finish its objectives instead of leaving them half accomplished and wasting all the sacrifices that has been made," but eventually he dropped the point.[43]

On August 14, after his return from Korea, Dulles commented on the negotiations in a memorandum to the Under Secretary. He said the visit "ended with a very good relationship," which could not be maintained if the Koreans should "think we have forgotten about them and work only with the British, French, Indians, etc." Because the Koreans had felt this way about the armistice, Dulles continued, "We had a narrow escape from disaster. We had to use up all the bargaining power we possessed to get President Rhee to go along with the Armistice [i.e., a mutual defense agreement, U.S. support for an extensive ROK military buildup, and a billion-dollar economic development program]. Now we face the problem his going along with the political conference. . . ." He went on,

> . . . the ROK in my opinion will not go into a roundtable conference dominated by the "great powers." . . . The ROK feel that in the past they have always been sacrificed to such great power interests. . . . The U.S. cannot be expected in this matter to "sell" the conference to Rhee because it is not the type of conference which the U.S. itself believes in."[44]

Problems Connected with
the Political Conference

Believable or not, a political conference was specified in the Armistice Agreement of July 27, 1953, to begin within ninety days. Negotiation soon began with the Communists in Korea (first by Kenneth Young, then by Arthur Dean), but they promptly reached an impasse. Meantime, Rhee started again to threaten unilateral action. Ambassador Briggs's assessment in October 1953 suggested that Rhee was still not convinced that the United States would not support him in such a move and that only a firm decision by the United States, made known to him, would provide a deterrent.[45]

While the Koreans dragged their feet and threw up roadblocks in various negotiations on economic and military matters, Rhee wrote another letter to President Eisenhower on February 4, 1954, which was so incredibly insulting in tone that Assistant Secretary Robertson prevailed on ROK Ambassador Yang to have it withdrawn. A revised and watered-down version was sent on March 11. The letter again asked American help for military action against the Communists, and made either it or an enormous military assistance program the price for ROK participation in the forthcoming political conference in Geneva (replacing the one supposed to have been held within ninety days of the armistice). "We have nothing to look forward to except a new round of fruitless talks at Geneva. Our allies may find reasons to insist on these endless conferences, but we Koreans can set aside our original determination no longer."[46]

During May, American representatives tried to persuade Rhee to join a common front with other non-Communist nations at the Geneva conference, but to no avail. Rhee continued to insist on prior withdrawal of Chinese Communist troops. He said he would keep silence on his objections provided the U.S. secretly agreed to join the ROK in an attack on the Communists if the Communists accepted the UN side's unification proposals. After numerous U.S. concessions and compromise on language, a final stumbling block was security guarantees in the event of non-withdrawal of north Korean forces. On May 21, Briggs and Dean reported that their final attempt to negotiate with Rhee had failed, and commented, "Sincerely sorry could not influence him. His stand has noticeably hardened since fall of Dien Bien Phu and he constantly wonders if USA is on winning side."[47]

After the conference, the ROK raised objections to the draft report of the Sixteen to the UN Secretary General, and, with the U.S. supporting it, was able to gain substantial concessions from the other nations on the language. The only major point on which the ROK failed was its insistence on deleting the qualification "by peaceful means" from references to unification. Thus, on September 17, Kenneth Young reported to Ambassador Briggs,

At three-hour meeting [with Sixteen] I made strong and determined effort resolve revisions desired by [ROK Foreign Minister] Dr. Pyun. With help [Pyo Wook] Han's able convincing advocacy ROK viewpoint, result far better than anticipated. Substance all points gained except Para 13 on armistice. . . .[48]

What was it that led Rhee to this almost unbelievable obstinacy in his dealings with the strongest power on earth? Certainly his motivations included his unquestioned deep personal anti-Communist convictions, his genuine and profound desire for reunification, and his real concern for the security of Korea, which in his view had been twice betrayed by the United States in the twentieth century. In addition, his political power in Korea rested in large part upon his proven ability to deal successfully with the United States as an independent nationalist leader (however much the Communists might call him an American stooge).[49]

There were at least two other factors. One was Rhee's bazaar mentality, seeking to bargain for maximum concessions from the United States in economic and military aid, using the threat of independent action as lever. This attitude was exemplified in Briggs's and Dean's cables during the attempt to line up Korea with other Geneva Conference participants in May 1954. Thus, on May 6, Briggs and Dean commented, "Arrival other mission [by retired General James Van Fleet] has to some extent complicated timetable." The next day, they reported, "President seeing General Van Fleet at 2:30 and obviously wants to see what he can get out of him before making any final commitments."[50]

Another source of Rhee's intransigence was the encouragement he received from individual Americans, some of them influential, who applauded his firm anti-Communist stand. Apart from his "kitchen cabinet" of long-time American associates, his supporters included such men as retired General Van Fleet (former commander of UN forces in Korea) and former U.S. Ambassador (to Canada) James Cromwell. The latter was in Korea at Rhee's invitation for an extended visit during the May negotiations and made strong public criticisms of "pro-Communists" in the U.S. Government.[51]

It is beyond the scope of this study to go into the proceedings of the Geneva Conference itself, the public record of which is contained in the publication, *The Korea Question at the Geneva Conference*.[52]   The United States and its allies were thinking in terms of a key role for the United Nations Commission for the Unification and Rehabilitation of Korea (UNCURK, established by the UN General Assembly resolution of October 7, 1950, as a successor to the former UNCOK) in the elections, an idea that Rhee resisted because he resented UNCURK's role in the 1952 political crisis (see Chapter 5). The Communists, on the other hand, wanted a neutral nations supervisory commission, which the allies in their final report of the political conference compared to the Neutral Nations Supervisory Commission established by the armistice.[53]

The allies' report of November 11, 1954, to the United Nations on the political conference contained their two principles for peaceful unification, which underlay all subsequent UN General Assembly resolutions on Korea:

(1) The United Nations, under its Charter, is fully and rightly empowered to take collective action to repel aggression, to restore peace and security, and to extend its good offices to seeking a peaceful settlement in Korea; and

(2) In order to establish a unified, independent and democratic Korea genuinely free elections should be held under United Nations supervision for representatives in a National Assembly, in which representation shall be in direct proportion to the indigenous population in all parts of Korea.

ROK Foreign Minister Pyun, however, made it clear in his proposal to the Conference on May 22, 1954, that for the Republic this meant elections in south Korea in accordance with the constitutional processes of the ROK; and that after the elections, the new National Assembly might amend the ROK constitution if it chose. This reflected substantially the same "elections in north Korea only" formula that the ROK had supported since its formation.[54]

The Unification Question
After the Geneva Conference, 1954-1960

Rhee's Continuing Opposition: His Visit to Washington

In an effort to improve relationships with President Rhee and the ROK, which continued to be very difficult in the political, economic, and military fields, as well as on unification policy, President Rhee was invited to visit the United States. After some blowing hot and cold, he accepted (but not without asking a price), and came to Washington in August 1954. Among other things, he was honored with the opportunity to address a joint session of Congress. His attitude on unification, however, did not perceptibly change. Upon his return to Korea, he told the principal U.S. representatives there that the purpose of his trip had not been to get U.S. aid, but to achieve unification of Korea; he had offered a military plan, since U.S. policy for peaceful unification had failed; since there had been no interest in this plan, he had not presented it. He attacked planned American redeployment (see Chapter 3), and concluded (for the thousandth time) that Korea must now determine its own course, regardless of U.S. assistance. He also mounted a vitriolic anti-U.S. campaign, which the U.S. officially protested. Nevertheless, an internal assessment by the Department's Bureau of Intelligence and Research concluded that Rhee,

> having observed at first hand the cool response in the United States to a call for militant action, has probably revised his misconception of US opinion based on previous residence in the U.S., and is thus less likely to undertake action to reopen hostilities in Korea.[55]

In April 1955, at the height of the crisis over the presence in south Korea of Communist personnel of the Neutral Nations Supervisory Commission (NNSC, see Chapter 3), the ROK National Assembly unanimously passed two resolutions, one urging that the United Nations and the Sixteen abrogate the Armistice Agreement, cooperating with the ROK, and the other recommending that the ROK Government do so. In June, during a conversation with Ambassador John Allison from Tokyo, Rhee irrelevantly said he had decided to announce that "Korea no longer regards itself bound by the provisions of the Armistice Agreement," but then conceded that he did not intend to act unilaterally. He apparently had in mind the return of Kaesong, his concern for which has already been mentioned (page 49, above). Nothing further came of these schemes; the UN Command's expulsion of the NNSC inspection teams alleviated the Korean tensions.[56]

The following year, the uprisings in Poland and Hungary stimulated a south Korean campaign for north Koreans to take similar action, with Rhee again taking a belligerent line. In November, there were reports of ROK military planning for a move along the demilitarized zone. On December 18, 1956, in a conversation with the visiting Assistant Secretary of State Robertson, Rhee played the familiar litany once more, criticizing U.S. softness on Communism and stressing the dangers to the ROK.[57]

New Initiatives at the United Nations

The continuing hypersensitivity of the south Koreans to any hint of U.S. softness toward the Communists, or any willingness to compromise on the unification issue, was repeatedly illustrated. For example, in January 1957, the annual UN General Assembly resolution contained slightly modified wording. It called on UNCURK, among other things, to "observe and report on elections throughout Korea." The ROK National Assembly responded to the UN General Assembly discussions with resolutions again calling for abrogation of the Armistice, and opposing elections throughout Korea as disparaging ROK sovereignty. The U.S. Embassy in Seoul commented that the National Assembly's action was motivated by a desire for international attention, plus the new Chairman's desire to show his support for Rhee's policies, together with real uncertainty regarding the meaning of the new language.

In American representations to the ROK, an attempt was made to meet their concerns by explaining that the new language was not intended to call for nationwide elections, but rather that it was intended to maximize the advantage that the ROK enjoyed, in contrast with the north, by having its own elections observed by UNCURK. This advantage might be highlighted by a north Korean refusal to permit UNCURK observation of elections scheduled in the north later that year.[58]

Despite ROK rigidity, attempts were made by the U.S. and other countries to breathe some life into the UN unification formula, which was becoming an empty litany. Thus in 1957 U.S. Ambassador Walter Dowling (who succeeded William S.B. Lacy in 1956) noted that the Communists in responding to the U.S. statement in the Military Armistice Commission on force modernization on June 21, had repeatedly referred to peaceful settlement of the Korean problem, perhaps to lay the groundwork for proposing a second political conference at the forthcoming UN General Assembly session (as proposed by north Korean Premier Kim Il Sung the same day).

The Ambassador recommended seizing the initiative on the unification issues, as in Germany, utilizing the north Korean suggestion and focusing on projected north Korean elections in August, perhaps with an offer of UNCURK supervision. UNCURK was approached by the Embassy, at Department of State suggestion, and was favorable. However, the Australian Government opposed an offer of UNCURK supervision of north Korean elections on several reasonable grounds, and the idea was dropped.[59]

In October 1957, the Irish delegate to the United Nations General Assembly, speaking in the Special Political Committee, suggested that free elections in Korea might be brought about by substituting an independent international commission of nonaligned countries, designated by the United Nations, for the UN supervision formula which had by then become well established. This idea had some support in New York, but was totally unacceptable to Rhee and his supporters. It was unpalatable to the United States, as well, because it opened the door to manipulation of the unification issue by the Communist nations or by unsympathetic nonaligned countries.

A month later, when a "progressive" ROK National Assembly member endeavored to make political capital out of the peaceful unification issue by proposing political reforms in the south and certain contacts with the north, Rhee was furious and was only with difficulty dissuaded from ordering the arrest of all Assembly members who signed the "questionnaire" containing the proposal. In reporting the incident, the U.S. Embassy commented, "Seems likely line taken by Cho [Bong Am] indicates wider support in Korea for such ideas than previously indicated and will have increasingly greater appeal as disappointment over failure unify country increases.[60]

The Chinese-North Korean Initiative of 1958

The Communists may have seen an opportunity in such events, for in February 1958 they undertook a major unification campaign linked with the withdrawal of Chinese Communist troops from north Korea. On February 5, the north Korean leader, Kim Il Sung, with Chinese Communist endorsement, put forward a proposal involving (1) simultaneous withdrawal of all foreign troops from Korea, (2) free all-Korean elections under neutral nations supervision with "democratic rights and guarantees," (3) negotiations between north and south Korea on the election, on cultural and economic contacts, and freedom of movement, and (4) reduction of armed forces in north and south to minimum levels. These points were similar to the Communist proposals at Geneva in 1954. Omitted was the idea of a second international conference, which the Communists had often advanced in statements since 1954. The Communist initiative was dramatized by the hijacking of a ROK civilian aircraft, possibly timed deliberately for the purpose.[61]

On February 7, 1958, the Chinese Communist statement of support for the north Korean proposals was given to the British chargé d'affaires in Peking, with a request that it be transmitted to the Sixteen. This note touched off consultations with the Sixteen and a series of exchanges of notes between the British, on behalf of the Sixteen, and the Chinese Communists, over a period of about a year, during which the Chinese troops were withdrawn. Many of the Sixteen were disposed to show more flexibility than the United States on a unification formula--the Canadians, for example, proposed referring to Korean elections under United Nations "auspices" instead of "supervision." The ROK continued suspicious and rigid, speaking in its notes of April and June 1958 to the Sixteen of elections in north Korea only. Korean suspicions were intensified by leaks of an internal State Department message soliciting field views and calling for confidential contacts with the Japanese and British. In the end, no changes of position resulted from all the activity, either in Korea or elsewhere.[62]

Indications of Shift in Korean Public Attitudes

In Korea, however, unification was becoming increasingly important as a political issue. In March 1958, Ambassador Dowling expressed doubt that "the ROK government's position now accords with majority public opinion, which has undoubtedly been impressed by announcement Chicom withdrawal." Young people, such as a college student on trial for an article in the school newspaper, were calling for "a new fatherland" based on a form of socialism. The conservative opposition Democratic Party wanted to support the UN formula for unification, rather than the harder government position, although it showed little sympathy for more radical approaches.

A Korean ambassador even confidentially proposed to Ambassador U. Alexis Johnson in Bangkok a deal to exchange Chinese Communist membership in the UN for an agreement to free elections throughout Korea and a possible buffer zone along the northern boundary of a united Korea. The ROK Government's Office of Public Information, for the first time, was showing interest in research on north Korean affairs. The Minister-Counselor of the Korean Embassy in Washington (Han Pyo Wook) delivered a speech to the American Academy of Political and Social Sciences on April 11, 1959, in Ambassador Yang's name, suggesting the possibility of simultaneous elections in north and south Korea, but it was subsequently denied that this represented official thinking.[63]

In the Fall of 1959 (when the UN General Assembly was involved in its annual exercise on the Korean question), the north Koreans mounted a propaganda barrage aimed at withdrawal of U.S. forces, dissolution of UNCURK, and holding of all-Korean elections, orchestrated with letters to world parliaments, including the ROK National Assembly. An attempt by UNCURK to solicit north Korean views had gone unanswered, like all previous UNCURK overtures.[64]

Despite foreign impatience, domestic unhappiness, and Communist blandishments, Rhee maintained the same opinion. In October, when Under Secretary of State Dillon called on him, Rhee's "speech was hesitant and halting and he had difficulty remembering names and places." But he was impatient with the lack of progress on unification, and said that the only way to achieve it was through military force, although he conceded that he would abide by the U.S. approach and follow peaceful means. After the infamous ROK election of March 15, 1960, Rhee aroused foreign concern with his renewed cry for a march north to liberate Korea from the Communist aggressors.[65]

In fact, of course, Rhee was quite right: the only short-term means of reunifying Korea was through military force, which neither side dared to try for fear of losing its friends and support or touching off a wider conflict. The north

Koreans, once they had put themselves back together again after the Korean War, turned to internal subversion and revolt in the south as the next best alternative. For the longer run there was non-violent competition between north and south for internal progress and external support; this was the course of action the United States tried to sell to its south Korean clients. Under these circumstances, the unification issue, and the annual UN General Assembly debates, had by the end of the Rhee regime become simply a propaganda battle and popularity contest, in which the Rhee regime seemed to be losing.[66]

The Unification Question in the
Second and Third Republics, 1960-1965

The New ROK Government and
New Unification Initiatives, 1960-1961

The year 1960 was one of dramatic political change in the United Nations as well as in Korea. The Rhee regime collapsed in April as the result of a student uprising (see Chapter 5). In the UN General Assembly session that Fall, many new nations were admitted to membership, and the Soviet Union, led by Nikita Khrushchev in person, endeavored to put an end to the traditional American leadership.

The United States promptly took advantage of the change of Korean government to urge greater flexibility in approaching the unification problem. The interim Prime Minister, Huh Chung, publicly affirmed on June 23 to American news correspondents that his administration did not accept the unbending "march north" policy of his predecessor, and pointed out that 100 seats in the National Assembly were being reserved for north Korea, as in the past. At the same time, he said that trade and postal exchange with the north was impossible under present circumstances. The U.S. Embassy observed that Huh's views "make clear that ROKG[overnment] not prepared for time being at least to embark on uncertain waters of direct negotiation over unification issues."[67]

When President Eisenhower visited Korea in late June 1960, Chang Myon (John M. Chang), who two months later was to become Prime Minister, handed him a letter reaffirming the Democratic Party's support for the UN formula for unification and the hope for a "bipartisan" front on this policy in Korea. On June 24, Secretary of State Herter marked the tenth anniversary of the Korean War with a special press statement.[68]

However, when the Democrats came to power in Korea after the July 1960 elections they seemed to qualify somewhat their support of the UN formula as they encountered the same political problems as their predecessors. The Foreign Minister's statements in the National Assembly, for example, spoke of UN "observation" of elections in the south, but "supervision" in the north. In the U.S. Embassy's view, these statements reflected apprehension at the growing "unreliability" of the United Nations as the role of neutral nations grew. At the same time, other Korean political leaders were worried about new American initiatives in East Asia under the incoming U.S. Democratic administration; one dissident Democratic Korean Assembly member privately suggested the need for a "new coating" on the ROK unification program, and more independence of the United States to protect Korea's own interest.[69]

There were also new ideas from abroad. Thus a Canadian Embassy officer in November 1960 discussed with State Department representatives an Indian proposal (attributed to Krishna Menon) for a good offices commission composed of half a dozen neutral nations, to study the Korean question, presumably reporting to the UN on means of unification. In the following year, the Indonesians proposed an international conference on Korea, which the U.S. also opposed; and in 1962, the leader of the Indonesian UN General Assembly delegation suggested a good offices commission of nonaligned nations, without specifying how it would be linked with the UN.[70]

The north Koreans, for their part, made the "first significant post-armistice departure from standard North Korean unification proposals" in a liberation anniversary statement by Kim Il Sung on August 14, 1960. In a bitterly anti-American speech, Kim advanced the idea of a north-south federation, with a supreme committee composed of representatives of both regimes. Kim suggested a conference to discuss this and other previous proposals. All were promptly rejected by the ROK interim government. The north Korean federation idea was subsequently supported by Khrushchev in the UN General Assembly.[71]

The United Nations Debate on Korea, 1960-1961

The U.S. sought to maximize UN support for Korea by trying to develop modified language for the annual General Assembly resolution which would attract wider sponsorship, including that of Canada and New Zealand. In March 1961, it was agreed at a meeting of Commonwealth representatives in Washington (the Koreans not present) to incorporate Canadian and New Zealand suggestions for a softened UN resolution referring to elections under UN "auspices" rather than "supervision." However, when the idea was proposed to the ROK Government, its leaders reacted almost as negatively as Rhee would have. Their Ambassador in Washington, Chang Lee Wook, protested strongly that the change might reinforce the Koreans public's impression of weakening American support "and thus aggravate neutralist pressure" within the ROK. The ROK representative to the UN publicly protested the U.S. initiative in concert with other Western powers "behind the stage without giving Korea enough time to study it." The ROK House of Representatives passed a resolution opposing any change in the established UN formula--"a pointed reminder," the U.S. Embassy commented, "that both ROKG and US must tread slowly and carefully in dealing with this most sensitive Korean question." The final agreed draft language therefore evaded the contentious issue by simply referring to previous resolutions.[72]

As it turned out, the substance of the Korean resolution did not come to debate in the UN General Assembly in the 1960-1961 session for lack of time; the issue was joined, instead, over a neutralist move in the 1961 resumed session to invite both north and south Korea to participate in First Committee debate. This was cleverly frustrated by Ambassador Adlai Stevenson, then U.S. Representative to the UN, who suggested an amendment that north Korea (which had incautiously repeated its attacks on past U.S. and UN policies in Korea) first "accept the competence and authority of the United Nations in the Korean question," and that in the meantime the representative of the ROK, which had accepted, be admitted to participation. But the U.S. delegation made some gloomy predictions as to what might have happened if the resolution itself had come to a vote. The Japanese, newly admitted to the UN, played a key role in maximizing support for the ROK.[73]

Unification and the ROK Military Leadership, 1961-1965

Soon after the 1961 UN debate, the unification issue came to the forefront in domestic Korean politics. A National Unification League, backed largely by college students, took advantage of the freedom under the Chang government to plan a meeting with counterparts from the north at Panmunjom (site of the Military Armistice Commission) to discuss national unification. It was likely that covert north Korean encouragement was involved, but the initiative struck a responsive chord among many young south Koreans. The Chang government itself moved to prevent any such meeting; but the seizure of power by a military junta on May 16, 1961, definitively ended such activity. The League's plans were one of the main reasons cited by the junta for their coup d'état.[74]

Once again, the United States moved in the new situation to promote Korean support of peaceful unification, and won a public proclamation from the new military government in June 1961, of a policy of peaceful unification under UN principles. The State Department also suggested that the U.S. Embassy in Seoul promote support for a proposal for Korean unification through UN-supervised elections in north and south (similar to the proposition the Embassy had rejected the year before). Overlooking no possibility, the Department suggested in October that UN Day would be a good time for an appropriate reiteration of Korean support of the UN position; the Koreans, often obliging in small things, did so.[75]

From this time forward, there was no major difference between the ROK and the U.S. on unification policy, although there was ROK resistance to American and other foreign suggestions to avoid the annual UN debate, and a continuing question over what the ROK delegation would do if north Korean representatives were admitted to UN debate on the Korean question. Fortunately, the work of friendly delegations in getting the UN resolution through was facilitated from 1962 onwards by the split between the Soviets and Chinese; the vote favoring the seating of the ROK only, in December 1962, was far better than in 1961, and drew a telegram of gratitude to the U.S. from the ROK Foreign Minister.[76]

By 1965, the Koreans were somewhat more relaxed and realistic about UN support. The Political Committee adoption of the usual seating resolution got front-page treatment in the ROK press, which hailed the event but observed that the tactical victory really amounted to a practical stalemate, and suggested "it might be time for a new government policy at this time." One independent paper (*Hankook Ilbo*) added that the ROK should free itself from the "time-worn habit of relying on the UN for the same conclusions since both the deployment and balance of power at the UN have become not altogether compatible with our national interests." This shift in Korean attitudes had been foreseen by the Embassy in 1961, prophetically commenting on the traumatic maneuverings of that year regarding the UN debate:

> . . . it seems likely that any conservative or liberal-conservative ROKG will hereafter be less and less inclined to place ROK fate in hands of an organization in which Korea's trusted friends seem to be increasingly outnumbered by neutralists and by new found countries which are unreliable, ignorant or disinterested as far as Korean question concerned. ROK also has not accepted unqualified UN competence and authority re question Korean unification and it has only given its specific acquiescence and support to UN formula as now constituted. . . . Increasing "unreliability" of UN may also spark new demands for approaching unification for means outside UN. . . . Before ROKG can be convinced new initiative or changes in current UN formula desirable, US must be in position to assure ROKs convincingly that UN will remain in future, as in past, secure and firm defender of legitimate interests free Korean people, a point on which they are increasingly doubtful.[77]

3

Politico-Military and Security Issues

Political, military, and security considerations were closely intertwined in Korean affairs during the whole 1945-1965 period. The external threat from north Korea was magnified by south Korean leaders for their own purposes, yet it was very real, and required adequate defense if political and economic progress were to be made. Lacking resources to meet the threat by themselves, the south Koreans were heavily dependent upon the United States both for a deterrent U.S. military presence and for equipment and training for Korean forces. At the same time, the size and quality of defense (except during the Korean War) were limited by both U.S. and Korean budgetary considerations.

Internal security problems, also, were very real, threatening the very existence of the Republic in its early years. These problems were partly due to south Korean mismanagement and political opportunism, and partly to the painful heritage of the Japanese occupation; but to a considerable if debatable extent, they were aggravated by the north Koreans. U.S. assistance in this area was more difficult and controversial than external defense, because of Korean sensitivity, American concerns over human rights, and differing cultural values.

For clarity of discussion, these interrelated matters are analyzed under five headings: the military threat; U.S. defense responsibilities; problems of U.S. forces in Korea; military assistance; and internal security. A final section deals with the despatch of Korean forces to Vietnam.

The Threat Prior to the Korean War

U.S. policy from 1947 contemplated the withdrawal of U.S. forces from Korea. By mid-1949, as the withdrawal was being completed, the security of the fledgling Republic looked shaky. The internal security situation was not yet under control, and at the same time there was an escalation of incidents along the 38th parallel. These had begun before independence; in the week ended June 4, 1948, they rose to a new high of 48, some of which involved American patrols. (It is generally believed that the incidents were initiated from both north and south.)

In May 1949, north Korean forces gradually advanced into south Korean territory below the hills overlooking the city of Kaesong, very close to the parallel; they constructed fortifications as they came. The ROK forces attacked and drove the north Koreans back, but not before some artillery rounds had landed in the city. North Koreans also penetrated the line in the nearby Ongjin Peninsula, actions that the U.S. Embassy termed "a continuation of the war of nerves along the parallel."[1]

In August 1949, there was a north Korean attack near Ch'unch'on in central Korea. In September, the ROK Foreign Minister addressed identical notes to the twenty-one governments that had recognized the Republic, noting the threat to its security, and predicting even larger attacks in future unless friendly governments could "find a solution for this dangerous situation within the near future." In October, a memorandum from ROK Defense Minister Sihn to President Rhee gave a projected timetable of north Korean actions and predicted a north Korean invasion of the south in March 1950. He was only three months off.[2]

The Embassy, at State Department request, evaluated the security situation in June 1949, and concluded that although there were many indications of trouble,

> . . . it is the considered view of this Mission that neither South Korea nor North Korea, with what would appear to be fairly evenly balanced forces, is likely in the foreseeable future to assume the risks associated with a deliberate allout invasion. . . . It cannot be ruled out that the removal of the stabilizing force may in the end contribute to the initiation of a general conflict.

Noting the intensification of military preparations in the north, the Embassy said that the ROK Army "would give an excellent account of itself against the North Koreans." At this time, the U.S. was worried about a south Korean attack as well as a north Korean one, and--as President Rhee publicly noted in May 1949--had insisted on the deployment of civilian police along the 38th parallel, with ROK military forces in reserve, as a means of preventing ROK unilateral action.[3]

The difference between the ROK and the Americans in appraising the threat continued. The Koreans at first welcomed the prospective withdrawal of foreign troops, but then opposed U.S. withdrawal until they could develop their own armed strength. The U.S. forces withdrew anyway, although the timetable was stretched out by six months, and Korean nervousness increased as aid to their own forces arrived slowly and in far less amount than they wanted. In

May, 1949, the differing appraisals showed vividly in a heated encounter between the President and Ambassador Muccio, in which the Koreans wanted assurance of U.S. support of a kind the Ambassador could not give.

> The President then asserted it had been suggested the U.S. had decided it is not worth while to try to defend Korea. . . . The story of the contraction of the U.S. defense line had been spread all over Korea. . . . He would be grateful if President Truman and the State Department could help him clarify this situation.[4]

The only assurance of this character that President Rhee received was one he attributed to General MacArthur in October 1948: the General, he said, told him, "I will defend Korea as I would my own country--just as I would California." In August 1949, Rhee wrote to President Truman to emphasize the danger from north Korea and ask more aid. Truman's reply followed the same general lines as General Wedemeyer's appraisal (see page 93 below).[5]

In May 1950, the ROK pulled out all stops in a campaign to dramatize the security threat. Defense Minister Sihn, at a hurriedly-called press conference, announced that the arrival of two divisions of "Chinese Communist troops" in north Korea had raised the force level there to 183,100, plus paramilitary organizations, for a total of 300,000. Sihn's statement detailed north Korean force composition, including a tank brigade, mechanized cavalry, heavy guns, and so on. (A defecting north Korean officer in 1955 told of the training of three divisions of Koreans from China in 1949, and described deployments of forces for attack in the Spring of 1950.) The impact of Sihn's statements on Americans was diluted, however, by the recognition that they were intended to maximize Congressional action on Korean aid.[6]

American skepticism continued until the invasion came. In part this was due to an unwillingness to believe the Soviets would either launch an invasion or allow their north Korean "puppets" to do so. Ambassador Muccio, in the 1949 conversation above referred to, told President Rhee that the best defense was "a good, strong and good government in Korea . . . that will satisfy the aspirations of the Korean people"; that U.S. aid was sufficient for Korean defense short of an international conflagration, which the U.S. was seeking to avoid; and that "it was not up to us here to prepare for a hot war. Should that unfortunately come about, the military would have to get in and take over direction." These statements reflected the American consensus at the time.[7]

Perhaps the most revealing indication of the American appraisal of the risks to Korean security was the insouciance about KMAG personnel. In the Spring of 1950, there was uncertainty about who would replace General Roberts as Chief of the U.S. military advisory group, or when; yet "General Roberts's wife ill, hence [he] may have to leave earlier than planned." There was also doubt about the replacement of the KMAG Chief of Staff, and all other senior officers were to be replaced at the same time. When the invasion came, neither the Chief of KMAG nor the Chief of Staff was in Korea.[8]

Aside from some reevaluation of military assistance levels (see pages 94-95 below), the principal response to Korean concerns was the UN General Assembly resolution of October 21, 1949, which (in operative paragraph 1[a]) specifically charged the UN Commission with the responsibility to "observe and report any developments which might lead to or otherwise involve military conflict in Korea." This proposal had been foreshadowed by the El Salvador delegate to the Commission, who recommended in the Spring of 1949 that the Commission should have military observers. Such observers did arrive in Korea soon enough to verify the defensive disposition of the ROK Army just before the invasion.[9]

U.S. Defense Responsibilities

Originally, the United States saw its responsibility toward Korea as a joint one with other countries in an international trusteeship to assure viability as an independent state. This first phase ended with the breakdown of negotiations with the Soviet Union in 1947 and separate elections in the south in 1948. In a second phase, the United States sought to disengage itself from direct involvement in Korean defense by strengthening the ROK security forces, withdrawing U.S. forces, and substituting the umbrella of United Nations collective security.[10]

The north Korean attack in 1950 opened a third phase, in which the United States, under the UN umbrella, in fact assumed the lion's share of defending an independent south Korea by force of arms. In the light of the Communist assault, Korea assumed a greater importance in U.S. national interest calculations. Thereafter, the Koreans successfully engaged the United States in a bilateral mutual defense treaty, which--together with the deployment of U.S. forces in Korea--they have since regarded as the major source of their security. This "fourth phase" continued throughout the remainder of the twenty-year period under review, with no substantial change in U.S. defense commitments or deployments.

Force Levels and Deployments

The principal issues concerning U.S. defense responsibilities--apart from military assistance, discussed above--were U.S. force levels and deployments in Korea; U.S. responsibilities, under UN resolutions, for the Unified Command; the related issue of responsibilities under the Armistice Agreement of 1953; the negotiation and implementation of the Mutual Defense Treaty of 1954; and the containment of risks of south Korean unilateral military action.

In 1945, three U.S. Army divisions (6th, 7th, and 40th) comprising the XXIV Corps of Lt. Gen. John R. Hodge, occupied Korea. Their task at that time was to disarm the Japanese forces and to maintain order pending international negotiations for a transitional government of Korea. The 40th Division very soon departed, and military energies focused on problems of military government administration and negotiations with the Soviet authorities. U.S. troops were occasionally called upon in civil disturbances, but basic reliance was placed on the Korean police. The remaining forces of the two combat divisions were withdrawn gradually after the establishment of the Republic of Korea; the last regimental combat team departed on June 29, 1949, leaving a 250-man provisional advisory group as the sole U.S. military deployment.

Very soon after the outbreak of hostilities in June 1950, President Truman committed air and naval support to Korea--first to protect American citizens, then (following the UN Security Council resolution of June 27) in support of Korean forces. In early July, following General MacArthur's personal survey of the situation, elements of the U.S. 24th Division were deployed to Korea from Japan. A buildup followed which reached a peak level of five U.S. divisions and supporting units, plus a British Commonwealth division (comprised of units from Australia, Canada, New Zealand, and the United Kingdom), a Turkish brigade, and smaller land, naval, and air contributions from ten other nations (Belgium, Colombia, Ethiopia, France, Greece, Luxembourg, Netherlands, Philippines, South Africa, Thailand). The United States mounted a major effort to promote contributions of men and material from as many countries as possible, principally to preserve the international character of the defense effort as the first collective security action of the United Nations.

Following the signing of the Armistice Agreement (after difficult negotiations with the south Koreans, as well as with the enemy--see Chapter 2), the United States undertook to redeploy the bulk of its forces out of Korea, while building up the ROK forces and seeking (with very limited success) to persuade other countries to leave their contingents in the United Nations Command. The redeployment was, however, deferred until after the 1954 political conference, and the plans kept secret, on the basis that the U.S. would lose bargaining power if they became known.[11]

President Rhee, who had written a protest to President Eisenhower on March 11, 1954, was given the President's reply on March 22, and took it mildly, observing that it was clear the U.S. wanted to reduce its personnel, which was understandable. However, in September, Ambassador Ellis Briggs protested to the Prime Minister at a ROK general's statement that the Koreans were uninformed of redeployment plans, which was only one aspect of the general anti-U.S. campaign being conducted at the time. At a rally on September 28, protests against U.S. troop withdrawal were among the themes; this was followed by a demonstration in front of the Embassy and an ultimatum that unless the demonstration received satisfaction in regard to the termination of U.S. redeployment, they would return on October 1 and blockade the Embassy indefinitely. Ambassador Briggs, asked by Washington to call Rhee's attention to misleading Korean statements about U.S. troop withdrawal each time such statements appeared, responded that further such representations would be anticlimactic; that what would most likely restrain Rhee would be public indications from Washington of distaste for his behavior.[12]

In early 1955, senior U.S. commanders favored either total removal of U.S. forces (preceded by a campaign to build up Korean confidence in their own forces), or retention of a token force such as a regimental combat team; they also favored releasing operational control of ROK forces. State's Bureau of Far Eastern Affairs opposed such action, pointing out that ROK leaders recalled that the north Korean attack had come only a year after the previous U.S. withdrawal. The Joint Chiefs of Staff disagreed among themselves as to the desirability of total withdrawal. In the end, the retention advocates carried the day.[13]

The only subsequent major changes in U.S. forces, up to 1965, involved conversion to pentomic divisions in 1957 (when the 24th Division was redesignated as the 1st Cavalry Division) and the rotation of U.S. Air Force units in and out of Korea in place of the previous permanently assigned wing, as a part of the force modernization program (see pages 98-99, below). At a Washington meeting discussing modernization in September 1957, while the Secretary of Defense (Quarles) said that plans called for no U.S. divisions to remain in Korea after June 30, 1961, Secretary of State Dulles said that if Rhee went along on Korean force reductions, the U.S. was honor bound to keep two divisions there. From 1960 to 1963, actual U.S. manning levels were allowed to fall to around 52,000 without any visible organizational changes; in March 1965, actual strength dropped to 48,000, but apparently the under-strength was not observed by the Koreans.[14]

In 1958, when the Chinese Communist forces withdrew from Korea, the Japanese government voiced concern that the United States might respond by withdrawing its forces: their Embassy counselor in Washington expressed the view that the Communists were not sincere in withdrawing, but wanted to put the United States on the defensive and gain support for Chinese respectability.[15]

U.S. internal consideration of U.S. deployments continued, however. In late 1960, the National Security Council sponsored a net evaluation study of limited war situations in Korea and Taiwan, assuming both sides used nuclear weapons. In 1962, a working-level Bureau of Far Eastern Affairs evaluation held that the political effects of withdrawing one division from Korea would be (1) to arouse renewed Korean fears of abandonment, (2) to cause loss of prestige for the current Korean government and reduce prospects of its cooperation with the U.S., (3) to cause Korean demands for more autonomy of command, (4) to increase the likelihood of independent ROK negotiations with the north (a possibility regarded as more likely during the 1961-63 military government period than before or since).

Although proper advance preparation might mitigate the effects, the Bureau did not believe the time for withdrawal was then ripe, nor could such a time be foreseen. The Joint Chiefs of Staff objected to moving a division from Korea to Okinawa, because it would weaken the position in Korea and possibly reduce flexibility of deployment in the Pacific, and because of moving costs and logistics. While Governor Averill Harriman (then Assistant Secretary of State) favored the redeployment, the Secretary of State (Christian Herter) concurred with the Deputy Secretary of Defense (Roswell Gilpatric) that withdrawal at the time was inadvisable.[16]

The following year, Deputy Under Secretary of State Johnson opposed the proposal of the Chairman of the Joint Chiefs of Staff (Maxwell Taylor) to withdraw both U.S. divisions from Korea and base Korean defense on nuclear weapons. Johnson's objections were based on geopolitical grounds as well as on Korean problems. He noted among other things that such a plan would be criticized as "racist," contrasting as it would with the European policy. Johnson also noted,

> Even in the coups of the last few years our conventional forces have placed a certain limit on the extremes to which events could move in South Korea and provided a shield between North and South Korea, reducing the danger of civil strife involving the two parts of the country.

Moreover, he said, studies had shown that U.S. troop withdrawals would have little effect on the U.S. balance of payments, because of the need for a compensating increase in aid. Thus, "on balance the political, military and economic factors seem to weigh against taking such action." But in future, with better mobility, a reduction might be considered.[17]

In 1965, Ambassador Berger successfully opposed planned reductions in actual manning levels (as part of a worldwide effort to conserve dollars) to 48,700, from the then existing 55,000 (out of a table of organization level of 70,000). He noted that it would be difficult to conceal such a shortage for long, and that it would have adverse political as well as military effects.[18]

The United Nations Command and Operational Control

In its third resolution after the outbreak of the Korean War, the United Nations Security Council on July 7, 1950, recommended that all UN members "providing military forces and other assistance . . . make such forces and other assistance available to a unified command under the United States," and requested "the United States to designate the commander of such forces." General MacArthur was designated the first United Nations commander. In a letter of July 15, President Rhee placed the Korean forces under MacArthur's command. The Agreed Minute of Understanding that accompanied the 1954 mutual defense treaty (and as subsequently revised) replaced that letter as the basis, not for command, but for operational control of Korean forces.

Korean Forces' Performance. There was much American criticism of Korean combat performance from the very beginning of the Korean War. Some of the criticism was unjustified, and American evaluators differed; but all of it bothered the Koreans. In the dark days of the Chinese drive southward in early 1961, ROK Ambassador Chang Myon (John M. Chang) referred to uncomplimentary American press reports in a conversation with the Secretary of State (Dean Rusk), and "asked if something could be done to moderate the tone of the U.S. press." The Secretary said, "the Department had received the impression that the ROK troops were acquitting themselves very well.[19]

International Contingents. The long history of U.S. diplomatic efforts to keep at least token contingents of other UN members in the UN Command is beyond the scope of this study, but many man-hours were expended in arm-twisting and assorted blandishments to prevent or retard the withdrawal of Philippine, British Commonwealth, Turkish, Greek, and other units. Secretary Dulles, for example, appealed to President Ramon Magsaysay in March 1955 to keep the Philippine unit in Korea; in August, Dulles discussed Commonwealth force levels with Sir Anthony Eden. Representations by U.S. ambassadors continued throughout ensuing years.

The Korean Role in the United Nations Command. Despite their acceptance of the UN Command as the price of an international presence, the Koreans were sensitive about their subordinate status in it. In early 1955, they were pressing for placing ROK military officers in staff positions within the UN Command (UNC), and "officers such as General Chung Il Kwon" were "particularly anxious for ROK regain control own armed forces." The Koreans also objected to having the UNC headquarters in Tokyo, rather than in Seoul, and the decision of July 18, 1956, to move it was enthusiastically greeted by ROK officials as "response of UN to people's demand and sign of increasing UN confidence in Korea." In 1956, the Koreans were suggesting that a ROK officer be appointed Deputy United Nations Commander--an idea that the Department of State opposed because of the UN character of the command and anticipated objections by allies.[20]

In September 1960, after the Rhee regime was replaced by that of Chang Myon, a senior U.S. general (Palmer) visiting Korea made public remarks opposing a reduction of Korean forces (then the policy of the new ROK government) and objecting to the loss of many experienced Korean officers through "political pressures." The United Nations Commander, General Carter Magruder, supported Palmer's position, as did many ROK officers; but the ROK Chief of Staff vehemently protested Palmer's action as interference in Korean domestic affairs. The incident blew over; but it illustrated ROK sensitivity over its relationship to American military commanders. General Magruder's and General Carter's concern was well-grounded; for the same unrest which the Chief of Staff cited in justifying his removal of the six generals in question eventually led to the coup d'etat of May 1961.[21]

Challenges to UN Operational Control. The first problem with the operational control of the United Nations Commander (CINCUNC) over ROK forces came during the political crisis of 1951-52 (see Chapter 5), when President Rhee appointed a Joint Provost Marshal General with jurisdiction over a special group of internal security and intelligence troops. This officer, General Won Yung Duk, reported directly to the President and was not responsive to UNC control. However, his interference with regular military operations was kept small both by CINCUNC pressure and by the resentment of the regular military forces.

As soon as the Korean Navy was established, the ROK wanted to use it to keep Japanese fishermen out of a large area of the surrounding seas. The United States endeavored to avoid involvement by permitting establishment of a separate Coast Guard, which had no U.S.-provided equipment or assistance. At times during the Korean War period the danger of ROK naval action against Japanese ships was serious. The issue was not resolved until ROK-Japan relations were normalized in 1965.

In 1953 and 1954, President Rhee threatened to order unilateral military action by his forces, but no such action was ever taken. No further serious threat was posed to UN operational control during his administration, although requests were made to the UN Commander for withdrawal of certain units in cases of civil disturbance. The United States was nevertheless sufficiently concerned at the possibility of unilateral military action so that American representatives directly counseled senior Korean military commanders against it, in accordance with U.S. policy directives (see page 79, below).

During the "second republic" period, in October 1960, Assemblyman Yang Il-tong announced his intention to press for restoration of ROK government control over its own forces, and questioned the constitutionality of former President Rhee's July 15, 1950 letter putting Korean forces under UN command. The American chargé d'affaires called on Prime Minister Chang to point out that the basic authority for UN operational control was actually the 1954 Agreed Minute, and that this Minute was also the basis for needed U.S. assistance. The Defense Minister subsequently made a public statement reaffirming UNC operational control.[22]

The military coup d'état of May 16, 1961 was in itself a major contravention of UNC operational control, and one of the first U.S. concerns thereafter was to reassert it. The military government, after some hedging, finally acknowledged operational control, including the UN Commander's right to approve designations of senior ROK commanders. However, the Capital

Defense Command (responsible for preventing counter-coups) remained outside UNC jurisdiction, and the question of personnel jurisdiction was always an open one thereafter because of the nationalist attitude of the military leaders.

At the time of the coup d'état, General Magruder had issued orders calling on military commanders to support the constitutional government. Accordingly, in 1962, when the ROK government indicted General Kim Ung-Soo for having obeyed General Magruder's orders, among other things, the Department instructed the Embassy to make strong representations opposing such charges. The original indictment accused Kim of having instructed artillery elements of the ROK VI Corps to return to their positions on orders of the UN Commander, and of having disseminated copies of statements by General Magruder and Chargé d'Affaires Marshall Green, supporting the constitutional regime. This portion of the indictment was withdrawn. The "revolutionary prosecution office" explained the action publicly on the basis that the revolutionary court respected the importance of UN operational control, although it had the right to punish its own traitor in its own way. General Kim's ten-year sentence was remitted by Park Chung Hee as head of the military government.

The continuing problem of operational control was again demonstrated in 1965, when the ROK Defense Minister notified CINCUNC at ten o'clock one morning of six proposed changes of senior ROK commanders, requesting concurrence, and publicly announced the changes at one o'clock that afternoon without further consultation.[23]

The Armistice Agreement

The main problems for the United States in its relations with Korea regarding the armistice, concluded July 27, 1953, involved the activities of the Neutral Nations Supervisory Commission; the limitations on weapons types imposed by the armistice; the Korean role in the Military Armistice Commission; the threat of ROK unilateral abrogation of the Armistice Agreement; and violations of the Agreement by military incursion--chiefly by the north Koreans--and by infiltration. (Military violations, as a chiefly military matter, are not discussed here.)

Neutral Nations Supervisory Commission (NNSC). Although the Communists had originally proposed the NNSC and suggested the four nations composing it, they obstructed its activities in north Korea from the first. The south Koreans bitterly resented the presence of Communist representatives in the south, whom they accused (with some reason) of espionage and propaganda. The four NNSC members never agreed on any substantive issue, the Czechs and Poles invariably supporting Communist allegations. The net effect was to cloak illegal reinforcement of Communist strength and equipment (in violation of the

Armistice Agreement, which limited both sides to the number of troops and the numbers and types of weapons in Korea when hostilities ceased).

President Rhee therefore demanded that the NNSC inspection teams (NNITs, of which there were five on each side in designated ports of entry, plus ten mobile teams) be removed from the ROK. The UN Commander (Hull) shared this view, and told the Swedish and Swiss representatives in May 1954 that the United States would appreciate their withdrawal by their governments (thus effectively terminating the NNSC). The Swedish and Swiss governments had themselves voiced their unhappiness with the operation of the NNSC the previous month in notes to governments on both sides.[24]

The ROK government grew more insistent in its demand for removal of the NNSC. There were demonstrations outside three NNIT compounds in August. Ambassador Briggs sympathized with the ROK position. The UN Command on one occasion refused to permit inspection of an alleged violation requested by the Communist side, citing past Communist obstruction. However, other Communist-requested inspections continued for several months without major incident, as both the Ambassador and CINCUNC sought to restrain the ROK, lest the appearance of coercion hamper delicate international negotiations to eliminate the problem.

The United States consulted with the Sixteen (nations who had contributed forces to the UN Command), who agreed that the Swedes and Swiss should be encouraged to end the NNSC by withdrawing from it. In the Fall of 1954, the senior Swedish representative to the NNSC suggested the removal of the resident inspection teams. However, State and Defense were unable to agree on a U.S. position, with State favoring the Swedish slow-and-steady approach and Defense (especially the field commanders, Generals Hull and Taylor) wanting total and immediate elimination of the NNSC.[25]

In January 1955 the Swedes and Swiss responded to continued pressures applied by the U.S. in coordination with the United Kingdom and France. Similar notes addressed to the principal governments on both sides favored the abolition of the NNSC, or, if that could not be arranged, a substantial reduction in NNSC activities. The Chinese rejected the abolition of the Commission, but accepted a reduction in strength. The United States responded that while it favored total elimination, it would accept the stationing of a reduced Commission within the Demilitarized Zone (DMZ, a strip four kilometers wide between the opposing forces), where it could continue to accept reports from both sides. General Hull objected to this position.[26]

The ROK manifested renewed impatience with lack of action, although it indicated acquiescence in a reduced NNSC within the DMZ. At the same time, north Korea began to play up NNSC activities in its radio propaganda coverage. In March 1955 the Swiss formally stated their unwillingness to go beyond a reduction in NNSC activities, while the ROK started publicly to assert its right to unilateral action if necessary to throw out the Communist "spies"--a position assailed in both the Korean and Swedish press as an "ultimatum."

Nevertheless, within the NNSC itself, the Swedes proposed both reduction of personnel and withdrawal of the teams to the DMZ. The proposal was discussed in April; the Communists opposed it vigorously and the Swiss gave no support. However, the Czech and Polish representatives counterproposed a 50 percent reduction by cutting the teams from four representatives to two, and the Chinese informally suggested to the Swiss that the number of teams be reduced.[27]

On May 3, 1955, the four members of the NNSC unanimously agreed to propose withdrawal of four of the ten resident NNITs, and reduction of the remaining six to two representatives each. This solution was unacceptable either to the ROK or to the U.S. military authorities. Hence, although the Communist side in the Military Armistice Commission accepted the NNSC proposal, the UNC side did not.

Since the United States could not reach internal agreement on its own position, the proposal remained unanswered for over three months. The matter was referred to President Eisenhower in a conference on May 11, in which he supported the Secretary of Defense (Anderson) in a suggestion to authorize General Taylor, as field commander, to suspend the provisions of the Armistice Agreement relating to the NNSC and NNITs. Prime Minister Macmillan of the United Kingdom sympathized with this approach, but the United Kingdom eventually decided against it. The Swedes registered their impatience with the continuing delay in the U.S. decision.[28]

For a time, Ambassador Briggs and his successor, William S.B. Lacy, were successful in keeping President Rhee from drastic action, by assurances that progress was being made. In July 1955, however, the ROK acted on its own--not only because of impatience with NNSC negotiations, but also because of concerns growing out of the U.S.-Soviet Summit meeting and the beginning of U.S. talks with the Chinese Communists in Geneva. The ROK demanded return of "its territory" south of the 38th parallel in the west, removal of NNSC personnel from the ROK, and abrogation of the Armistice Agreement. These demands were accompanied by a planned program of "popular" demonstrations of growing intensity, to protest the NNSC teams. On August 6, the ROK delivered an ultimatum to the NNSC (through the ROK representative on the Military Armistice Commission) to evacuate its personnel from the ROK.

U.S. troops prepared to defend the NNSC personnel. U.S. pressure (including a call on Rhee, at Washington's instruction, by Ambassador Lacy and General Lyman Lemnitzer, now the UN Commander) avoided extremes of violence, and Rhee backed down on his ultimatum, but the net result was to complicate the diplomatic problem of disposing of the NNSC. Neither the U.S. nor the Swedes or Swiss were prepared to respond to duress.[29]

The Korean demonstrations slacked off, but did not stop, as U.S. representatives explained that they were hindering rather than helping the desired results. Meantime, State finally persuaded Defense to accept a compromise by which the May 3 reduction proposal would be accepted, with the understanding that the Swedes and Swiss would be asked to pull out of the NNSC entirely by October 15 (the deadline to be kept quiet); if NNITs had not been withdrawn by then, CINCUNC could act unilaterally to remove them. After further consultation with the Sixteen, and with the Swedes and Swiss, and notification in general terms to the ROK, the UNC was authorized to accept the May 3 proposal. On August 29, 1955, a joint letter was signed by the senior representatives of both sides on the Military Armistice Commission, informing the NNSC that there were no objections to carrying out the reduction. This was accomplished by early September.[30]

The Swiss and Swedes then continued their negotiations with the Communists to bring about a removal of the remaining NNSC personnel from the ROK. (The Swiss, in particular, were unwilling to move for the total abolition of the NNSC; and although Swedish views were sympathetic to abolition, the Swedish Ambassador in Washington (Beheman) gently pointed out the possible utility of having "the Swiss and Swedes in the DMZ to be available to identify the aggressor in the event of a renewal of hostilities by the Communists. . . ."

The main hope for success appeared to lie in a Communist desire to preserve some part of the NNSC institution. Soviet commentary on the demonstrations in the ROK in August had been relatively mild, noting among other things that some U.S. troops had been injured in defending NNIT compounds. But the negotiations moved very slowly. Rhee was by no means satisfied with the NNIT reductions; after October 15, his impatience again mounted. In November 1955 he set a ninety-day limit to ROK tolerance, and critical propaganda began again. Meantime, State prevailed on Defense to postpone the deadline for unilateral CINCUNC action until January 1, 1956--partly to avoid adverse reaction in the UN General Assembly--and this "absolute deadline" was later postponed again. Rhee, also, postponed his limit.[31]

In January 1956 the UN Commander introduced a new consideration: he wanted to bring a new type of weapon into Korea in the form of all-weather jet fighters, to offset jet aircraft introduced into north Korea, and wanted the NNITs out of Korea to facilitate this action. He proposed a single action to suspend both relevant articles of the Armistice Agreement, so as to permit weapons modernization and dissolution of the NNSC. State did not agree, preferring less drastic action. The Swedish Foreign Office raised the same question, in some annoyance, with U.S. Ambassador Cabot, pointing out that modern weapons would violate the Armistice whether or not the NNITs were present. Reporting the conversation, Cabot recalled that he had been instructed to intimate to the

Swedes that introduction of weapons was not the U.S. intention in seeking the removal of the NNSC, and that he had twice done so a year previously.[32]

The modern weapons issue (discussed below) was, as the Swedes pointed out, a separate one from that of the NNSC, but the two were interrelated, and there was a tactical problem of whether to act on both fronts at once or handle them separately. (The U.S. Embassy in Seoul reversed its previous position, and supported the CINCUNC desire to act on both at once.) This question, plus ROK impatience and the growing unlikelihood of effective action by the Swedes and Swiss, were considered in U.S. and Allied consultations during the Spring. Meanwhile, the chargé in Seoul (Carl Strom) bought some more time from President Rhee.

Still another new dimension of the problem was a Chinese Communist note, received by the British chargé d'affaires in Peking on April 9, 1956 for transmission to all states members of the UN Command. Referring to Swiss and Swedish representations regarding the NNSC, it said the problem could not be resolved without attention to the more fundamental question of withdrawal of foreign troops and unification, and proposed, on behalf of the Chinese and north Koreans, an international conference with the nations concerned. The note, in effect, ended the possibility of Swiss and Swedish action.

After a month of consultations with the Swiss and Swedes and among the Sixteen, the British delivered an agreed response to the Chinese on May 28, on behalf of the Sixteen. It rejected the conference proposal, stated that the NNSC was an inequitable burden on the UN side, and said that the UN Command would announce its position in the Military Armistice Commission. The UNC did so on May 31; the substance of the note to the Chinese had leaked to the press in the meantime. The ROK rejected anything short of eliminating the NNSC.[33]

On June 2, the Chinese responded directly to a Swedish note of March 16, accepting its proposal for withdrawal of the NNITs subject to provision for possible future inspections. (The Swiss had now become firmer than the Swedes on unconditional withdrawal.) After discussion within the NNSC, an agreed NNSC recommendation for withdrawal with "no change in the legal status of the NNSC" was sent to both sides of the Military Armistice Commission on June 5. The Communist side accepted it, subject to the continued right of inspection (which it had some legitimate claim to do, because of confusion in the language of the British note).

CINCUNC, in reporting this action, concluded that the arrangement would not serve UNC objectives. After consulting again in Washington with the Sixteen, and despite last-minute attempts to bring about voluntary NNSC withdrawal, the U.S. gave a go-ahead for unilateral removal of the NNITs from south Korea. This was accomplished without incident by June 9. Reporting by the UNC to the NNSC continued for a time.[34]

The ouster of NNSC personnel from the ROK drew relatively little world attention, and the NNSC itself subsequently received scant attention. Non-Communist reaction was not unfavorable; even the Swiss minister in Stockholm privately expressed gratification that the problem had been eliminated. The UN Command continued to favor total abolition of the NNSC; the Swiss and Swedes blew hot and cold on the issue.

In 1958, however, U.S. Ambassador Walter Dowling in Seoul responded to a Washington inquiry by saying that Swiss and Swedish participation in NNSC was useful: the presence of an internationally-recognized body in the Demilitarized Zone was in itself a deterrent to renewed hostilities, and helped to focus world attention on Communist aggression in Korea. Withdrawal might signal relaxation, and make it more difficult to maintain Allied support for the U.S. position. Moreover, the Swiss and Swedes, as objective observers, contributed indirectly to the support of the U.S. and Allied position on the Korean question. The Ambassador observed that no ROK opinion had recently been voiced, but that the Swiss and Swedes were then travelling freely in the ROK, as well as in the north.[35]

In March 1958, at the time of the Chinese troop withdrawal, the Communists also implicitly acknowledged the value of the NNSC by asking it to supervise and inspect the withdrawal. The NNSC considered the request at a meeting on March 14, but did not agree to supervision.[36]

The Swiss and Swedish members of the NNSC continued to be valuable sources of information on north Korea, which they were able to visit from time to time. They frequently came to south Korea on quiet personal visits. By 1962, the climate in south Korea had changed sufficiently so that the UN Command member on the Military Armistice Commission, with Washington and ROK government clearance, invited two Polish and two Czech members of the NNSC for a visit to Seoul on October 6 and 7. The visitors had no contacts outside MAC personnel, but they were reported to be "favorably impressed by appearance orderliness and prosperity in Seoul."[37]

Weapon Modernization. The language of the Armistice Agreement limiting weapons of both sides to the numbers and types present in Korea at the cessation of hostilities quickly proved onerous to the UN Command for three reasons. (The Agreement similarly limited the numbers of military personnel, but force levels were not a problem, since no need to increase them was seen.)

--First, Communist frustration of NNSC activities, plus intelligence reports of Communist violations, aroused fear of a buildup on the Communist side with a resulting danger to the UN forces. As noted above, illegal Communist intro-duction of jet aircraft into north Korea caused great concern; and in early 1957, the Far East Command called attention to north Korean superiority in artillery, with twice as many divisional weapons as the ROK.

--Second, the introduction of improved weaponry into the ROK--"modernization"--was seen as the only way of bringing about a reduction in ROK troop strength.

--Third, the replacement of obsolete equipment was a difficult logistic problem. American production of many of the World War II types of weapons used in Korea had already ceased, or was being phased out. Moreover, nuclear-capable weapons, a major and growing basis for U.S. military strength in this period, were denied to the UN Command under the Armistice Agreement because they had not been used in the Korean War.

In June 1954 a memorandum on possible policy changes from the Korea desk officer in State (William G. Jones) reflected the thinking in State and Defense. It suggested that since the division of Korea was permanent for practical purposes, in the aftermath of the abortive Geneva conference, the UN Command should be relieved of the constraints of Armistice provisions "made onerous for it by Communist violations." From that time on, much thought was given to the method by which these constrains might be removed.

While State and Defense agreed on general principles, they differed on tactics. State favored a gradual approach to modernization, because of world opinion and the risk of jeopardizing the entire Armistice Agreement. Defense favored prompt and forthright action on both the restrictive issues--the NNSC (discussed above) and weapon limitations.

Separate action was first taken on the NNSC issue. For a time the State policy on modernization, based on a legal opinion by State's Legal Adviser (Phleger) and transmitted to Defense in May 1956, was that obsolete and worn-out equipment might be replaced with new items "within the terms of Paragraph 13(d) as a matter of interpretation." Defense was not satisfied. At a State-Defense conference in September 1956, the Chairman of the Joint Chiefs of Staff (Radford) bluntly stated the military intention to introduce atomic weapons and warheads into Korea and the resultant need to suspend Article 13(d), which in his view could not be "interpreted" to permit them. State and Defense lawyers subsequently confirmed this judgment.[38]

In the end, the Defense view prevailed. The United States in the Spring of 1957 undertook to get the support of British Commonwealth and other members of the Sixteen for a publicly announced suspension of Article 13(d). The legal rationale, although difficult, was developed by the Legal Adviser for the NNSC case, but it required effective demonstration of violations by the Communist side. Curiously, the Defense Department was unable to develop a completely convincing brief showing such violations, a fact which bothered the British. Nonetheless the senior UNC member announced in a Military Armistice Commission meeting on June 21, 1957, that the UN Command considered itself relieved of its obligations under Article 13(d). On June 29, he notified the NNSC that there would be no more UN Command reports on replacement of weapons, aircraft, and equipment (although reporting of personnel continued).

The Communist side continued to report, but the NNSC ceased to submit monthly evaluations to the Military Armistice Commission.[39]

The ROK reaction to suspension of Article 13(d) was of course enthusiastic, but a new problem was raised: if the United States brought in atomic-capable weapons for its own troops, the Koreans wanted them, too; otherwise, they saw themselves in second-class status. World reaction to the suspension was milder than expected. Non-Communist opinion generally supported the action, on the basis of the need to restore the military balance in the light of Communist violations. Communist comment "was heavy and vituperative, but there was nothing striking or new. . . ." The north Koreans called for withdrawal of foreign troops and a political conference. The UN Command filed a report with the United Nations in August 1957, in anticipation of debate in the UN General Assembly. In the following year, the Chinese pulled their "volunteers" out of Korea. Nevertheless, for several years thereafter they did attend meetings of the Military Armistice Commission.[40]

Threat of ROK Unilateral Action. Given the strongly anti-Communist sentiments of the Korean conservatives, and especially those of President Rhee, coupled with the strength of Korean aspirations for unification, the United States was greatly concerned even before the Korean War at the possibility of a ROK military adventure against north Korea, once it had gained a measure of military strength. Up to mid-1949, the time of heavy north Korean assaults on the 38th parallel, American advisers had civil police stationed in front of the ROK military units to guard against any such ill-advised ROK initiative.

After the armistice was concluded, the possibility of ROK unilateral action became a major U.S. concern. The armistice and the abortive political conference of the following year were intensely frustrating to Rhee, who believed (not without reason) that his hopes for unification had been dashed by outside decisions in which he had not been fully consulted. He himself firmly believed that the only possibility of unification was through force, and viewed the issue emotionally and somewhat irrationally. Both publicly and privately, he talked and planned for a "march north for unification," the Korean phrase for which *(pukchin t'ongil)* became a national slogan. The U.S. judgment in the field was that in the last analysis Rhee would not order an attack--in which ROK forces would certainly be "cut to ribbons" by Chinese forces--nor would his military commanders really prosecute such an attack. Nevertheless, Rhee had already shown his independence in the unilateral release of prisoners; the events of 1953 might have given him an exaggerated view of his ability to influence U.S. policy by toughness; and the effective barring of unilateral action presented severe psychological problems for the Koreans.[41]

The American responses to this problem, after formulating the policy in NSC 167 (see Chapter 1, page 18), were a Presidential letter in November 1953, informing Rhee that the United States would not support unilateral renewal of the conflict, plus discreet notification of a few senior military commanders to the same effect; U.S. military dispositions to protect themselves if such actions occurred; and plans to gain advance warning and to prevent effective implementation of an ROK attack order, including limitations on ROK logistics. In March 1954, top ROK military leaders flatly informed Rhee that he could not hope to achieve unification through unilateral military action.[42]

Through 1954 and 1955, there were several indications of continued planning for unilateral action, at Rhee's behest. In September 1954, CINCUNC noted reports of Korean plans for unilateral action intended to embroil U.S. forces with the Communists. In February 1955, unverified intelligence reports spoke of meetings in which Rhee told Korean military and civilian leaders to prepare for military action against north Korea.

On July 31, 1955, Rhee (in the context of his campaign against the NNSC, as noted above) called on the north Koreans to withdraw from Kaesong and the Ongjin Peninsula, indefensible territory south of the 38th parallel that the north Koreans had retained under the Armistice Agreement. The U.S. Ambassador (Lacy) and CINCUNC (Lemnitzer) called on Rhee under instructions, but Rhee observed that no reference had been made to the use of force. Senior military leaders subsequently assured the Ambassador that they opposed such action, and the Embassy concluded that while Rhee had the capability to manufacture an incident, his power to initiate military action against the north had declined.

In October 1955, however, there were more belligerent ROK utterances, and renewed reports that Rhee had ordered plans for the retaking of Kaesong and Ongjin. The Embassy responded by ostracizing one of the few senior generals who supported Rhee in such plans (Yi Hyung-Kun). A State Department memorandum of January 1956 reported a plan for a covert ROK Army raid on the Chinese.[43]

From then on, although Rhee and his ministers continued to pay lip-service to *pukchin t'ongil*, evidence of actual activity declined. Reporting a reply by Rhee to written press questions in mid-1959, which renewed the ROK demand for Allied support to drive out the Communists and unify Korea, the Embassy commented that this had been the only repetition of such comments for the past year. The successor regimes of Huh Chung (1960) and Chang Myon (1960-61) manifested no intention of unilateral action; on the contrary, they explicitly supported the UN formula for peaceful unification, which Rhee had never done. The military regime, when it came to power in 1961, eventually also supported the peaceful unification formula.

The Mutual Defense Treaty

From the time of its establishment in 1948, the ROK sought formal American assurances for its security. In May 1949, for example, United Press reported that President Rhee was asking for a mutual defense pact. While in actuality he had not formally requested one, he had repeatedly expressed to Ambassador Muccio his "hope for some kind of agreement by which the United States would guarantee Korean independence and protection in case of attack."[44]

Following the north Korean attack, ROK demands for an American commitment became more insistent. In 1952, Foreign Minister Pyun Yung Tai called for a security pact, noting the recent American conclusion of such a pact with Japan; but the Secretary of State (Dean Acheson) replied that the already demonstrated "clear evidence of our concern for Korea would not be materially strengthened by a paper indication of such resolve. . . ."

The next year (1953), the U.S. Ambassador in Seoul (Ellis Briggs) noted the real Korean fears of abandonment, and observed that while "it is true that the U.S. is for all practical purposes already committed by the magnitude of its sacrifices in Korea to defense of ROK not only in present emergency but also in event of future aggression, I believe that commitment should be brought into open, not only for favorable effect on relations with Korean government and people, but also for deterrent effect on potential future aggressors." He pointed out that the Koreans' desire for such a commitment should be utilized to gain maximum concessions from them in return--notably, acceptance of an armistice agreement. This view eventually prevailed over Washington reluctance, largely because of Rhee's obduracy, as noted above.

In the Rhee-Dulles meetings in August 1953, a Mutual Defense Treaty was drafted and initialled. Its provisions were largely equivalent to the treaty with Japan, as the Koreans demanded, but not to the NATO treaty, as the Koreans had asked. A ceremony for exchange of ratifications was scheduled for March 18, 1954; but the American side called it off on a few days' notice without substantive explanation (as a means of applying pressure for Korean compliance with economic agreements). The final act was not consummated until November 1954. In the interim the Koreans, consistent in carrying out Rhee's pressure tactics, asked for still further strengthening of the treaty provisions.[45]

Ratification of the Mutual Defense Treaty was accompanied by an Agreed Minute of Understanding on military assistance and two appendices--one of which, dealing with ROK force levels, was classified. The Agreed Minute was subject to recurring negotiations, but the Mutual Defense Treaty itself went unquestioned for ten years.

In December 1964 (when U.S. policy toward Korea was under review) U.S. Senator Church proposed the withdrawal of all U.S. troops from Korea, except for a token force. This statement, widely reported in Korea, prompted a member of the Korean National Assembly (Ch'a Ch'i-Ch'ol) with 17 supporters to introduce a bill on January 23, 1965, calling for revision of the treaty so that the United States would be obligated to intervene immediately upon invasion of the ROK, and U.S. forces could be withdrawn from Korea only by mutual agreement. On January 25, in the course of testimony before the National Assembly on the despatch of Korean troops to Vietnam, the Foreign Minister said that the government proposed to open negotiations to revise the treaty. These actions were motivated in part by opposition to despatch of troops to Vietnam, as well as by continuing fear of U.S. abandonment. In May 1965, as Korea was being requested to send troops to Vietnam, the Prime Minister said that the ROK would like to revise the treaty to include defense assurances similar to the NATO treaty, but the U.S. Ambassador (Winthrop Brown) pointed out the impossibility of such action.[46]

Problems of U.S. Forces in Korea

U.S. military forces were in south Korea at a strength of two Army divisions or more from September 1945 until 1970, except for a period of less than two years preceding the Korean conflict. A generation of Koreans thus grew up under a massive foreign military presence. In general, this presence was tolerated surprisingly well; American soldiers were a symbol of both liberation and security, first against the Japanese, and then against the Communists. Nonetheless the foreign presence led to a series of difficult diplomatic problems. Of these, the four most significant were local currency advances, the legal status of U.S. forces, community relations, and labor relations. (The problem of U.S. prisoners of war was not an issue in relations with the ROK.)

Local Currency Advances

During the American Military Government period, 1945-48, one of the reasons for government budget deficits and inflation was that American military requirements for local goods and services were paid for by drawing on the Korean monetary system. Such expenses had largely been brought under control in the final year of the occupation, with dollar reimbursement on a pay-as-you-go basis, so that the new ROK government began operations with a modest dollar reserve and a budgetary balance.

The outbreak of hostilities in 1950 brought foreign forces back to Korea, with their need for local facilities, products, and services. To pay for them, the finance officer of U.S. forces Korea (USFK) reached an agreement with the ROK Foreign Minister on July 6, 1950, under which the Bank of Korea would advance local currency *(won)* to the U.S. forces, and the ROK government would be reimbursed at an unspecified future time in whole or in part, at the rate of exchange prevailing on the day when the finance officer made actual expenditures.

Washington authorities, however, called for a new agreement which would leave the reimbursement question open. A new agreement between the U.S.

Ambassador (Muccio) and the ROK Finance Minister (Chay Soon-ju) was therefore reached on July 28. The ROK undertook to provide local currency to the
Commanding General, USFK, as he requested; the Commanding General could
use other currency if desirable. Settlements for currency used would be between
the ROK and governments concerned, and would be deferred to a "time or times
mutually satisfactory to the respective governments and the Government of the
ROK." Records were to be kept of amounts of currency received and transferred. The Defense Department set up a dollar reserve account against such
advances, although the agreement did not call for it. The existence of the
reserve account does not seem to have been officially communicated to the
Koreans, but they were doubtless aware of it.

Wartime conditions in Korea resulted in rapid inflation. The Koreans saw
in the *won* drawings, which soon ran into millions of dollars, a major cause of
inflation, and in reimbursement to them a major tool for coping with it.
Politically, this was a convenient argument, because it enabled the ROK Government to transfer blame to the foreigners. Nevertheless, Embassy reports in the
Spring of 1951 acknowledged that unreimbursed *won* expenditures by UN forces
were a significant contributing factor in inflation, although the Korean
government budget deficit on regular account, poor tax collections, maldistri-
bution of rice, and the wartime difficulty of meeting consumer demand were
also basic problems.

In March 1951, as some element of normalcy returned to Korea, the ROK
chargé in Washington conveyed President Rhee's request for early reimbursement of 50 billion *won* in advances (equivalent in Korean reckoning to $21
million), the proceeds to be used for buying consumer goods to control inflation.
The State Department representative (Noel Hemmendinger) pointed out that
under the July 28 agreement, settlement was to be after cessation of hostilities.
In June, the issue reached the ROK National Assembly. From this time until
eventual settlement in 1954, the question of reimbursement for *won* advances
was a major irritant in Korean-American relations.

The question was also a bone of contention between the U.S. State and
Defense departments. Defense (principally the Department of the Army)
opposed any settlement of *won* advances until after the termination of hostilities.
Military authorities cited the World War II precedent. They also held that the
least the Koreans could do for their own defense was to pay for local requirements of the Allied forces. They pointed out that the dollar expenditures being
made by the United States for Korean defense, including equipment and supplies
for the Korean forces, were vastly in excess of the *won* drawings, and that
reimbursement should be suspended for later use as an offset and a bargaining
lever in eventual financial settlement. In their view, the *won* drawings were not
a major factor in Korean inflation. Additionally, they wanted rigorous U.S.
controls over the Koreans' use of dollars. State officials, on the other hand,

attached more weight to the inflationary impact of the local currency drawings; beyond this, they saw a growing political problem for relations with the ROK caused by Korean fixation on the issue as a basic remedy for a problem of great public concern, as well as by Korean nationalist sensitivities.

Whatever the merits of reimbursement as a principle, however, there was an additional problem of calculating the conversion of *won* into dollars in a period of rapid inflation. Although technically the conversion rate was not the same thing as the rate of foreign exchange, as a practical matter the two rates could not be kept separate politically or psychologically even if it was arithmetically possible; and Rhee had a fixed idea that inflation could be controlled by keeping the dollar-*won* exchange rate constant (an idea which also conveniently maximized ROK dollar claims).

The first tangible step toward settlement was a three-way compromise among ROK demands and the State and Army positions, under which the ROK Ambassador (Yang Yu-Chan) on September 27, 1951, received a check for $12,155,714 in payment for *won* sales to individual members of the UN Command through July 31. This payment, intended largely as a political palliative, did not affect the much larger amount of local currency advances for official military uses, nor did it resolve the question of current settlement for accumulating balances.[47]

On December 7, 1951, a high-level Korean-American conference reached agreement in principle on current settlement for advances, subject to conclusion of a CINCUNC-ROK economic aid agreement which would provide for U.S. concurrence in allocation and use of Korean foreign exchange. The aid negotiations bogged down over Korean objections and State-Defense differences; and the Koreans in January 1952 threatened to suspend *won* drawing privileges when currency circulation in Korea reached 600 million *won*. The Army took its side of the case to the U.S. Congress; a Presidential envoy was sent to Korea to resolve the over-all economic impasse; an agreement was signed on May 24, 1952, providing for settlement at a rate of 6,000 *won* per dollar of drawings since December 31, 1951, plus monthly U.S. partial payments of $4 million, plus monthly dollar settlements for *won* sales to UN personnel, plus yearly settlements to be negotiated.[48]

The actual payments, however, were grudgingly and belatedly made, partly for bureaucratic reasons and partly because of the political crisis of 1952 (see Chapter 5). After total payments to the ROK had reached $74 million the arrangement broke down because the UN Command insisted on revising the conversion rate from 6,000 to 18,000 *won* per dollar, effective September 1952, and the Koreans refused to agree. Again, the Koreans threatened to suspend *won* advances. CINCUNC recommended a global settlement for all remaining balances at $65 million (or a total of $139 million, against the Korean claim of

$171 million), but the Army Controller, on the basis of an elaborate computation, recommended $50 million.

Negotiations ensued among CINCUNC, Army, the Army's Office of Civil Affairs and Military Government, Treasury, and State, and the matter finally went to the National Security Council, which set up an interagency committee chaired by a Treasury representative to resolve the problem. On February 20, 1953, CINCUNC negotiated a global settlement with the Koreans for $85,000,000, of which $3 million was for drawings subsequent to December 16, 1952 (the original ROK settlement deadline) at 18,000 *won* per dollar.[49]

The February 1953 settlement also provided for continuing purchases of *hwan* (the new Korean currency, worth 100 *won*) at 180 per dollar, but specified that the rate was subject to quarterly adjustment based on changes in the Pusan wholesale price index. The U.S. authorities endeavored to adjust the rate in the light of continuing inflation, and in October refused to continue payments at 180 to 1. The Koreans retaliated by suspending local currency advances and blocking UN Command *hwan* accounts. The UN Command commenced paying its obligations in U.S. Treasury checks and greenbacks, and sold commodities on the local market to raise *hwan*. After about two weeks of this economic warfare, which was related to the broader issue of economic aid as well as currency advances, the ROK government accepted an Agreed Minute of Understanding accompanying the Mutual Defense Treaty, including a 500-to-1 exchange rate. Only then was the currency advance problem finally resolved, after much unnecessary complication and emotion on both sides over a period of more than three years.[50]

Status of U.S. Forces

The term "status of forces" refers to the legal and administrative arrangements relating U.S. and other foreign troops to the Korean polity and economy. Korean legal jurisdiction over the acts, civil and criminal, of U.S. and other foreign military personnel has been the crucial problem. Other problems include the use of Korean facilities and areas by U.S. and other foreign forces; entry and exit of military personnel; and customs, tax, and other privileges and exemptions for foreign forces, both collectively and individually.

Prior to the Korean War. During the U.S. Military Government period, all Americans and other official foreigners were exempted from Korean jurisdiction and subject to U.S. military jurisdiction. All Korean claims arising from the occupation were settled by the Initial Financial and Property Settlement of September 12, 1948, which transferred sovereignty from the United States to the Republic of Korea. Upon withdrawal of American combat forces in 1949, personnel of the Korea Military Advisory Group (KMAG) were attached to the U.S. diplomatic mission and given what amounted to diplomatic immunity. The original draft of the KMAG agreement provided for exclusive U.S. jurisdiction over criminal offenses by KMAG members; the Korean negotiators insisted on deleting it, and the U.S. side acquiesced, against the advice of military legal advisers in the field. An internal State memorandum noted that the status of forces agreement with the United Kingdom contained no such provision.

Soon after U.S. forces were committed to the Korean hostilities, the United States requested and obtained from President Rhee an exchange of notes, signed at the temporary capital of Taejon on July 12, 1950, granting exclusive jurisdiction to the U.S. over criminal acts of its military personnel. In the emergency circumstances of the time, this act appeared almost *pro forma*; but as the military situation stabilized and the impact of the foreign presence was increasingly felt by the civilian population, the inability of the ROK government to act in numerous cases of murder, rape, robbery, and other misconduct caused Korean frustration and resentment, fed by too frequent manifestations--both real and imagined--of foreign condescension and discourtesy. As a new nation struggling for existence and identity, Korea was extremely sensitive in matters of its sovereignty, independence, and equality, and the privileged status of foreign forces was a constant irritant.

Promise and Procrastination, 1952-60. In early 1952 (a time of great political instability in Korea), U.S. Army authorities in both Washington and Tokyo (then the locus of the UN Command) favored the negotiation of a "full-blown" civil affairs agreement with the ROK, which would have dealt with the whole range of UN Command responsibilities and activities in Korean affairs (and could have turned Korea into a virtual UNC protectorate). State opposed such action because of Korean sensitivity, intensified by insecurity regarding their future, by their lack of confidence in the UN as having failed to realize their political aspirations, and by their having already yielded the exercise of sovereignty to alien agencies over a wide range of internal affairs. The agreement was never made, although a Korean Civil Assistance Command (UNCACK, later KCAK) exercised broad functions in domestic Korean economic, social, and supply matters for about four years, with foreign personnel stationed in detachments throughout the country.[51]

In the following year, as part of the concessions made to gain President Rhee's acquiescence in an armistice agreement, Secretary of State Dulles pledged publicly in a joint statement of August 7, 1953, to negotiate a status of forces agreement (SOFA) with the ROK. In the discreet words of a State Department background memorandum, "This assurance was repeated on many occasions, but various circumstances prevented the opening of negotiations for several years." After two largely abortive beginnings and a final difficult three-year negotiation, a SOFA was ultimately signed in 1965.[52]

The intervening twelve-year period saw mounting Korean resentment--genuine and widespread, unlike some issues drummed up by Rhee or his successors for tactical purposes. It was met by adamantine opposition on the part of U.S. military leaders to any arrangement which would subject American boys to Korean justice, or make the U.S. liable for Korean property claims. A considerable number of influential U.S. Congress members also opposed the idea.

The Embassy in Seoul and the Department of State were caught in the middle, confronted on the Korean side with repeated Foreign Ministry and Korean Embassy representations, as well as periodic press campaigns, signature drives, and Korean National Assembly debates, while on the U.S. military side there was refusal to start down the slippery slope of negotiations.

The first Foreign Ministry note asking for SOFA negotiations was sent in late 1954. In May 1955, the ROK Foreign Minister (Pyun) submitted a draft agreement and asked for negotiations. The Department of State told the U.S. Embassy to postpone the issue and avoid any negotiation which raised the criminal jurisdiction question, but indicated that the U.S. would be "willing negotiate on other subjects usually covered by SOFA piecemeal as necessity arises." There was also an exchange of correspondence with CINCUNC, who pointed out the additional problem of consulting with other nations in the UN Command.[53]

Following conclusion of a treaty of friendship, commerce, and navigation in 1956, and with settlement of Korean utility and property claims against the UN Command under way, the ROK Foreign Minister (Cho Chung-hwan) reopened the SOFA issue in a note of January 5, 1957. The U.S. Embassy in its report suggested that in view of growing Korean self-assertiveness and capability, some movement toward Korean demands might be necessary. Several unfortunate incidents involving American actions offensive to Koreans-- especially a U.S. military police raid on the Korean village of P'aju near the front lines, and killings by American sentries around the perimeters of U.S. installations--stimulated Korean protests and calls for SOFA negotiation. However, the Girard case in Japan had aroused U.S. Congressional ire, and action was therefore delayed again.[54]

In November 1957, CINCUNC and the U.S. Ambassador met with the ROK Foreign and Home Ministers at the Foreign Minister's initiative. The latter, attributing the idea to Ambassador Dowling, suggested negotiating individual agreements on various aspects of a SOFA (as the Department's 1955 instruction had indicated). In a subsequent letter, the Minister proposed five agreements: procurement-taxation-customs, claims, entry-exit, facilities and areas, to be negotiated over a two- or three-year period, and criminal jurisdiction, to be indefinitely deferred.

The Embassy responded negatively to the Foreign Minister (pointing out that a technical state of war existed) but recommended to the Department that negotiations for separate agreements be started in response to ROK government and public demand. This recommendation was rejected in Washington the following year, after protracted interagency discussions. The rejection was justified on the basis of (1) inadequate Korean legal-judicial procedures, (2) adverse American congressional and public attitudes, (3) failure to achieve a Korean political settlement such as Secretary Dulles had envisaged when he made his pledge, (4) concern that negotiation of even non-controversial aspects of a SOFA would enhance, rather than diminish, demand for criminal jurisdiction. However, the instruction to the Embassy in Seoul expressed willingness to discuss other than criminal matters with the ROK government "with view determining what problem areas may exist and, where possible, take such US action as may be appropriate."[55]

The Koreans endeavored to build this minor concession into a basis for discussion of problem areas, which they identified in terms similar to the agreements they had proposed the previous year; but the Department, after more interagency discussion, emphasized that the United States did not want to negotiate any agreement, although informal working-level arrangements might be necessary. Various forms of direct and indirect Korean pressure ensued, including compensation demands by Korean property owners and press outcry over continuing "G.I. incidents."[56]

In May 1959, CINCUNC (Decker) and the Ambassador (Dowling) again proposed phased negotiations, calling attention to the effect that the impending SOFA with the Republic of China (Taiwan) would have. In June, the Vice Minister of Foreign Affairs proposed negotiating a facilities and areas agreement with no reference to SOFA. A draft was developed in the field, and agreed in January 1960. Defense developed a counter-draft. Korean pressure mounted. In March, the National Assembly unanimously called for "earliest conclusion" of the SOFA promised by Secretary Dulles in 1953. Finally, Washington authorized commencement of negotiations on SOFA aspects other than criminal jurisdiction. It was stipulated that the United States would not pay compensation for military use of Korean property. In a note of March 30, 1960, the ROK Foreign Ministry accepted these conditions; but before any action was taken, the Rhee government was toppled by the student revolt.

SOFA Negotiations, 1961-1965. The SOFA issue again came to the fore after the new "Second Republic" came to power in mid-1960. The Democratic Party, which dominated it, had stood since 1957 for a status of forces agreement; and public pressure continued. The U.S. Embassy pointed out to Washington that the United States could either respond positively to this political problem, or remain firm with the likelihood of eventual capitulation, thus suggesting once again to the Koreans that "intransigence and bluster are best ways to negotiate with U.S." The Foreign Minister (Chyung Il-Hyung), in a call on the Secretary of State in November, handed him an aide-memoire on the subject, recalling the nine ROK Foreign Ministry notes since 1954.

The pattern of Korean representations and American temporizations began again. It was accentuated by a controversy over an American defense con-

tractor's employee, R.W. Jenkins, who was counseled by the USFK Judge
Advocate not to pay a traffic fine levied by a Korean court, and by a unanimous
ROK National Assembly call for "earliest conclusion" of the SOFA promised
by Dulles. Finally, after a Defense legal team had studied Korean judicial and
legal processes, State succeeded in persuading Defense of the political necessity
of SOFA negotiations, eventually including criminal jurisdiction. The Embassy
in Seoul was authorized on April 5, 1961, to inform the Foreign Ministry
accordingly--subject to reservation on property compensation. The first
negotiating session was held on April 18, 1961, but no U.S. negotiating draft
was available, and the military coup d'état of May 16 supervened.[57]

Less than a month later, a Foreign Ministry officer told the U.S. Embassy
that the new ROK government wanted to resume the SOFA negotiations. Not
surprisingly, Washington instructed the Embassy that the time was not ripe, but
that the United States would reconsider "when government organization and
legal system of ROK have returned to normal." The Koreans bided their time
until March of the following year, when the holdover civilian President (Yun
Bo-Sun) told a press conference that a SOFA "must be concluded as quickly as
possible." More "G.I. incidents" evoked student demonstrations, which in the
Ambassador's view were not government-inspired. One of these, on June 8,
1962, at Seoul National University, was so serious that it drew an expression of
regret regarding American actions from the State Department spokesman. Three
days later, State proposed to the White House the reopening of SOFA negotiations. They commenced in September, and continued for almost three years,
with 82 plenary meetings and innumerable working sessions. A full status of
forces agreement was concluded following the state visit to the United States of
President Park Chung Hee in 1965.

The main issues in the three-year negotiations were--as they had always
been--criminal jurisdiction and compensation for UN forces' use of property.
On the former, the Koreans wanted, first, assurances of their sovereign equality
both absolutely and in comparison with language in U.S. status of forces
agreements with other nations--particularly Japan, China, and the Philippines.
Second, they wanted leverage to control the constant incidents of American
misconduct. State and Defense continued to differ between themselves on a
negotiating draft of a criminal jurisdiction article until January 1964, at which
time Defense agreed to language which did not explicitly assert a total waiver
of Korean jurisdiction. The Koreans responded with demands for language
similar to that of the NATO agreement (which had been given to the
Philippines). In the end, President Park settled with Secretary Rusk for a
German-type formula during his state visit to the United States.[58]

On compensation for use of Korean facilities by U.S. forces, the United States
gained its point that the ROK should be responsible for reimbursing Korean citizens, but the U.S. agreed to assist in the processing of claims. There was con-

troversy concerning provisions for hiring of Korean employees by the U.S. forces: the United States successfully insisted upon its right to hire its employees directly, but partially conceded to Korean objections on a no-strike provision by accepting a seventy-day time limit. The Koreans unsuccessfully endeavored to obtain rights to search parcels carried by the Army Postal Service, as well as other shipments to "non-appropriated fund activities" (chiefly social clubs) of the U.S. forces. A final minor disagreement involved the status of "invited contractor" personnel--the extent to which they would benefit from privileges extended to the UN military establishment. The Koreans were concerned that Japanese nationals might be hired, gain privileged status, and thus draw public criticism.[59]

Community Relations

Faced with growing resentment and frustration by the Koreans at their inability to act on real and fancied injustices at the hands of foreign troops, the United States put increasing emphasis on improving psychological and social relations of its personnel with the Korean community, and on minimizing irritants to these relations.

The principal U.S. action, inaugurated while hostilities were still in progress and continued throughout the period here studied, was Armed Forces Assistance to Korea (AFAK), begun as a largely voluntary program by U.S. military personnel to furnish materials, advice, and even labor to help rebuild the devastation caused by the war--especially schools, hospitals, churches, and orphanages, plus disaster relief. The program was institutionalized and supported from the U.S. military budget at a level of several hundred thousand dollars a year. It proved immensely popular because it responded to community needs at the grass-roots level in a way that few other American assistance programs did, often with considerable enthusiasm on the part of individual U.S. military units and personnel. The budget squeeze eventually forced the termination of official dollar support for the program; but in early 1965, the Embassy in Seoul was endeavoring to continue support by utilizing the local currency proceeds of surplus agricultural product sales under Section 104c of Public Law 480. By this time, most needed commodities for building were available in Korea at cheaper than American prices.[60]

The other major U.S. action in the community relations field was the Community Relations Program, involving binational effort to develop American understanding of Korean people and their culture, to develop better educational and social facilities on U.S. military posts, to promote binational social intercourse under civilized conditions, to clean up the sinkholes of vice and corruption that had grown up around the gates of American military enclaves, and to control the Korean and American criminal elements that were victimizing

both sides. This program was so successful that the Embassy in 1961 saw no
need for a Defense Department Civil Action Team.[61]

Labor Relations

The U.S. forces in Korea had trouble with labor relations even during the
American Military Government period. At that time the problem was interrelated with the over-all labor policies of the Military Government, which were
ambivalent because, on the one hand, American organized labor insisted on freedom of Korean labor to organize, bargain collectively, and strike; yet, on the
other hand, leftist and Communist elements took advantage of the situation to
call strikes and demonstrations in a continuing effort to embarrass the American
administration and bring it down. American military officers, moreover, often
had little sympathy for Western-style labor freedom in the face of their many
problems of administering the underdeveloped Korean economy; and the
Koreans themselves had virtually no tradition of responsible, free organized
labor activity.

After the outbreak of Korean hostilities, U.S. forces became one of the
largest employers of Korean labor. Again they were at a disadvantage. The
Koreans, led by ambitious labor leaders, sought to exact American-style benefits
and high wages at a time when budgetary and other economic constraints, both
in dollars and in local currency, set limits on what the Americans could pay.
The UN Command, for its part, saw no reason why it should go beyond prevailing Korean practices as to wages and conditions. The actual UNC labor practices, however, were often inferior to the standards prescribed in Korean laws
--some of which were American-inspired--and it was easier to criticize the
Americans than local industrialists, especially when American organized labor
continued its international concern for its brother organizations abroad.

There were at least four significant categories of Korean employees of the
UN Command: the regular civilian employees, on hourly wages and monthly
salaries; the Korean Service Corps, a quasi-military labor service organization;
the so-called KATUSAs (Korean soldiers attached to the U.S. Army), who were
actually in Korean military service and assigned into American units for purposes of both reinforcement and training; and the employees of individuals,
messes, and "non-appropriated fund activities." Each of these categories had its
own problems, and the negotiations were frequently difficult, approaching and
sometimes actually reaching the strike stage.

One of the first real strike threats arose over regular Korean employees'
demands in early 1956 for a 100 percent wage increase in the face of rapidly
mounting inflation. The need was real, as eventually demonstrated by a UN
Command wage survey, but no funds were available. State brought pressure on
Defense to respond to the workers' demands and avert a strike, which would
make the American position much worse. Wage concessions were eventually

made (an 86 percent pay increase), but the U.S. Army affirmed and maintained its position that it would not enter into collective bargaining with any labor organization.[62]

Two years later a union in the port city of Inch'on accused the U.S. Post Exchange management there of violating the Korean labor law and mistreating its employees, and threatened a strike, supported by the Korea Federation of Trade Unions. The Embassy investigated, and concluded that the issues were exaggerated on both sides, but that the Army authorities had been unwilling to make minor and reasonable concessions urged by the ROK Bureau of Labor.[63]

In 1965, the Korean Service Corps threatened a strike. It was averted at the last minute when U.S. Army authorities indicated to leaders of the Foreign Organizations Employees' Union that they were prepared to make most of the concessions sought by the Service Corps. The issues included wages and benefits, recognition of the union as bargaining agent, and the status of the Service Corps.[64]

Utilities Claims

During and after the Korean hostilities, American forces were heavy consumers of Korean public utility production--particularly electricity. In response to Korean pressure for payment of past and current utility supply, as well as other claims against U.S. forces, the United States in September 1955 proposed negotiations based on specified preconditions: no payment for combat damage; no payment for past utility services until pay-as-you-go arrangements had been concluded.

Negotiations began on December 16, with the Koreans objecting to the preconditions. After over a year of exchanges of communications in the field and with Washington, the ROK shut off the power to the U.S. I Corps installation at Uijongbu on February 16, 1957, for failure to conclude an appropriate power contract. Twelve hours later, after Ambassador Dowling's personal intervention with President Rhee, the power supply was resumed. On July 3, a contract was signed for current supply of electricity to USFK, with an agreement expected soon for settling past claims on the basis of general principles that had been worked out.[65]

Military Assistance

Formative Stages

American military government authorities early in 1946 recognized a need for Korean military forces, and established a Department of National Defense to train them. In response to Washington insistence that such a program might hinder negotiations for a unified government, the department was renamed, but organization of a small force known as the Korean Constabulary began in 1946, and some of its first recruits became the leaders of the Korean armed forces in later years. Policy planning in the Spring of 1948 for the establishment of a separate south Korean government called for equipping and training the Korean Constabulary as part of the preparation for expeditious U.S. withdrawal. Under this plan (NSC 8--see Chapter 1, pages 4-5), "modified infantry division type equipment for a period of six months" was transferred from the departing U.S. 6th and 7th divisions to the ROK forces, without charge to the ROK. By the end of the year the "six-month stockpile" commitment had been "substantially" met, although some items (e.g., 30 percent of the ordnance items) were being procured from the United States.

At approximately the time of the transfer in September 1948, the U.S. set up a 250-man provisional military advisory group to organize and train the Korean armed forces, which originally numbered 50,000 men for the Army plus a small coast guard of 5,000.[66]

Assistance Before the Korean War

In February 1949, President Rhee told visiting Army Secretary Royall of his military assistance requirements, and went on to say "he would like to increase the Army, provide equipment and arms for it, and then in a short time move north into North Korea," which would be legal in view of the UN recognition of the ROK; "he saw nothing could be gained by waiting." When Royall suggested that this idea was tantamount to expecting the removal of U.S. forces, Rhee said he would not object, provided the U.S. furnished good advice and equipment. However, Ambassador Muccio pointed out that this statement did not mean (as Royall wanted to interpret it) that U.S. troops should be withdrawn at once. General Wedemeyer, on a survey mission in February 1949, told the Koreans that "what was essential here was a small, compact, well-trained and equipped force thoroughly loyal" (the last qualification probably a reference to the Sunch'on-Yosu mutiny of 1948).[67]

As the north Korean threat appeared to grow, and as the situation in China deteriorated, the ROK clamored for more military aid for a larger force. The ROK National Assembly raised the Army force level to 100,000 (it had actually reached 65,000 in February 1949). In November 1949, President Rhee forwarded a request for equipment for this level, plus a reserve force of 50,000, and for improved equipment for the coast guard. The U.S. military commander, General Coulter, noted that his command could not meet such requests under existing policy, and called for an American policy review as to whether they should be met--observing that the Korean economy alone could not support the proposed force levels, but implicitly favoring increased aid. The Ambassador concurred. Subsequent policy review did increase support levels to 65,000 men for the Army, but not to the levels desired by the Koreans.[68]

Rhee had asked in his letter of November 2, 1948 for establishment of a U.S. military and naval advisory mission in Korea. Such a group (KMAG) was authorized by NSC 8/2 in March 1949. A draft agreement was first sent to the Ambassador in Seoul on July 6, 1949 for negotiation, and a revised one in October (to take account of new U.S. legislation). After minor adjustments, the agreement was signed in January 1950, giving the provisional advisory group permanent status and doubling its authorized size (to 500). The Embassy, noting a progress report from the Chief of KMAG to the Minister of National Defense in December 1949, concurred in the report's "warm praise" of Korean military improvement and commented,

> There is rapidly being forged that rarity in Asia--a well-trained, cloaked, fed, housed, loyal army that is eager to fight and, even with the comparatively limited quantity of arms and equipment on hand, should give a good account of itself if need arises.[69]

The Embassy report spoke highly of KMAG performance and observed that, with a cooperative Defense Minister, the Korean security forces had welcomed American advice and adopted American methods and standards.

Throughout 1949, both the ROK and the U.S. Embassy urged that the Korean armed forces be given better equipment, and the Ambassador recommended provision of equipment for the entire 100,000-man armed force, rather than the 65,000 authorized by NSC 8/2. Reference has already been made to Rhee's exchange of correspondence with Truman (page 65). In September, Ambassador Muccio sent to Washington the recommendations of the Chief, KMAG, for a military aid program within a prescribed $10 million dollar ceiling, but observed, "in the unfortunate event of the outbreak of large-scale hostilities between North and South Korea, the over-all amount of $10 million would obviously be inadequate to keep the security forces of the Republic of Korea in the field for any extended period of time."

At the Ambassador's request, KMAG made supplementary recommendations in the light of reports of increasing north Korean capabilities; these totalled over $18 million, chiefly for artillery, limited aid to the new Korean Air Force, and further strengthening of the Korean Coast Guard. Ambassador Muccio suggested that the additional amount might be financed from the fund appropriated for use in the general area of China. But in November, Washington cut assistance below $10 million, which action the Ambassador viewed as weakening support to the Korean forces below a safe minimum.[70]

Toward the end of 1949, Rhee began to act independently to increase his military capability. He purchased a naval patrol craft with Korean funds; and he invited retired U.S. Air Force General Russell Randall to Korea to make recommendations for a Korean air force (not previously planned by the U.S.). Randall's recommendations were supported by Ambassador Muccio.[71]

In December, representatives of the Mutual Defense Assistance Program visited Korea to discuss the proposed 1950 program, and revised the previous recommendations, but within the $10 million ceiling. The Embassy again considered this program "patently inadequate." Subsequent events proved the Embassy correct; in any event, only an insignificant amount of the equipment under the proposed program had reached Korea at the time of the invasion.[72]

The Postwar Buildup

In the first few traumatic days of the Korean War, the outnumbered and outgunned ROK armed forces were badly damaged, and many months were required to reconstitute them. The military assistance problems of the wartime period are beyond the scope of this study. However, the military cost of the Korean War was estimated in 1954 as "at least $10 billion," and subsequent estimates have run much higher.[73]

The military advisory group (KMAG) continued functioning through the war, but as an element of the unified command. It was largely responsible for the reconstitution of the ROK forces. During his assignment as Commander of the Eighth Army in Korea, General James Van Fleet in particular devoted much energy and attention to the rebuilding of the ROK Army, and established a close personal relationship with President Rhee.[74]

In 1953, a commitment for building up ROK forces was made as part of the price for Rhee's acquiescence in an armistice (see Chapter 2, page 49). General Van Fleet returned to Korea as head of a mission to plan the fulfillment of this commitment, pursuant to President Eisenhower's letter to Rhee of April 16, 1953, and a directive to Van Fleet from the Secretary of Defense on April 26.

The mission had problems. Van Fleet favored a buildup to as many as 35 Army divisions, on a basis of 5 ROK divisions for each US division withdrawn, while the Commander of the Eighth Army and the Economic Coordinator were thinking in terms of cutting back, since they were concerned at costs to the United States and the inflationary impact of force expansion in Korea. Rhee, puzzled and suspicious, had an opportunity to play one side against the other (an opportunity that the Americans had frequently given him since 1945), and to take a hard line toward the Geneva negotiations in the hope of getting further concessions.[75]

In the end, an Agreed Minute of Understanding was signed in conjunction with the Mutual Defense Treaty in 1954, after months of very difficult bargaining. A confidential Appendix B to the Agreed Minute set Korean force levels at 720,000 men, including 20 active Army divisions, and committed the United States to supply and equip them, although not at U.S. standards. At this time, the Armistice Agreement prevented introduction of new types or additional numbers of weapons into Korea, so that ROK requirements could be very largely met from the inventories of U.S. units being withdrawn.

Difficulties were encountered very soon in fulfilling the program. One was Korean unhappiness at not being consulted in formulating plans and programs. In October 1955, Assistant Secretary of State Robertson wrote to the Assistant Secretary of Defense (Gray), referring to an American-Korean conference in June and July where this problem became evident, and urged that American military authorities encourage Koreans to participate in preparing lists of requirements, as well as consult them on administration of agreed programs. Subsequently, a Military Assistance Advisory Group (PROVMAAG/K) was established within the U.S. military command to facilitate joint planning.[76]

The most serious difficulty, however, was that while the Communist forces were building up their capability, in violation of the Armistice Agreement, the United States was encountering severe budgetary constraints on its own dollar aid programs, and at the same time the huge Korean armed forces were threatening to choke off civilian economic development. Concurrently, U.S. forces in Korea were being reduced, and even the small troop contributions of other nations were being reduced or withdrawn.

When the United States, as a partial answer to this dilemma, unilaterally suspended certain portions of the Armistice Agreement (see pages 77-79 below) and started to modernize its own forces, the Koreans were very unhappy not to receive modern weapons, including atomic weapons, at the same time. In February 1959, when the Draper Mission visited Korea, General Draper noted, "With deficiencies presently existing in firepower, mobility and communications equipment, ROK forces may be completely outmoded in the very near future and will be little use when hostilities resumed." Subsequently, the Koreans did receive modern weapons--for example, Hawk and Nike-Hercules weapons were planned for Korea in 1961 and classified agreements signed in 1963 and 1965-- but not until that doughty old warrior, Rhee, had left the Presidency.[77]

Minor program difficulties involved examples of corruption and waste on both sides, such as the "raw cotton case" (involving irregularities in procurement of cotton for uniforms), difficulties over rental for loaned U.S. naval vessels, and a controversy over the disposal of scrap and salvage. There was also a flurry over the authorization for an expansion of the military advisory group to a thousand persons in 1960, because the Koreans objected to an increase in support costs. An informal understanding on this matter was eventually preferred to an amendment of the 1960 mutual defense assistance agreement.[78]

Budgetary Constraints and Force Reductions

Even before the Korean War, the military assistance program had encountered difficulties because of the shortage of U.S. funds and the pressure on the weak Korean economy of a large military force. In the early 1950s, the military planners discounted economic problems in their concern at what seemed the worldwide weakness of Free World forces against the Communists, and U.S. money was more freely appropriated to meet the threat. It was enough to say that five Korean divisions could be fielded for the cost of one American division. During this period, the economic assistance program was subordinate to the United Nations Commander, who gave higher priority to military security than to Korean economic development. However, grandiose plans for over a million Koreans under arms in 35 army divisions, discussed during the Van Fleet mission in 1953, were considerably pruned.

By the mid-1950s, the military drag on Korean economic progress was clear. It was most evident in the defense budget and in the counterpart fund. Large quantities of consumer goods were being brought into Korea for sale on the civilian market--partly to meet the civilian need, but also partly to generate local currency which went into the counterpart fund and then was released by the U.S. to pay the larger part of the expenses of the Korean military establishment.

As military pay and operating costs mounted, they soaked up more and more of the counterpart funds, leaving less available for investment in civilian economic expansion. On the other hand, military requirements were partly responsible for a distortion of the whole U.S. economic assistance program in favor of saleable consumer goods, and in this way, also, delayed Korean economic rehabilitation and growth. Military expenditures were somewhat inflationary, besides--increasing Korean price levels and still further adding to the demand for counterpart money to support the 720,000-person military establishment.

The provision of U.S. military equipment had no large direct effect on the Korean economy, but it involved very high dollar costs to the United States. Some trade-off was theoretically possible: smaller Korean forces could be given more sophisticated equipment. However, U.S. budgetary pressures were increasingly limiting the amount of military assistance available worldwide, and Korea's requirements had to compete with those of other nations within the declining over-all levels.[79]

Budgetary constraints not only ran counter to military security considerations-- they also ran into major political problems. Ambassador Lacy outlined them in a memorandum to CINCUNC (General Maxwell Taylor) in May 1955. The ROK military establishment, he said, was the strongest single stabilizing force in Korea and a significant factor in the general Far East situation. Within Korea, if ROK force reductions were mandated before tensions in the area eased --particularly before the promised force goals were reached--ROK morale would be shaken, and ROK forces might be withdrawn from UNC operational control. Rhee's political influence, built in large part on his success in getting military aid from the United States, would be diminished, with an adverse effect on the economic stabilization program then beginning. There would also be adverse political effects in other Asian countries.[80]

The assessments of the Joint Chiefs of Staff throughout most of the post-Korean War period held that from a military standpoint, the 20-division Korean Army, plus the two U.S. divisions in Korea and other available supporting forces, were no more than adequate for a holding action against a joint north Korean-Chinese assault. The withdrawal of the Chinese forces across the Yalu in 1958 made only a small difference in the assessment. By 1965, CINCUNC (General Hamilton Howze) was reluctantly willing to concede, in the face of strong pressures from the State Department and U.S. economic agencies, that reduction to a 500,000-person Korean force might be an acceptable risk, although he maintained that the result would be a hazardous weakening of the defenses along the 38th parallel.[81]

Despite the political and security risks, economic problems obviously necessitated a cutback. In June 1956, when President Rhee said that he wanted to stop all flow of counterpart funds to the military budget, the Chairman of the ROK Joint Chiefs of Staff (General Yi Hyong-kun) responded that the only alternative was reduction in the numerical strength of the Army, compensated by better training and firepower.

Asked by the Department of State for an assessment in October 1956, Ambassador Dowling recommended a reduction of Army forces to 10 active and 10 reserve divisions, accompanied by introduction of atomic-capable weapons, addition of sophisticated aircraft, and replacement of worn-out transport and communications equipment. If this were done gradually over a three-year period, reductions in both defense assistance (MDAP) and economic aid funds might be possible by fiscal year 1960. The Ambassador noted the same political problems as his predecessor, and added the problem of unemployment of discharged veterans, but thought these problems were manageable. He added, with prescience, that nuclear weapons for the U.S. forces might help offset ROK force reductions but would create a clamor for similar weapons for the Koreans, who otherwise would seem "not allies but mercenaries."[82]

In June 1957, after discussion in the National Security Council and Presidential decision, Ambassador Dowling and General Lemnitzer were instructed to propose a reduction of ROK forces to President Rhee, together with a modernization program, the proposal to be timed with the U.S. announcement of suspension of Armistice limitations on force improvement. The proposal was tied squarely to the Korean economic problem: "The [U.S.] President is convinced that a substantial reduction of Korean forces is essential to help the economic situation in Korea." A reduction of four divisions by the end of fiscal 1958, with no addition to the existing ten reserve divisions, was "the minimum President Eisenhower is willing to accept now. . . . A further reduction may ultimately be made to 11 active divisions including Marines and 12 to 15 reserve divisions. . . ." In the following month, replying to Rhee's letter of June 19, Eisenhower added the problem of U.S. budgetary constraints.[83]

Rhee welcomed modernization but raised objections to force reductions, and Eisenhower on August 21 reiterated his position. Rhee then resorted to the familiar demonstrations--the National Police reported that 366,500 persons demonstrated in the first seven days of September, and students marched past the U.S. Embassy on September 21. However, the real focus of concern by Rhee, the government, and the public at this time was mostly on modernization to compensate for reductions; there was considerable popular sympathy for reducing the burdensome force levels. The underlying concern was that American interest and support for Korea was declining.[84]

In subsequent months, difficult negotiations dragged on with the Koreans using every conceivable argument to maximize force modernization while avoiding troop reductions. The Acting Foreign Minister wondered how the U.S. could reduce aid to Korea while spending money on politically unreliable Yugoslavs, Indians, and Japanese. The Middle East crisis and the Quemoy crisis were both cited as reasons for suspending reductions; the Chinese withdrawal from north Korea made relatively little impact. Impossibly large demands for modern weapons, ships, and aircraft were put forward.[85]

In the end, the Koreans settled for a reduction of two divisions, rather than four, plus supporting unit reductions, and a new force ceiling of 630,000 in place of the former 720,000 (which meant an actual reduction of around 60,000, since the old ceiling had not been reached.) Some modern equipment was to be provided, particularly to the Air Force. Two divisions were deactivated in December 1958, and a revised Appendix B to the Agreed Minute was signed in November. CINCUNC commented earlier in the year that the presence of atomic-capable weapons in Korea had been instrumental in obtaining ROK agreement.[86]

The conservative political opposition seized the troop reduction issue, and adopted a position favoring substantial further reductions as a means of speeding economic development and stability. However, when the opposition came to power in 1960, it encountered another political obstacle to reductions: the political power of the military establishment itself. The prospect of force reduction may have been a contributing factor in the military coup d'état of 1961. Thereafter, force reductions became politically impossible until the economic burden of the ROK forces began to jeopardize the Park government's economic development goals. By that time, the United States wanted Korean forces for the effort in Vietnam, which again postponed the force reduction issue.

In May 1959, the Country Team in Korea completed a study of five-year cost projections for various Korean force levels, at the request of the State Department. The study concluded that in the face of rising enemy capabilities (assuming, at the time, growing Soviet nuclear support for the Chinese), 26 full-strength divisions would be needed to contain a Chinese-North Korean ground offensive with non-nuclear weapons. The existing 21 Korean divisions (18 ROK Army, 1 ROK Marine, 2 U.S.) if fully equipped, might hold without nuclear weapons but would have to give up a considerable portion of south Korea. Thus no reduction was considered to be militarily justified for 1959-1963; if reductions were made they would have to be evaluated in the context of over-all U.S. objectives. On the economic side, however, the long-run effects of reduction would be a gain in Korean gross national product.[87]

Meanwhile, the U.S. General Accounting Office reviewed the military assistance program to Korea, and made highly adverse findings, reinforcing a steady flow of information critical of Korea on political, economic, and military grounds, and making further Congressional cuts in U.S. aid levels likely. In February 1959, the Draper Committee visited Korea as part of its worldwide study of U.S. assistance programs. In a farewell call by General Draper and CINCUNC (General Hull) on President Rhee, Hull suggested a further reduction of active divisions over a two- to three-year period, with a corresponding increase in reserve divisions.[88]

After Rhee's government was overthrown and the Democratic Party controlled the new government, attention was once more given to force reductions. For a time, the shoe was on the other foot: a *New York Herald Tribune* article on August 4 reported the concern of American officials that the new government might reduce the ROK Army by as many as 200,000, as pledged in the Democratic Party platform, an action which might invite aggression from the north.

In September 1960, the Country Team commented on reported ROK government plans for force reductions (plus increases in budget and pay scales) by saying that force level requirements were unchanged; the problem was what was economically supportable. The Koreans were now trying to threaten the United States with force reductions in order to get more U.S. aid, without taking necessary and possible budgetary measures of their own. Ambassador Walter McConaughy (who had replaced Dowling in 1959) thought that reductions of up to 100,000 might be acceptable if properly made, but deferred a final decision pending further study.

In the end, a revised Appendix B was negotiated, and signed December 30, 1960. It reduced maximum U.S.-assisted strength from 630,000 to 600,000; increased the readiness of reserve divisions from 60 days to 30 days; and eliminated the need for annual review of the Appendix, but continued joint annual review of force levels. Eventual establishment of regular (career) armed forces was also envisaged.[89]

Five-year planning for Korean military assistance began in 1958, and was repeated annually thereafter. In commenting on plans for fiscal 1963-67, the Country Team in Seoul concluded that the projection of current trends indicated that no counterpart funds would be available for non-military activities in Korea after 1965, despite the economic development needs, and that there was no foreseeable way of filling the gap. Yet economic progress "is one of the imperatives of ROK political life. . . . Any ROK government that fails of achievement in this respect cannot stand." Thus, reasonable economic expansion was necessary to stability, and therefore necessary for U.S. interests. This evaluation was made in March 1961, just before the military coup; hence considerable time passed before much could be done about it.[90]

Military Assistance Planning After 1960

For obvious reasons, innovation in military assistance was virtually impossible for a considerable period after the military coup d'état of May 16, 1961 (for example, in analyzing a major political crisis in 1963, Ambassador Samuel Berger referred to a possible U.S. decision on ROK force reductions, which he himself had favored for economic reasons, and pointed out the difficulty of dealing with the ROK government on the issue at the time.) Nevertheless, U.S. consideration of force reductions continued.[91]

In October 1963, Ambassador Berger submitted a penetrating and thorough-going analysis of U.S. military assistance policy and its impact on Korea. It pointed out that a good deal of the Koreans' poor-mouthing about the defense burden was based upon a feeling that the United States was obligated to them, rather than upon economic facts. The Koreans' own defense expenditures were not an unreasonable share of their total economy, and their feelings about the diversion of resources from economic development were unrealistic in the assumption that without the military burden, they could have received the same total aid for economic purposes alone. Nevertheless (the analysis continued), the Koreans had been encouraged in high consumption levels and other economic distortions by the large American aid program, and it seemed doubtful that economic discipline could be imposed on the scale necessary to achieve objectives of the 1964-69 military assistance program then being considered, which would reduce annual assistance from the previous $200 million to about $150 million, even before Congress made its own cuts. The United States had "unwittingly compounded this problem when due to a windfall in local currency deposits following devaluation of *hwan* in 1961 we agreed to cover about 94 percent (160 billion *hwan*) of 1961 defense budget (198 billion *hwan*)," compared to about 50 percent previously.[92]

The general thrust of the Ambassador's conclusions was that U.S. aid policies--including those for economic assistance, which had been largely justified by the need for military budget support--should be modified so that the Koreans would have to face up to ordering their own priorities within a diminishing U.S. aid contribution. In this way, the Koreans themselves might find force reductions necessary. Ambassador Berger also noted that American officials formulating the ROK defense budget were still looking on financial and economic considerations as secondary, "producing an increasingly acute competition between military and development demands on available resources."

This reasoning led to pressure on the Korean government for economies, and in November 1963 the ROK Cabinet approved a jointly-developed reduction of about 10 percent in the total military budget. However, the Defense Minister begged the Ambassador "to ward off such cuts as may be contemplated in the ROK force level and the U.S. Forces Korea," pointing to the usual catalogue of dire political consequences. At this time, Washington agencies were thinking in terms of an even lower defense budget, as well as force reductions.[93]

In the Fall of 1963, President Kennedy apparently asked the Defense Secretary (Robert McNamara) and the Secretary of State (Dean Rusk) to look into the problem of Korean force reductions; the actual examination was done by Deputy Defense Secretary Gilpatrick and Deputy Under Secretary of State U. Alexis Johnson. General Howze, the United Nations Commander (CINCUNC), had made specific (and relatively modest) force reduction recommendations, and Ambassador Berger proposed that the time was ripe to do something about them, since the new civilian government (about to be elected) would be in a strong position for the time being. However, neither the Department of the Army nor the Joint Chiefs of Staff accepted CINCUNC's recommendations. Moreover, in January 1964, the Ambassador altered his own idea of timing, because the new ROK Government was faced with so many difficult problems and decisions were being forced on it by the United States (economic stabilization, U.S. aid reduction, settlement with Japan, currency devaluation).[94]

By 1964 (when Military Assistance Program [MAP] funds for Korea were reduced to $153 million), continuing military modernization programs were in jeopardy. A proposed further cut in fiscal year 1965 was seen by State's Bureau of Far Eastern Affairs as cancelling virtually all new modernization programs except the introduction of F-5 aircraft, and as having the usual adverse political effects in Korea. These cuts were primarily due to altered Congressional attitudes, not yet greatly affected by the problem of Vietnam.[95]

Military assistance was one of the principal questions at issue in the State Department's policy review of Korea in the Fall of 1964. The eventual conclusion, concurred in by Defense only with great reluctance, was to work for a reduction of forces to approximately 500,000, coupled with emphasis on force modernization together with a package of capital investment assistance (see Chapter 1, page 34). Although the modernization program was undertaken, no change in ROK force levels was accomplished.

Offshore Procurement

The U.S. military assistance program included the purchase of materials for dollars in foreign countries to supply U.S. forces, known as offshore procurement (OSP). During the Korean War, a great deal of such purchasing was done in Japan for the supply of the United Nations forces, including the Koreans. The intent was both to save money for the United States and to benefit the supplying countries. The Koreans resented such aid to the Japanese, and asked that similar procurement be undertaken in Korea. In the mid-1950s a small procurement program was begun, for U.S. force requirements, not only as a source of dollars for Korea but also as a means of educating Korean industry to comply with established standards, specifications, and production schedules.

As U.S. assistance levels began to decline, the Koreans saw in offshore procurement a means of increasing their foreign exchange, and proposed that materials be purchased in this way for the Korean forces as well. Such action required an exception to the normal policy, which precluded "dollar procurement [of] any item which is to be provided source country under MDAP." However, in 1957 Ambassador Dowling argued for an exception the Korean case and in 1959 Assistant Secretary J. Graham Parsons supported the Country Team arguments. After further discussion and review, an offshore procurement program for Korean forces was finally authorized, with the understanding that over time the procurement of OSP items would gradually revert to the ROK defense budget.[96]

In ensuing years, the issue of "MAP transfer"--i.e., ROK assumption of the costs of MAP items procured in Korea--became a major issue in ROK-U.S. relations, the United States utilizing it as a negotiating lever and endeavoring to phase it out so as to conserve diminishing assistance dollars for items not available in Korea, the Koreans trying to have their OSP cake and other military assistance, too. For example, in 1963 the Koreans were bringing great pressure on the Embassy to reverse the decision to transfer soybeans to the ROK budget; and in 1964 there was a Korean campaign to have the MAP transfer program suspended for five years. In May 1966, the Minister of National Defense regarded MAP transfer as such an important issue that his own future might depend on it.[97]

Internal Security

U.S. Role Prior to ROK Independence

Korea's internal security problem has involved a blend of Western cultural impact, rising expectations, political infighting among rival political leaders and groups, incompetent and time-serving government, scarce and badly-distributed resources, Marxist ideas, youthful revolt, a violent tradition born of the long Japanese occupation, police repression also largely inspired by that occupation, and--leavening the whole loaf--Communist agitation and subversion trained, financed, and encouraged from the north.

The ill-informed and poorly-financed early American approach to this complicated problem added to its difficulty. It was easy for American military government officers to see the Communists as responsible for all unrest and subversion (since they clearly were responsible for much of it) and equally easy for liberals in both the United States and Korea to see the heavy military hand as responsible for all evils. Syngman Rhee's approach to the problem when he assumed power in 1948 was no better than that of the military government, although he had legitimacy where the Americans did not.

A conservative British observer in August 1946 (a month before the terrible bloodletting in the southeastern city of Taegu) reported the discovery of "an extensive plot to sabotage American military installations and stir up trouble in southern Korea." In September, he commented that the Communists in the north were diverting much of their assets into propaganda in the south, taking advantage of the American commitments to political freedom.

> Communist agents . . . with bulging wallets have bought over most of the press and spread skillful propaganda which their disunited opponents . . . have as yet done little to counter. . . . Everywhere under the surface the Communist propaganda makes steadily creeping headway. . . .[98]

The problems of the American command in dealing with internal security are described in the monthly activities reports of the U.S. military government (USAMGIK) and the successor South Korean Interim Government (SKIG). Major reliance was placed on a police force that utilized Japanese organization and techniques (despite American attempts at reform) and some of the Korean personnel who had worked for the Japanese. There were two major peaks of subversive activity during the pre-independence period, and a third attempt, which had only very limited success, just before the elections of May 1948. (At this time the north Koreans apparently organized a training school for subversives at Kangdong.) General Hodge, in a statement to the Korean people on February 13, 1948, regarding the wave of strikes then in progress, referred to the letter that the strike leaders had sent him, and said,

> . . . [the strike leaders] harked back to their attempt to take over the government by revolution in October, 1946, when they killed many patriotic Korean policemen and government officials in the bloodiest riots known to present-day Korea. They harked back to March, 1947, when they again tried to take over the government in South Korea by force. . . . Insofar as I can find out no Korean voluntarily joined in the strikes. . . . The damage done in this effort to destroy South Korean democracy and to hurt the economy of your country was accomplished by a few hundred stooges.[99]

Subversion Prior to the Korean War

There was relatively little disorder during the May 1948 elections, but the new Republic of Korea immediately faced fresh challenges, as well as a continuation of the troubles of the previous era. The first major incident was a revolt by elements of two ROK Army regiments (then still referred to as Constabulary) in the southern cities of Yosu and Sunch'on in October 1948. Loyal forces put down the revolt in a week, after considerable loss of life, and most of the ROK troops remained loyal, but the incident demonstrated a disturbing degree of Communist infiltration of the Constabulary. It also demonstrated deficiencies of Constabulary training and equipment, and highlighted the risks of U.S. troop withdrawal. By chance a U.S. Embassy officer (David E. Mark) was in the area at the time, witnessed some of the action, and prepared a careful, detailed account of the affair.

After the Yosu/Sunch'on revolt, the dissidents joined other rebels in the nearby Chiri Mountain area, which with Cheju Island and one or two other regions remained centers of guerrilla activity for some time. Although the general level of violence was considered no higher than before the May elections, it was upsetting to Koreans, some of whom might have been "developing an attitude of siding with the ultimate victor as they see it." Both Ambassador Muccio and the U.S. military commander (General John B. Coulter) endeavored to reassure the ROK government and people, uneasy at the prospect of U.S. troop withdrawal. An American military officer was given part of the blame by Koreans for permitting Communists to penetrate the Constabulary.[100]

The Ambassador, commenting on Defense Minister Lee Bum Suk's report to the National Assembly on "internal insurrections after April 1948," said that although the report was an honest attempt to present the facts, it failed to recognize government inefficiency and veniality, and police brutality, among other things, as contributing causes. In March 1949, the Embassy reported:

> The American Mission in Korea is in a sense, attempting to grapple with the dilemma of how to bring the Koreans down to earth. On the one hand, through the ECA mission, it strives to give Koreans some of the economic tools . . . [and] advice. . . . In the area of national security, the Korea Military Advisory Group performs the same functions. . . . The U.S. Information and Education program attempts to educate Koreans to the realities of what life in a Communist state means, to the improving picture of current Korean affairs, and to the hope that there is a bright future by working through the present government.[101]

U.S. assistance to the Korean police was never very influential except in the area of new weapons and techniques. One reason was that President Rhee did not want the United States deeply involved in this area of his political strength; moreover, U.S. advisers were not always of the highest competence.

For well over a year after independence guerrilla bands continued active, particularly in the countryside, and south Korea evolved its own version of what came to be known elsewhere as the fortified hamlet program. There was a constant flow of frightened country folk into the towns and cities, adding to already difficult economic and social problems. By the spring of 1950, however, with American assistance, the Korean security forces managed to get on top of the problem.[102]

Lack of information was one of the main Korean shortcomings. In 1949, the new Defense Minister, Sihn Sung Mo, first learned the seriousness of the subversive problem from Americans. Once aware of it, he moved vigorously, with American military assistance, and by May 1949, both Cheju Island and the Chiri Mountain area had been substantially brought under control.[103]

One ingenious device used in the drive against the Communists was a National Guidance Alliance, which offered "protection to repentant leftists in the form of immunity from arrest under the National Security Law, and assistance in keeping a job or finding a new one. The Alliance also conducts courses of reindoctrination for converts, and publishes propaganda. . . . It maintains surveillance over converts. . . ." In a nationwide drive for "voluntary surrender" in October-November 1949, up to 70,000 converts were expected. The success of this operation marked a reversal of the tide of dissidence owing to improved security and some gain in Korean confidence and well-being. By April 1950, an internal State Department memorandum noted the relative success of the ROK against the guerrillas, comparing it favorably with the situation in the Philippines at the time. This success was attributed to the threat from the north (facilitating mobilization of anti-Communist support), U.S. military assistance and effective Korean utilization of it, plus at least some measure of popular support for the regime.[104]

Wartime Subversive Activity

The guerrilla problem reemerged behind the fighting lines in 1950, often in the same traditional centers of resistance, where up to thirty or forty thousand of the defeated north Korean forces remained. These were not considered a great threat, but tied down forces and hampered government operations. In mid-1951, it appeared that the Communists might be once more reverting to internal subversion, as the commencement of cease-fire negotiations indicated the failure of outside attack. A careful Embassy study in south Korea from Japanese times, when remnants of the Korean imperial forces had become a "Righteous Army" against the occupying forces in the 1900s demonstrated the long history of the problem.[105]

The bitter experience of the Korean War, including brief but draconic north Korean administration of large areas in the south, made the south Korean people firmly anti-Communist, and the north Koreans were never thereafter able to win any appreciable popular support in the ROK. Increasingly effective ROK action, with U.S. assistance, put an end to organized guerrilla activity by 1955, when the last special anti-guerrilla army and police operations were terminated. During this period, however, there were several cases in which the ROK armed forces faked guerrilla activities for political purposes. These included one case in which American soldiers were shot near Pusan in 1952 to create an impression of great danger, and the notorious faked "guerrilla" assault on the town of Kochang to impress a Korean legislative team.[106]

Internal Security After 1955

By 1955, counter-subversion had become a major U.S. government concern throughout the Free World, with its own developing expertise and country plans under the "1290-d program." The Embassy in Seoul submitted numerous analyses of ROK countersubversive capability, and specific programs were drawn up to improve it. In April 1955, the Embassy called attention to the plethora of ROK government agencies involved, their shortcomings, the degree of political involvement and infighting among them under Rhee, and the divided and piecemeal character of U.S. government assistance. The Embassy wanted more assistance for the police as the primary focus of U.S. assistance in this area, but the Eighth Army intelligence officer disagreed, holding that the Korean police were adequate, despite their inefficiency, to deal with the Communist threat. The State Department concluded that the Communist threat by then was more potential than actual. Responsibility for police assistance was transferred from the U.S. Army to the economic assistance program in 1956, although that program in turn was controlled by the commander of U.S. forces until 1959.[107]

Although the Korean counter-subversive capability improved, the north Korean challenge to it grew, and the problem was compounded by continuing ROK internal political and economic difficulties. In 1957, Communist emphasis shifted from espionage to political and subversive missions. There was little strictly military information gathering. A total of 236 enemy-controlled agents were caught in the ROK in 1957, an increase of 25 to 35 percent over previous years, and some of them seemed to be of higher caliber than before. Most arrived by small boats along the irregular west coast.

However, the ROK security agencies retained effective control, and some of their claims of increased subversive activity were exaggerated. U.S. authorities assisted with equipment and a modest training program, and endeavored to emphasize better ROK agency coordination. (These steps helped lay the groundwork for what later, as the ROK Central Intelligence Agency, became a "sorcerer's apprentice" far transcending the advisers' intentions.) Americans also emphasized improved coast-watching capability--not only because it was greatly needed, but because if was the area least likely to be politically manipulated.[108]

The internal security problem after the collapse of the Rhee government in 1960 involved domestic discontent and demonstrations of all kinds, in which the extent of external inspiration and participation was difficult to determine. The military junta, upon taking power in May 1961, banned all political activity and imposed firm security controls, which greatly inhibited subversion. Upon return to civilian government in early 1964, however, the internal security problem re-emerged--both as genuine internal discontent and as activity inspired from the north.

The most serious example of internal discontent in this latter period was the demonstration against normalization of relations with Japan, an issue deliberately seized upon by the opposition in an attempt to bring down the Park government (see Chapter 5). In February 1965, the ROK government asked the Embassy in Seoul for tear gas and gas masks for police use in anticipated riots on the Japan treaty issue. The aid was provided, on the basis that successful police containment of disorders would avoid the use of military forces.

Despite efforts to avoid such American aid becoming generally known (by supplying the materials through military channels). the opposition leader discovered it, and exploited the issue politically in an open letter of protest to the commander of U.S. Forces on April 21. After Washington policy clearance, General Hamilton Howze, the U.S. commander, responded on the 23d that the U.S. had supplied standard riot control materials, such as tear gas, to the Korean armed forces under successive Korean governments, and stated, "These materials are not 'poisonous chemical weapons.'"[109]

Responding to a worldwide inquiry on U.S. public safety assistance programs in August 1965, the Embassy noted that there was stepped-up north Korean infiltration, together with vulnerability resulting from the turmoil over the Korea-Japan treaty. Although the ROK Central Intelligence Agency now had over-all responsibility for security, there were still the same old problems of coordination among agencies, which might be the most serious deficiency, and of anti-infiltration controls along the demilitarized zone and the coast. Needs for counter-intelligence training and for additional equipment were also noted.[110]

A preliminary U.S. survey of internal security program requirements in the Fall of 1965 was accompanied by an upsurge of incidents of subversive violence, together with increasingly belligerent propaganda from north Korea. An interagency survey team was assembled in Washington late in 1965; and in mid-1966, in reference to its report, the Country Team in Seoul recommended immediate attention to improving ROK capability for detection, surveillance, and apprehension of north Korean agents as a first-priority program. (In subsequent years, the north Korean challenge built up to a climax in 1968, when an attempt to assassinate President Park came alarmingly close to success; but eventually the renewed north Korean effort at subversion failed, without ever having aroused any notable response among most of the south Korean people.[111]

ROK Troops to Vietnam

As the French position in Indochina deteriorated, the Koreans offered troop support: their Ambassador in Washington (Yang) suggested a ROK division be sent to help the Laotians; and Rhee, in June 1954, reaffirming previous troop tragedy for future. . . ." In a letter to Ambassador Briggs in July, Rhee said he was willing to send three Army divisions, and, observing that "Koreans cannot survive in Communist-dominated Asia," he called for quick and resolute U.S. and Free World action. The American response to these overtures was to put them tactfully aside.[70]

The Koreans again made their offer in 1961, when General Park Chung Hee, as leader of the military junta, told President Kennedy that Korea could supply troops for Vietnam. Without U.S. involvement, Korean *karate* instructors were sent to Vietnam. The renewed 1963 offer of Korean combat forces was repeated on a personal basis by ex-Prime Minister Kim Hyon Chul in early 1964. The United States by this time was more favorably disposed toward the idea, but at first encouraged engineer, medical, and technical assistance rather than combat troops, because the nature of the war at that time did not appear to argue for such intervention.[71]

In May 1964, the ROK press "showed immediate, favorable response to U.S. appeal for free world countries aid Vietnam fight against Communism." The ROK government also favored sending Korean forces. The Korean motives were complex. There was sincere desire to push the Communists back, along the lines previously indicated by former President Rhee. Additionally, the Koreans welcomed an opportunity to repay what they saw as a debt to the United States and the Free World for defense against the 1950 aggression. On a more calculating level, the Koreans saw an opportunity to increase their leverage on the U.S. in terms both of financial and military assistance and of American commitment to the Korean cause. The latter appeared particularly important as the critical stage in normalization of relations with Japan approached. Moreover, there would be opportunity for gaining battlefield experience and (as later developed) for earning substantial amounts of American dollars.

In mid-1964, U.S. officials proposed to the Koreans that they send a mobile station hospital (MASH) to Vietnam, along lines developed by Korean consultations in Vietnam. After a pause to develop the necessary request from the Vietnamese government, a hospital unit was sent. The Koreans continued eager to send combat forces, but the U.S. discouraged the idea. In December, the U.S. proposed that the Koreans send combat engineers and a transportation company to Vietnam, in a contingent totalling two thousand men.

The ROK government considered that approval of the National Assembly for this action was necessary. The political opposition seized the opportunity to argue against it, although the Ambassador (Berger) endeavored to dissuade the principal opposition leader (ex-President Yun Bo-Sun) from doing so. However, National Assembly approval was obtained on January 26, 1965, and the forces were dispatched, with "reluctant approval" of the opposition and the press. The U.S. was still concerned to avoid any suggestion that Korea was sending combat troops, so as not to arouse speculation as to Vietnamese weakness. The Embassy was therefore instructed to emphasize to the ROK government that the infantry battalion accompanying the ROK contingent to Vietnam would have no combat role other than security for the Korean force.[72]

By April 1965, the situation in Vietnam had reached a point where additional troops seemed necessary. The U.S. Ambassador to Vietnam (Henry Cabot Lodge) carried to Seoul a message to President Park from President Johnson along these lines. In May, the Koreans received a vague request from the Vietnamese government for combat troops--apparently uncoordinated with the United States. The Koreans seized upon it as in accord with their own desires, and as a means of maximizing concessions to be gained at the time of President Park's impending visit to Washington.

In subsequent months, a proposal was formulated to send a combat division to Vietnam, at the invitation of the Vietnamese. Consent of the National Assembly was again obtained, despite the political crisis surrounding the Korean-Japanese treaty, and by September, ROK Forces Vietnam had become a part of the military effort there. According to a ROK government public opinion survey in September, 57.6 percent of those among the sample polled who were aware of the despatch of troops to Vietnam approved of the action.[73]

As the Ambassador pointed out in his evaluation of the proposal for sending a Korean division, this action added "a new dimension" to the ROK-U.S. relationship. A voluntary major Korean contribution toward U.S. and Free World interests added impetus to ROK requests for various forms of military and economic assistance and effectively suspended U.S. efforts at reducing both American and Korean military force levels. In direct maintenance costs alone, it was estimated in June 1965 that annual overseas allowances paid by the United States for the initial ROK regimental combat team would amount to $2,700,000; for the balance of the division task force, $7,500,000--still much less, of course, than the cost of an American division. An effort was made to keep these payments secret, but the ROK Defense Minister made an allusion to them in his explanatory statement before the National Assembly.[74]

4

Korean International Relations

From the time of its formation, the Republic of Korea recognized that the United States was the principal source--indeed, almost the only source--of the political, economic, and military assistance it needed. The United States was looked upon as an "elder brother" with corresponding status and responsibilities. Although the Republic of Korea was constantly apprehensive of American abandonment, often skeptical of American motives, and doubtful of American policies, its international relations--so long as Syngman Rhee, the Republic's first President, directed them--were concentrated almost exclusively on the United States. Japan was viewed during most of the period as an enemy. Some attention was paid to the United Nations and to a few friendly countries; but the primary south Korean concern was to influence the United States to maximize its aid, minimize its interference, and exercise its world leadership in ways that accorded with Korean needs and attitudes.

At the same time, however, south Koreans were increasingly conscious of their own identity. Rhee himself appealed to his people not only for his ability to get aid and concessions from the United States, but for his willingness to stand up to the Americans. ROK assertiveness increased following the military coup d'état of 1961, although continued dependence on American assistance limited Korean freedom of action.

The United States, once it had at least partially discharged its promise of Korean independence through the establishment of the Republic of Korea in 1948, wanted to achieve a graceful withdrawal from its role as Korea's guardian. This was to be accomplished by means a minimal program of economic and military development and the encouragement of the ROK as a peaceful, democratic state that could look out for itself under the general protection of the United Nations. One element in achieving this goal was to make the ROK a full-fledged member of the international community. Accordingly, the United States constantly encouraged the south Koreans to broaden their international contacts by campaigning for broader recognition, by establishing diplomatic relations, and by joining international organizations.

The Korean War increased the importance of south Korea to the United States, which then provided massive military and economic aid and entered into a formal alliance with the ROK as part of American anti-Communist containment policy. The United States nevertheless continued to encourage the expansion of ROK international relations. As for North Korea, American policy was insofar as possible to isolate and belittle or ignore it.

ROK Foreign Policy

Until 1960, Syngman Rhee personally managed ROK foreign policy, assisted by his Austrian wife. (As a result, his Foreign Ministry was largely inconsequential until the late 1950s.) He showed little enthusiasm for expending effort on more than a handful of foreign countries--partly because he jealously conserved foreign exchange, partly because he would not maintain relations with countries he considered soft toward Communists, but also in large part because he preferred to concentrate on the United States. Additionally, Rhee until 1959 refused to accept dual accreditation of foreign envoys in Tokyo, because of his anti-Japanese position.

In actuality, it would have been difficult for the Koreans during those years to establish meaningful diplomatic intercourse on a broad scale, because they had little or nothing of their own to offer and were generally viewed as American proteges. They could not have formulated really independent foreign policies unless they were willing to run the risk of losing American aid, and it was unlikely they could get aid anywhere else so long as they clung to a rigid anti-Japanese and anti-Communist position.

Nevertheless, the Koreans shared with the United States one good reason for expanding diplomatic recognition: the ongoing popularity contest with the north Koreans. It was important to both the ROK and the United States that the world support the United Nations position on Korea, as formulated in the December 1948 General Assembly resolution: that the ROK, though it did not control all Korean territory, was nonetheless the only legitimate government in Korea. The Korean question was part of the Cold War, and any increase in north Korean legitimacy, prestige, or recognition represented a loss for the Free World side, with consequences for domestic Korean political stability. The annual debate in the UN over the Korean question was one of the Cold War battlegrounds, watched closely by the Korean public as well as by the world at large.

When new African and Asian nations started to swell the UN membership ranks, the south Koreans--with American encouragement--recognized the need for support of the ROK case among them. This was difficult for the Koreans to get; they had little to offer the new states for their votes, and American persuasion did not always work. Nevertheless, the Koreans tried hard. The year 1960, when sixteen new states joined the UN, was a watershed in Korean international relations, coinciding with a year of dramatic political developments within the ROK itself.[1]

After 1960, successive Korean governments sought increasingly to expand their international contacts, with a considerable measure of success despite continuing north Korean competition and the distaste of new nations for Cold War involvement. The United States continued to encourage and support them in this expansion. There was additional motivation on both sides: growing emphasis on Korean economic development argued for maximizing foreign trade and investment in Korea, especially as a counterweight to prospective Japanese contributions; and the eventual elimination of the American aid burden, both economic and military, would be facilitated by a greater Korean involvement with the Free World as a whole. One of the first new ROK international initiatives was an international community development conference in May 1961, just prior to the military coup d'état, with U.S. support and encouragement.

Exemplifying the new Korean emphasis was the ROK Foreign Minister's remark to a State Department official (Yager) in 1962 that during the Rhee regime the ROK had established diplomatic relations with 13 countries (16 by American calculations), while the new ROK government had established relations with 29 countries since November 1961. The Foreign Minister also thought that the ROK could advance Free World interests by strengthening its relations with the Afro-Asian neutrals, which distrusted the white man. He acknowledged, however, that the ROK had difficulty in getting established in African countries, and had been unable to establish relations with any Arab country--even Jordan; hence the Koreans had finally agreed to establish relations with Israel.

The Department officer, strongly supporting the ROK position, noted the U.S. interest in having the Koreans extend technical assistance to the less-developed countries in such matters as rice-growing. At the end of the year 1963, the Foreign Minister held a press conference in which he characterized the main goal of ROK foreign policy as "independent diplomacy," to be achieved by strengthening ROK ties with neutral nations to the point where the ROK could serve as a bridge between the neutral nations and the West. By 1965, the ROK was recognized by 76 countries.[2]

In its competition with north Korea, the ROK faced the same problem as West Germany--the reluctance of many countries to take sides in the Cold War. Paralleling the German Hallstein doctrine, the ROK long refused to maintain relations with any country that recognized north Korea, even while the Koreans were seeking neutral support. For example, ROK relations with Mauritania were broken off in December 1964, despite American advice, after Mauritanian recognition of north Korea. On the other hand, the ROK was willing to post a consul general in Cairo, despite the presence of a north Korean trade mission there, because the United Arab Republic did not formally recognize the northern regime.[3]

Relations with the United States

The paragraphs that follow are intended as a general overview and appraisal of ROK relations with the United States, since the entire book examines them in detail.

The Koreans had long been a tributary state of China, and they shared the Chinese cultural tradition despite their exposure to Japan and the West. Thus they could, and did, fit their complete early dependence upon the United States into a Confucian mold, in which the United States had the status and responsibilities of an elder brother. The Koreans exerted their influence to maximize American aid, minimize American interference, and induce American foreign policies that accorded with Korean needs and attitudes, especially in regard to Japan and the Communists. At worst, the Korean approach was condemned as "mendicant mentality" (to use the late Hahm Pyong-Choon's term in a *Foreign Affairs* article). At best, it was a pragmatic acceptance of the inevitable.

Syngman Rhee had begun life as a revolutionary, and devoted his life to the cause of Korean independence from Japan. However, his long residence in the United States had turned him into an arch-conservative in his views on communism, and had made him suspicious of U.S. policies toward the Soviet Union. These views were reinforced, both for him and for his conservative countrymen, by the division of Korea. He probably believed in all sincerity that he had a duty to educate the United States on the evils of the Communists, not only for Korean security but for that of the Free World.

Rhee distrusted the State Department (except for John Foster Dulles) as much as, or more than, conservative American Republicans. He regarded it as both pro-Communist and pro-Japanese. He had his own unofficial American advisers with whom he had been associated during his years of exile, the so-called "kitchen cabinet" of such men as Staggers, Goodfellow, Williams, Oliver, and Staggers's son-in-law, Harold Lady. Through these men, and anyone else who would listen to him (including Congressmen, military officers, missionaries, clergymen, and journalists) he sought to exert influence directly upon the American Congress, Administration, and public, to the constant annoyance of the State Department and the Embassy in Seoul.

Rhee tended to trust American military men more than diplomats--especially Generals MacArthur, Clark, and Van Fleet--and tried to utilize them in end-runs around American diplomatic representatives. From 1951 until 1959, the American military commander controlled the U.S. economic aid program to Korea--a complication of channels which maximized Rhee's opportunities to frustrate overall American policies.

From the moment of his return to Korea in October 1945, Rhee endeavored to impose his own anti-Communist policies on the United States. He early argued for a separate anti-Communist regime in south Korea, and had no use for American attempts to reach an understanding with the Soviets. Upon the foundation of the Republic of Korea in 1948, he adopted a strong anti-Communist and anti-Japanese posture, focusing his own and the nation's attention on these issues at the expense of urgent problems of political and economic development. Fearing the Communists, and worried over the possibility of American abandonment, he sought to get a treaty of mutual security, or at minimum a treaty of friendship, from the United States. He was given no satisfaction on either idea until the final stage of the Korean War. Fearing the eventual reemergence of Japan, he objected to American policies which strengthened Japan, especially after the San Francisco Treaty of 1951 restored Japanese sovereignty.

The nadir of Korean-American relations came between 1952 and 1955, when Rhee saw the glittering prospect of a reunified anti-Communist Korea slipping away because of what he considered American weakness, and at the same time perceived American policies as strengthening Japan at the expense of Korea. During this same period he was struggling to assert domestic political control against a powerful opposition which drew considerable moral support from American conceptions of democratic process, expressed in an unsympathetic American press, and (as he saw it) some more tangible opposition support from certain American officials. The war had brought vast economic destruction and rapid inflation, which American assistance seemed unable and even unwilling to remedy. Viewed in this light, Rhee's extreme recalcitrance, described in the frustrated telegrams of Ambassadors Muccio and Briggs, is understandable. Moreover, Embassy reporting in late 1952 recognized American failure to consult with the Koreans in advance concerning policies of utmost importance to them.[4]

Actually, Rhee's accomplishments in winning benefits for his country from the United States during this period through stubbornness and unilateral action were noteworthy. His release of Korean war prisoners in June 1953 and refusal to accede to an armistice or a political conference, at a time when the United States desperately wanted to end the fighting, gained him a mutual defense treaty, a billion-dollar economic reconstruction program, the training and equipping of a 700,000-person army, and a 1954 visit to the United States, where he addressed a joint session of Congress. His demonstrations against the inspection teams of the Neutral Nations Supervisory Commission helped induce the Americans to suspend one of the articles of the Armistice Agreement so as to expel Communist representatives. These and other lesser successes confirmed his countrymen in their view that he was uniquely qualified to handle the all-important problem of dealing with the United States, and that his rough tactics paid off. In reality, of course, Rhee's tactics would not have worked, had it not been for an American re-evaluation of Korea's strategic and political importance, but it is arguable that under weaker leadership, Korea would have benefited far less from American assistance.

The United States, for its part, until 1960 accepted Rhee as his country's inevitable leader during his lifetime, despite the difficulties of dealing with him, and despite American hopes for a more democratic political regime. In 1960, however, the United States was constrained to give moral support to his overthrow. During the two short-lived civilian administrations that followed, the general nature of the Korean relationship to the United States did not greatly change, although the beginnings of a greater self-reliance and independence appeared along with a greater short-term responsiveness to American guidance. Subsequent to the military coup d'état, there was a period of great strain and some return to the eyeball-to-eyeball confrontations of the early 1950s (although more effectively coordinated on both sides), accompanied by growth of both pragmatism and independence on the Korean side. By 1965 a new era of friendly ROK-U.S. relationships was signalled by the official visit of Park Chung Hee--now a duly-elected civilian President--to the United States; but the new era had more equality and independence of action on the Korean side than ever before.

Relations with Japan

For most Koreans in the years after their liberation in 1945, Japan was still the enemy that had devastated them in the sixteenth century and oppressed them during most of the twentieth. They recalled that the United States had abandoned them to the Japanese in 1905. They resented what they took to be preferential treatment of Japan by the United States, and in particular the economic benefits accruing to Japan from U.S. procurement during the Korean War. When they emerged in 1948 as a new and struggling state, the Koreans were assertive about their sovereignty, and covered their feelings of inferiority and fear with exaggerated demands for Japanese reparations and apologies. They expected the United States, as their "elder brother," to back them up in these demands. For many years, such Korean emotions overshadowed the very real substantive issues involved in Korean-Japanese relations. The same was true to some extent on the Japanese side: the Japanese were somewhat contemptuous of their former colony, and tended to feel that their occupation of Korea had done more good than harm.

Mindful of this background, the United States worked constantly to improve relations and mutual understanding, and to encourage negotiation of outstanding issues. During President Rhee's administration, however, little could be done.

Rhee, whose public posture was more anti-Japanese than any of his countrymen, was unwilling to normalize relations with Japan except on his own extreme terms, and seemed quite content with a situation of continuing hostility, in the confidence that the Americans would have to provide for his nation's economic and security requirements anyway. He probably feared that closer relations with Japan would inhibit the development of Korean national consciousness and identity. Moreover, the Japanese made a convenient scapegoat for domestic difficulties. Moreover, convinced that the State Department was pro-Japanese, Rhee was not responsive to U.S. advice on Japanese relations.

Nevertheless, there was a growing awareness among Korean leaders generally of the need for a settlement with Japan, if only for the sake of speeding economic development. The negotiations under Rhee, though they produced virtually no tangible agreement, did promote understanding of the substantive issues and of the negotiating process. When full-scale negotiations resumed under the military regime in late 1961, therefore, most technical questions could be speedily dealt with, leaving only the final political decisions to be made. The Japanese by 1962 had realized clearly that strengthening the ROK was in their own interest. Both sides had gained in strength, confidence, and capability.

The United States managed to maintain pressure on both sides to work for a settlement without becoming over-identified with either, despite constant attempts on each side to enlist American support for its positions. Although the political opposition in both the ROK and Japan endeavored to utilize the impending normalization of relations against the two governments, their efforts were overcome by as mixture of strategy, persuasion, and common sense. Final exchange of ratifications came in December, 1965, rewarding patient and discreet American effort over seventeen years.

The Substantive Issues

As a basis for reviewing the sixteen years of negotiations leading to normalization of Korean-Japanese relations, the main substantive problems at issue in the negotiations are discussed in the following paragraphs. Two of the issues--Korean claims for art objects taken by the Japanese and for return of gold bullion held by the Japanese central bank in Korea--did not involve the United States. The other issues were fisheries, property claims, Korean residents in Japan, sovereignty over Tokto Island, ROK-Japan trade, diplomatic relations, and ship ownership. A relatively minor question, not discussed here, was the marine communication cables linking Korea and Japan, which were largely under U.S. military control until Japan regained its sovereignty.

Fisheries and the "Rhee Line." Rich fishing areas near Korea in the East Sea (Sea of Japan) are of major economic importance to both Japan and Korea. During the American occupation of Japan, the Supreme Commander, Allied

Powers (SCAP, i.e., General MacArthur) designated outer limits for Japanese fishermen, often referred to as the "MacArthur Line." As soon as the ROK obtained its independence, the Koreans started policing the Korean side of the MacArthur Line, although legally and in the U.S. view, all waters beyond the Korean three-mile limit were high seas. In the Spring of 1949, ROK forces seized six Japanese fishing boats, which act was formally protested by the Diplomatic Section of SCAP to the ROK diplomatic mission in Tokyo. This and subsequent communications went unanswered except for a noncommittal acknowledgement of December 22, 1949. The Korean capture of Japanese fishing boats and crews continued during and after the Korean War, with periodic variations of activity and repatriations of boats and men, the latter often after U.S. representations.[5]

As the date of Japanese resumption of sovereignty approached, and just prior to opening negotiations with Japan, President Rhee on January 18, 1952 unilaterally proclaimed his own line, roughly corresponding to the MacArthur Line that was to be abolished with the end of the American control in Japan. The move, coming in the midst of ongoing Korean War hostilities, took both Japan and the United States by surprise. The Japanese protested this act as incompatible with international usage regarding freedom of the seas and conservation of natural resources. U.S. naval authorities took measures to prevent the use of Korean naval vessels for enforcing the new "Rhee Line" (sometimes referred to as the "Peace Line"). The United States officially informed the Koreans that it would not support ROK enforcement action against Japan, and called attention to the desirability of solving the problem through an equitable fishing agreement. This position was not made public nor communicated to the Japanese.

The Koreans, however, continued to patrol up to the Rhee Line with their navy and seize Japanese vessels--sixty-three in one summertime period of less than a month. The Japanese established their own patrols, and the risk of clashes grew in the midst of the ongoing war. Accordingly, on September 27, 1952, CINCUNC (General Clark) established a "Sea Defense Zone," ostensibly for security against Communist incursions, but designed in actuality to keep Japanese fishing boats out of areas close to Korea. The line (unbeknownst to the Koreans) more or less corresponded to a patrol line already established by the Japanese. CINCUNC's move upset the State Department and displeased the Japanese, but it mollified Rhee.

Although a U.S. naval task force was made responsible for enforcing the zone, Rhee ordered his Chief of Naval Operations to seize any non-UN vessels in the zone and bring them to Pusan. CINCUNC forbade such action. The United States was caught in a dilemma between the Koreans and the Japanese, but finally reiterated to the Koreans its non-support of the Rhee Line and stated that the UN Command alone was responsible for enforcement as a military measure against enemy attack or infiltration. The Japanese agreed to cooperate in restraining their fishing vessels, but in February 1953 protested a lower-level U.S. naval order prohibiting all entry into the Sea Defense Zone. In July, after the Korean armistice, the Japanese requested removal of the zone, and CINCUNC suspended its enforcement in August.[6]

Meantime, general Korean-Japanese negotiations had broken down, and the ROK Navy again started enforcing the Rhee Line in September. The Japanese, with their own political crisis and strong domestic interests, strongly protested, although they privately indicated to American officials their willingness to limit the Japanese fish catch in the former zone and concede to the Koreans those fishing grounds that had been set aside for them during the Japanese administration of Korea. The U.S. Embassy in Tokyo estimated in March 1954 that Japanese losses of boats and catch as a result of Korean activities might be around $9.5 million. The two embassies in Seoul and Pusan differed on policies to be followed, each favoring its host country; Defense wanted to withdraw logistic support from the Korean Navy; State wanted to keep the Koreans quiet as the political conference on unification approached. The Koreans released some of the Japanese fishing crews they had detained, but arrested others. The efforts of the U.S. good offices mission, described below (page 129), improved understanding of fisheries issues on both sides, but did not produce any immediate change in positions, although some detained fishermen were released.[7]

Despite constant U.S. representations, the Koreans continued to support the Rhee Line. They organized a "Coast Guard" to enforce it, separate from the ROK Navy, so as not to violate CINCUNC operational control. Seizures of Japanese boats and crews continued, as did periodic releases, depending on the climate of relations with Japan. On May 25, 1959, answering a Korean circular note to chiefs of diplomatic missions in Seoul, the U.S. Ambassador (Dowling) reiterated the "fundamental disagreement of the U.S. Government with the proclamation of [the Rhee Line]. . . ."

In 1960, as the Rhee administration approached its domestic nemesis, it was again in a phase of vigorously enforcing the Rhee Line as a tactic in the general negotiations with Japan then in progress. There was resultant resentment and hardening of positions on the Japanese side, and a crisis in Korean-Japanese relations seemed in prospect. The United States was greatly concerned, not only because of the regional problem, but also because of the issue's implications for the forthcoming Law of the Sea Conference, where the United States would need all the support it could get. It therefore reiterated its position in strong terms in an aide-memoire of March 9, 1960 in Seoul and another of March 16 read by the Secretary of State (Herter) to the ROK Ambassador (Yang). As of March 15, 1960, according to the Japanese, the box score since establishment of the Rhee Line in 1952 stood at 170 Japanese fishing boats and 2,209 fishermen captured; of these, 19 boats and 1,990 men had been returned to Japan.[8]

After the fall of the Rhee government, the United States expected improved ROK relations with Japan. However, the Japanese repatriation of Koreans to north Korea had stirred anti-Japanese feelings. Although Acting President Huh Chung, who had headed the Korean negotiators in the latest round with Japan, was personally anxious to move toward settlement, he was impeded by the political climate. There were rumors, moreover, that Japanese fishermen were seeking to take advantage of the new Korean regime. Rhee Line incidents therefore continued. The United States asked the Japanese to exercise restraint, but the Japanese Foreign Office maintained that it was no more able to enforce restraints on its fishermen in waters off Korea than the United States could with its own fishermen in Latin American waters.[9]

When the Chang Myon government came to power, it also felt constrained to reaffirm the Rhee Line publicly to placate domestic interests. Before any significant progress was made in negotiations with Japan, the Korean military coup occurred; and the military in their turn reasserted support of the Rhee Line--in part, again, in deference to Korean public opinion, but also in part as a bargaining chip.

The fisheries issue continued as a major domestic political problem in both Korea and Japan, and the Koreans continued seizures of Japanese fishing vessels at least until late 1963. In the end, in the final 1965 settlement, the Japanese conceded exclusive Korean fishing rights only within a twelve-mile limit off the Korean coast. Other areas were covered by a conservation agreement of the kind which had been urged by the United States for many years.[10]

Reparations and Property Claims. The ROK government, supported by public opinion, consistently believed that it was entitled to reparations from Japan for damages and indignities to persons and property during Japanese rule. Korean estimates of this damage ran up to $1.3 billion. In addition to real property and other assets, the claims involved compensation allegedly due to Koreans who were forcibly taken to Japan and other territories for labor during World War II. The Japanese did not agree to this view. They were prepared to pay a price for normalizing relations, to assist in Korean economic development; but they believed that any obligations they might have had toward the Koreans were met by the surrender of Japanese property claims in the peace treaty of 1951 with the United States, and they pointed out that Japanese had owned 85 percent of the property in Korea. (The U.S. Ambassador [Muccio] confidentially estimated in early 1950 that 95 percent of industrial property in Korea had been owned by Japanese.)

The United States was involved in this issue because it had seized all Japanese assets within its zone of occupation in Korea, both public and private, except what personal property the repatriated Japanese had been able to carry with them. The seizure of private assets was a dubious step under international law, with potential for embarrassment. The United States had turned over all Japanese property in its custody to the ROK in the Initial Financial and Property Settlement of September 9, 1948, except for what little had been sold off before then, and except for Japanese farmland sold to 500,000 tenants under the U.S. Military Government land reform of 1948. The Japanese had accepted these actions in Article 4(b) of the peace treaty. However, the Japanese Foreign Office in a March 1952 note to Korean negotiators contended that Japan still had valid property rights in Korea, since international law did not permit the American military government to transfer full rights. The Japanese went so far as to suggest that Korea was liable for damage to Japanese property during the Korean War.[11]

The chief Korean negotiator (Ambassador Yang) asked for a U.S. interpretation. Assistant Secretary of State John Allison responded with a note on April 29, 1952, affirming that Japan had been divested of all property rights by the treaty. The note also stated: "The disposition of such assets . . . is relevant, however, in the opinion of the United States, in the consideration of the arrangements contemplated by Article 4(a) of the Treaty." The Japanese were informed of this exchange, and the United States stated that negotiations concerning property claims were a bilateral matter between the ROK and Japan. The U.S. position was not made public.

When the Korean chargé in Washington (Han Pyo-Wook) asked for an interpretation of the U.S. Military Government's Ordinance 33, vesting Japanese property, a State Department officer (McClurkin) pointed out to him that the matter should not be pressed too far, since the Japanese might react with regard to Korean claims under that ordinance for assets in Japan of corporations formerly based in Korea. In such event, the United States would support the validity of SCAP orders which in effect relieved the Japanese of such obligations. Concurrently, U.S. representatives were telling the Japanese that their claims to privately owned property in Korea were "legally uncertain and politically futile." Korean-Japanese disagreement over property claims, aggravated by considerations of "face," was the chief proximate cause for breaking off the 1952 talks.[12]

The following year, all American efforts to get Korean-Japanese talks going again foundered on President Rhee's uncompromising attitude. The U.S. Embassy in Tokyo finally commented in June 1954 that the basic "facts are simple: ROK expects to collect large sum of money from Japan, and Japan has no intention of paying it. . . . This is basic deadlock which no U.S. 'good offices' likely to remove." Despite subsequent feelers and communications between both parties and the United States, there was little further progress for some time.[13]

In July 1956 the ROK Foreign Minister wrote the Secretary of State to ask for a U.S. demand that Japan "publicly and officially" renounce its claim to former Japanese property. In his reply of September 10, the Secretary simply reaffirmed the American position that it was up to the two countries to negotiate their differences, adding that the United States would offer its good offices on the invitation of both governments if its participation would be useful. Subsequently, after checking with the Japanese Foreign Ministry, the U.S. released to the Koreans in October the official U.S. Government interpretation of Article 4 of the peace treaty (essentially the same as given to Ambassador Yang in 1952). The Japanese withdrew the "Kubota remarks" (see below, page 129) and their claims to Japanese property in Korea, for which President Rhee thanked Secretary Dulles in a letter of January 23, 1958. In 1959, reflecting a considerable evolution of thinking on both sides, there was talk of a negotiating deal as part of which the Japanese would offer assurances through the United States of a commitment of economic assistance to Korea.[14]

As the prospects of a real settlement drew nearer, under the Chang Myon government, another issue came to the fore: the legal implications of a Japanese settlement with the Republic of Korea, representing only part of Korea, for the entirety of Korean claims. This was a difficult problem for Japan, where the Socialist opposition tended to support north Korea. The Japanese confidentially raised this subject with the United States, which maintained in view of UN recognition that the ROK was competent to negotiate a settlement. This issue disposed of, actual figures began to be mentioned to U.S. officials: the Japanese in May 1961 (just before the coup d'état) were thinking of $50 million to settle claims (largely for personnel compensation, bullion, etc.); $250 million in grant aid; and an undetermined amount of long-term credit. The Koreans were thinking at that time of a total of $1 to 1.2 billion over a ten-year period, about half of which would be in grant assistance.[15]

Over the next four years, there was hard bargaining over amounts and categories, with the United States urging the Japanese to be forthcoming and acting as an informal communication channel between the two governments. The conversation focused increasingly on economic development. The Koreans began to be apprehensive over the effect of large-scale Japanese capital input and trade on Korean political and economic independence.

To reassure the Koreans, as well as to help assure orderly and non-duplicating use of U.S. and Japanese funds, the United States promoted formation of an international consultative group on development assistance to Korea, with World Bank participation. The final settlement was far removed from the original property claims: Japan gave Korea a total commitment of $800 million, including grants, concessional development loans, and commercial credits; the settlement included amounts to settle property claims considered valid by the Japanese, and fishery development loans. The United States, for its part, repeatedly reassured the Koreans that it would not take advantage of Japanese aid to reduce its own economic assistance program.[16]

Status of Korean Residents in Japan. Although the American military forces carried out a large-scale repatriation of Koreans after World War II, about 700,000 Korean nationals chose to remain in Japan and some discontented south Koreans (including north Korean agents) filtered illegally into Japan. A few of these expatriates prospered, but most were poor, discontented, somewhat crime-prone, and discriminated against by the Japanese. The north Korean regime cultivated them and encouraged them in anti-ROK sentiments and leftist causes. The ROK, for its part, was not really interested in their welfare except to the extent that its national prestige and security were involved. Accordingly, ROK negotiators insisted on full rights for Korean nationals in Japan, but the ROK consistently refused to accept the repatriation of Koreans whom the Japanese wanted to deport, and would not seriously consider a repatriation program unless the Japanese paid the costs.[17]

The United States was concerned with this issue for three reasons. It was one of the many stumbling blocks in Korean-Japanese relations, which the Americans wanted to improve. In particular, it became involved in the fisheries problem, because the Japanese started to apprehend illegal Korean entrants who had come since World War II, put them in detention camps (chiefly at Omura), and refused to release them unless the Japanese fishermen held by the Koreans were released. Most significantly, it became a Cold War issue because the Japanese, frustrated in their attempts to deal with the troublesome Korean community, allowed the Japanese Red Cross to negotiate with the north Korean Red Cross, at the latter's initiative, for a large-scale voluntary repatriation program to north Korea on Soviet ships. This program began in 1959, following signature of an agreement between the two Red Cross societies on August 16. It was renewed annually for several years, until over 100,000 people had been moved to north Korea, accompanied by vociferous protests by the ROK.

Unable to prevent the repatriation program to north Korea, the United States sought unsuccessfully to persuade President Rhee to acquiesce in it, while seeking to assure that the repatriation that occurred was in fact voluntary. The United States also suggested that the ROK undertake a repatriation program of its own, but when the Koreans found that the United States would not pay the costs, they lost enthusiasm. After Rhee was overthrown, it was hoped that Huh Chung, head of the interim government, would accept the repatriation; but he manifested the same attitude as Rhee. After the Chang Myon government took over in south Korea, the United States sought to dissuade the Japanese from renewing the repatriation program, but was unsuccessful. Although repatriation continued thereafter as an irritant, applications for the program eventually ceased and it died a natural death.[18]

In the initial round of Japanese-Korean negotiations, the legal status of Korean residents in Japan was not a major concern, and in January 1952, early agreement seemed possible, although the Japanese Justice Ministry had various technical problems. However, the Japanese wanted to get rid of five to seven thousand undesirables, and in July 1952 asked U.S. cooperation in arranging for their deportation. The Ambassador to Korea (Muccio), then visiting Japan, pointed out the difficulty of absorbing them in wartime south Korea.[19]

In mid-1958, the Japanese held ninety-three illegal Korean entrants from the ROK in detention camps, refused to repatriate them, and announced their intention to parole those who had been detained over three years, although the ROK wanted them returned for prosecution as subversives. The American Ambassador (Dowling) urged the Foreign Ministry to submit a compromise proposal and name a date for resumption of talks on the fisheries issue. The detainee problem was temporized, with private U.S. assistance, and in March, an exchange of detainees and fishermen took place, which Japanese Prime Minister Kishi attributed in part to the U.S. aide-memoire of March 16 (see page 119 above).

Sovereignty over Tokto (Takeshima) and Tsushima Islands. The only real territorial issue in Korean-Japanese relations concerned a rocky, uninhabited island about 140 miles off the Korean east coast, termed Tokto by the Koreans, Takeshima by the Japanese, and Liancourt Rocks by Western charts. The land in question was virtually valueless, except as a seal breeding ground and fishing base, but a great deal of attention was devoted to it. Tsushima, a sizeable and well-populated island in the straits between Korea and Japan, had been completely under Japanese control since the Meiji Restoration of 1869; the Korean claim to it was largely fanciful and for effect, and was never seriously pushed.

American involvement with the Tokto problem began with its use by the U.S. Air Force as a bombing target. In June 1948, a bombing run hit some fishermen on the island. Neither the Korean nor U.S. governments had been aware of this operation, and first learned of the incident from the local press. During the Korean War, the island was used by aircraft returning from north Korea to dump unexpended bomb loads, and its use as a target was recognized by agreement with the Japanese.

Despite general dissemination of this information, the UN naval commander in Pusan was unaware of the arrangements, and permitted the ROK Chief of Naval Operations to send a "scientific expedition" to Tokto in September 1952. It suffered no damage, but reported the bombing of a fishing crew, which was protested by the ROK Ministry of Foreign Affairs two months later in a note that asserted ROK sovereignty over the island.

In August 1951, the Assistant Secretary of State (Rusk) stated in a note to the ROK Ambassador (Yang) that Tokto had been under Japanese jurisdiction since 1905, had apparently never been treated as part of Korea, and had not previously been claimed as such. In a note of December 4, 1952, the U.S. Embassy in Seoul reaffirmed the 1951 position, but added that "preparations have . . . been expedited to dispense with the use of Dokdo [sic] Island as a bombing range."[20]

There ensued a Korean campaign to assert its sovereignty, involving expeditions to the island, firings on Japanese vessels in the vicinity, and an exchange of notes with the Japanese. The U.S. Embassy in Tokyo pointed out that the

American position in the 1951 and 1952 notes had never been communicated to the Japanese, and suggested that the United States publicly announce its view that sovereignty rested with Japan.

A legalistic exchange followed between the Department and the Embassy in Tokyo, in which the Embassy pointed out among other things that the omission of Tokto (Takeshima) from the peace treaty involved the United States in the determination of sovereignty. The Department, however, believed that the United States should not be involved in the dispute, and that if the problem could not be settled between the two countries, it should be referred to the International Court of Justice. In 1954, the Koreans established a lighthouse on Tokto; the Japanese reacted with a circular note proposing to submit the question to the International Court. Tokto continued to attract periodic attention on both sides throughout the course of the normalization negotiations, but in the end the Japanese abandoned their insistence on settling the issue in the text of the over-all agreement.[21]

Trade. The United States from the beginning of its economic aid program for Korea sought to promote and facilitate trade with Japan as a natural market and source of supply. Korean agricultural and marine products were needed in Japan, and Japan was the obvious source of equipment for Korea's largely Japanese-built industrial plants. However, President Rhee was intensely suspicious of Japan's economic intentions, and he sought to manipulate trade for Korea's political advantage, with negative result. He also objected to American purchases in Japan, particularly during the Korean War. The Japanese government, for its part, came under pressure from its own domestic producers to exclude Korean products. Aside from these political problems, such trade as did take place under an open account agreement of June 1950 resulted in a heavy payments deficit for Korea, amounting by mid-1954 to $44 million. Trade was somewhat better balanced thereafter, but the previous deficit remained. Eventually, it was forgiven by Japan as part of the over-all settlement in 1965.

One example of U.S. intervention in the trade field was its influence on the Japanese in 1958 to permit the import of Korean laver (dried seaweed), a dietary delicacy which was at that time the major Korean export item to Japan. The Japanese Ministry of Agriculture was under pressure from domestic producers, but American representations convinced the authorities of the need to ease the difficult situation with Korea. Fortunately, there was also a shortfall in Japanese production at the time.[22]

Diplomatic Relations. Upon formation of the Republic of Korea in 1948, General MacArthur permitted the establishment of a Korean diplomatic mission in Tokyo. The first round of Korean-Japanese negotiations (just before Japan regained its sovereignty in 1952) produced agreement that the Japanese Government would tentatively recognize the Korean mission, according it privileges equivalent to a consular agency, until normal diplomatic and consular relations were established. In the 1952 negotiations, a treaty of friendship was discussed, but not formalized. Relations between the two countries thus had little formal basis during the Rhee administration, but the Koreans maintained their representative in Tokyo, with the personal rank of Ambassador, and a fairly large staff. In 1955, Rhee threatened to withdraw his representatives as an indication of his displeasure with the Japanese, but the U.S. Ambassador (Lacy) urged him not to do so.[23]

The Chang Myon administration undertook in the Fall of 1960 to reach a settlement with Japan. The Japanese government was prepared to normalize diplomatic relations. The Americans in January 1961 suggested to ROK Prime Minister Chang that his government permit an exchange of diplomatic missions. Chang agreed to the desirability of the action, but doubted that Korean opinion was yet ready for it. At the same time, the Japanese Socialist Party issued a statement attacking the Japanese government's policy of seeking normalization of relations with the ROK as unfair to north Korea. The Socialists also raised the specter of a Japan-Republic of Korea-Republic of China-Philippines military alliance (which had actually been under consideration by the United States as a long-range possibility), and alleged that recognition of the ROK would intensify the partition of Korea.[24]

The 1961 military coup interrupted efforts at normalization of relations, but the Korean diplomatic mission remained in Tokyo. The Japanese were gradually allowed to establish a quasi-official presence in Korea well before the formal normalization was achieved in 1965.[25]

Ships. Since ships were movable, they were a particularly complicated problem in separating Korean from Japanese property after World War II. In October 1947, it was decided by a U.S. government interagency committee that all ships of Korean registry in Japan be returned to Korea, which was then in urgent need of them. Those owned by Korean companies and individuals would be returned to them by the U.S. military government in Korea; others would be vested, as with other Japanese property. The documents listed sixty-four "Korean ships in Japan" and ninety-three "Korean fishing vessels in Japan." However, the problem was still unresolved in the ROK view in 1949, and President Rhee asked the U.S. Embassy for documentation.[26]

Conferences ensued in June 1949 between the Koreans and SCAP authorities in Japan; they broke down because the SCAP authorities were "bound by instructions from Washington making actual ownership of vessels and their locus of August 9, 1945 the test, and Korean representatives insisting that place of registry of vessels as well as their locus on August 9, 1945, were critical." Of 194 vessels that Korea claimed from Japan, 20 had been returned, 25 were wrecked, 116 could not be found, and the remainder were returnable or subject to Korean proof of ownership. At the same time, the SCAP representatives claimed five large cargo ships and 110 fishing vessels from Korea. The cargo ships had been sent to Korea by the occupation authorities on a temporary basis, but one had fallen into north Korean control, one had sunk, and the ROK had sold the other three to private Korean interests.[27]

In September 1949 the Korean Embassy in Washington raised the question again, citing a ROK estimate that under the American formula it was entitled to 300,000 tons of shipping in Korean waters on August 9, 1945, and could substantiate its claim to much of this total. The Department, while maintaining the U.S. position, suggested that SCAP not press its claim for the five cargo ships and recognized Korea's need for shipping. The U.S. Embassy in Seoul responded, "The Korean Government seems to have complete knowledge of the problem of ships and is apparently making a successful negotiation in the matter on its own account." However, the ships remained one of the issues in the ROK-Japan negotiations of succeeding years. In 1951, SCAP ordered the Japanese government to turn over to the ROK all vessels registered with the Japanese Government General of Korea on August 9, 1945. The Korean reaction was to demand all vessels in Korean waters on that date.[28]

The Normalization Negotiations

Except for certain aspects of early discussion in 1951 and 1952, the United States never actually participated in the negotiations between the Republic of Korea and Japan. In 1953, a two-man good offices mission was authorized to participate within narrow limits, but never did so, although it conferred separately with both governments and made suggestions. Mediation was often considered, but never actually tried. On March 25, 1960, the Secretary of State (Herter) said that the United States had "never at any time offered our good offices," a statement that was perhaps literally correct but understated the U.S. role in encouraging progress toward normalization.[29]

First Rhee Visit to Japan, 1950. General MacArthur sought to initiate closer ROK-Japan ties through a personal invitation for President Rhee and his wife to visit Japan. They did so in February 1950, accompanied by a small staff, and met Japanese Prime Minister Shigeru Yoshida and other officials. Rhee held a press conference on February 18, conciliatory and friendly in tone, but nothing specific came out of the trip.[30]

First Round of Negotiations, 1951-1952. Signing of the U.S. peace treaty with Japan in September 1951 provoked an outburst of anti-Japanese pronouncements by President Rhee, reflecting a genuine fear of future Japanese economic and military domination, and the desire to stimulate the United States into explicit security guarantees as a counterbalance to Japan's restored national identity. The signing also led to Korean recognition of the need to consider future relations. Preliminary conferences between the Koreans and Japanese started on October 13 (six months before Japan regained its sovereignty) with offensive Korean statements, Japanese resentment, and private American hand-holding. The Koreans were "incredibly unprepared," although the chief delegate, Ambassador Yang Yu-chan, proved an able debater.[31]

The United States took the position that the two parties should negotiate between themselves, but that the U.S. "would consider furnishing mediator only if requested by both interested parties, and ourselves convinced mediation required achieve agreement." This position was to be repeated again and again throughout the next dozen years. However, SCAP observers did sit in as observers on discussions concerned solely with the status of Koreans in Japan and with ship claims. The Koreans sought to expand the talks into negotiations on the whole range of issues, but SCAP maintained that its good offices were restricted to the two specified topics.

The Koreans and Japanese in November 1951 agreed on a six-point agenda (diplomatic relations, nationality claims, fishing, marine cables, commerce and navigation) and presented draft proposals on property claims and on fisheries. There was talk of a visit to Korea by a Japanese representative (Matsumoto), but although the Koreans at first were positive, Rhee rejected it. Formal talks began in Tokyo on February 15, 1952, but soon reached an impasse, and adjourned indefinitely on April 24.

Second Rhee Visit, 1953. In an effort to improve the climate, which had steadily worsened since the suspension of negotiations, CINCUNC (General Mark Clark) sent President Rhee a personal invitation to visit him in Tokyo, which was accepted after hesitation and an initial refusal. Prime Minister Yoshida extended a dinner invitation, but Rhee would not accept it, and his meeting with Yoshida during the visit in January 1953 was correct but chilly and sterile. Nevertheless the atmosphere for renewed talks improved.

Second Round of Negotiations. Encouraged by the United States, and concerned at improving the government's image for their forthcoming election, the Japanese took the initiative in proposing the reopening of negotiations, which began in Tokyo on April 15, 1953, headed by ROK Minister Kim Yong-sik and by Kanichiro Kubota on the Japanese side. The Koreans were willing to negotiate because they calculated that they could get a better deal from the Yoshida government than from a successor. Five subcommittees were established, on property claims, fisheries, shipping, nationality, and conclusion of a basic treaty. The talks were negatively influenced, among other things, by continuing Korean seizures of Japanese fishing vessels; sessions were suspended from July to October, and came to an explosive end on October 21 because of an intemperate remark by the Japanese chief delegate, Kubota.[32]

The Kubota Remarks and Informal U.S. Mediation Efforts. According to subsequent Korean statements (which though somewhat overplayed were essentially correct), Kubota told the Koreans on October 21, 1953 that repatriation of Japanese from Korea, disposition of property by the American military government, and establishment of an independent Korean state before the peace treaty with Japan, were all violations of international law; that the description in the Cairo Declaration of Korean "enslavement" was wartime hysteria; and that "Japan's compulsory occupation of Korea for 36 years was beneficial to the Korean people." Kubota subsequently apologized, and asked to have the remarks stricken from the record, but the Koreans chose to make the statement a major substantive and propaganda issue, while the Japanese were reluctant to make a formal withdrawal because of the effect on Korean property claims, as well as for considerations of face.[33]

The breakdown came at a bad time from both the Japanese and the U.S. points of view. The Japanese were about to hold a parliamentary election, and the Koreans held nearly 500 Japanese fishermen, which was a topic of major Japanese concern. The State Department was trying to "keep Rhee quiet" and "buy time for the political conference" which was to follow the recently-concluded Korean armistice. The Koreans asked for American mediation. Accordingly, while the U.S. Ambassador in Tokyo (at secret Japanese Foreign Office urging) dissuaded Prime Minister Yoshida from retaliating against Korea, the United States named Niles Bond, a career diplomat, and the State Department's fisheries expert, Julian Harrington, as a good offices mission. They and the two U.S. embassies sought to bring the two sides together by working out a formula for dealing with the problem of the Kubota statement, as well as by trying to promote accommodation on substantive issues.[34]

Meantime, there was an exchange of letters between Rhee and Secretary Dulles, which dealt with Korean-Japanese relations as well as with economic reconstruction problems. The two issues were interrelated because Rhee believed that the American program to aid Korea was designed to aid Japan. Replying on December 10, 1953, to the barrage of criticism in Rhee's November 10 letter, Dulles spoke of U.S. efforts to bring about a peaceful Korean-Japanese settlement, and said among other things, "We are prepared to provide observers for the [Korea-Japan] negotiations . . . when they are resumed, and through these observers we are endeavoring to find a basis for the resumption of the talks. . . ."[35]

Subsequently, Rhee "contemptuously" rejected a proposed Japanese apology for the Kubota statement, which American officials in Tokyo and Seoul had helped to draft in confidential consultations with representatives of the two governments--an act that angered both U.S. embassies. The U.S. observer mission was terminated, amid charges by Rhee that Bond was "pro-Japanese." Assistant Secretary Robertson, then in Korea trying to keep Rhee from upsetting the post-Armistice political discussions, suggested to Washington the appointment of a "U.S. mediator of great prestige," and the suggestion was conveyed to the Koreans, with the additional proposal of talks between ROK and Japanese ambassadors in Washington. American mediation was also discussed during Rhee's mid-1954 visit to Washington. In the end, however, the proposal was never implemented.[36]

Efforts continued at finding a suitable formula for ending the impasse over the Kubota statement. In May 1954 a Japanese Foreign Ministry official (Okazaki) announced to the press that Japan was willing to withdraw the statement. However, the ROK Foreign Minister (Pyun) told the Embassy that the Japanese, if sincere, should send a formal note of apology. By June, the U.S. Embassy in Seoul doubted that it had any more leverage with the Koreans, and the Embassy in Tokyo believed that Washington was expecting too much of it. In Embassy Tokyo's view, American efforts on the Kubota statement had simply encouraged the ROK to stiffen their demands. In August, the Japanese said they were willing to resume talks if an American observer was present and both sides reexamined their claims positions; but Embassy Tokyo agreed with Ambassador Briggs's assessment in Seoul: "What is lacking is neither a formula nor negotiating opportunity but belief that interests of ROK will be better served in friendship than in animosity to Japan. . . ." The State Department agreed that further U.S. pressure would be futile for the time being, and American efforts slackened.[37]

Finally, in the 1957 preliminary talks, the Koreans accepted a Japanese withdrawal of the Kubota statement, and President Rhee in a letter to Secretary Dulles on January 13, 1958, expressed his appreciation for the U.S. role.[38]

Non-aggression Pact. In January 1955, the Japanese confidentially reported that the Koreans had suggested secret discussions looking toward formal resumption of negotiations. The Japanese agreed, and such talks commenced between the Korean Minister (Kim) and a Japanese Foreign Office representative (Tani). These talks soon led to the idea of a Japan-Korea non-aggression pact to meet Korean fears of Japan. (Such a pact had also been suggested to CINCUNC [General Hull] by Minister Kim in December 1954.) Minister Kim, reporting this to U.S. officials as his idea, asked for a U.S. guarantee.

The Japanese, however, did not want such a guarantee because it "would have the appearance of teacher supervising activities of schoolboys." The State Department pointed out that in the long run the United States favored a mutual defense treaty among the free nations of Northeast Asia, and that in the meantime Korea was protected by the Mutual Defense Treaty with the United States; hence the United States was not disposed to offer additional guarantees. Tani then drafted a trilateral declaration of adherence to Article 2 of the UN Charter, as cited in the San Francisco peace treaty. In February 1955 the Secretary of State approved in principle the participation of the United States in such a declaration. However, when the idea was broached at higher levels, neither the Japanese nor the Koreans were very enthusiastic about it, and it eventually disappeared, although Japanese Foreign Minister Shigemitsu raised it again in April 1956 with Ambassador Allison.[39]

Anti-Japanese Campaign. Beginning in the Spring of 1955, President Rhee ordered an all-out campaign against the Japanese for their allegedly growing pro-Communism and their overtures toward north Korea and other Communist countries, as well as for their refusal to meet Korea's "just" demands. In June, there were demonstrations and riots in front of the American Embassy in Seoul, which the State Department protested to the ROK Ambassador. Later that month, Ambassador Allison came from Tokyo to meet with President Rhee and Ambassador Lacy in Seoul, in an endeavor to promote a better atmosphere; but the two ambassadors concluded that "nothing less than a miraculous revelation will cause [Rhee] to depart from his deep-seated prejudice." The campaign abated, however, and in early 1956 the Japanese took a conciliatory line. Meetings between the Japanese and the ROK Minister resulted in an agreement in principle on release of some Korean illegal entrants and Japanese fishermen. In April, the ROK Acting Foreign Minister (Cho Chung Hwan) publicly noted some progress in Korean-Japanese relations, and thanked the United States for its good offices, to which he attributed the improvement.[40]

Third Round of Negotiations, 1958-1960. In January 1957, the U.S. Embassy in Seoul concluded that Rhee was "increasingly anxious for a settlement with Japan, although on his own terms." He had injected, as a new element, a demand that Japan return to Korea four political figures whom he regarded as subversives; nonetheless he seemed trying to be reasonable. The United States again sought to influence both sides toward resumption of negotiations, and helped in communication while exploratory conversations were going on. One of the principal issues in these conversations was the American interpretation of the effect of Article 4(b) of the San Francisco peace treaty on Korean property claims, which was to be in a U.S. note publicly released when both sides desired it.[41]

In December, it was agreed to reconvene the negotiations in March 1958, and both Japanese and Korean officials expressed their gratitude to the United States for its assistance. Rhee, in his letter to Secretary Dulles on January 23, 1958, asserted Korean determination to achieve a satisfactory solution, but reasserted his reservations about Japan and sought assurances against aggression from China, the USSR, or Japan. Dulles made a tactful, general response on February 1, reassuring Rhee that "the United States stands firm in its resolve to see Korea free from domination by any power." The United States decided in advance not to offer good offices "unless and until it becomes evident that such an offer would resolve outstanding problems and encourage cooperation."

However, it continued its informal contacts with both sides, and assisted in overcoming a last-minute hitch involving the release of detainees and fishermen.[42]

Formal talks commenced in April 1958. They were suspended the next month because of a dispute over detainees, but resumed in October. However, neither side was willing to make a significant concession to the other. There was another recess, largely because of the Japanese-north Korean repatriation agreement. Negotiations resumed again in August 1959, with a new ROK chief negotiator, Huh Chung (who the following year would head the post-Rhee interim ROK government). The Korean negotiators were disposed to be realistic about the substantive issues, but Rhee continued in his rigid views. Nevertheless, in May 1958 a Japanese emissary (Kazuo Yatsugi) was permitted a secret visit to Korea, as personal emissary of Prime Minister Kishi. By early 1960, relations had again worsened; the talks were "bumping along at rock bottom," while fishing seizures mounted and the United States protested, making its views public on March 16.[43]

The student uprising in Korea in April 1960 terminated the third round of negotiations. The succeeding interim government favored settlement with Japan, provided repatriation to north Korea was halted, but was not able to move definitively because of domestic political pressures. In late April, acting President Huh Chung's assistant (Sul Kuk-hwan) indicated that Huh would be embarrassed at any further U.S. pressure, lest there be doubts as to ROK government independence. Huh did, however, decide to admit Japanese newspaper correspondents to Korea for the first time.[44]

Negotiations by the Chang Administration. As soon as the new administration of Chang Myon was installed in August 1960, the U.S. Ambassador (Walter McConaughy) called on the Foreign Minister (Chyung Il-Hyung), to point out that the new situation, with new governments in both Korea and Japan, provided a "uniquely favorable setting for resolution outstanding ROK-Japan problems." He hoped the ROK would not repeat the mistakes of predecessor governments on the repatriation issue, and generally urged a forthcoming Korean approach. The Foreign Minister "urged that the US play a 'leading role' in bringing both sides together." Shortly thereafter, the Japanese Foreign Minister (Kosaka) broke tradition by visiting Korea, and said afterward that the visit had gone well.[45]

Preliminary discussions between the two countries began in October, and continued thereafter despite several difficulties--the ROK protest at renewal of the Japanese repatriation agreement with the north Korean Red Cross in October; new Korean seizures of Japanese fishing boats in January 1961; Korean cancellation of a Japanese trade mission; political opposition in both countries. However, the Japanese grew increasingly discouraged at prospects for progress, because of the weakness of the Chang government.

Meantime, the United States continued exerting its influence behind the scenes on both sides to induce maximum mutual understanding and accommodation; but both U.S. embassies were instructed to avoid detailed involvement or support of either side. At the same time, an influential private Korean businessman (Pak Heung-Sik) undertook a private mission to Japan in March on behalf of Prime Minister Chang, to discuss outstanding problems with Japanese governmental and business leaders. A Japanese Diet delegation visited Korea in May 1961, and formal negotiations were expected to begin in September or October. However, relations were once again put in limbo by the military coup d'état of May 16.

Final Phase of Negotiations, 1961-1965. Soon after the military regime was installed in Korea in May 1961, both it and the Japanese showed cautious interest in renewed negotiations. Japan, convinced of the danger of chaos in Korea, and the need for economic development to avoid chaos, was prepared to furnish economic assistance to Korea in an appropriate international context (see page 135, below). The Koreans wanted to maximize economic development. After the United States decided to work with the military regime in July, it again encouraged both sides.

Exploratory talks resumed in August, but the beginnings were not auspicious. A U.S. presidential message to both countries was considered, but postponed, lest it seem to exaggerate the U.S. involvement. Efforts by the U.S. embassies in both Seoul and Tokyo helped convince both sides that prompt negotiations would be desirable, and a special Korean emissary (Kim Yu-Taek) was sent to Tokyo to pave the way. However, the Korean chief negotiator (still Huh Chung) refused to serve because he considered Michisuge Sugi, whom the Japanese had named, to be of insufficient rank.[46]

Formal negotiations finally began in Tokyo on October 20, 1961, with a new Korean chief negotiator (Pae Ui-Hwan), and a staff of twenty-three, mostly technicians. On the 24th, Kim Jong-Pil, second most important figure in the military regime, arrived for independent discussions. From this time onward, various direct contacts, both overt and secret, between Korean and Japanese government heads paralleled the negotiations, sometimes to the concern of watching U.S. representatives. In November, the head of the Korean military regime (General Park Chung Hee) had a ninety-minute personal talk with Japanese Prime Minister Ikeda at Tokyo, at Ikeda's invitation, on Park's way back from a Washington visit. This meeting was a major milestone on the route to settlement, and its success (despite later misunderstandings) was attributed by the Japanese to the U.S. Secretary of State's (Rusk's) "spadework in Seoul" during his earlier visit to Japan and Korea.[47]

During the first half of 1962, the Japanese moved slowly because of approaching elections and Japanese economic problems, endeavoring to pressure the United States into balance-of-payments concessions as a price for rapprochement with Korea. Mindful of this factor, the United States nonetheless urged both sides to move toward settlement. The chief of the U.S. aid mission in Korea (James Killen) briefed Japanese officials on Korean development needs and U.S. programs. The idea of a special U.S. representative was considered, but shelved. In August, as formal negotiations resumed after a recess, President John F. Kennedy sent letters to both heads of government (Park and Ikeda) expressing American hopes for settlement as of importance "to both countries, to the United States, and to the Free World." In 1964, Embassy Tokyo commented on this period: "After years of urging on our part [the Japanese Government] made firm decision to push ahead toward Korean settlement as necessary in Japan's own interests."[48]

Thereafter, agreement was gradually reached on the basic issues. The general magnitude of a claims settlement was decided in November 1962 in the course of a visit by Kim Jong-pil to Tokyo, leaving fisheries, with the related Rhee Line issue, as the major problem. The United States exerted strong pressure for settlement, and after the 1963 elections in both countries, despite mounting domestic political difficulties in both Korea and Japan (including political use of press reports of U.S. diplomatic pressure in March 1964), the essential lines of a fisheries agreement had been worked out by early 1964. Various minor differences remained, however, and final agreement was inhibited by Korean opposition political pressures as well as by the suspicions, rivalries, and bargaining instincts of both sides. The Koreans captured more fishing boats. The United States considered, but shelved, the idea of offering a $100 million development loan program to the ROK as an incentive, and of holding tripartite meetings to promote resumption of negotiations. President Lyndon Johnson sent a personal message to President Park in July 1964, urging settlement. Finally, after Sato had succeeded Ikeda as Japanese Prime Minister, formal talks resumed in December. A Japanese Foreign Ministry official (Ushiroku) visited Korea in February 1965, and initialled a treaty of basic relations. On April 3, Korean and Japanese representatives initialled agreements on the principal outstanding issues.[49]

The opposition party in Korea, led by ex-President Yun Bo-Sun, seized on the normalization issue as a means of bringing down the Park administration. It had encouraged student demonstrations in March 1964, inhibiting the negotiations then in progress. In April 1965, it began again, and Yun remained intransigent, despite assurances of the U.S. Ambassador (Winthrop Brown) of U.S. support for the legal government and for legal processes. President Park was invited for an official visit to the United States "primarily for his ability to conclude a settlement with Japan" against such opposition. Following his return, agreements were signed on fisheries, Korean residents, art objects and cultural cooperation, property and claims settlement, economic cooperation, and settlement of disputes (e.g., Tokto).

American reaction to the signing was restrained, because of continuing political opposition in both countries, but President Johnson sent congratulatory messages to both Sato and Park, who released the messages to the press and responded with genuine appreciation for the American contribution. There were opposition anti-ratification drives in both Korea and Japan. The moderate political forces in Korea were not wholly in favor of such action, however, and the U.S. privately sought to encourage them not to block the treaty. In the end, the ROK National Assembly voted for ratification, 110 to nothing, with no opposition members present, on August 14, 1965; there were no significant demonstrations. The Japanese pushed ratification through the Diet over Socialist opposition with "blitzkrieg" tactics in November, and the ratification exchange ceremony was held in Seoul on December 18. State Department statements recognized both the ROK ratification and the final exchange.[50]

International Consultative Group

Although both Koreans and Japanese at various times spoke of an international consortium or consultative group to coordinate foreign assistance to Korea, the first official mention of such an idea seems to have been by the ROK chargé d'affaires (Koh Kwang-lim) under the Chang Myon government in January 1961. In a conversation with a State Department official (David Bane), Koh attributed to Professor Edwin O. Reischauer (then at Harvard University, later Ambassador to Japan) the concept of an American guarantee that economic assistance from Japan would not lead to political domination. Reischauer had noted, also, according to Koh, that Korea would require aid from many nations, which would have to be coordinated. At the time, the Department reaction was not enthusiastic, but the idea grew both as a way of reassuring the Koreans and as a parallel to multilateral coordinating arrangements in other countries.[51]

The Development Assistance Committee (DAC) of the Organization for Economic Cooperation and Development discussed aid to Korea in December 1962, but little interest was shown, in the absence of a settlement with Japan, and there was considerable embarrassment when failure of the discussions was reported in the press. A Korean Foreign Ministry official in November 1963 proposed to the Canadians that they participate with the United States, Japan, the United Kingdom, France, Germany, and Australia in a $1.9 billion consortium with World Bank sponsorship to cover the foreign exchange requirements of the Korean five-year development plan. In 1964, both Korean and Japanese press stories referred to the idea, and the Japanese Foreign Ministry was considering a proposal for a DAC consultative group.

The United States floated the idea of a consulting group in the DAC meeting of July 1964. In March 1965 the ROK Foreign Ministry formally proposed to the United States the establishment of an international group, initially without Japan, but in the U.S. and World Bank view, Japanese participation was essential. A consulting group, including Japan, was eventually formed and held its first meeting in London in May 1986, although the World Bank was still not committed to it at that time.[52]

Japanese Nationals in Korea

The presence of Japanese in Korea was a highly sensitive issue. Initial American attempts to continue temporarily the Japanese administration of Korea in 1945 had caused Korean resentment and misunderstanding, not wholly overcome by a prompt change in U.S. policy under which all Japanese nationals were discharged and repatriated. Accordingly, when the Koreans learned that the United Nations Command had brought Japanese technicians into Korea during the Korean War, they objected strenuously. In September 1952 the U.S. Ambassador in Tokyo (Robert Murphy) quoted CINCUNC (General Clark) as telling him that 1,700 Japanese were employed in Korea, mostly as employees of contractors, to perform technical functions such as dredging and construction work for which Koreans could not be obtained. CINCUNC said he would avoid the use of Japanese where possible, but would use them as necessary and "would take measures, if necessary, should there be ROK obstructionism." The Japanese were removed before a major confrontation occurred.[53]

As a footnote, a reverse movement also occurred: the American forces moved a number of prominent Koreans to Japan in the dark days of the early war period, and employed them in various capacities for a number of years. A few more were given what amounted to political asylum in the Korean political crisis of 1952. Many among these people refused for several years to return to Korea because of their fear or distaste of the Rhee administration; one of them was Chang Lee-Wook, former president of Seoul National University, who became ROK Ambassador to Washington, 1960-1961, under the Chang Myon government. Another, Sonu Chong-won (an associate of Chang Myon) became a political issue when Rhee demanded his return for trial in Korea as one of his conditions for reopening negotiations with Japan.

Relations with China

Next to the United States and Japan, China bulked largest on the ROK international horizon. Korea had been a tributary state in the traditional Chinese world order until 1895; its politics and culture had been as thoroughly Confucianized as those of China. The Chinese had stationed Yuan Shih-kai, one of their ablest officials, as Resident-General in Korea for a number of years, in an unsuccessful effort to keep Korea in the Chinese orbit and out of Japanese clutches. Republican China had accommodated the Korean Provisional Government in exile from 1919 to 1945, and had given it some support during

World War II. Some small Korean units fought for the Chinese Nationalists against the Japanese (and more Koreans fought with the Chinese Communists). China was represented on the first UN commission on Korea, which oversaw the birth of the Republic of Korea, and was the first state to recognize it. Moreover, the only significant foreign population in south Korea--around 35,000 people, mostly shopkeepers and small businessmen--was Chinese.

However, when the ROK gained its independence, China was already in the last phases of its civil war. For Rhee, even aside from U.S. influence, there could have been no thought of establishing relations with the Communists. The Communist menace solidified relations between Rhee and President Chiang Kai-shek, head of non-Communist China, because they faced a common danger; and also, perhaps, because Chiang with only a distant island under his effective control was in no position to threaten Korea, or to play a strong role in its domestic affairs. Upon the outbreak of the Korean War, Chiang offered a division of his troops to the United Nations Command, and General MacArthur was inclined to accept it; but the offer was refused by the United States on both political and strategic grounds.

Rhee and Chiang continued to cooperate in various schemes for a regional defense alliance (see pages 138-139, below); there were exchanges of state visits; the respective diplomatic missions were at the Embassy level even when most diplomats in Seoul were ministers, and the Chinese diplomatic staff-- located in the same compound that had housed the nineteenth-century Resident-General--was comparatively large. Formosa became one of the early markets for the limited flow of south Korean exports. But the potential benefit to either nation was limited by the small effective size of both, and their status as client states of the United States. Moreover, the Koreans had some suspicion and antipathy toward the Chinese. This feeling was largely for historical reasons; but there may have been Chinese efforts to influence Korean affairs in ways favorable to them. The U.S. Political Adviser (Joseph Jacobs) had such thoughts in 1948, and Ambassador Muccio reported his suspicions of such intrigue during the Korean War period.[54]

The United States naturally welcomed friendly relations between two of its friends in East Asia, and was sympathetic toward efforts to build regional security arrangements. However, the practicality of these arrangements was seen to be small, owing to Rhee's anti-Japanese attitude and to the lack of enthusiasm of other Asian states. There was no other major U.S. interest involved. Accordingly, the United States played no significant role in ROK-Chinese relations.

As early as 1960, however, at least one thoughtful ROK Foreign Ministry official (Yun Sok-hun) saw the implications for Korea in what he already perceived as "impending change in U.S. policy toward China." He commented that if any American deal were consummated with China that "did not include provision for the reunification of Korea or otherwise helping to advance a solution for the reunification of this divided nation, then the Korean people would be plunged into deep dismay." He thought that the only real hope within the foreseeable future for Korean reunification was "in the context of some overall settlement of the China question."[55]

Relations with the United Nations

The United States proposed ROK membership in the United Nations soon after the General Assembly resolution of December 12, 1948, had recognized the Republic as the only legitimate government in Korea. The Soviets, however, vetoed the proposal, and nothing further could be done unless north Korea, which had in effect defied the UN, were also admitted. In January 1960, the Japanese Foreign Minister (Fujiyama) asked the Secretary of State (Herter) why the United States had not requested the admission of the ROK and of south Vietnam at the 1959 UN General Assembly session. The Secretary replied that the decision was a pragmatic one: there was no prospect of admission and a rebuff would have hurt the prestige of both countries. ". . . The U.S. had decided that fruitless debate on this issue would do more harm than good and therefore we would wait until an appropriate occasion arose." No such occasion ever did arise.[56]

However, the ROK was permitted to establish an observer mission at the UN, and its representative was admitted to the annual committee debate on the Korean question (see Chapter 2, pages 56ff). By 1965 the ROK was a member of all UN specialized agencies except the International Labour Organisation (ILO); it participated in the Economic Commission for Asia and the Far East (ECAFE); and it had an active Korean Association for UNESCO (the United Nations Economic, Social, and Cultural Organisation), which was active in the cultural and publishing field in Korea.

The United Nations was represented in Korea pursuant to successive General Assembly resolutions--first by the temporary commission (UNTCOK) that observed the 1948 elections; then by a United Nations Commission on Korea (UNCOK); and from 1950, after the outbreak of the Korean War, by the seven-member United Nations Commission for the Unification and Rehabilitation of Korea (UNCURK). Of the member nations of the latter commission, only Australia, the Philippines, Thailand, and Turkey maintained resident representatives in Korea, with the Australians taking the most active role. There were also a principal secretary and staff from career UN Secretariat personnel. UNCURK's role in unification is discussed in Chapter 2. The Commission also observed all major ROK elections, usually with ROK cooperation because the international presence was a source of legitimation.

In addition, a United Nations Korea Reconstruction Agency (UNKRA) was established by General Assembly resolution in October 1950 to apply international contributions (largely American) in repairing war damage and making limited capital investment. During most of its eight-year existence it was directed by a retired U.S. Army general (John Coulter), who enjoyed good personal relations with President Rhee. However, UNKRA relations with the UN Command and with U.S. economic aid programs were always troublesome because of difficulties in defining responsibilities and jurisdictions, bureaucratic rivalries, and parochialism. During a short period after the outbreak of the Korean War, before UNKRA was established, the UN Secretary General stationed a personal representative in Korea.

Multilateral Security

The first significant ROK endeavor to go beyond the United States and the United Nations in its security concerns came in response to the north Korean forays across the 38th parallel in 1949 (south Korean forays in the opposite direction were not mentioned). The British Minister (Vivian Holt), as a personal initiative, suggested to the Koreans that they should bring this violation of the peace to the attention of friendly governments, instead of leaving the matter to the UN Commission. Accordingly, on September 3, before the annual UN General Assembly session, the ROK Foreign Minister (Im Pyong-chik, or Ben C. Limb) sent identical notes to friendly governments, including the United States, protesting the policies and actions of the north Koreans.[57]

In addition to the north Korean actions, the worsening situation in China and the concurrent U.S. troop withdrawal in mid-1949 sharpened Korean concerns for their security. In May 1949, President Rhee told a United Press correspondent that Korea favored a Pacific security pact along the lines of NATO, with the United States playing a similar role, but without Japan. In August 1949, Chinese [Nationalist] President Chiang Kai-shek visited Rhee at Chinhae (Rhee's south coast retreat, and the ROK Navy headquarters), and they proposed a conference of Asian leaders to be held at Baguio in the Philippines. However, Rhee's subsequent press comments showed that whereas he and Chiang were primarily concerned with defense, Philippine President Quirino was thinking primarily of economic development.[58]

Diverse Asian viewpoints and ambitions, and Rhee's anti-Japanese policy, among other factors, aborted the Pacific security proposal. In the end, only an ineffectual "Asian Peoples' Anti-Communist League" (APACL) eventuated. Nevertheless, the APACL survived Rhee's downfall and was still in existence in 1965 as a consultative body and propaganda agency, with the Koreans and Chinese as the principal sponsors.

After the Korean War, Rhee again undertook to stimulate a meeting of Asian leaders at Chinhae in April 1954 for informal discussions. Again it was abortive. However, the Koreans continued to support the idea of a defense alliance; for example, several Korean newspaper editorials in January 1958 discussed a possible "Northeast Asia Treaty Organization," and government statements called for a Free Asian alliance to counter neutralist Afro-Asian activity. On January 13, 1958, the government-sponsored newspaper *Korean Republic* alleged that the United States was sending up trial balloons on a Northeast Asian alliance, and suggested Korea, China, and Vietnam as a nucleus. In fact, the United States was interested in such a proposal, but recognized that hostilities, rivalries, and differences of interests and views among the nations of the area made it impracticable at the time.[59]

As an outgrowth of a four-nation meeting in the Philippines in January 1961, the ROK Foreign Minister (Yi Tong-won) in September 1964 proposed a conference in Seoul among the foreign ministers of Australia, the Republic of China [Taiwan], Malaysia, New Zealand, the Philippines, Thailand, and the Republic of Vietnam (south Vietnam). The Koreans saw the conference as a means of strengthening the defenses of the area against Communist subversion, in the light of the worsening situation in Vietnam, and of promoting economic and cultural cooperation, as well as enhancing ROK prestige.

After some initial pondering, the United States decided to support the idea; so did the Thai Foreign Minister. The participation of Japan was a problem, since relations with Korea were not yet normalized; for this reason, the conference was postponed but eventually became the first full-dress international conference to be held in south Korea. This meeting was the beginning of the Asia and Pacific Council (ASPAC), marking another milestone in Korea's achievement of an international personality.[60]

5

Korean Political Development

It has been a consistent part of U.S. policy on Korea since 1945 to make Korea not only independent and united, but democratic. In the beginning, given the revulsion from the Fascist dictatorships in Germany, Italy, and (as the Americans saw it) Japan, plus widespread hostility toward the Communist dictatorship of the Soviet Union, any other American policy would have been inconceivable.

Americans in 1945 did not realize the implications of this policy of implanting democracy. They did not see it as intervention or interference, because they viewed democracy as the natural state of society, which would be achieved by liberating Korea from foreign control and providing tutelage. Although they foresaw that the process would take time--Franklin Roosevelt originally spoke of a forty-year trusteeship--the Americans had no conception of the difficulties, nor any doubt as to the universal validity of their democratic goals and standards.

American policy formulations in regard to growth of democracy in Korea grew more sophisticated with the passage of time (see Chapter 1), but the objective remained. It was natural, particularly as the importance of Korea to the United States grew after the Korean War and the amounts of economic and military aid multiplied--not to speak of American lives lost--that the U.S. government and people should expect their protege to conform to Free World standards as set by the United States--to be a "showcase of democracy in Asia."

It is true that American concern for security against Soviet communism, particularly after the Korean War, somewhat eclipsed concern for democracy. Nevertheless, authoritarian rule in Korea, and violations of individual liberties and due process there, not only were repugnant to the American scale of values; they called into question the real benefit of the assistance given, and affected similar American goals in other countries. The gap between American and

141

Western European standards and Korean political performance became a major problem in Korean-American relations.[1]

As of 1965, Korean progress toward what the U.S. public would call democracy appeared both limited and irregular. However, real economic progress had begun to attract favorable American public attention as an alternative validation of past assistance. Additionally, there was a growing realization in well-informed circles, both government and private, of the practical and moral questions involved in advocacy of any specific set of political institutions and standards for Korea or any foreign country, however sincere or well-intended. A strong element of critical scrutiny nevertheless persisted, in both official and non-official American attitudes, and although the pursuit of democracy in Korea no longer had such priority, it continued as a significant element of American policy.

American influence on Korean political behavior was exerted principally by informal and relatively subtle means. Despite the responsibility attributed to it by Koreans for division of the country, and its equivocal three-year military government record, the United States enjoyed great prestige in Korea because of its reputation for wealth, freedom, and military power; its victory in World War II; and its liberation of Korea from Japan. Past contacts between the two nations--largely through missionaries--had been generally friendly. Through informal social and professional contacts, technical assistance, and large programs for information and exchange of persons, the United States sought to capitalize on this prestige to stimulate the growth of democratic political institutions.

In addition, however, American opinion, both Congressional and public, was a significant influence on the Koreans not only because of their economic and military dependence on the United States but also because of national pride and the desire for American approbation. The prospect of decreasing U.S. appropriations was sometimes expressly invoked by American officials in urging Koreans to moderate their political behavior, and it figured implicitly in all U.S. requests or suggestions. In critical periods, such as elections, the United States encouraged the presence of American journalists as a means of inhibiting Korean political excesses, and welcomed American editorial comment. The presence of the United Nations Commission on Korea also supported this objective, as well as helping to bring the favorable aspects of Korean political process to world attention.[2]

Actual American intervention in Korean politics, however, was slight in the active sense; its greatest impact was passive, through Korean perceptions of its potential. Pressure was applied in certain crises and specific situations, some of which are discussed below. The strongest American influence was applied to bring about the return of civilian administration in 1963 (see Chapter 6, pages 217-225, below).

Principal Problems

Inexperience and Factionalism

In 1945, Korea had had no experience with democracy, except for a few token Japanese reforms. Her political leaders had had little administrative experience, and had done little planning for their nation beyond revolutionary schemes against the Japanese. The political activists, moreover, were divided into two broad groups of Leftists and Rightists; each of these groups was fractionated among contending individuals and their followers. The Leftists favored sweeping economic and political reforms of a generally socialist character; they were by no means all Communists, but the Communists among them had the drive and organizational skills to play a growing role, probably an eventual dominant one if events had run their natural course. The Americans distrusted the Leftists, both for their socialism and for their susceptibility to outside Communist control.

The Rightists included most of the Christians, most of the small group of native landowners and businessmen and most of the American-educated and English-speaking people. Some of this group were regarded as pro-Japanese or "national traitors" by the Leftists and by the general public. The Right generally supported the exile Provisional Government, headed by Kim Koo. This group had led a tenuous existence in China since 1919 and in turn was tenuously connected with Syngman Rhee and his supporters (including Rhee's "Korean Commission") in the United States. The American government experience with Korean exiles in China and the United States, and particularly with Rhee, during World War II had left an unfavorable impression of all of them. Nevertheless, Americans were more comfortable with Rightists, who voiced less jarring political and economic ideas and could make themselves understood.[3]

Not only had the Koreans had no experience with democratic government; they had had virtually no experience with any modern government above the clerical level, except on the receiving end. The Japanese colonial regime, which brought elements of modern administration and economy to Korea, admitted very few Koreans to posts of senior responsibility or technical competence in either government or industry. Those who were admitted were ostracized by their compatriots. Except for limited experience in churches, schools, and certain industries and businesses, the Koreans were cut off from the modern sector in their own country. Higher education was denied most of them. To the extent they understood democracy, it was a disembodied ideal or a textbook subject. Their admiration for it as a concept was beyond question; their understanding of it as a political method was totally lacking, and their early experience with it was disillusioning.

As early as 1947, Rhee publicly said that American-style democracy was not suited to the problems of his country. A leading member of the conservative opposition (Kim Young-Sun, later Chang Myon's Finance Minister) said somewhat the same thing to a U.S. Embassy officer on his return from a trip to the United States in 1956. An Embassy appraisal in December 1958 noted,

> Little genuine conviction exists among Korean officials of the basic concepts of democratic government. . . . The population has even less understanding in these areas. . . . Danger exists that current malpractices . . . are being identified by Koreans with democracy and free enterprise.

The Embassy prophetically added,

> It is entirely conceivable that at some future date, . . . democratic and free enterprise institutions could be rejected in favor other alternatives less desirable in terms U.S. policy.

After the military coup d'état in 1961, its leader and subsequent President, Park Chung Hee, criticized American democracy in his writings.[4]

These facts, together with a strong element of self-seeking among rival Korean politicians, led Americans initially to doubt Korean capacities for self-government, just as President Roosevelt had doubted them. British advice in the formative period reinforced this view. But the manifold problems of the American occupation forced an early transfer of sovereignty. Self-government was achieved but its policies, practices, and accomplishments remained in doubt both by the United States and by the Korean population.[5]

U.S.-Soviet Differences:
Left-Right Polarization

American difficulties and differences with the Soviets, both practical and ideological, interacted with the Korean Left-Right split. Each conflict reinforced the other, with the unification issue and the course of future Korean political evolution as the principal foci. The Soviets had already fortified the 38th parallel in 1945. They explicitly stated at the first Joint Commission meeting that they expected Korea to be a state friendly toward them. Americans could draw dire interpretations from this view, in the light of the experience in Western Europe. The Communists and Leftists had tried to consolidate governmental power in a People's Republic led by left-leaning Lyuh Woon-Hyung before the Americans arrived, taking advantage of the three-week interregnum after V-J Day. Frustrated in this attempt, some of them sought thereafter to discredit and destroy the American military government by taking advantage of the political freedoms that Americans tried to preserve. On the other hand, many Rightists supported the legitimacy of the Provisional Government. There was violence and bloodshed, involving the Rightist-dominated police. Polarization constantly increased; American efforts to build a moderate, middle-of-the-road coalition failed for several reasons, including the assassination of two key figures (Lyuh Woon-Hyung and a moderate rightist, Chang Duk-Soo) in 1947.[6]

When the ROK obtained its sovereignty in 1948, Rhee moved firmly against the Communists and against all Leftist opposition, often in ways that distressed American officials and public. (He also evoked anti-Japanism, but here he was far less specific or active so far as domestic affairs were concerned.) The need for intensifying internal security against the Communist subversive threat was clear (see Chapter 3, pages 103-108); but such action could, and did, cloak actions to suppress or inhibit all opposition, however valid. As early as April 1949, the Assistant Secretary of State (Walton Butterworth) expressed to the Koreans "the necessity of preventing the Korean government, in its struggle against Communism, from losing the support of the people by becoming static and anti-progressive." Such views were repeatedly expressed by Americans at all levels both in and out of government in succeeding years. They may have inhibited ROK government excesses to some extent.[7]

The Problem of Legitimacy

Distrusting all Korean politicians and groups, ill-informed on the local situation, trying to keep the Korean political picture from crystallizing until agreement with the Soviets could be reached, yet faced with the need to maintain public order and provide for minimal public needs, the Americans refused to confer authority on any Korean political group or individual. Instead, after an abortive attempt to continue the Japanese administration on an interim basis, they established a military government and recruited Koreans individually to operate it under the direction (later "advice") of Army colonels, within a legal and organizational structure largely taken over from the Japanese.

This government, despite efforts to Koreanize it as a South Korean Interim Government (SKIG), never had any legitimacy in the eyes of the people, who had had their own unified national government since the seventh century. Contending Korean political leaders, none of whom had been given any real authority, could therefore agree on criticizing the Americans, even if they could agree on nothing else. (It should be noted that the Political Adviser in Tokyo [Atcheson] foresaw this problem in October 1945.)[8]

Although the legitimacy problem was satisfactorily resolved with the establishment of the Republic of Korea, the Left-Right polarization continued, as did the Communist determination to overthrow the ROK and vice versa. Factionalism continued within both major political persuasions. The legacy of the early post-World War II period in Korea was therefore unfavorable to the growth of democracy, not only because of individual rivalries for power, but because of a fundamental lack of political consensus.

American Organizational Problems

Further complicating the problem were conflicting views among American agencies and a lengthy chain of command. The American Military Governor was subordinate to the senior troop commander, the Commanding General of XXIV Corps (General Hodge); Hodge for some time reported to Washington through General MacArthur's headquarters in Tokyo. There were two State Department advisers in Korea, one political (successively Merle Benninghoff, William Langdon, Joseph Jacobs) and one economic (Arthur Bunce), who differed basically between themselves and often with the military, who were not obliged to follow their guidance in any event.

Growing recognition of this problem, plus criticism of General Hodge's policies, led to the recommendation that a civilian High Commissioner be appointed to head the American administration. No action was taken on this proposal until after the Republic of Korea was established; thereafter, until the Korean War, a unified American mission under Ambassador John Muccio controlled all aspects of U.S. operations in Korea, although conflicts continued among Washington agencies.[9]

Within the State Department in Washington there were also organizational problems. A separate office for occupied areas was concerned with Korea policy in the early years, as well as the Office of Far Eastern Affairs; the latter was headed by John Carter Vincent, who was under attack by conservatives for his reporting from China. Korean affairs were handled within a division of Japan-Korea affairs, in which Japanese concerns predominated. In any event, the War Department played the main role in Korean affairs until 1948, because it had the civil affairs responsibility.

The Korean War brought a renewal of organizational difficulties, with an international component added. Most serious among these, and continuing until 1959, was the fact that the American economic and military aid program was subordinated to the Commanding General of the United Nations Command, who also commanded the forces in Japan; thus the Ambassador in Korea, despite his theoretical supremacy, was deprived of direct control over the levers of economic and military assistance. President Rhee ably exploited the differences in view between Ambassador and CINCUNC.[10]

Lack of Resources and Planning

During the formative years, Americans were inhibited from moving effectively in the political, economic, and social fields in Korea by insufficient resources and lack of policies or planning, as well as by communication problems. This was partly due to disinclination to undertake positive programs until agreement on a national administration had been reached with the Soviets; it was also due in part to the low priority given to Korea in allocating American resources. Additionally, Americans in the immediate postwar period tended to suspect as socialistic or Communist many programs of national development of the sort now taken for granted.

To some extent, similar problems reappeared after the Korean War, but they were gradually resolved as American understanding and operating techniques in economic aid improved, and as it again became evident that Korean unification was a forlorn and long-range prospect. Rhee's squeaky wheel during the armistice negotiations, plus his anti-Communist stand, helped to get the necessary grease of large-scale U.S. aid allocations. It is ironic that the full potential benefit of rapid economic progress, based on an eventually successful American aid program, was reaped by the least democratically-oriented government in Korea's postwar history. The Economic Adviser in Korea (Bunce) observed in 1947:

> . . . It may be one of the great tragedies of history that the concept of individual freedom and democracy has been associated with a reluctance to support or initiate the basic economic and social reforms desired by the masses of the people.[11]

Moreover, the absence of effective policies and plans enhanced the American tendency to impose piecemeal reforms on Korea in the American image. One example was the establishment of Seoul National University in 1946, which resulted in months of strikes and disorders. Although the problem became part of the ongoing confrontation between Left and Right, the Political Adviser commented that the new university organization was copied from the models of American state schools. "The result proved again that the validity of experience in the United States is no guarantee of its equal validity in Korea. . . ." Lord Curzon had tried the same thing in India at the turn of the century, with equally unfortunate results.[12]

Nationalism

The Koreans had struggled throughout the Japanese occupation for their independence, and their resistance had centered around symbols of their national identity, particularly their language. Wilson's principle of self-determination of nations had been one of the sparks that set off the great Korean national uprising of 1919. The spirit of independence and nationalism burst out in the nationwide anti-trusteeship demonstrations after the Moscow conference in 1945, which included a strike by Korean officials of the American military government. It also sparked early demands for punishment of "national traitors," among whom were some of the relatively few experienced Korean administrators and technicians.

This fierce independence, coupled with growing doubts and criticism of the efficacy of American principles and programs, led to the need for Korean leaders to prove that they were not under the thumb of the Americans. At the same time, these leaders had to show that they could maximize American assistance and support. The problem appeared in the formative stages of the Republic of Korea, as Interim Government officials associated with the Americans were dismissed, and American advice was often disregarded.

Part of Rhee's domestic prestige was built on the capacity he demonstrated to stand up to the Americans and yet get their aid. During his administration, opposition leaders solicited American support for their cause; yet when the opposition controlled the government in 1960 and 1961, the United States had extreme difficulty in negotiating a new comprehensive aid agreement because it involved clauses that the Koreans considered to infringe their sovereignty. The military leaders who seized power in 1961 were motivated in part by their contempt for what they saw as toadyism toward the Americans by senior Korean generals (probably coupled with jealousy for the fruits thereof), and nationalism was a greater problem during the period of junta control than at any other time.

Nationalistic feelings, coupled with long experience in manipulation by Japanese and other external forces, led to sensitivity and suspicion on the part of Rhee and other Koreans (especially in times of political crisis, as in 1952) that Americans might intervene in domestic Korean affairs. Opposition groups nevertheless strongly solicited American help for their efforts to take power, thus reinforcing government concern. Rhee's suspicions of the United States reached a peak at the time that William S.B. Lacy was assigned as Ambassador to Korea, after he was reported to have assisted (as Deputy Chief of Mission in Manila) in installing Ramon Magsaysay as President of the Philippines. Rhee mounted an obstructionist campaign against Lacy from the moment of his arrival in Korea, a principal feature of which was the ROK Government harassment of American businessmen in the summer of 1955. Lacy resigned after six months.

Such nationalist sensitivities led to misunderstandings as to the nature of American contacts with non-governmental individuals and groups, political or otherwise, and required some American circumspection. (The abrupt departure of an experienced Foreign Service Officer, Gregory Henderson, from Seoul in 1964 at the demand of the ROK Government is an illustration of this sensitivity.) Contacts nevertheless continued, as one means of supporting political freedom as well as for information-gathering purposes.[13]

Establishment of an Independent Government

South Korean Interim Government (SKIG)

In October 1945, Dr. Syngman Rhee was welcomed back to Korea as a nationalist leader after an American exile of forty years. Although he initially advocated the unity of all Korean political groups, his anti-Communism soon emerged. In early 1946, he started campaigning for establishment of an independent anti-Communist government in south Korea through general elections, and grew increasingly critical of American policies.

General Hodge and the State Department were principal targets of his criticism. Rhee's tactics became increasingly embarrassing and irritating to the United States, but the confrontation continued until a separate regime became assured through UN action. (By April 1948 Rhee was telling his supporters to stop the criticism, because he would need all the help he could get.) At the same time, other Korean groups, particularly the Left but including many moderates, opposed a separate regime because they did not want action that would foreclose the possibility of unification.[14]

The American Military Government took tentative steps toward self-government in the South through the establishment of the South Korean Interim Government (SKIG) in 1946. The U.S. authorities installed a Korean moderate, An Chae-Hong, as Civil Administrator (a position loosely comparable in theory to prime minister, taken over from the organization of the Japanese Government General). Safely conservative Koreans were named heads of all the government departments. A Korean Interim Legislative Assembly (KILA) was constituted, half by loosely-supervised election and half by appointment (a device adopted to offset the expected conservative dominance of elections). The Assembly convened on December 12, 1946.

However, the American Military Governor had the final authority, and exercised it firmly. The Military Governor's staff, as American "advisers" to the Korean department chiefs, also retained considerable *de facto* authority. Moreover, the Civil Administrator was of different political persuasion than the department heads, and the national police chief worked directly and enthusiastically with the Americans. With some notable exceptions, the body of law remained basically Japanese; so did government practices and much of the personnel. Especially in the police, in consequence, SKIG had little significant Korean identity or legitimacy. Reflecting this view, Rhee's American agent, Robert Oliver, wrote the Assistant Secretary of State for Occupied Areas (General Hilldring) in April 1947:

> . . . My own conviction is that military government was devised as an instrument by which a defeated and guilty people might be held in subjection for a period of punishment. I do not believe there is any justification for imposing it upon a friendly and liberated people. . . . It is dangerous because of its separation from the people who are being governed . . . because professional military men are accustomed to being obeyed and to giving orders categorically. . . .[15]

Constituent Assembly, 1948

The transition from SKIG to an independent government in the south was eventually begun through the election of May 10, 1948, with UN blessing (see below, page). Although the American Military Government drew up a draft constitution in early 1948 (after the Military Governor had vetoed an attempt by the Interim Legislative Assembly to enact one the previous year), the new National Assembly called on an eminent Korean jurist, Yu Chin-O, for an independent draft. It was prepared with little or no American advice. At Rhee's insistence, the original parliamentary form was altered to give the President strong powers.

The U.S. Political Adviser commented that the constitution "makes no change in the old strongly centralized system of government established by the Japanese" but "at this stage there is nothing that can be done about it." Subsequently, a "Law of Governmental Organization" was enacted, once more with no direct American input; the Political Adviser again noted the high degree of centralization, and observed that the President's emergency powers might be criticized by the UN Commission and the Soviet Union.[16]

While plans were proceeding in the south, the northern regime in February 1948 announced its own draft constitution, "virtually a carbon copy of constitutions imposed on other Soviet-satellite countries," and in May the draft was adopted by unanimous vote of the north Korean People's Council, subject to approval of a future all-Korean assembly.

Despite this step, two south Korean leaders --Kim Koo, who had headed the Provisional Government in exile, and a leading moderate, Kimm Kiu-Sic, chairman of KILA--called for a meeting with leaders of the north to discuss unification, and called on their supporters not to participate in the separate southern elections. The meeting, often called the Conference of the Four Kims, was held in late April 1948. It served to shift the interest of the leftists and middle-roaders away from the May 10 election, leaving a clear field to the Rightists.[17]

Establishment of the Republic
of Korea Government

Within a week after formation of the National Assembly in south Korea, Rhee's spokesman in Washington (Im Pyong-Chik, or Ben C. Limb) was in touch with the State Department, asking to explore problems of the transfer of sovereignty, to discuss economic aid plans, and to provide military security. The United States gave *de facto* recognition to the Republic of Korea on August 12, 1948, and sent a Special Representative, John J. Muccio, pending *de jure* recognition.

Among the many concerns of transition to independence, three were prominent: the fate of the government organization and personnel that the Americans had built up over three frustrating years; the financial and legal aspects of the transfer of jurisdiction and sovereignty; and the security of the fledgling nation. Although inauguration ceremonies for the Republic were held on August 15, 1948, the actual transfer of authority and functions was far from complete.

ROK Organization and Personnel. The United States had inherited a government structure from the Japanese, and a considerable number of its working personnel. The Japanese had been sent home, and significant organizational modifications had been made, particularly in education, welfare, justice, and the relationships of provincial to national government (the Home Affairs Department, for example, had been abolished; the broad police responsibilities in economic and social areas under the Government General had been curtailed; new departments of Health, Welfare, and Labor had been established; and the courts had been given greatly increased independence). Some of the modifications were made in the few months immediately preceding the turnover of authority to the Koreans. The basic Japanese structure was still recognizable, and Japanese bureaucratic procedures had largely resisted American attempts at change. But the Americans were proud that they could pass on a functioning structure to the new Republic, and sought to protect it.

After his election as President, Rhee wrote the Military Governor on July 26, 1948, noting that some officials had resigned, and asking that personnel be encouraged to remain. He said that initially only department heads (or ministers in the new government) would be newly appointed; "changes at lower level will come only gradually and after careful study, if at all." The Military Governor issued a memorandum on August 13:

> Government of the ROK will take over a government in full operation with property, equipment, funds, personnel, functions, and responsibilities. All of its activities and functions must go on without interruption during the transfer. . . . Each minister of the Government of the ROK will be invited to confer with the respective directors of the departments and offices of the South Korean Interim Government regarding details. . . . When it is agreed by the minister, the director, and the American advisor that the necessary arrangements have been made it will be reported to the Commanding General, USAFIK [U.S. Army Forces in Korea], who will make official announcement the specific time at which the authority and functions of the Department are transferred. . . .[18]

In practice, the transfer did not go smoothly. ROK ministers and SKIG directors were mutually suspicious, jealous, and protocol- and face-conscious, and Rhee's subsequent appointments belied his July 26 letter. By the end of October, internal ROK Government organization had been largely worked out and formalized, except for the Ministry of National Defense (still awaiting passage of the Army Organization Law) and the Office of Public Information, which was of special interest to Rhee.

Despite Rhee's July assurances, personnel changes were "numerous and sudden," replacing military government appointees with new men chosen "largely on the basis of previous personal connection with and loyalty to the superior rather than on the basis of professional qualifications." In March 1949 the U.S. Embassy sorrowfully reported that although on the previous August 15 the government· had had a cadre of at least partially-trained officials, whose training "was considered one of the important efforts of the Military Government in Korea in view of the vacuum created in administrative experience by the departure of the Japanese,," about 94 percent of the officials at the level of section chief (equivalent to office director in the U.S. government) or above had been replaced. On the other hand, the new Cabinet members, mostly chosen for their personal relationships with Rhee, were not anti-foreign; on the contrary, their foreign education and deracination was a source of government weakness.[19]

The Financial and Property Settlement

The financial and legal aspects of the transfer of sovereignty were negotiated in an Initial Financial and Property Settlement, a draft of which had been prepared in Washington for the new Political Adviser and Special Representative of the President (Muccio) to bring with him to Korea.

Serious problems arose in the negotiations. Some of them were associated with inevitable Korean nationalist feelings; but much of the difficulty centered around the disposition of ex-Japanese property--of which the United States retained a considerable amount on free leasehold as well as by purchase, for the use of its large Mission staff--and around the ROK assumption of a $25 million surplus property loan that had been negotiated by the Military Government in 1946 in its capacity as the government of Korea.[20]

As a result of controversy and delay, the agreement was not signed until September 11, 1948; and, since the ROK insisted on its ratification by the National Assembly, it did not enter into force until September 20, which is perhaps a more accurate date for the commencement of ROK sovereignty. However, strong Korean criticism and ROK Government pressure had forced the transfer of jurisdiction over the police on September 2.

Under Article XI of the Financial and Property Settlement,

> The Government of the Republic of Korea agrees to continue in full force and effect all existing laws, ordinances, public acts, and regulations of the United States Army Military Government in Korea and/or of the South Korean Interim Government until repealed or amended by the Government of the Republic of Korea.

Article XIII provided that control over accounts, properties, and facilities of the Korean government should be transferred within thirty days, or as soon thereafter as the new ROK government was prepared to accept the transfer. A ninety-day transition was provided for control over former Japanese property and relief and rehabilitation supplies. Article LX rewrote the surplus property loan. Other articles dealt with various aspects of property and finances.

Defense

For a transitional period, the Commanding General, USAFIK (General John Coulter, replacing General Hodge) retained operational control over the ROK security forces, including the police. This was provided in a separate agreement between Rhee and Coulter on August 9, 1948, which terminated automatically with the withdrawal of U.S. combat forces in June 1949.

Korean Political Leadership and Institutions

American Influence Before Independence

The United States throughout World War II had been exposed to the importunities of contending Korean exile groups and would-be leaders, each of whom criticized the others, and none of whom appeared to have a real claim to represent the Korean people. Accordingly, the United States chose not to support any of them at the outset, apparently envisaging a democratic process within Korea under benign international guidance through which indigenous groups and leaders would emerge.

This process, however, was frustrated from the beginning by the inability of the United States and the Soviet Union to agree; by the Left-Right polarization among the Korean people; by the fierce ambition and factionalism among Korean groups; and by the thirst for immediate independence from foreign control. Additionally, the United States was unwilling at first to concede real political power to any Korean individual or group, because the unpreparedness of any of them to lead a modern state seemed so evident.

Among the various exile leaders and groups, Syngman Rhee had achieved the greatest individual stature both in the United States and, probably, in Korea. This prestige is demonstrated by the fact that the Left-oriented People's Republic, hastily established in Seoul in September 1945, before the Americans arrived, named Rhee *in absentia* as its president. Rhee had been active on the American scene for many years, and had a devoted following of both Koreans and Americans despite many detractors and enemies. His association with the Provisional Government in exile and his early nationalist activities gave him a claim to legitimacy. His rigid anti-Communism and his Christian faith (he was an ordained Presbyterian minister) made him attractive to many conservative Americans; but his stubbornness, his imperiousness, and his importunities for political recognition and support had alienated the State Department.

The alternatives to Rhee, however, were not promising. The leaders of the Provisional Government in China had not been in their homeland since 1919, quarrelled among themselves, and showed little capacity to run a government. Two of them--Kim Koo, president of the Provisional Government, known for his assassination of Japanese officials, and Kimm Kiu-Sic, leader of a moderate group affiliated with the Provisional Government and chairman of its nominal legislature--nevertheless played significant roles in early postwar Korea. The Leftists, although they had able men among them, were suspected by the Americans--some with good reason--as playing the Soviet (or north Korean) game. One of them, however, Lyuh Woon-Hyung, the chief organizer of the former People's Republic, later became a central figure in an American-sponsored moderate coalition (see below, page 154).

Few of the other political figures or groups that emerged within south Korea showed special promise initially. Some of them were open to charges of collaboration with the Japanese. Noteworthy, however, were the wealthy businessman and philanthropist, Kim Sung-Soo, who headed the conservative Han'guk (Korea) Democratic Party; Song Chin-U, editor of the principal Korean-language daily newspaper during the Japanese regime; and Chang Duk-Soo, a moderate rightist.

With some reluctance, and after controversy and hesitation, the U.S. Government finally permitted Rhee to return to Korea in October 1945. As already noted, Rhee soon started promoting a separate anti-Communist government for the south, with himself as its head. On instructions from Washington, the American Military Government then endeavored to build a middle-of-the-road political coalition that would avoid the Left-Right polarization while resisting Communist domination. In doing so, it worked primarily with Lyuh Woon-hyung, Kimm Kiu-Sic, Chang Duk-Soo, and An Chae-Hong.[21]

Coalition efforts were given impetus by the Communist-inspired uprisings in the Fall of 1946 and their violent suppression by the Rightist-dominated security forces. Kimm Kiu-Sic became chairman of the new Interim Legislative Assembly, and An Chae-Hong became Civil Administrator of SKIG. Lyuh, however, who had the most prestige among non-Rightists, refused to take an Assembly seat or otherwise enter the military government. He was assassinated in July 1947. Chang Duk-Soo was assassinated in December. The other moderates were no match for Rhee and the Rightists, particularly since the Rightists, as already noted, dominated the military government machinery and particularly the police. Kim Koo, Rhee's major remaining rival, was assassinated in 1949, leaving only the Han'guk Democratic Party to challenge his leadership.

In July 1947, the U.S. authorities brought to Korea as General Hodge's political adviser an elderly Korean, Philip Jaisohn (Korean name, So Chae-Pil), who had started his activities as a political reformer in 1884, had been driven into exile, and had acquired American citizenship and a medical degree. Dr. Jaisohn sought to neutralize Rhee's political dominance and support a moderate coalition, but he was an old man long absent from the country, and did not have the connections or time to overcome Rhee's head start.[22]

One other early American political enterprise was a national youth organization, the National Youth Corps, intended to harness youthful enthusiasm to useful purposes, including security. As head of the Corps, the U.S. authorities installed General Lee Bum-Suk, a soldier trained by the Chinese Nationalists who had commanded Korean resistance fighters against the Japanese in China. Lee had his own leadership ambitions, but twice was used by Rhee (as Prime Minister and Defense Minister, 1948-1949, and as Home Minister during the crisis of 1952) and never reached a top political position on his own. His youth corps base was weakened when Rhee ordered a merger of the many rival youth groups, including Rhee's own and those of other Rightist politicians, in 1949.

American Influence After Independence

With the establishment of the ROK as a sovereign nation, U.S. influence was concentrated chiefly in the economic and military areas. The United States sought to restrain Rhee and his successors from obvious political errors and excesses, and to advise and inform them in political matters, but rarely asserted positions to the point of confrontation. The chief areas of U.S. political concern, where advice and influence were chiefly applied, were fair elections, civil liberties, adherence to constitutional process, maintenance of a non-Communist political opposition, better education and information (including freedom of the press), public administration, and justice. The problem of succession to Rhee concerned Americans as he grew older and weaker.

The American input in these areas was chiefly subtle and informal, except for certain critical periods (1950, 1952, 1959, 1960, and 1963). A major source of U.S. influence was negative: Koreans undoubtedly were deterred from doing some things they otherwise might have done, because of their recognition that a bad American press and critical Embassy reporting would adversely affect economic and military aid levels. There was fear of the possibility of American intervention. The Koreans probably also wanted American approval for their policies and actions.

Some potential Korean leaders were aided in their political fortunes through "leader grants" to visit the United States, there to see and be seen with prestigious Americans; they also were aided by entree to the American diplomatic and military establishment in Korea. The U.S. information program in Korea tried to promote citizenship education. Aid to Korean education, especially teacher training, was a major objective in the American aid program, and had an obvious political significance. The American input in primary school texts which derived from the military government period undoubtedly had a strong influence on a generation of Korean youth, despite a nationalistic drive to re-edit them when the Republic gained its sovereignty. It is notable, for example, that the college students who sparked the protests of 1960 against the rigged elections had been primary school students in the pre-Korean War period.

The United States and Syngman Rhee

During most of Syngman Rhee's long residence in the United States (chiefly in Hawaii), he maintained uneasy connections with the exiled Korean Provisional Government in China, and for a time was its president. He also developed an independent power base among expatriate Koreans in Hawaii and on the mainland, and a "Korean Commission" which he headed to represent the Provisional Government (and himself) as a sort of embassy to the United States and other countries. Revered by some of the Korean community, he was reviled by others. Although his talents were recognized, he was unable to bring the various exile Korean groups together. His arrogance and unwillingness to share power or responsibility with others handicapped him in his relations with the Koreans as well as with the U.S. government. Moreover, as his biographer and associate, Robert Oliver, points out, he built his career and his aspirations on a few relatively simple and firmly held principles, which made compromise difficult.

These same problems soon led to trouble with the American command in Korea after Rhee returned, even though General Hodge initially tried to accord him respect and consideration. He was in the forefront of the anti-trusteeship demonstrations of December 1945. By February 1946 he was forming his own would-be governmental organization and advancing his own utopian platform, the "National Program of the Representative Democratic Council of South Korea" (building upon a group originally organized by the American Military Government to represent the Korean people).

Rhee utilized his own channels and connections to gain American support against the American military government, and in favor of his own proposal for a separate interim government. In early 1947, he personally visited the United States for this purpose. His fight with General Hodge grew bitter and personal. In October 1947, his Austrian wife, Francesca Rhee, said at a dinner, "Many people speak of Dr. Rhee as the future President of Korea. He is now the President of Korea." By October, Rhee claimed to have organized his own election machinery throughout south Korea, which he offered to put at the disposition of the United Nations. In February 1948, General Hodge tried to bring about some unity among Rhee, Kim Koo, and Kimm Kiu-Sic, but in vain.[23]

The U.S. Political Adviser (Jacobs), himself a political conservative, sized up Rhee in early 1948 as follows:

I am inclined to believe that [Rhee's] popularity has waned considerably. . . . Rhee is rather the outstanding leader in a confused, ill-informed society lacking in leadership--no doubt a bad, self-seeking and unwise leader, but nevertheless a dominating, shrewd, positive, feared character. His large following has nothing to do with love or veneration for the man, at least in this third year of his return to his homeland. It is in my view the result of a wide belief that Rhee is the source of all present and future power in South Korea. Although treatment of him by the United States and events at times should have created doubts on this score, his unfailing success, through a variety of circumstances, in stealing every important and historic public show in South Korea confirms and reconfirms this belief.[24]

After the American military government ended, U.S. relations with Rhee through a new representative, Ambassador Muccio, were more cordial but still difficult. Not only was Rhee unyielding in his own views, but he utilized a kitchen cabinet of American associates without official status, and a number of conservative supporters in the United States, to support and propagate his ideas, as he had done during the American occupation. One analysis of the period suggested that "instead of leaning on the advice and counsel of official American representatives in Korea, the President is inclined to utilize instead the advice and counsel of this kitchen cabinet." He utilized the group, also, as "intermediaries to U.S. Government agencies in Korea, and to influence American public opinion by lobbying activities." This tendency toward independent action--plus a shrewd capacity to play Americans off against one another--continued to plague U.S. relations with him at least until 1957.[25]

Rhee was essentially a traditionalist and a resistance fighter, an admirer of the traditional virtues, who saw leadership in the negative terms of struggle against Communists, against Japanese, against his rivals, even against Americans when necessary. On the other hand, Rhee looked to the United States as virtually the sole source of Korea's support and defense, particularly during the Korean War. Ambassador Muccio observed in 1951, "I have never been able to sell him the idea that support depends in the last analysis on what the Korean people do and that his main task is to give proper guidance and inspired leadership to his own people. . . . Unfortunately, in his senility, he thinks that he and Korea are synonymous." Nevertheless, Rhee was a shrewd politician, a patriot, and a national symbol. He remained as Korea's unchallenged leader until, twelve years after independence, his declining faculties no longer permitted him to play the game.[26]

Despite his three years of feuding with the military government--or perhaps because of them--Rhee derived much of his prestige from his countrymen's perception of his ability to manipulate and influence the United States. When this ability was in doubt, as it was during Rhee's dispute with the United States over the Agreed Minute in 1953 and 1954 (see Chapters 3 and 6), his power position was undermined. Commenting on the concurrent political turmoil over constitutional amendments in 1954, the U.S. Embassy noted that Rhee's intransigence had evoked unprecedented open criticism of the government by the opposition; there was even the possibility that he might be replaced, if the military supported such a move. As the Embassy foresaw, Rhee was "too shrewd for that," and maintained political control. Nevertheless, a period of unprecedented opposition successes followed, and these in turn led to repression in Rhee's name, but without Rhee's old skill, ending in the debacle of April 1960.[27]

In early 1955, as Ambassador Briggs departed from Korea, he commented on Rhee's economic naivete, his simplistic bipolar view of the world, and his "passionate ambition to see Korea unified in his lifetime," to achieve which

> he would gladly see us embark on World War Three tomorrow believing this inevitable anyway. . . . This bipolar and oversimplified view of affairs renders Rhee difficult to deal with and intolerant of obstacles. . . . Finally, Rhee now recognizes that he is old, but he refuses to select a successor. If he remains in office he would probably be increasingly stubborn, irrational and exasperating. The world, nevertheless, will be a smaller place when he leaves it.[28]

The Succession Problem
and Alternative Leadership

Three possible forms of succession to President Rhee were foreseen by American observers from the early 1950s: a constitutional succession by one of his supporters following his death (or his departure from office, which was considered improbable); a constitutional succession through victory of the opposition at the polls; and some form of extralegal succession, violent or otherwise. Rhee's advanced age obviously necessitated consideration of what would happen on his death; but there was no American desire to force either that or any other form of succession because of the lack of visible alternative leaders.

U.S. government assessments considered violent succession unlikely until repression and public discontent began to mount in 1959. In April 1955, an internal State Department assessment observed that all major Korean power groupings were weakened by factional divisions; there were no individual leaders with stature or prestige to gain preeminence; and although the army had the potential to decide the succession, no leaders could involve it in political action except to prevent government collapse. Moreover, Korean concern over relations with the United States would militate against an unconstitutional regime.[29]

By 1956, it began to appear that Rhee had finally decided upon Lee Ki-Poong, a long-time associate, as his principal lieutenant and successor. Lee was head of the Liberal Party, Speaker of the National Assembly, close confidant, and distant relative. Rhee adopted Lee's elder son as his own son, and supported Lee despite his defeat by an opposition candidate for the vice-presidency that year. Unfortunately, Lee himself was a sick man; his sickness was a major element in the deterioration of the political situation in 1959. Thus prospects for a peaceful and constitutional succession within the pro-Rhee forces were uncertain.[30]

Among opposition politicians, the three who had achieved preeminent status were Shin Ik-Hi (P.H. Shinicky), Cho Pyong-Ok (P.O. Chough), and Chang Myon (John M. Chang). Chang, a noted Catholic educator of good character and reputation, was considered to have good standing with the Americans, but had shown himself to be lacking in personal courage. Cho had been national police director under the American military government, and had remained on good terms with Americans. Shin, who had been in exile in China, owed nothing of his political reputation to the United States, but had proved himself an able politician in the Interim Legislative Assembly and in every ROK National Assembly term thereafter.

Shin Ik-Hi was the principal opposition candidate for President in 1956. With an opposition organization behind him that for once was fairly united, he had such broad popular support that an election victory was conceivable; but he died of a cerebral hemorrhage ten days before the election. Chang, his running mate, was narrowly elected Vice President, causing four years of political uncertainty during which Chang himself lay low for fear of assassination (which was once attempted) and sent feelers to the United States for temporary asylum in case Rhee should actually die. In 1960, Cho was the opposition candidate for President, but he died of cancer in Walter Reed Hospital in Washington, D.C. before the public campaign began.

In the turmoil following the fraudulent election of March 1960, another old Rhee associate, Huh Chung, emerged with behind-the-scenes American support as the constitutional successor to head an interim government, because Chang had resigned the vice-presidency in protest before the Rhee government fell. Chang, almost by default, gained political ascendancy for a brief and confused period of parliamentary government, during which the "old faction" of his own Democratic Party, led by an aristocrat named Yun Bo-Sun, turned to opposition.[31]

The military coup of 1961 was a form of succession which, although foreseen as a possibility, had been rated as highly improbable. It brought men virtually unknown to most Americans into positions of leadership, utilizing the military organization that Americans had created, trained, and equipped to defy American political policies. Another older-generation figure, Yun Bo-Sun, came surprisingly close to Park Chung Hee, the junta leader, as a vote-getter in the presidential election of 1963; but the young military group was not thereafter seriously challenged in its control of Korean politics until a younger-generation opposition leader (Kim Dae-Jung) again ran up a close vote in 1971.[32]

The United States could have moved in the crisis of 1952 (see Chapter 6, pages 187-191, below) to put Chang Myon in power, but elected not to do so, nor to challenge the constitutional change pushed through by Rhee to ensure his popular re-election. Thereafter, the U.S. role was limited to insistence on constitutional process (as, for example, the installation of Huh Chung as acting President in April 1960, and the retention of Yun Bo-Sun, President of the brief parliamentary regime, as nominal President during part of the Korean military government period). The United States maintained readiness for such limited contingency action as might protect lives and public order in an emergency.

At the time of the military coup, in 1961, the American Chargé (Marshall Green) and the Commander of the United Nations Command (Carter Magruder) both called for support of the constitutional government; but the U.S. government elected to utilize neither its own 50,000 troops nor the UN operational control over the ROK forces to challenge the junta's political control.

Political Parties

One of the first acts of the American Military Governor (Arnold) in 1945 was to announce his willingness to confer with Korean political groups, but not with individuals. This announcement encouraged ambitious individuals to organize "parties," many of which existed in name only. Within a few weeks, approximately fifty parties had asked for consultation; by 1947, 422 south Korean groups asked for consultation with the U.S.-USSR Joint Commission on the establishment of a unified government. In one sense, this plethora of political parties was good, because it demonstrated the freedom of discussion and viewpoint under the democratic American regime in south Korea, and resulted in a much larger number of groups on the non-Communist side than on the Communist side. On the other hand, such proliferation both reflected and encouraged the natural Korean tendency toward factionalism and political infighting, and made the development of a political consensus all the more difficult.[33]

A partial brake on this process was the enactment of Military Government Ordinance 55, which required political parties to register and set certain minimal standards. Like other American measures, this ordinance was later used by the ROK government for its own political ends, happily citing the American source.[34]

Parties of both Left and Right increasingly opposed American policies during the occupation, most on the Left calling for cooperation with the north, and most on the Right demanding immediate elections in the south to set up a separate government. (The Rightist Han'guk Democratic party was a partial exception, because some of its leading members were principal officials of the South Korean Interim Government.) Political activities frequently involved demonstrations, violence, and illegal actions on both sides. Next to the Communist party, the greatest problem in early months was the Left-oriented

People's party, which had replaced the self-constituted People's Republic when U.S. authorities denied it governmental status. On the Right, as already noted, the greatest problem was Rhee.

The Americans did not outlaw the Communists nor any other major political grouping, but sought to control political activities by prosecuting violations of law, while promoting a middle-of-the-road coalition. The U.S. discovery and prosecution of a large-scale counterfeiting operation, together with constant pressure by the Rightist-dominated police, seriously weakened the Communist party. The People's party gradually disintegrated into extreme-Left and moderate fractions; many of the latter joined the moderate coalition that the Americans promoted. The moderates were given a modest political base when the Military Governor appointed forty-five members of the Korean Interim Legislative Assembly who were nominated by the Left-Right Coalition to counterbalance forty-five elected Rightist members. As stated above, however, the coalition effort did not prevent the Rightist groups from dominating the Korean political scene.

Once the Republic of Korea was established, the United States played a largely passive role in political party development, but its representatives kept in contact with politicians of all major groups, and favored opposition as well as government leaders with trips to the United States, while making clear to everyone the American conception of healthy political development. Such modest steps may have encouraged opposition politicians in their bid for power, and may have been a factor in the opposition of the opposition Democratic Party in 1956. Certainly the Democratic party platform reflected political principles attractive to Americans.

In 1958, reporting on Democratic party prospects, the U.S. Embassy in Seoul commented:

> . . . the Democratic Party merits the attention of the United States as a strong force in present-day politics and as the possible administration party after 1960. As the Party has grown stronger and come to play a major role in a two-party system, the Embassy has given it a proportionate emphasis, together with the Administration and Liberal Party. Efforts to influence it to adopt a more positive and constructive approach to the conduct of government have had and probably will have only limited success, because of the Opposition's tradition of criticism and obstruction. Increasingly careful attention and planning should be devoted to the Democratic Party, however, as the 1960 elections approach, inasmuch as a Democratic victory would require and hold great potential for the exercise of American influence to effect a basic improvement in government in Korea.[35]

Elections

The idea of elections in Korea, as a means of ensuring that the government would be considered legitimate and representative of the people, was quite generally shared by Korean leaders as well as the American authorities from the outset. However, different Koreans had different ideas. From early 1946,

Syngman Rhee and many of his Rightist supporters insisted on separate elections in south Korea.· Others wanted all-Korean elections. The United States was reluctant to take steps that would prejudice the prospects of unifying the American and Soviet zones, but perceived the need for increasing Korean participation in government.

In October 1946, an election of sorts was held in the south for representatives in a Korean Interim Legislative Assembly. After the Soviet Union had refused to cooperate with the United Nations, a general election in the South under UN observation on May 10, 1948, led to the establishment of the Republic of Korea. Thereafter, general elections were held in the south in 1950, 1954, 1958, 1960, and 1963 for representatives in the national legislature; in 1952, 1956, 1960, and 1963 for President; and in 1952, 1956, and 1960 for local assemblies and executives. There were by-elections in other years to fill vacancies.

The United States took a keen interest in all elections, because in the American view they played in key role in the general U.S. objective of democratic development--both structurally, in providing an expression of the people's will, and symbolically, in offering to the world a demonstration of American-style democracy operating in Asia. In general, after the ROK gained its sovereignty in 1948, the U.S. role was limited to promoting a free atmosphere and fair practices through (1) discreet influence on the leadership, (2) overt observation of the campaigns and elections by U.S. Embassy personnel and coverage of them by the U.S. Information Service, (3) encouraging the UN Commission to carry out its own observations as thoroughly and vigorously as possible, (4) encouraging the presence of foreign newsmen.

For a brief period, from 1955 to 1958, the electoral process and the legislature appeared to be a vehicle for the emergence of a two-party system, raising the possibility of a peaceful change of political power. Free political institutions, however, were too fragile and superficial a conception--even with such encouragement as the United States and the UN could offer--to resist basic drives for power and influence. Some of Syngman Rhee's supporters determined to suppress the trend toward an opposition electoral victory, and massively rigged the 1960 elections. They were aided by the natural death of the principal opposition leader, Cho Pyong-Ok. The appeal of free elections, and indignation over government excesses, were strong enough to provoke a student revolt that toppled the Rhee administration. The election that followed probably marked the high point of freedom in Korea (although a great deal of money was spent on them, some of which allegedly came from covert American sources), but the very scope of the ex-opposition victory turned out to be one cause of its subsequent weakness in government.

The last general elections within the scope of this study were held in 1963, in large part because of strong American pressure, to legitimize the power of the new military leadership. They demonstrated that the civilian politicians remained so divided among themselves, so concerned with their individual power positions and attitudes, at the expense of large-group cooperation, that party politics on the Western model was not yet viable.

The 1946 KILA Election. The State Department files offer very little information on the election of October 1946, carried out by the American Military Government for forty-five seats in the Korean Interim Legislative Assembly (KILA). Except in Seoul, the election was indirect: village heads chose representatives to county assemblies, which in turn designated provincial representatives; these in turn named the representatives to KILA. Nearly all the men so chosen were of Rightist persuasion, since Rightists were in fairly effective control of south Korean politics and administration, especially the police.

Recognizing this fact, and under instruction from Washington to work for a political coalition that would reduce the Left-Right polarization, the U.S. military commander (Hodge) asked for nominations by the Coalition Committee that had been formed of moderate Leftists and centrists, and appointed forty-five of these nominees to the Assembly to counterbalance the elected Rightists. One of KILA's few accomplishments, in a little over one year of existence, was an election law that it passed after much dispute and after modification by the American Military Governor (who had veto power).

The American authorities in Seoul wanted to conduct a new election under the KILA law, regardless of negotiations in the Joint Commission with the Soviets, because of the apathy of KILA and growing Korean demands--especially by the Rightists--for such an election. Washington, however, preferred to wait until international auspices could be worked out as contemplated by the policy paper then in force (SWNCC 176/30). Rhee and his followers, failing to bring about a new election, announced in November 1947 that they would conduct one themselves unless General Hodge set an election date before the end of the year; but this challenge was overtaken by the arrival of the UN Commission.[36]

The 1948 Election. The UN General Assembly resolution of October 1947 called for elections throughout Korea to form a government, and named a nine-member United Nations Temporary Commission on Korea (UNTCOK) to bring such elections about and observe them. To no one's surprise, the Soviet and north Korean authorities refused to cooperate. Following a decision by the United Nations Interim Assembly that elections would be held in areas open to UN observation, and despite opposition by some Koreans, the American Military Government conducted elections in its zone of occupation on May 10, 1948, for 200 representatives to a constituent assembly.

The UN Commission consulted extensively with the Military Government during the preparatory period and called for a number of modifications of rules and policies, most of which were made--ranging from extensive changes in the election law, release of political prisoners, and liberalization of security regulations, to the change of election date from May 9 to May 10 to avoid coincidence with an eclipse of the sun.

In addition, the American command undertook a massive program of public education, devoting "practically the entire staff" of its information and public relations office to "popularizing the elections and events growing out of it. . . ." A total of 15,299,900 pieces of printed matter, 81,000 posters, and 48 radio features were produced; 1,215 radio receivers and 90 public-address systems were distributed; 117 speakers addressed over 400,000 people; a special information train travelled 2,900 miles and presented 39 performances, reaching 60,000 people; a special motion picture, "The People Vote," was viewed by eight million. The director of the Military Government's Office of Civil Information (James Stewart), on the basis of interviews with newsmen, officials, and citizens, credited this massive campaign with being the principal cause of a voter registration estimated at 92 percent of those eligible.[37]

The election itself was the subject of an exhaustive report on July 10 by the Military Governor (General Dean). The report held that the ability of the Korean people to hold "fair, honest, and efficient elections" had been demonstrated. However, leaving nothing to chance, Americans were omnipresent during the election to be sure that Korean honesty and efficiency were maintained. For example, all shipments of ballots, boxes, etc. throughout Korea were accompanied by American personnel. For this reason, the Political Adviser noted, "the attached report is classified as 'restricted.' For international reasons, it is inadvisable to stress overly United States participation publicly at this time."[38]

Members of the UN Commission, which observed the elections, as well as U.S. Mission observers, acknowledged that they were honest, efficient, legal, and democratic; and they were accepted as legitimate by most Koreans, thus effectively accomplishing their main purpose of constituting a representative government. However, the Syrian UNTCOK delegate (Mughir), in an unauthorized press release three days after the event, noted that the "remarkable efficiency" should give rise to a certain degree of caution and reservation in our appraisal of that efficiency." The delegate may have had in mind, not only the American role, but the major role played by a volunteer local defense group, the *hyangbodan*, which was organized to guard against Communist interference. According to General Dean's report, "This vigilante-type body of men was organized from citizens and members of youth groups and armed with clubs. . . . [It] served a good purpose although (inevitably) there were a few reports of excesses committed by some members of the Corps." Given the thorough Rightist organization of the country, a bias toward the Right was virtually inevitable, the more so because the moderates--still hoping for unification--had encouraged their adherents to abstain from the election.[39]

The 1950 Election. Under the terms of the ROK Constitution adopted in July 1948, the first National Assembly was limited to a two-year term, while the President and Vice President were elected by the Assembly for four years. Subsequent Assemblies were to have four years in office. In the Fall of 1949, however, there were second thoughts about the two-year term. President Rhee (who had been elected by the Assembly the previous year) referred to the problem in a September 30 press conference, noting among other things that it would be appropriate for a newly elected Assembly to elect the President in 1952. By March 1950, Rhee was proposing that elections be postponed until November.

The question of election postponement became part of the larger problem of ROK political and economic inadequacies, as the United States saw them, and American representatives applied strong pressure to Rhee and his ministers to bring about reforms. On April 4, the Ambassador (Muccio) called on Rhee and gave him an aide-memoire that had been cleared with Washington. The document was basically concerned with inflation, but it had a final paragraph, added at the Ambassador's suggestion, referring to Rhee's message of March 31 proposing election postponement. "The holding of the elections as scheduled and provided for by the basic laws of the Republic appears to [the U.S.] Government as equally urgent with the taking of necessary measures for the countering of the inflationary forces. . . ."

When Rhee asked "what he could do to satisfy the Secretary [of State] and Mr. Hoffman [Administrator of the U.S. Economic Cooperation Administration]," the Ambassador replied, "(1) cause passage laws, budget and taxes, and (2) hold elections before end May." Rhee had the aide-memoire translated and distributed to the National Assembly, but it was not made public until the gist was reported in Washington press despatches. The elections were held on May 30, in a "commendably free and peaceful atmosphere," observed by the UN Commission and Embassy personnel. They resulted in a "rebuff for the Administration, legislature, and rightist political parties"--thus laying the groundwork for the political crisis of 1952.[40]

The 1952 Election. The Presidential election of 1952 is inseparable from the political crisis of that year, discussed in Chapter 6, pages 187-91. Conducted with general freedom, but in an atmosphere of wartime tension and political repression, it resulted in a 74.6 percent majority for Rhee--probably greater than he would have received in a really free election, but nonetheless reflecting the real majority opinion among the electorate.[41]

The 1954 Election. In 1954, the newly-organized Liberal Party was vigorously supported by the government machinery in returning an Assembly favorable to Rhee. Embassy observers sought comfort in observing that it was a real election, freer than in many other countries, but acknowledged that it was "a rough election with widespread official and unofficial pressure being brought to bear in varying degrees. . . ." Election committees were ineffectual, plain-clothes policemen were often present in polling places; ballot-stuffing was reported for the first time; the evidence pointed to "resurgence of old authoritarian traditions coupled with the development of a one-party system," and boded ill for the future of the "democratic framework established here in 1948." There is no indication in the files that the United States took any particular action regarding the election except for the usual spot observations; American attention was largely focused on the difficult military and economic problems then at issue, complicated by Rhee's stubborn intransigence. More-over, anti-Communism rather than civil rights was the theme then dominant in Washington.[42]

The 1956 Election. The political atmosphere moderated somewhat after 1954 as Lee Ki-Poong, a moderate, consolidated his control of the Liberal Party under Rhee's auspices. Nevertheless, there was a crisis in November 1954, when a constitutional amendment was forced through the legislature to remove the prohibition on a third term for Rhee. The consequence of these developments was a strong trend toward a two-party system. The trend was demonstrated in an Assembly by-election in December 1955, regarded by both major parties as a test run for the 1956 presidential election, and termed by the U.S. Embassy a turning-point in Korean politics. For almost the first time, both candidates capitalized on their party affiliations and received strong party support; the two major candidates got the great majority of the votes cast; and persuasion of voters was more in evidence than coercion.[43]

In the months before the presidential election the United States was twice brought into the campaign by newspaper stories. First was a November 1955 United Press International despatch that cited a "usually reliable American source" as saying that the United States "might reject Rhee and support someone else in next year's elections." The ROK government sought to prevent publica-tion of the story in Korea, but was only partially successful; the Liberal party then issued a sharply critical statement.

In January 1956, Rhee's ambassador to Washington (Yang) told the press on two occasions that American economic aid would be suspended if Rhee were not re-elected. The statement was widely criticized in the Korean press. Rhee made a statement which while correct was not a complete disavowal of his Ambassador's view. Americans, accustomed to Ambassador Yang's verbal excesses, sought to play the episode in a low key while privately offering assurances of non-intervention. Both stories, and the reaction to them, showed how large a potential role American influence was perceived to play in Korean politics. At the same time, opposition leaders were privately calling on the United States for support of their cause.[44]

American representatives, in the course of normal diplomatic contact, encouraged the leaders of the opposition Democratic party to improve their organization and campaign and to hold firm against government pressures. The United States also informally encouraged attention to the campaign by American news media. Otherwise, the United States maintained a position of neutrality and non-intervention in the campaign and election. UNCURK, for its part, decided to engage in "limited, informal, and unobtrusive" observation.[45]

The Democratic party mounted a vigorous and imaginative campaign for its candidates, ex-Assembly Chairman Shin Ik-Hi for President and ex-Prime Minister Chang Myon for Vice President, against Rhee and Lee Ki-Poong for the Liberal Party. The Democratic slogan, "We can't live, let's try a change" *(mot salgetta, kara poja)* had great popular appeal. At the same time Rhee's forces allowed Cho Bong-Am, an ex-Communist with strongly socialist views, to head a ticket for the mildly socialist Progressive Party.

There was a surprising degree of press freedom, and a relative--though by no means complete--reduction of the traditional official pressures on the electorate and candidates. Newspapermen attributed the press freedom to Rhee's recognition that his extreme anti-U.S. and anti-NNSC positions of 1953 and 1954 had lost American public support, and his consequent endeavor to convince the United States that he was not a dictator. It was apparent to U.S. Embassy observers that the opposition would score a very large vote, but it seemed inconceivable that they would be allowed an actual victory, even if their following should entitle them to it.[46]

The charged atmosphere of Korea's first real political contest for the presidency was greatly heightened by the sudden death of Shin Ik-Hi, the Democratic presidential candidate, ten days before the election. Although it was established that the death was natural, there were demonstrations and some violence. However, under Korean law, the candidacy was vacant, and attention then focused on the vice-presidential contest. As the vote count came in on May 15, it was clear that Rhee would be re-elected; but to the surprise of many observers, the vice-presidential vote was extremely close. Ballot-counting in the large city of Taegu, an opposition stronghold, was suspended. There were rumors of opposition plans for violence, in conjunction with the impending funeral of Shin Ik-Hi, if the election results were rigged.[47]

In these circumstances, the American Chargé (Strom) asked and received authority to approach the two principal Democratic party leaders, Chang Myon and Cho Pyong-Ok, counseling restraint and moderation and the avoidance of violence. This was done through Embassy officers, and the ROK government was quietly informed of the action, with suggestions that manipulation of the vote count might have serious domestic consequences.

Counsels of moderation prevailed. The opposition vice-presidential candidate was allowed to win the election and assume his office--a historic event in Korea.

In the Embassy's view, the presence of nine foreign correspondents during the campaign and election may have played a role in Rhee's decision to accept the verdict of the vote count. Rhee himself won about 55 percent of the total vote; the remainder of the presidential ballots went chiefly to Cho Pong-Am (about 24 percent), and to the deceased Shin Ik-Hi, who probably would have had many of Cho's votes if he had lived.[48]

Observers agreed that by Korean standards, the election was in general free and fair, although official pressures on the electorate, as usual, were not absent. However, according to one report, the vote of the entire First ROK Army had been "delivered" by order of the commander (Paik Sun-Yup). While the Army probably did not all vote as ordered, this instance of military power applied to politics, in direct contradiction of American training doctrine, may have been one of the factors in the politicization that led to the 1961 military coup d'état.[49]

Despite the massive popular protest registered in the 1956 vote, there was little or no change in Rhee's policies. On the contrary, it appeared that Rhee would utilize his two main power bases--the police and the local bureaucracy, and the Liberal Party under Lee Ki-Poong--as "loyal instruments of his will in essentially same way as in past. . . ." The U.S. Embassy appraisal was that Rhee had "failed to recognize the significance of the May 15 election except in terms of a challenge to his 'rightful' authority. . ." and had therefore failed to turn the emotional climate of the election to his advantage. "While his tactics may succeed in maintaining order in future as in past, their inflexible continuation creates increasing danger of trouble ahead."[50]

Following the 1956 elections, two strains of thought among Rhee's supporters became increasingly evident: the desire for Western-style moderate politics, on one hand, and the determination to maintain control, on the other. There was discussion of compromise constitutional amendments that would prevent Chang Myon's accession to the presidency and establish greater parliamentary control. Rhee would have none of them. He reshuffled his cabinet to install his stalwart supporters, and put the national police "under the command of a heavy-handed officer who owed personal allegiance to him." The Army command was also reshuffled. Liberal party discipline was tightened.[51]

Firm action was taken in the August 1956 elections for local councils and executives, by amendments to the basic law and by effective organization and pressure, so that about 70 percent of Liberal candidates won. The pressures were such that on July 27, 1956, opposition Assemblymen led a protest demonstration in downtown Seoul, in full view of the U.S. Embassy, and scuffled with police sent to stop them. The Embassy recommended a critical U.S. Government press statement. The State Department, although it decided to make statements only in response to questions, instructed the Embassy to inform ROK government officials (but not Rhee) "informally and discreetly" of U.S. concern regarding election interference, and to encourage UNCURK officials to do likewise. Lee Ki-Poong's reaction to such representations--blaming the Home Minister for the tactics used against the Assemblymen, and complaining that he was "powerless to influence events any more"--was a signal of the coming shift away from moderation and toward increasingly blatant power tactics. Nonetheless, UNCURK observers concluded that on the whole, the 1956 local elections were generally fair.[52]

The 1958 Election. The growing Liberal party division between the "soft" (moderate) and "hard" factions became evident in debates in late 1957 over revisions to the election law, and in a crisis over the rigging of a local election for the mayor of Chinju. Mounting opposition popularity posed the real danger of a Liberal party defeat in the 1958 Assembly elections and in the 1960 presidential election as well; yet undue pressure might further weaken ROK government prestige, both domestically and internationally. The opposition was becoming increasingly confident and active. The U.S. Ambassador, in reporting the election bill debate, commented that the "controversy over it is evidence that considerable segment Korean political leaders remain ready disregard democratic principles in order to preserve power." Embassy officers exerted informal pressures for a reasonable compromise on the bill, which was eventually achieved in January 1958, at the price of resignations by some of the opposition party leaders.[53]

In the event, however, moderate policies prevailed in the May 2, 1958 Assembly elections except for treatment of the "progressive" or socialist forces. The Embassy reported that the conduct of the elections and the behavior of both major parties "were at high-point in Korean politics. . . . Two major parties, as a result of the development of a strong two-party system, dominated the elections heavily and developed strong campaigns based on major issues, in a style approaching that of the more advanced democratic countries." Both the Liberal and Democratic parties had coherent platforms for the first time. The Liberals won a majority, favored by improving economic conditions and by continuing weaknesses in the opposition, which "prevented the development of a protest vote." However, the Democrats succeeded in gaining over one-third of the Assembly seats, and thus the power to block a constitutional amendment. This success whetted their appetite for power and reinforced the concerns of the Liberals. There were few reported election irregularities, but there was vigorous criticism of those that occurred. The "progressive" elements (Progressive and Democratic Reformist parties) were harassed and muzzled, but their fate, as small and suspect minorities, was of little general concern. Their principal leader, Cho Bong-Am, who had scored a large presidential vote in 1956, disappeared; his subsequent trial and execution became a *cause celebre* (see Chapter 6, pages 193-194).

Both UNCURK and the U.S. Embassy observed the elections. UNCURK's role was low-key, and there were rumors (subsequently denied) that the ROK had rejected election observation by the Commission. Embassy officers made ten observation trips of three to five days each throughout the country in the three months preceding the election, as well as some observations on the election day itself. Otherwise there was little U.S. involvement. In the Embassy's view, the Administration probably calculated that its victory was assured and that it therefore did not need to use heavy-handed tactics.[54]

After the election, however, the Administration and the Liberal party showed concern over its implications for the 1960 presidential election. The danger was highlighted in a by-election in October 1958 in a supposedly safe rural Liberal Party constituency. Despite various forms of evident election rigging, the Democratic candidate scored very nearly as many votes as the Liberal. Liberal party leaders acquiesced in an investigation, largely (according to a Democratic source) because of U.S. Embassy and UNCURK intercession "which, he believed, had brought the true facts of the incident to the attention of top Liberal party leaders. It might be noted that Seoul political circles in general appear to have drawn this conclusion."[55]

The Elections of 1960 and Subsequent Years. Beginning at the end of 1958, the Liberal party's "hard faction" moved to ensure victory in the 1960 presidential election by whatever means necessary, thus bearing out Ambassador Dowling's 1957 evaluation. Their heavy-handed tactics produced an atmosphere of growing political repression, which eventually exploded into the downfall of the Rhee regime and--a year later--of its democratic successor. The heavily rigged March 15, 1960 presidential election; the unprecedentedly free July 29, 1960 elections for a two-house parliament under the revised constitution and the subsequent local elections; and the elections in October and November 1963 to legitimize the military government, are all related to the broader political situation of the Republic in those years, and are therefore discussed in Chapter 6, below.

ROK Governmental Institutions

Constitution. The original ROK constitution of 1948 was largely the work of a single constitutional scholar, Yu Chin-O, who was asked by Syngman Rhee to undertake the work soon after Rhee's election as Chairman of the newly-constituted National Assembly. Working with a committee of the Assembly, Yu drew upon various foreign models, but particularly that of Weimar Germany, and produced a draft providing for a parliamentary regime with significant socialist elements. American Military Government experts had prepared a draft constitution earlier that year (despite the fact that the American Military Governor had rejected a Rightist effort in the Interim Legislative Assembly to enact a constitution in 1947); but the American draft was largely disregarded.

Americans played no significant role in the infighting between Rhee, who wanted a strong presidency for himself, and the conservative Han'guk Democratic party, which wanted a parliamentary regime with its own leader, Kim Sung-Soo, as Prime Minister. Rhee won; the result was a curious hybrid providing for a prime minister with little power, under a strong President who shared power in only token respects with his cabinet. An attempt was made in 1950 to restore provision for parliamentary government, but it failed (see Chapter 6, page 185).

During Rhee's incumbency, the Constitution was amended twice: once in 1952, largely to permit his own popular re-election, and again in 1954, to permit him a third term. These two amendments also dropped the office of Prime Minister and modified some clauses considered disadvantageous for foreign investment. The United States played no role in the amendments, although its own constitutional form supported Rhee's advocacy of a strong President. After the 1956 election put an opposition leader in place to succeed Rhee, there was renewed talk of a parliamentary regime, this time among Liberals. The obvious expediency of such an amendment led a State Department officer to comment to the ROK Embassy counselor in Washington in August 1956 that its passage "could lead to extensive disillusionment throughout the world. . . ." The idea was not formally proposed during Rhee's time.[56]

Following Rhee's resignation in 1960, a revised Constitution was enacted. Along with strengthening of language concerning individual rights, the new document provided for a genuine parliamentary system with a two-house legislature, largely because the Democratic party and its predecessor conservative opposition parties had favored such a system for so long that they could not alter their position. Nonetheless, some Democrats had private reservations about the suitability of a parliamentary structure for Korea.

When the military junta seized power in May 1961, it did not abolish the Constitution, but suspended many of its provisions, substituting its own emergency organic law. In 1962, the junta undertook the drafting of a new document--as before, in the form of sweeping amendments to the previous Constitution. The Koreans solicited the help of three foreign consultants, including Professor Rupert Emerson of Harvard University; there was no direct U.S. Government input. The amendments, adopted by popular referendum, restored a strong presidency and a unicameral legislature. The new Constitution remained in force until 1972.

Executive Branch. During most of Rhee's administration, the executive branch of the ROK government suffered from cronyism in appointments and frequent changes of personnel, as well as from overcentralization and from Rhee's reluctance to delegate authority (part of which was due to the incompetence of many of the office-holders). Low pay handicapped recruitment and encouraged corruption. In 1957, an Embassy report pointed out that the average tenure of ROK cabinet ministers since 1948 had ranged from a high of twenty-seven months for Foreign Affairs (an almost meaningless position during much of that time) to a low of seven months for Home Affairs and Agriculture.

Nevertheless, a 1956 Embassy report of a new law simplifying the government structure professed to find "certain small signs for the better" in the ROK bureaucracy, "for which both Koreans and Americans may take credit." Turnover at lower levels had declined; more career civil servants were being named to high positions; a growing number of middle-rank officials had had training and observation tours abroad (chiefly in the United States), and might be expected to apply this experience to raising the level of government performance.[57]

U.S. influence on structure and performance of the ROK government was chiefly indirect, through its technical assistance programs. A civil service training institute of sorts had been established under the American Military Government, and similar ROK institutions received U.S. support and guidance. The economic ministries and offices of the ROK, since they were in constant contact with U.S. officials concerning the large aid program and were held responsible for the use and accounting of some of the funds, were necessarily influenced by American practice. The United States informally endeavored to promote increased government efficiency through simplification, elimination of supernumeraries, and better pay. So long as the Japanese-trained or expatriate Old Guard were in control, such influence was minimal in its effect; but the dramatic improvement in ROK government efficiency since the mid-1950s suggests that the U.S. investment in training and its subtle influence (in both civilian and military sectors) had a long-run payoff.[58]

Legislative Branch. During the first four years of its existence, from 1948 to 1952, the ROK National Assembly was a major factor in Korean political affairs. It not only legitimated early basic legislation, but in some instances exercised significant initiative. However, from the very beginning there was a struggle for power between Rhee and the legislative leaders, which as early as 1949 led to the arrest of fifteen Assembly members, and which culminated in the political crisis of 1952. From that time on, the legislature became less and less significant, although on occasion it could and did embarrass the executive through investigations, interpellations, and votes against individual ministers.[59] It re-emerged into confused and tension-filled pre-eminence during the short-lived parliamentary regime, but from 1963 onward it had an ever-diminishing function in ROK governmental processes.

The United States provided the basic mechanical framework for a legislature in establishing the Korean Interim Legislative Assembly under the military government. The main contribution of KILA to Korea was probably its value as a training ground for the legislative process. (The American Military Governor exercised the same executive dominance that Rhee did.) After 1948, the American role in Korean legislative affairs was largely confined to the sending of certain Assemblymen to the United States for study and observation; informal continuing contacts with legislative leaders; and the assignment of a local U.S. Embassy employee to attend all legislative sessions and prepare daily summaries of proceedings. On occasion, Embassy officers attended important debates; in only one instance, in the Security Law crisis of 1958, was such an officer refused admission. In a few instances, American officials intervened with legislative leaders in matters intimately connected with economic and military aid. When the role of the legislature as a democratic institution was in jeopardy, as in 1952, 1958, and 1961-1963, the United States privately sought to influence the ROK government so as to preserve it. The steady decline in power and influence of the legislature over the years demonstrates the lack of American success. Nevertheless, the continuous existence of the National Assembly, despite its vicissitudes, from 1948 to 1961, and its re-establishment in 1963, were perhaps in part a result of American influence.

Judicial Branch. As one of its eleventh-hour reforms in 1948, the American Military Government established the court system as a separate branch of government with considerable autonomy. This act was one of the relatively few basic American breaks with the Japanese governmental tradition. The 1948 ROK Constitution (in theory, at least) preserved the separation of judicial powers. In addition, several legal reforms under the Americans introduced such new concepts as habeas corpus and adversary proceedings, and increased somewhat the prestige of judges. Following the establishment of the ROK, a small-scale program of technical advice and exchange of experts continued with both official and non-governmental U.S. funding (the latter particularly from the Asia Foundation). The judicial branch struggled, with indifferent success, to maintain "some semblance of independence from the Executive."[60] As the issue of a status of forces agreement came to the fore after the Korean War, the Koreans had an incentive to improve their judicial and legal system, so that they could meet the criticisms of Americans who were unwilling to relinquish American citizens to Korean criminal jurisdiction.[61]

Judicial independence, however, was one of the sacrifices to political expediency made in the last years of the Rhee regime--particularly in 1959, when ten-year judicial appointments came up for renewal. The Korean military regime superimposed military "revolutionary courts" on the civil system (as the Americans had superimposed military "provost courts" in 1946), but these courts were abolished when their political purposes were accomplished. By 1965, the Korean courts were sufficiently acceptable in American eyes to permit signing a status of forces agreement that recognized Korean jurisdiction over U.S. nationals--although the number of Americans actually tried in Korean courts or serving sentences in Korean prisons was small.

The sovereignty exercised by the American Military Government from 1945 to 1948 injected the United States into the Korean legal system through over two hundred decrees of the Military Governor, which were continued in effect under the terms of the Initial Financial and Property Settlement. Some of these decrees, when invoked subsequently by the Koreans, were a source of no little embarrassment. For example, Military Government Ordinance 88 was the authority for the closing of a major opposition newspaper in 1959; and Military Government Ordinance 55 was invoked in the same year as authority for requiring the major opposition party to make embarrassing reports to the ROK government.

Labor Problems

During the American Military Government period, labor policy was one of the most troublesome governmental areas because the authorities in Seoul were caught between the insistence of American organized labor on freedom of organization, collective bargaining, and strikes, on the one hand, and the growing Communist ability to exploit these freedoms to their own advantage, on the other. The Koreans themselves had experience only with the draconian Japanese model of industrial relations; expectations of workers (encouraged by the Left) were unrealistic, and their understanding of economics was small; while industrialists continued in the paternalistic Japanese style but with less financial resources or responsibility. Both Leftist and Rightist labor organizations proliferated, but they often dealt with political as much as economic issues. The American authorities were ill-equipped to deal with the problem. American military officers emphasized law and order, with some resultant excesses by the conservatively-oriented police. The riots in the Fall of 1946, which resulted in pitched battles in Taegu and other cities between workers, students, and citizens and the police, began with a railroad strike; in some instances, American troops had to be called to restore order. The problem reached such dimensions that it required a policy paper of the State-War-Navy Coordinating Committee (SWNCC); work on such a paper was apparently begun in 1946.[62]

In April 1947, the Communist labor federation called a strike of railroad, electric, and telephone workers, apparently timed to coincide with a visit by a delegation from the Communist-oriented World Federation of Trade Unions. Conservative Korean and American authorities arrested 29 leading members of left-wing political parties. About a week previously, the Military Government had arrested several union leaders because they had called an "unauthorized" union meeting. The entire sequence of events, compounded by inept handling of the WFTU delegation, made lurid reading in the American press and elsewhere.[63]

The SWNCC paper (No. 376) was approved on September 23, 1947. It gave a brief history of the Korean labor movement and of American Military Government acts and policies toward it; but reaffirmed the policy of encouraging development of democratic labor organizations and safeguarding labor rights.[64]

After its establishment, the ROK did not feel compelled to provide the same degree of freedom to labor, especially Communist-oriented labor. Unions continued in existence, but were largely geared into the network of organizations supporting Rhee; the union of electrical workers, for example, could be counted on to demonstrate against U.S. policies whenever Rhee wanted them to. Rhee strongly objected to the activities of some American labor experts. After one idealistic but somewhat naive Oregonian had encouraged labor to demand its rights, soon after the establishment of the Republic, Rhee managed to prevent the assignment of a labor attache to the American staff for many years.

The United States continued to press quietly for improved labor conditions. At the same time the American military forces, as one of the largest employers in Korea, were not happy at the efforts of Korean labor unions to organize their local employees, or to force expensive compliance with the very liberal provisions of the (partially American-inspired) labor law. The issue of labor treatment resulted in several strike threats against the U.S. forces, and eventually became one of the difficult issues in the negotiation of a status of forces agreement (see Chapter 3, pages 85-92).

Workers were among the many groups that demonstrated for improved conditions during the short-lived Chang Myon government. The military junta, however, applied rigid controls to labor along with other groups in society. When civilian government was restored, however, a rash of labor disputes erupted in Korea in December 1963 and early 1964. Up to January 15, there were 140 labor disputes involving 16 unions and over 100,000 workers, all involving demands for wage increases of 50 to 100 percent. This development resulted both from the long period of military control and from the inflation of the previous two years. The U.S. Embassy, in analyzing the trend of affairs in labor in July 1964, noted that organized labor was more economically than ideologically oriented, but that its leadership was "more concerned with maintaining itself in power and with its relationship to the regime than with the development of the labor movement or labor conditions. . . ."

Accordingly, the Embassy suggested that the best policy for outside institutions to follow--be they the U.S. government or the International Confederation of Free Trade Unions (ICFTU)--was to develop the prestige and functions of the ROK Government's Office of Labor. ". . . Any real development of trade unionism, regardless of administrative machinery or leadership, will be dependent on attainment of an increasing measure of stability in the ROK economy." Implicit in these observations is not only the continuing immaturity of the labor movement at the time, but the fact that the growth of the Korean economy depended heavily upon cheap labor--a fact hardly calculated to encourage independent trade unionism.[65]

Peace Corps

In October 1961, the then ROK Ambassador to the United States (Chung Il-Kwon) expressed an interest in having a Peace Corps contingent in Korea. At the time, the United States was not enthusiastic about the proposal for obvious political reasons, and it was not pursued further. In October 1965, however, the Far East regional director of the Peace Corps (Ross Pritchard) visited Korea. Discussion with the country team of the pros and cons of a Peace Corps contingent led to agreement that it could make an important contribution in Korea, especially in English teaching. Ambassador Chung had by now become Prime Minister; his 1961 request was therefore used by Ambassador Berger as a peg for inquiry as to whether Korea would like Peace Corps volunteers for English instruction. The Prime Minister reacted favorably, and at year's end the topic was being explored with the ROK government. The Peace Corps subsequently set up a sizeable operation in Korea.[66]

Youth Problems

During the Kennedy and Johnson administrations, youth were a focus of interest and concern worldwide. This was particularly true in Korea, where students had toppled the Rhee regime. In early 1965, the U.S. Embassy responded to a worldwide State Department inquiry by listing programs it had undertaken in past years and appraising Korean young people's attitudes and motivations.[67]

Among the past programs listed was "a program of education for responsible democratic citizenship," initiated by the U.S. Information Service (USIS) in 1962 (in which the USIS Director, Huntington Damon, took strong personal interest), "which has been adopted in the school system of five provinces."

> Based on the Columbia University citizenship project, it has been adapted to Korean educational requirements by the Central Educational Research Institute (CERI) to instill the following five concepts into elementary and secondary school students: (a) dignity and worth of the individual, (b) cooperation and community service, (c) taking responsibility, (d) respect for the law and public property, and (e) choosing good leaders. . . .

Other programs listed by the Embassy were the use of foreign lecturers and returned Korean scholars under the Fulbright program to talk on American political processes and democratic concepts of government; special seminars in support of U.S. policy objectives; U.S. policy materials for officers in the troop information and education program of the ROK armed forces and for Ministry of Education editors working on school textbook revision; USIS publications increasingly oriented toward university and high school students. Embassy and USIS officers were devoting "considerable attention and time to working with hard-core leaders of some of the more difficult student groups and universities in Seoul. Personal contact has been maintained with student leaders at Seoul National University who represent leftist elements ranging from mild to extreme."

The report contained the following summary of student attitudes:

> . . . Korean students are motivated by the twin drives of individualism and nationalism rather than by intellectual or philosophical interests. They respond to new ideas or new political movements pragmatically, asking in effect, "What's in it for me?" This is not to deny the presence of youthful idealism. . . . The events of April, 1960 . . . show that there is a foundation of healthy patriotism among students. As individuals they seek security, freedom, and an outlet for self-expression; as Koreans they seek national independence, economic growth and increased respect and prestige among nations.
>
> . . . The students in particular are concerned about the industrialization and modernization of Korea. They desire fast action and shortcuts to industrial progress and are consequently now tempted to think of communism and socialism less in terms of ideology than as a means of achieving economic progress quickly. . . . Youth in Korea are prone to indignation about the perennial problem of corruption in government. . . . Korean youth still reflects a vague and hard-to-define feeling of resentment towards foreign influences. They are eager, however, to develop friendships with individual foreigners, particularly Americans. . . . Another attitude prevalent among some students is an idea that western-style democracy has not solved Korean problems. . . . At the root of their attitudes on this point is the feeling that Korea has not made as much progress as it should, despite massive American aid. . . . Underlying all other attitudes of Korean youth is a strong desire for reunification of their country. . . . In any youth program for Korea, the United States should avoid trying to use a primarily doctrinal approach to promote Western ideas of democracy and government. . . .

One American attempt to respond to the appeal of communism and socialism "as a means of achieving economic progress quickly" was a project promoted by the U.S. Information Service in the Fall of 1964. To offset criticism of the lack of south Korean economic and industrial progress in comparison with north Korea (a common attitude encouraged by north Korean propaganda), USIS arranged to have the ROK Economic Planning Board sponsor a seminar for fifty college student leaders to acquaint them with the facts of ROK power and industry during the previous nineteen-year period, followed by a tour of Korean factories. The expenses were paid by USIS, and transportation was furnished by U.S. Forces Korea (the U.S. component of the UN Command). The students, as a result of the tour, prepared articles for their school newspapers (with illustrations made available by USIS); and the EPB official who directed the program reversed his previously negative attitude on the utility of such activities for students. In addition, contacts were established for the USIS officers involved.[68]

Corruption

Like other developing countries undergoing rapid change, Korea had large amounts of corruption at all levels of government and society from the time of its liberation. The problem was compounded by lack of resources, by the economic and social confusion of the American Military Government period, and by the effects of the Korean War. It was the subject of constant complaint by the Koreans themselves, and a constant source of worry to the Americans. Corruption not infrequently involved U.S. funds or aid goods, and thus was of immediate concern to the responsible U.S. authorities, whatever their moral views. One celebrated case in 1954 was the diversion of considerable quantities of U.S.-supplied raw cotton from their intended use (for military uniforms) to civilian consumption. This case became a political football in Korean circles, since it allegedly involved the Defense Minister (Sohn Won-Il) and other high officials.

Charges of corruption were frequently directed at President Rhee and more particularly at his Austrian wife. Such charges were made, for example, in connection with National Assembly investigation of financial institutions in 1955. Commenting on the charges, the U.S. Ambassador (Briggs) said that no evidence had been uncovered in this or other cases that implicated the Rhees directly. "The Rhee's live simply and unostentatiously, almost austerely," he observed. ". . . The personal probity of the President has not to my knowledge been effectively challenged during my tour of duty in Korea." Again in 1958, an assistant to General Van Fleet told a Department officer that "a number of correspondents in New York, including Edward R. Murrow of CBS, have 'incontrovertible proof' that Mrs. Syngman Rhee has 'at least' $15 million salted away in New York and Swiss banks and . . . might be proceeding at the rate of $8 million a year."

Responding to inquiries about such charges, an Assistant Secretary of State (Macomber) wrote in a letter of December 4, 1958 to Senator William Fulbright, ". . . there is no evidence that U.S. aid funds have been diverted in any way to Mrs. Rhee's personal use [or] that either Mrs. Rhee or her relatives are engaged in any questionable activities." If ill-gotten millions were accumulated by either of the Rhees, they were certainly not drawn upon after their departure from Korea in 1960; their life of exile in Hawaii was supported largely by the Korean community there, and Mrs. Rhee in 1973 was living a comfortable but simple life in Seoul, in the house which had been given Rhee in 1949, shortly after his return from the United States.[69]

In early 1961, the deputy director of the U.S. aid program in Korea, Hugh Farley, became so concerned with the endemic corruption that he resigned his position in protest, and returned to the United States to mount a campaign to stamp it out. As a result of his unpublicized but strong representations within the U.S. government, the question of corruption became the subject of a staff inquiry and an annex to the report of the presidential task force on Korea (see Chapter 1, page 29).

Although anti-corruption statements were included in subsequent U.S. policy papers, no satisfactory means of American attack was found for a problem so deeply involved with the basic issues of Korean society. For that matter, the young Korean military idealists of 1961 could not cope with it, either:

> The military government based its moral claim to power in Korea importantly on the corruption issue. Its record after 10 months is curiously characteristic of totalitarian power. Finding a land where corruption is sewn into almost every seam of life, it used its immense controls not to eliminate corruption but rather to concentrate it--to reduce the breadth of the area in which corruption operated while increasing its depth.
>
> Draconian measures and constant surveillance reduced, at first sharply, then gradually less so, the constant round of pettifogging corruption entwined into most previous contacts between civilians and the govt. Strongly recognizing the need for 'unbudgeted funds,' especially for coming political activities, it set out to obtain these in far better-plotted, intensive ways, concentrating this activity almost entirely in the hands of the ROK CIA [Central Intelligence Agency] which developed special men and means for this function. The obvious risks involved in this very concentration have been further reduced by controls over the press and free speech, and, even, by the implication of threat and force. Thus far and on these terms, the operation has been a stunning success, netting larger sums than ever before with infinitely less publicity and making childish the comparison of the efforts in this area of previous Korean governments.[70]

Communications and the Press

The United States maintained great interest in communications in Korea as an obvious focal point for promoting both economic and political development. Aid and technical assistance were devoted to telecommunications and to various mass media, including motion pictures and radio. The U.S. Information Service (USIS) took over from the American Military Government's Office of Civil Information when the ROK became independent, and continued in close relations with newspapers and other mass media. Journalist exchanges were a conspicuous part of the exchange of persons program; USIS materials were supplied in quantity to mass media; USIS news and documentary films were shown extensively in Korean movie houses. USIS mobile units themselves entertained countless thousands of rural audiences.

Press. During the American occupation, an initial policy of total press freedom was succeeded, when hostile political elements took advantage of it, by a certain amount of censorship and control. Thus, in September 1945, anyone who wanted to start a newspaper was permitted to do so, and many did; a few months later, Military Government Ordinance 88 required licensing, and some forty dailies were so licensed. In 1949, an Embassy officer (Stewart) attributed the "ridiculously large number of daily papers" in Seoul to Military Government policies.[67]

The ROK Government began immediately to exert control over the press in 1948. An early move was to install a trusted Rhee lieutenant in a formerly Japanese-owned newspaper and turn it into a government mouthpiece. Opposition papers were harassed in varying degrees, but outright censorship and closure were very rare. Until the end of the Rhee regime, a considerable degree of press freedom prevailed within largely tacit limits. Partly this was due to continuing American influence, backed by American control of newsprint supply; but partly, also, it probably came from the Koreans' own experience under oppression and a genuine regard for press freedom. Rhee himself as a young man had been involved with opposition movements and their newspapers.

Another problem of the Korean press was the immaturity and irresponsibility of many of the reporters and editors. Underpaid and competing for circulation and attention, pressmen frequently printed unsubstantiated gossip and rumor and often resorted to blackmail based on their power of exposure. The United States endeavored to promote high journalistic standards of ethics and operation, both through training and exchange visits and through encouragement of professionalism. Thus, in June 1957, representatives of 34 daily newspapers met to form a Korea Newspaper Publishers' Association. An Editors' Association had been formed the previous April. Although the Embassy report does not explicitly say so, the influence of Embassy and USIS personnel and programs was instrumental in this development, which the Embassy regarded as "a reflection of the growing maturity of the newspapers in Korea."[68]

In 1959, however, press freedom became one of the many casualties to the new hard political line as the 1960 election approached. On April 30, one of the two major opposition daily newspapers *(Kyonghyang Sinmun)* was closed by the ROK Government, ironically by means of revoking its license under authority of American Military Government Ordinance 88. The Embassy got word that ROK officials themselves were divided on the wisdom of the move, and that President Rhee himself was not wholly sold on it. Accordingly, the Ambassador (Dowling) publicly commented on May 1,

> American public opinion has long held that suppression of the press is not a remedy for press errors. The intent of the American Military Government in promulgating Ordinance 88 was clearly to curb Communist subversive propaganda which threatened Korean internal security at that time.

Subsequently, in the course of a call on Rhee, the Ambassador expressed the hope that he would reconsider the closure decision; and public statements were made by the State Department in Washington and by a visiting State Department officer in Seoul. Vice President Chang, who had been publisher of the closed paper before his election in 1956, appealed to various foreign representatives for help--a move that hardly encouraged reconsideration by the ROK government.

In the end, despite U.S. action (or possibly because of them), the paper stayed closed until the Rhee government fell.[69]

Press freedom re-emerged in the new order that followed Rhee's departure, and with it the old abuses. The military coup re-imposed press controls, and maintained them thereafter in varying degrees. In 1964, in the course of a political crisis, opposition forces in the reconstituted National Assembly managed to water down government proposals for a press control law, and the administration for a time was denied the degree of control it desired. However, the press after 1961 never again enjoyed the degree of freedom it had before 1959, despite all the pressures that the U.S. was able to apply.[70]

Book Publishing. In August 1949, an observant Embassy officer (Gregory Henderson) discovered that of approximately 230 books translated into Korean from the end of World War II to 1948, "it seems safe to say that approximately half . . . were Communist." The number dropped off sharply thereafter.

> The first two years of American Military Government permitted a Communist proportion of publishing and translation to appear that was literally overwhelming, while doing almost nothing to translate and publish books showing a democratic or non-Communist way of life and thought. . . . Of those which deal with politics and economics, the proportion is practically 90 percent. [These facts are] an inescapable and striking illustration of how the Communists used a U.S. Military Occupation and the principles of free publishing to their advantage. Just as striking . . . is the lack of a similar opportunity taken either by Military Government or by non-Communist Koreans to present democratic points of view by the translation of basic Western texts. . . .

In response, the State Department proposed financial assistance to book publishers and provided a list of titles available for translation or distribution. A subsidized program of book translation and publishing continued thereafter for a number of years.[71]

Telecommunications. U.S. aid in the telecommunications field is beyond the scope of this survey. However, the minor problem involved in reestablishing civilian telegraphic traffic between Korea and foreign countries after the liberation illustrates the tedious bureaucratic obstacles that beset U.S.-Korean relations both then and afterward in this and other fields.

In December 1945, the Chief Signal Officer of the U.S. Army (Stoner) telegraphed the Radio Corporation of America, asking RCA to initiate communications between the United States and Korea for press purposes and for the official and personal needs of military personnel. RCA agreed, and on January 17, 1946, direct service was opened between Seoul and San Francisco, at first handling only government, press, and military traffic. However, upon the initiative of the American military authorities in Korea, RCA accepted Korean civilian messages, paid for in Korean currency.[72]

In February 1947, the Assistant Secretary of State for Occupied Areas (Hilldring) wrote the Civil Affairs chief of the War Department (Noce), noting RCA's problems in financing its operations in Korea. He advocated a system of controlled payment of dollars to RCA for the local currency it had collected, and pointed out the desirability of continued RCA operations to provide a communications link between Korea and other countries.

The War Department, however, took the position that it had no funds for expansion of communications traffic, even into essential activities such as those involving foreign trade. Advancing an obviously circular argument, General Noce quoted the military commander in Korea as saying that the economy there did not warrant any expansion of existing communications service, and that a decision to do so would have to be made on political grounds. In rebuttal, Hilldring noted that refusal to provide international telecommunications would be "a departure from the general policy of this government . . . which is to provide the best possible communication service to all parts of the world." The War Department was unmoved.[73]

In August 1947, RCA wrote to a State Department officer (Whitman), stating that as of September 1, no messages would be accepted unless paid for in dollars, since no authorization had been given RCA to convert the Korean currency it had collected into dollars, and since the Korean operation was losing money in any event. In November, presumably after further bureaucratic exchanges, State replied that nothing could be done in the absence of foreign exchange resources or earnings in Korea, but noted that certain traders were earning dollars for exports (hence, implicitly, could be expected to pay dollars.)[74] The files contain no record of final settlement; presumably RCA limped along until the ROK Government was established. It was a telephone operator on the RCA international circuit, Mary Lee, remaining in Seoul after the ROK government and much of the population had fled before the Communists in June 1950, who was on hand to connect Ambassador Muccio in Suwon with General MacArthur in Tokyo for their first conversation on the Korean War.

6

U.S. Involvement
in Major Korean Political Crises

In Chapter 5, the statement was made that American influence on Korean political behavior was exerted principally by informal and relatively subtle means. Moreover, much American influence was passive. American wealth, freedom, and military power--which had expelled the hated Japanese--gave the United States great prestige in the eyes of Koreans; accordingly, American patterns of political and social behavior had influence even in the absence of overt activity by the U.S. government or its representatives.

A complete chronicling of all American actions which might have had some influence on Korean political development would have been far beyond the scope of this study of U.S.-Korean relations. Instead, the method followed was to select nine crisis periods in Korean political history from 1948 to 1965, and examine the record of U.S. action in each. Those selected were the parliamentary crises of 1949 and 1950; the survival of the Republic of Korea government in the early days of the Korean War; the constitutional crises of 1952 and 1954; the trial and execution of Cho Bong-Am; the National Security Law crisis of 1958; the fall of the Rhee government in 1960; and the "military revolution" or coup d'état in 1961.

Parliamentary Crises of 1949 and 1950

In March 1949, the American Chargé d'Affaires (Everett Drumright) reported that the ROK government "after a shaky start" was now "settling down." Government corruption and inefficiency were problems, but the latter at least was gradually improving; training of security forces was "well along"; economic conditions were "now on upgrade," with adequate food stocks and slowed inflation.[1]

183

However, the ROK government faced serious challenges. The menace of Communist-inspired subversion was still not wholly under control (see Chapter 3, pages 104-105), and the north Koreans were building up their armed forces, yet the United States was preparing to complete the withdrawal of its combat forces. The Democratic Nationalist party, an expanded version of the Han'guk Democratic Party, was endeavoring to regain the power it had lost at Rhee's hands in the formation of the government. Other political elements were still supporting peaceful unification with the north. Rhee was under heavy U.S. pressure for economic reforms. Amid all these challenges, the National Assembly was demonstrating "remarkable" independence of the Executive, and Rhee felt compelled to consolidate still further his already preponderant influence and control.

Arrest of the Young Progressives

One of Rhee's moves was to suppress the "young progressive group" in the National Assembly, led by Vice Chairman Kim Yak-Su. This group opposed Rhee's conservative policies, favored a socialist approach to national development, and demanded withdrawal of U.S. forces. Two members of the group were arrested in May 1949 on charges of illegal contact with the Communists. In June, eight more were arrested, five of them (including Vice Speaker Kim) for violating the National Security Act by presenting an unauthorized petition to the United Nations Commission on Korea. These moves evoked U.S. Congressional criticism. On June 25, Rhee acknowledged to the U.S. Ambassador (Muccio) that the arrests were "unfortunate," and said

> he realized action of government might be regarded as 'undemocratic practice.' . . . He went on to explain conditions in Korea today vastly different from those in most countries . . . justified action taken against Assemblymen on grounds it necessary nip Communist plots in bud. . . .[2]

In November 1949, Kim Yak-Su was brought to trial. Embassy personnel were present, and reported "an even more astonishing lack of evidence against the defendant than characterized the first hearings of [arrested Assemblymen] No Il Hwan and Lee Moon Wun. . . ."[3] Although the personal sympathies of junior Embassy officers were strongly with the defendants, the line between loyal opposition and subversion was a difficult one to draw in the circumstances. U.S. representatives officially confined themselves to support for basic human rights and freedoms. (Kim and No were still in confinement when the north Korean invaded Seoul and liberated them, but whether they were actually Communists or Communist agents is not clear.)

Assassination of Kim Koo

Kim Koo, President of the former Provisional Government in exile, was Rhee's only real remaining rival with established national credentials as an independence leader, and one of the few prominent Koreans who publicly opposed "the armed solution to the [38th] parallel." Analyzing his assassination in 1949 and the trial of the killer (a young Army lieutenant, who got a mild sentence and was eventually released), the U.S. Embassy concluded that "both Army and Government might sleep more peacefully if Kim Koo were gone." The Embassy noted, also, that the Army's actions in the case "implied that it had begun to operate in the field of politics."[4]

The assassination of Kim Koo, like the arrests of Assemblymen, evoked strong American public criticism of Korea. The files do not indicate that the United States made any official representations regarding either case.

Constitutional Amendment Proposal of 1950

Undaunted by the fate of the "progressives," the conservative opposition Democratic Nationalist party put forward a constitutional amendment in March 1950, which would have established a "semi-parliamentary" regime with a Prime Minister responsible to the National Assembly. The proposal was motivated partly by Assembly irritation over Rhee's independent actions--including expenditure of funds beyond legal authorization--and partly by Rhee's failure to put enough DNP members in his cabinet, or to consult the DNP, despite DNP support for his election.[5]

Rhee refused any compromise. He announced that he would appeal directly to the people if the amendment passed, and conveyed the impression that its passage would result in the withdrawal of American aid. In the end, the proposal failed to pass, and Rhee's power was further strengthened.

The United States took no official stand on the amendment, but "when asked their views privately, Embassy officers . . . indicated a concern lest the controversy over the Constitutional amendment, and indeed the success of the amendment itself, might lead to unstable government, which Korea could not afford at this time." They also suggested that such fundamental action might better be taken by the new Assembly after the scheduled May elections. However, in reaction to statements before the National Assembly by Rhee's spokesman about the possible withdrawal of American aid, the chief of the economic aid mission in Seoul (Arthur Bunce) wrote to the Prime Minister (Lee Bum-Suk) on March 3, with a copy to the Chairman of the National Assembly (Shin Ik-Hi), "restating traditional ECA position that 'American economic assistance is not used to influence the political decisions of the people of any participating country.'" This statement encouraged the proponents of the amendment.[6]

On March 8, an Embassy officer (Harold Noble) called on Madame Rhee to say that an attempt by the President to appeal to the people over the heads of the Assembly, which was not provided for in the Constitution, would be "a revolutionary act . . . very harmful to orderly government in Korea and . . . would adversely affect the program of American aid." Madame Rhee called the President, who "quite frankly told [Noble] it was his intention to appeal to the people through a plebiscite," and went on to state his own views on government. Noble commented:

> In my view Dr. Rhee has a mystical conception of his own role in history and of his relationship to the Korean people and he truly believes that he today represents the feelings and longings of the Korean people just as he has ever since 1919, whereas the National Assembly, being made up of selfish power-hungry persons, does not.[7]

Survival of ROK Government, 1950-1951

In the first days and weeks after the north Korean invasion of June 25, 1950, the uncertainty of ROK government leaders from Rhee on down as to their own fate, and their feelings of impotence before north Korean heavy tanks and massed troops against their own light weapons, led to a good deal of irrationality and in some cases a *sauve-qui-peut* mentality that made effective government very difficult. Rhee himself, after an apparent initial impulse to flee, had to be persuaded by the Americans to move to safety. The skeleton U.S. Embassy staff, and particularly Ambassador Muccio himself, gave encouragement to the Koreans and assisted them in making the necessary decisions and arrangements. Without this support--particularly in the days before the American policy was decided and announced--it is quite possible that the ROK government would have disintegrated. One of the Ambassador's first moves was to urge replacement of the eccentric Buddhist Home Minister by the Democratic Nationalist leader, Cho Pyong-Ok, who had been national police director under the American military government. Rhee did so.

American influence on Korean government operations remained strong for at least a year thereafter. In May 1951, Rhee discharged his Defense Minister, Sihn Sung-Mo (as well as Home Minister Cho); an Embassy officer commented, "It was probably the strong stand which Generals Ridgway and Van Fleet took in holding the military leaders, including specifically Captain Sihn, responsible for the debacle of the 6th ROK Division, together with the continuing agitation in the National Assembly against Sihn, which finally forced the President's hand."[8]

During this period, also, the American military command assumed responsibility for many areas of normal Korean government responsibility--partly out of necessity and partly because of its desire to maintain control over its battlefields and supporting areas. A United Nations Civil Assistance Command, Korea (UNCACK) was established (later the Korea Civil Assistance Command, KCAC) with its own personnel operating both in the capital and in the provinces in a manner reminiscent of the American Military Government period. Control over economic assistance was transferred from the Ambassador to the United Nations Commander in late 1950, and was not returned until 1959. The consequence was that there were three major centers of political power in Korea: the ROK government, the U.S. Embassy, and the UN Command headquarters controlled by the U.S. military. A theoretical fourth center was the United Nations Commission for the Unification and Rehabilitation of Korea (UNCURK), established to replace UNCOK in October 1950, which occasionally asserted itself. The divergences among these power centers came to the fore in the 1952 crisis.

The Constitutional Crisis of 1952

Summary of Events

The confrontation between Rhee and his political enemies in 1952 was a watershed in Korean history and in Korea-U.S. relations. It demonstrated the frailty of Western-style democratic institutions in Korea and the impotence of the United States to sustain them. These facts were obscured by the superficial reappearance of parliamentary and party processes for a few years thereafter, but the lesson in retrospect is clear.

As the fighting lines stabilized in the Spring of 1951, the old Korean political rivalries came to the fore. The Constitution provided for election of the President by the National Assembly in 1952; but the Assembly was increasingly critical and hostile toward Rhee. The elderly Vice President, Yi Si-Yong, resigned in May 1951, professing sympathy for the Assembly's criticisms, and the Assembly elected the opposition leader, Kim Sung-Soo of the Democratic Nationalist party, to succeed him. The idea of a Constitutional amendment to establish a parliamentary government, such as had been defeated in 1950, was again discussed.[9]

Rhee's response to these developments was to propose a constitutional amendment of his own for direct popular election of the President and Vice President, and to build political forces to secure its passage. His followers worked to bring the non-DNP groups in the National Assembly together as a government majority. In October 1951, the government put forward formal amendment proposals for direct presidential election and for a bicameral legislature (the upper house of which would be more responsive to presidential direction). However, the amalgam of non-DNP groups (called the Republican People's Political Association) could not be brought into line. The amendment proposals failed when voted on in January 1952.[10]

Rhee then departed from his traditional suprapartisan position and stimulated the organization of a mass party to support him. He put trusted and ruthless supporters in charge of key security agencies, organized a military Provost Marshal General Command independent of UN control, and encouraged the organization and strengthening of various groups to mobilize popular support through both persuasion and terror. He proposed a recall campaign for removing from office those Assemblymen who failed to follow his leadership. Assembly by-elections in February 1952, and the first local elections of the Republic's history in April and May, all gave Rhee supporters a virtually clean sweep.

Even some of Rhee's loyal and long-time supporters differed with him on his high-handed tactics, and (like the opposition leaders) approached the Americans for help in moderating his policies. But the Korean public in general was little moved. In one Embassy observer's view, the acquiescent public attitude was "somewhat akin to the attitude of soda-pop hawkers at a prizefight; they glance up occasionally at the fighting but their only real concern is the operation of their own businesses."[11]

At first the Assembly remained firm against pressure, with some American encouragement (see below, page 191). On May 7, 1952, it approved and publicly announced a Constitutional amendment to establish a quasi-parliamentary system, thus triggering the required thirty-day waiting period before final vote. It seemed probable that an Assembly election for President, required before August 15, would not return Rhee to office.[12]

Flying in the face of all counsels of moderation, both domestic and foreign, Rhee had a new Constitutional amendment drafted and submitted to the Assembly on May 14. Essentially similar to the one defeated in January, it offered small compromises in respect to confirmation of Cabinet and diplomatic appointments. As the vote on the May 7 proposal neared, events moved rapidly toward crisis. There was a rising crescendo of government-inspired "popular demonstrations" designed to intimidate opposition Assemblymen. Rhee told the U.S. Ambassador on May 23 that he couldn't leave office so long as his enemies threatened Korea and Korean unity, and that he would bring them to heel.[13]

On May 25, without consulting UN military authorities, Rhee declared martial law, using as a pretext the killing of four American soldiers (who may have been sacrificed for the purpose by the Koreans). Despite American pressures, he undermined the authority of his own Army Chief of Staff (Lee Chong-Chan), who opposed his policies. A campaign of intimidation and harassment against the National Assembly continued for a month, during much of which a quorum could not be mustered. Twelve Assemblymen were arrested for participation in a vague Communist (or was it Japanese?) plot, but no good evidence was ever produced for it. At one point, an entire busload of Assemblymen was held captive to prevent the conduct of Assembly business. Press censorship was imposed; for a time Voice of America radio relays on domestic stations were banned. Rhee threatened to dissolve the Assembly, although under the Constitution he had no such power. (This threat, like the recall campaign, was never actually carried out.) In the end, Rhee had his way, with a few minor compromises. A last-minute upsurge of Opposition enthusiasm, partially based on a rumor of UN intervention, dissipated after soundings by opposition leaders at the American Fourth of July reception indicated that foreigners would not intervene. On July 5, the Constitutional amendments passed unanimously, and the crisis was over.[14]

The presidential election was held on August 6, and the inauguration on August 15. Rhee won 74.6 percent of the popular vote--probably more than he would have had in a completely free environment, but nonetheless a reflection of popular sentiment. Rhee also utilized the election to dispose of Lee Bum-suk. Lee's services as Home Minister and hatchet-man had been valuable during the political crisis, and he was expected to be Rhee's running-mate; but at the last minute a political nonentity, Rev. Hahm Tai-Yung, was put forward. Word of Rhee's support for Hahm was passed among the electorate, and he won.[15]

U.S. Attitudes and Actions

The United States and its UN allies were deeply concerned over the prostitution of democratic process that was manifest in the political crisis. A number of strong representations were made by Americans and other foreign representatives, including letters and messages from President Truman, the UN Secretary General (Trygve Lie), and UNCURK, criticizing the actions taken and insisting on moderation. However, if the crisis is viewed as a struggle between Rhee and the United States, it is clear that Rhee won resoundingly. If U.S. influence had any effect, it was only in marginal areas, such as to prevent actual dissolution of the National Assembly. His success may very well have encouraged Rhee in his subsequent opposition to U.S. security and economic policies. The basic issues were Rhee's own re-election and the reassertion of executive domination. He gained both points, and still kept an electoral majority. In a situation where Rhee was fighting for his own survival as the leader of his nation, he could not be expected to compromise or capitulate, unless the United States was prepared to overthrow him. This the United States was not willing to do.

Despite the massive U.S. and UN presence in Korea at this time, including the presence of five U.S. combat divisions, American influence in the Korean political situation was limited by a number of considerations. For one thing, the issue of democratic process itself was by no means a black-and-white one. As the Deputy Chief of Mission at the U.S. Embassy (Allan Lightner) put it,

> . . . [Rhee] is right when he talks about his popular support. . . . The Assemblymen . . . know as well as anybody that the people in their constituencies would follow Rhee rather than themselves on any given issue, if there were any way for the people to express their views. . . .

All this puts us in a rather peculiar position. . . . We must oppose the undemocratic methods that Rhee and his crowd are using . . .; at the same time when the constitutionally formed legislature completely ignores the mass of the electorate and stands on its constitutional rights alone, you can hardly say it is acting in a democratic manner either.

Lightner went on to note that the Embassy staff itself was not agreed on the Korean political outlook.[16]

Moreover, U.S. leverage on domestic affairs in Korea was weakened by disagreement with Rhee over both defense and economic policies. In particular, Rhee was engaged in an all-out campaign against an armistice, partly to improve chances for his re-election. Even if this had not been the situation, intervention in Korean politics was contrary to basic American principles and, if too obvious, could be utilized by Rhee to evoke nationalist reaction. Rhee did in fact protest foreign intervention in several diplomatic conversations. (Ironically, the American Ambassador saw evidence during the crisis that the Chinese Nationalists were seeking to broaden their influence in south Korea.)[17]

Still another problem was the divergence in view between U.S. military and civilian agencies as to the extent to which Americans should be involved. Continued large-scale fighting on the battle lines, the revolt of Communist prisoners on Koje Island, and the U.S.-Korean impasse over economic aid machinery, plus Rhee's anti-armistice campaign, all added to the difficulties. Military commanders were reluctant to get into political controversy which might affect security of their rear areas. Some of the military had sympathy and admiration for Rhee's firm anti-Communism. Rhee was sensitive to differences between U.S. military and civilian attitudes, and tried to play on them. Moreover, there was apprehension in Washington (probably recognized by Rhee, who capitalized on anti-Communism in his propaganda for American consumption) that opposition to him might result in public and Congressional reaction similar to that over China policy.[18]

Furthermore, U.S. intervention would have to result either in a radical change in Rhee's policies--which was highly unlikely--or in his replacement by a more effective Korean administration. Although there were several Koreans who were ready and willing to take Rhee's place, none of them was regarded either by the United States or by the majority of Koreans as clearly able to do any better than Rhee had done in promoting national unity, stability, and security.

To compound the American dilemma further, international support for the Korean cause was likely to be adversely affected by publicity regarding abuses of democracy in the ROK, since the preservation of freedom was one of the objectives of the UN action. The Communists could be expected to capitalize on any indication that the ROK was less than utopia, and the contributions of America's allies (not to speak of the American taxpayers) to the international military and economic effort would suffer if public opinion became disenchanted with it. Thus, the Embassy recommended that a briefing of the Ambassadors of the Sixteen be held to offset unfavorable press publicity and to point out the healthy aspects of the situation. On the other hand, the possible loss of international support was used as a lever on the Koreans.[19]

For all these reasons, while some thinking and planning was done by the Americans for intervention in the Korean political situation, the U.S. Embassy maintained a position of official neutrality among presidential candidates despite pressures by various Korean factions for support. Although the Embassy's own consensus (as expressed by the Ambassador) was that "Chang Myon's chances in an election held by the National Assembly are probably our best hope," any overt outside attempt to help him would cause a flare-up of Korean sensitivities.[20]

Actual U.S. actions were limited to a concerted attempt through diplomatic pressures (with occasional hints of adverse effect on economic aid) to preserve as much as possible of democratic process. President Truman referred to the problem in his letter to Rhee of March 4. The Embassy sought to "strengthen the Assembly's backbone by reassuring key members of the Assembly's right to vote independently . . .," but Rhee's tactics soon proved such assurances hollow. The support of the UN and UNCURK was sought, both through UN Headquarters and (for UNCURK) through the Australians. Approaches were also made to US allies. U.S. representations to Canberra succeeded in returning to Korea, as Australian representative on UNCURK, a diplomat (Plimsoll) whose ability to influence the Commission and the Koreans was already proved. Andrew Cordier visited Korea in March to express the concern of the UN Secretary General. The Australian Minister for External Affairs sent Rhee a message on June 4. The British Foreign Secretary proposed a nine-point UN ultimatum, but it was never acted upon. UNCURK sent Rhee its own letter on June 7, after previous oral representations, and the Embassy, on Washington instruction, formally supported it. Ambassador Muccio, on consultation at the time in the United States, sent a personal message to Rhee in late May. The State Department also endeavored, with partial success, to present Rhee with a common U.S. military-civilian front despite the differences in viewpoint already cited.[21]

Notwithstanding all such approaches, Rhee apparently perceived that America's bark, and that of the UN and other allies, were worse than their bite. He may have been deterred from some extremes of action, but not from the main lines of his strategy. He persevered, and he won. Although his positions were not enthusiastically supported by the Korean people, they did admire his ability to cope with the foreigners, with resultant bolstering of his domestic political position.[22]

The Crisis of 1954

Following his 1952 political victory, Rhee showed "determination to carry on his fight against the Assembly until he has succeeded in reducing it to a nonentity." U.S. Embassy observers noted with regret that Rhee, confirmed in his manipulative style of politics, continued to employ it rather than to reform or strengthen his administration or to move toward meeting pressing domestic problems. In October 1952, the Embassy assessed U.S. interests as follows:

> Since US interests in this area require a situation of internal strength in the ROK, the stability of the present regime is a matter of continuing concern to us. On the surface, Rhee's regime does provide the required minimum of internal order. Aside from the extensive controls attached to the office of the ROK President, the strength of Rhee's government is primarily based upon (1) US support and (2) Rhee's personal prestige. Over this latter factor we have no control and the personal prestige of an 80-year-old man approaching senility is an extremely precarious base for a nation's stability. Difficulties will arise as Rhee's grasp of the situation deteriorates. An even more dangerous prospect is that serious internal disorder will develop in the scramble to fill the vacuum when Rhee goes. In either case, the U.S. must be prepared to face these eventualities.[23]

In the 1954 general elections, accompanied by the familiar pressures, Rhee's Liberal party all but swept the field. He then pushed again for further constitutional amendments to permit him a third term; the previous Assembly, despite its 1952 ordeal, had refused to pass one.[24]

The ensuing political crisis did not bring formal U.S. involvement, but it did have consequences that brought Korea for a brief time quite close to Western-style politics. A constitutional amendment was formally proposed by the Administration forces in the fall of 1954 which would remove the two-term limitation on the presidency, and make certain other changes, including the abolition of the position of Prime Minister in the name of government simplification, and revision of economic provisions so as to encourage private enterprise and foreign investment. There was strong opposition to the amendments, and in the vote on November 27, 135 members supported it out of the total membership of 203. Since the required two-thirds, rounded off to the next highest whole number, was 136, the presiding Vice Chairman declared that it had failed. However, Rhee and some of his supporters (with the aid of a university mathematics professor) forced a reinterpretation, known as *sa-sa-o-ip* ("drop four [tenths], add five"). Rhee signed the amendments and pro-mulgated them on November 30.[25]

Although the Administration had made some compromises to maximize support for the amendments, the high-handed arithmetical reinterpretation strengthened the opposition. Over sixty National Assemblymen joined in a Comrades' Association to Safeguard the Constitution. Intensive negotiations followed, in which the traditional conservative opposition party, the Democratic

Nationalists, joined forces with other anti-Rhee elements led by ex-Prime Minister Chang Myon (John M. Chang) and others. A new, enlarged opposition party, the Democratic Party, emerged in September 1955, and managed to surmount its internal differences until it took power in 1960. During this period, the two large parties played key roles in Korean politics, which began to show a surface resemblance to the two-party system in the United States.[26]

Trial and Execution of Cho Bong-Am

For about two years after the formation of the Democratic party, the Korean political scene was characterized by relative freedom and moderation--highlighted by Chang Myon's victory in the vice-presidential contest of 1956, and by significant opposition gains in the Assembly elections of 1958, where the two-party system seemed to be working. However, the evanescent nature of the apparent growth of Western-style democracy became evident as Rhee and his supporters moved against the growing threat to their power. The first major retrograde move was the arrest of Cho Bong-am before the 1958 election. His subsequent trial and sentence to death were such a patent travesty of justice that the United States officially (and privately) protested. The protest had no effect.

Cho Bong-am had renounced his early Communist affiliations, and was elected as one of the small number of non-Rightists in the 1948 constituent assembly. Rhee named him the first Agriculture Minister, but he was dismissed in a few months. A man of considerable charisma and ability, Cho remained politically active, and in 1955 he organized a socialistically-oriented Progressive party. He won a million votes as a presidential candidate in 1956--partly because of the Democratic candidate's untimely death, but also because of the attractiveness of his party's program, which included advocacy of steps toward peaceful unification. Thus he was a political threat to both major political parties, and both were equally suspicious of possible secret ties with north Korea. He and his followers had been excluded, after considerable controversy, in the negotiations which created the Democratic party. When Rhee's forces moved against him, the Democrats were of no mind to help.

On January 14, 1958--shortly before the campaign began for the 1958 National Assembly elections--Cho was arrested, together with Assemblyman Kim Tal-Ho, his only avowed affiliate in the legislature. Originally, the indictment was reportedly to be based upon the similarity of the Progressive party platform to north Korean proposals for unification, plus the doubtful nature of Cho's 1946 disavowal of Communist connections. However, the actual indictment on February 8 was based on charges of espionage. The change was probably due to the weakness of the subversive case, plus Korean sensitivity to the international reaction that might result from the use of the peaceful unification issue. The following month, the Office of Public Information withdrew the registration of the Progressive party, ironically under authority of American Military Government Ordinance 55.[27]

The ensuing trial in Seoul District Court was attended by a Korean employee of the U.S. Embassy, and U.S. Army Counter-Intelligence Corps agents interrogated some of the trial principals. The prosecution's case sought to tie Cho to north Korea through a courier, Yang Myong-Sam, who admitted travelling to the north and receiving and transmitting money and instructions. Cho admitted receiving money, but denied being under north Korean instructions. Yang subsequently stated that his admission of transmitting instructions had been obtained under duress. On June 13, the prosecutor demanded the death sentence for Cho.

The State Department instructed the U.S. Embassy "unofficially" to reflect serious concern regarding the death sentence to appropriate ROK officials. Ambassador Dowling called on Lee Ki-Poong, Chairman of the National Assembly and leader of the government party, and discussed the Cho case among other things. The District Court did not impose the death sentence, but on October 27 the appellate court did so, under obvious political pressure. The State Department again asked the Embassy to approach Korean officials. Ambassador Dowling replied that in view of U.S. urging for the independence of the judiciary, such intervention would be inappropriate. He added that Rhee had reportedly been delighted with the death sentence. However, the Ambassador said he would consult with Lee Ki-Poong.[28]

Nine months later, in July 1959, the Government abruptly executed Cho. The State Department instructed the Ambassador to see Rhee and point out the damage, both international and domestic, that the action would cause. However, Rhee was away on a trip, so the Ambassador talked to the Foreign Minister. The latter "made the somewhat incoherent argument that the ROK Government must maintain a stringent defense against Communism, which he feared was not always understood abroad."

The Ambassador, in his report, attributed the execution to a decision of the "hard faction" of the Liberal party to impress the opposition with the determination of the Liberals to preserve their political power. He noted that while some moderates acquiesced in the execution out of conviction that Cho was a Communist, and out of belief in a firm anti-Communist stand, majority opinion was shocked and disturbed. He regarded the Liberal party decision as another indication that the Liberals had abandoned hope of restoring their popularity and were relying solely on repressive measures. He believed that such measures would continue except when they appeared to have an impact on U.S. and international relations, and pointed to the lack of international interest in the *Kyonghyang Sinmun* closing and in the Cho execution as well, as compared with the world outcry over the National Security Law affair (see below).[29]

The National Security Law Crisis of 1958

As Ambassador Dowling had foreseen, the moderate Liberal party policies of the mid-fifties did not long endure in the face of growing opposition power. The 1958 Assembly elections and various subsequent political developments demonstrated the threat. The leading Liberal moderate (and Rhee's principal lieutenant), Assembly Chairman Lee, was increasingly handicapped by a progressive systemic disease that hindered his speech and movement. He was therefore unable to resist the growing power of a "hard faction" in the Liberal party, which moved to assure continuation of power as the 1960 presidential election approached.

The struggle focused on a proposed amendment to the National Security Law in the Fall and Winter of 1958-1959. This struggle laid the groundwork for the debacle of 1960. Its outcome was a defeat for both the opposition and the United States, which tried repeatedly and unsuccessfully to weigh in at the highest levels on the side of democratic liberties.

Amendment Proposal

The original draft amendment to the National Security Law, introduced in the Assembly in August 1958, was purportedly aimed at Communist subversion but permitted tightened restrictions on political activity and press freedom. Embassy officers perceived, as did the opposition, that the loosely-drafted bill was a threat to Korean civil liberties. In fact, it called into question the growth of American-style democratic politics of which the United States had been so proud. A new draft, submitted in November, was an improvement in some respects but worse in others; the Embassy learned that one clause, at least, was drafted with the opposition in mind.[30]

Expression of U.S. Concern

Embassy officers discussed the problem with various government and Liberal party leaders, to demonstrate the serious consequences from the international point of view. Even the usually moderate Assembly Chairman, however, was bitter in his comments on press and opposition attitudes. The Ambassador also saw Democratic party leader Cho Pyong-Ok to ask a more constructive approach to the proposed legislation. In accordance with the Ambassador's recommendation, the State Department expressed its concern to Korean Ambassador Yang in Washington. This demarche angered Rhee, who saw it as intervention in Korean affairs and an example of Embassy support for the opposition.[31]

On December 8, 1958, the Minister of Finance (Song In-Sang, also a moderate) invited the Ambassador to lunch with the Foreign, Home, and Justice ministers. The Ambassador explained the U.S. concern. The Foreign Minister (Cho Chong-Hwan) said the measure was needed because the public was immature, and needed curbing; Koreans were too active politically, and in a democratic system, the public could not be too active. However, the following day the Liberal party informally offered tentative compromise proposals to the opposition. The Ambassador doubted that the Liberal party would agree to modification of key provisions unless it became evident that the attempt to curb press freedom would have strong repercussions in the United States. He went on to draw parallels with the 1952 crisis, and observed that the success or failure of the current move for repressive measures would be decisive for the political future of Korea.[32]

Passage of the Amendment and U.S. Reaction

On December 19, taking advantage of opposition members' tardiness at a meeting of the Legislation and Justice Committee of the National Assembly, the Liberal members passed the National Security bill in a three-minute session. The Democratic Assemblymen, joined by five independents, began a sit-down strike the same evening to prevent further legislative action. The next day, fighting broke out in the chamber. No meeting was held, but the Finance Minister told Embassy officers it was too late for compromise, and the bill would be passed in a few days.[33]

Ambassador Dowling recommended to Washington that an effort be made to stimulate American press coverage of the crisis, as the only way to convince the Koreans of the need to eliminate restrictive press provisions. The Ambassador repeated his plea for action on December 22, stating that "opposition now would be preferable in terms of U.S.-ROK relations, to later and perhaps more bitter controversy as well as more productive of results." In the absence of such action, he believed the United States would lose influence with both sides.[34]

The State Department's response was at first not helpful. The Korean press prominently displayed the Department spokesman's statement on December 23 that the National Security Law was a domestic affair of the ROK and he would not comment on it. However, Department officers conferred meanwhile and arranged for President Eisenhower to send a personal letter to President Rhee. Congressman Walter Judd, a long-time friend of Rhee, also agreed to send a letter, which expressed a similar general line. The Department made a statement on December 24 (hailed by the Korean opposition as unprecedented) hoping the National Security Law would not be used to hinder democratic development. Although a U.S. Development Loan Fund loan for hydroelectric development in Korea was approved on December 23, its public announcement was postponed and eventually made in March 1959.[35]

Unfortunately, events in Seoul moved too fast for the Presidential letter to have effect. While opposition legislators were forcibly confined to the basement restaurant, Liberal members of the Assembly passed the National Security Law with only inconsequential amendment. First Secretary William Jones of the U.S. Embassy was refused admission to the chamber, although the press was allowed--an action which was protested to the Koreans in both Seoul and Washington, and won an apology. The Embassy viewed both the content of the law and the manner of its passing as a "grave setback to the development of Korean democracy."[36]

When Ambassador Dowling delivered President Eisenhower's letter to Rhee in his vacation retreat at Chinhae on December 27, Rhee appeared uninformed on the details of what had gone on in the National Assembly, but sincerely convinced of the need for an amended National Security Law. He drew a parallel with the 1952 crisis, questioned the Embassy's contacts with the opposition, and suggested that Embassy reporting was distorted, like that of Ambassador Muccio in 1952. When the Vice Minister of Foreign Affairs refused to confirm or deny the Ambassador's statement that opposition Assembly members had been forcibly detained, Rhee ordered a full report, but it seemed unlikely that he would learn the whole truth. In January 1959, Rhee commented to the Ambassador (who called before leaving for consultation) that departures from normal democratic practice were necessary because of the struggle against the Communists.[37]

Political Consequences

The impasse between Liberals and Democrats continued into January. U.S. pressures also continued. There were two critical *Washington Post* editorials, and correspondents of several American newspapers and news services arrived in Seoul. Ambassador Dowling was recalled to Washington for consultation, where he presented a thoughtful analysis and recommendations for U.S. action. The Embassy was instructed to restrict senior U.S. contacts with the ROK to the most essential activities during his absence. The pressures had some effect, as demonstrated by the surveillance of the U.S. Embassy by "tough plain clothes elements of the national police" and challenging of visitors, which abated after a protest to the Foreign Ministry. Democratic Assemblymen attempted a march on the Embassy on January 13, but police intervened, and chased one photographer into the Embassy lobby.[38]

By January 20, tension had somewhat subsided. Democratic leader Cho Pyong-Ok met Assembly Chairman Lee, and a joint communique was issued. A UPI story the same day that the United States would informally encourage compromise got wide attention and some critical Democratic comment. Although small anti-National Security Law demonstrations continued, inter-party negotiations brought about some reduction of tension. The presence of American reporters may have prompted the government to keep the police as inconspicuous as possible. On February 2, an Embassy officer talked to Democratic leaders on the need to compromise and return to normal parliamentary procedures. He urged (to little avail) that the Democrats abandon their demand for an apology. On January 24, at a press conference, Secretary of State Dulles made a statement on the Korean crisis, concluding, "We want to follow that situation closely, and if we can, exert any friendly influence that will be welcomed or accepted, to try to keep Korea in the way of a model democratic country."[39]

Rhee himself was not swayed by developments. This was apparent when on January 29 he called the U.S. economic aid mission head (Warne) to see him about an office building project, and gave a lecture on the evils of the (Korean) Democratic party and the irresponsible things being said about Korea in the United States. He commented that the United States and the United Nations came close to interference in local affairs at times. On January 26, Rhee told an Associated Press correspondent that the amended law was needed to combat Communist subversive efforts, and maintained that the government had no intention of using it for political purposes. Asked about possibilities of revision, Rhee said he wished his American friends would wait and see, instead of talking about it.[40]

Although contacts continued, Liberals and Democrats were unable to agree on the basic issues separating them. Both sides appeared to be waiting to see what Ambassador Dowling would bring back from Washington. The Democrats wanted drastic revision in five articles of the National Security Law, as well as other legal and tactical concessions, while the Liberals were making virtually no concessions. On February 26, Cho Pyong-Ok told Embassy officers there was no prospect of Liberal concessions until Rhee decided to order a compromise, which was not likely; hence there was no reason for Cho to see Rhee, as had been suggested. Instead, he asked the Embassy to tell Rhee that the United States believed a compromise was necessary. The Embassy agreed that Rhee's intervention was necessary, but commented that Democratic intransigence had also contributed to the stalemate. Meantime, the Korean press reported meetings of the Director of the Office of Northeast Asian Affairs (David Bane) with Liberal and Democratic leaders during his visit to Seoul in late February.[41]

Following the National Assembly recess on March 20, a series of inter-party talks led to the formation of a ten-man consultative committee to compromise the legislative deadlock. However, nothing of substance was accomplished, and the bipartisan effort collapsed on May 11. The failure, due to rigidity of positions on both sides, suggested that so long as the current balance of power between the two parties continued, crisis rather than compromise would be the prevailing mode. In retrospect it seems clear, despite various recommendations for U.S. action, that the United States was unable to change the situation with the limited means and resources it was willing to employ.[42]

If the unwillingness of the United States to intervene in Korea needed any further demonstration, that demonstration was provided in May 1959. Retired Admiral Felix Stump, former commander of the U.S. forces in the Pacific, on behalf of the Freedoms Foundation, presented Rhee with the Freedoms Leadership Award. Here was a fresh demonstration of the differences among American attitudes that Rhee effectively utilized for his own purposes throughout his twelve-year administration, which, in Rhee's eyes and those of other Koreans, lent some credence to the view that the Embassy was not really representative of American opinion.[43]

Fall of the Rhee Government, 1960

The American policy of supporting Rhee's administration in Korea, while he lived, was based upon four considerations: (1) he had effective control in Korea, based on his prestige, his own political shrewdness, and the inertia of an established system; (2) there seemed to be no other Korean who had greater promise of effective leadership and maintaining political stability; (3) U.S. intervention in Korean political affairs, despite their obvious shortcomings by American standards, was risky and uncertain in its probable effect; (4) there was a good deal of American Establishment sympathy for Rhee's firm anti-Communist posture. At the same time, there was much criticism of American policy, both by the liberal American press and by academic figures in the United States and (privately) by Korean opposition leaders, especially in periods of political crisis. The United States endeavored to put pressure on Rhee and his government to moderate their policies; but such pressure was increasingly ignored.

Growing Repression; Ascendancy of the "Hard Faction"

Beginning with the National Security Law crisis of 1958, the overriding desire of the ROK government and Liberal party to assure continuance of power, plus Rhee's loss of finesse and perception as he grew more senile, made the Korean ruling group increasingly blatant in its indifference to democratic principles, and virtually impervious to American pressure. The obvious gap between democratic ideals and Korean reality aroused mounting opposition in the United States and abroad, called both U.S. and UN policies and programs into question, and played into the hands of Communist critics in United Nations debates.

Many U.S. officials were privately unhappy with continuing American inaction, and the Embassy in Korea warned Washington of the possibility of disorder if the trends of 1959 continued. But no course of U.S. government action to reverse these trends seemed feasible. American representatives continued to remonstrate, and Korean officials, with the "hard" faction in the ascendancy, continued to smile and ignore them. In September 1959, Rhee himself told Sydney Hook, the American conservative philosopher, with satisfaction of the numerous occasions on which he had refused to take American advice, adding that the U.S. Embassy was misinformed on Korean affairs and that he got along better with American military personnel than with civilians.[44]

Dress Rehearsal: The 1959 By-Elections

The resolve of Rhee's supporters to win the 1960 presidential election by any necessary means, despite Rhee's declining popularity and mounting popular support for the opposition Democratic party, was clearly demonstrated in two September 1959 by-elections. These elections, obviously dress rehearsals for the 1960 election, produced the largest victory margins for the Liberals in Korean history. The Democratic candidates withdrew before the final count, amid general gloom in opposition circles. UNCURK observers "witnessed more than a few violations of the Assembly election laws." Nevertheless, the government insisted that the elections were fair. One of the opposition leaders, in a talk with U.S. Embassy officers, observed that the continuation of existing trends would lead to violence. However, there is no record of any protest either by UNCURK or by the United States.[45]

The 1960 Election Campaign

In January 1960, the United States commenced to take a firmer stand toward Korea, based on experience with several 1959 crises (the north Korean repatriation problem, ROK Ambassador Yang's abuses of office in Washington, and the problem of U.S.-financed imports from Japan). The U.S. objective was to change ROK attitudes in matters directly affecting U.S. interests, and to "cause ROKG[overnment] to conduct its affairs as mature and responsible member Free World Community." It was concluded that the risk of irrational ROK reaction to such steps must be taken. "This decision most difficult since it evident ROKG in past has believed it could force U.S. back down out of fear that U.S. firmness might impair maintenance our military and political posture in Korea . . .; but "ROKG should be disabused of such belief." The new policy was applied to the exchange rate problem, to Korean relations with Japan, and ultimately to the problem of the March 15 presidential election; but the Korean leaders did not immediately get the message.[46]

In February 1960, the ROK government formally announced that the presidential election would be held on March 15--a much earlier date than normal, intended to disadvantage the opposition. Fate dealt struggling democracy a gratuitous blow: the most effective opposition leader and presidential candidate, Cho Pyong-Ok, died of cancer in Walter Reed Hospital in Washington. Nevertheless, the government and Liberal party pressed their attack, undeterred by the presence of UNCURK and Embassy observer teams. Campaign abuses, including beatings, became so frequent and obvious that they provoked student demonstrations.

The opposition Vice President, in an interview with the visiting U.S. Deputy Under Secretary of State (Loy Henderson) on March 12, commented that it was "difficult for Korean masses to understand why U.S. tolerated such defamation of democracy," and recommended a U.S. presidential letter to Rhee and an official U.S. statement. On election eve (March 14), in response to a press question on the situation, the State Department spokesman noted the American policy of non-interference and the difficulty of "maintaining democracy on the borders of Communism," but said in the course of his response, "This Government naturally has been concerned about the acts of violence which have taken place in connection with the preparations for the elections on March 15."[47]

The Election and Early Reaction

The elections themselves, attended by widespread and blatant abuses, delivered substantial and unbelievable majorities for Rhee and his chosen running-mate, Lee Ki-Poong (the latter now so feeble that he was virtually unable to campaign). Domestically, the public reaction ranged from widespread sullen resentment to rioting and violence. There was a tremendous outcry in the American press. In the south coast city of Masan, where the authorities refused to certify large numbers of voters, demonstrations escalated into hostilities between the police and the demonstrating crowds; a number of people were killed (largely students) and many more injured. Korean military authorities asked, and received, the United Nations Commander's permission to send troops in to restore order. The U.S. Embassy feared adverse political consequences from this decision, but in the event only fifty Korean Marines were used (with a reserve division standing by), and the CINCUNC decision was fortunately not publicized.[48]

The first U.S. government reaction to the elections was an Embassy recommendation to delay any action that might be interpreted as American support for what had happened. Announcement of an approved development loan was therefore deferred. On the other hand, the Embassy strongly recommended against holding back scheduled military and economic assistance allocations, because "such actions . . . would tend to undermine basic US objectives in Korea."

Stronger action was taken on the day after the election. The Secretary of State (Herter) called in the Korean Ambassador (Yang) and handed him a firmly-worded aide-memoire dealing both with the intransigent ROK attitude toward Japan (see Chapter 4, page 132) and with election abuses. The Secretary expressed his concern regarding American Congressional and public reaction to reports about the Korean election, which might adversely affect the American aid program. He noted that pressures in the election campaign "which exceeded the norm of democratic practice" were particularly distressing since there had been no real opposition candidate against Rhee. The Korean Ambassador's response was to deny intimidation, claim that American journalists were overly influenced by Chang Myon, and insinuate that Catholic influence was involved in the accusations.[49]

Following the Secretary's conversation, the State Department spokesman briefed the press. Regarding the ROK election, he said,

> . . . the Secretary also expressed his and this Government's concern over the many reports of violence and irregularities occurring in connection with the Korean Presidential elections on March 15. He reminded Ambassador Yang that although this Government has no intention of interfering in the internal affairs of Korea, it believes firmly in the free expression of popular will through fair elections and deplores any actions taken contrary thereto.[50]

The ROK government's response was not encouraging. The Home Minister and his deputy, and the chief of the national police, submitted their resignations, and a new Home Minister (Hong Chin-Ki) was appointed on March 23, but this appointment was not regarded by the Embassy as any improvement. Rhee once again called for a "march north" for unification. Noting the pointlessness of the large-scale coercion in the elections, the Embassy hypothesized that

> . . . for a few powerful placed individuals . . . these elections may have been approached as first crucial test their ability employ powers government to override all organized opposition and perpetuate their hold on power even after death President Rhee.

The reaction to such tactics in Korea had been greater anti-government feeling than at any time since the founding of the Republic, and lessening of popular confidence and respect for the United States and for democratic processes. Concurrently, there was mounting U.S. Congressional criticism of the lack of economic progress in Korea, and its police-state tendencies.[51]

Beginning a few days after the election, the U.S. Embassy initiated an exchange of views between Washington and the field as to what the United States could do to improve the situation. It was agreed that the United States should not do anything that would imply American indifference or approval of the conduct of the election; therefore such events as the dedication of a new fertilizer plant (an American aid showpiece) should be deferred. On the other hand, the Embassy was less willing than Washington to impose economic sanctions by slowing down military or economic aid, since this might have the reverse of the desired effect. The Embassy also noted (in the light of sad past experience) that the United States could not hope to act effectively to "prevent further dangerous erosion in ROK domestic and international positions" unless there was "full coordinated support from all US agencies concerned and adequate coordination with Congress," since "ROKs tend to feel that State

Department positions and pronouncements are not necessarily those of US Government as a whole, land ROKs have developed elaborate and not ineffective means for circumventing Department and of playing one US branch or agency against another." The Embassy further noted the need for clear speaking on the part of the United States, notwithstanding the domestic non-interference policy. "Our blood, money, reputation, and security are heavily invested in Korea. We have perhaps less reason to be passive observers here than anywhere else. . . ." The Department acquiesced in the Embassy's economic views, but stated that programs involving waste or misuse of American funds should be cut back or revised, and noted the likelihood of reduced aid appropriations for Korea.[52]

In the period of uneasy post-election quiet in Korea, the ROK government formula continued to be one of no compromise, and the opposition Democratic party showed signs of breaking up. Noting U.S. support for the retention of a healthy two-party system in Korea, the State Department instructed the Embassy to approach both Democratic and moderate Liberal party leaders. To the latter, the Embassy was to indicate the extent to which Korea had lost prestige in the United States and internationally, and the need for the ROK "immediately move to set its house in order, particularly before UNGA [General Assembly] convenes this autumn."[53]

The Second Round: Masan, the U.S. Aide-Memoire, and the Student Revolution

Before the Embassy could do much along the lines of its instructions, the lowering political storm broke. On April 12, the body of a student was recovered from Masan harbor, with "four wooden pegs driven through the right eye" (subsequently explained as grenade fragments). The police had denied any knowledge of the student's whereabouts since March 15. Crowds, first of students, then growing numbers of townspeople--to an eventual total of 40,000--went on a general offensive against the police, the Liberal party, and government. The police fired on the crowd, then fell back in confusion.

Again CINCUNC was asked for, and granted, permission to use Korean military forces. Rhee's reaction was a statement indicating that he was prepared to crack down on all anti-Administration activities, which he viewed as largely Communist-inspired. The Embassy reported that the situation required urgent action, since the ROK government was unlikely to act constructively unless pushed, and suggested several lines of such action. At the same time, Washington was drafting an aide-memoire (unfortunately delayed in transmission to Seoul) along lines similar to Embassy recommendations. Revised somewhat to include some of the recommendations, the aide-memoire was handed by Secretary Herter to Ambassador Yang in Washington.[54]

Forthrightly critical and implicitly threatening in tone, the aide-memoire reflected the policy "new look" in effect since January (see page 200 above).

It stated that the post-election disorders were a result of popular anger; that the situation had to be corrected to restore public confidence in democratic freedoms, in order to prevent Communist exploitation or other adverse consequences. The aide-memoire called for ROK investigation of election abuses, amendment of election laws, reopening of the opposition newspaper *Kyonghyang Sinmun*, repeal of restrictive amendments of the law on local elections, and implementation of constitutional provisions for an upper legislative house (included in the 1952 amendment but never enforced).

Concurrently with these developments, disorders were spreading through south Korea. Martial law was declared in Seoul and several other cities. Finally, on April 19, a crowd of up to 100,000 students and sympathizers demonstrated before the presidential palace in Seoul and demanded admission. The terrified palace guards fired point-blank at the demonstrators, a number of whom were killed. A complete breakdown of order in the capital ensued. A total of at least 115 people lost their lives and 730 were injured--mostly students and private citizens. Military forces were then called upon to restore order. This they easily did, aided by the students, with whom they generally sympathized.[55]

Rhee's Resignation and the U.S. Role

Ambassador McConaughy called on Rhee on the traumatic night of April 19, with only the Defense Minister (Kim Chung-Yul, a young and capable former Air Force commander) and the Home Minister (Hong Chin-Ki) present. Rhee, while he seemed to be in possession of his faculties, was obviously ill-informed on the situation. He blamed the Democrats, including Vice President Chang, and unnamed behind-the-scenes subversives, for all the trouble. He was not aware of the scope of the popular demonstrations. McConaughy endeavored to make Rhee realize the true nature of the situation, with "some limited measure of success"; but he "saw no evidence of recognition of basic issues or any disposition to come up with answers to them." This lack of recognition was highlighted two days later, when the Ambassador delivered the aide-memoire to the President. Rhee insisted that the troubles were a plot by Vice President Chang, supported by the Catholic archbishop, and dwelt on State Department naivete and misunderstanding of the situation.[56]

Although the United States government did not divulge the contents of the aid-memoire (which Rhee insisted to McConaughy should be kept strictly confidential), public statements in both Seoul and Washington left no doubt as to the U.S. position. After the Secretary met the ROK Ambassador on April 19, the Department spokesman issued a statement referring to the "profound and growing concern of this Government over the serious, continuing public unrest and acts of violence in Korea," and noting the U.S. Government belief "that the demonstrations in Korea are a reflection of popular dissatisfaction over the conduct of the recent elections and repressive measures unsuited to a free democracy." In Seoul, in response to press inquiries about Ambassador McConaughy's April 19 call on Rhee, the Embassy issued a statement explaining that the Ambassador had called to review developments and express concern that ROK government actions "would take into account the basic causes and grievances behind the disorders." At the height of the disorders in Seoul, the Ambassador issued a statement, after checking with a Cabinet member then at the presidential palace, calling upon both demonstrators and authorities to act "with a view to the immediate restoration of law and order and a settlement of justifiable grievances toward which the demonstrations are directed." This statement aided in calming the atmosphere in Seoul and--with other U.S. statements and actions--largely restored Korean public esteem for the United States. American press reaction was generally favorable, although the *Washington Star* supported ROK government actions and criticized American interference.[57]

After the Ambassador's second interview with Rhee, the Department informed Seoul that it was "both highly disappointed and concerned" at Rhee's lack of understanding of the situation, finding his charges of conspiracy preposterous and his proposed repressive course of action "a tragic farce and mockery." A firm line would continue to be followed by the United States; public statements would continue when necessary, despite Rhee's vexation at them; but no further demarche was contemplated until there was a clearer picture as to how Rhee would respond. Meantime, the Embassy should communicate U.S. government concern to a "variety of responsible and influential personalities," and plan for isolating Rhee and his supporters so as to replace them with a new administration, as well as for action in the event of Rhee's demise or overthrow. The contingencies foreseen by the Department included a coup d'état and a military takeover as a caretaker government.

American authorities were not alone in their concern: the ROK Chief of Naval Operations on April 20 urged the U.S. Naval Attache to press through the Ambassador and Rhee for Lee Ki-Poong's resignation. The CNO said that many high military and civilian officers believed it was necessary, but none had the courage to propose it themselves--Lee was so powerful that anyone who did would "lose his head."[58]

In the next few days, Rhee began to realize more fully the gravity of the situation as some courageous men, including a few of his own staff and Cabinet, and ex-prime ministers Huh Chung and Pyun Yung-Tai, explained it to him. On April 23, Vice President Chang resigned. On April 25, a demonstration led by two hundred university professors called for the resignation of Rhee and the entire government and the holding of new elections. By evening, forty to fifty thousand demonstrators were massed before the National Assembly building, and moving on Lee Ki-Poong's residence (which was destroyed). Once again, the

Embassy moved to calm the situation with a public statement, concluding, "This is no time for temporizing."[59]

The denouement came on April 26. With at least fifty thousand demonstrators marching toward the center of the city, Ambassador McConaughy telephoned the Defense Minister, shortly after nine in the morning, asking him to get Rhee to receive a delegation of students and issue a statement on new elections. Rhee did receive a group of five citizens, including two students. About an hour afterward, as the Ambassador, in company with CINCUNC (General Magruder), was proceeding to the presidential palace, Rhee issued a dramatic four-point statement indicating (1) his willingness to resign, (2) the holding of new elections, (3) the resignation of Lee Ki-Poong from all his positions, (4) action to amend the constitution for a parliamentary system.[60]

In Rhee's meeting with the Ambassador and CINCUNC, the Koreans present asked prompt U.S. support for Rhee's four-point statement, before troublemakers could adversely influence the population. The Ambassador tactfully indicated that it was time for Rhee to resign the presidency, and pointed to the need for some statement responding to public resentment at the police role in the election and subsequent events. Rhee and his advisers were somewhat vague on the specifics and details of their four points. At the end of the meeting, as he returned from the presidential palace, the Ambassador was given a tremendous public ovation. He then met with the press. Without specifically endorsing Rhee's four-point statement (the Department had instructed him not to do so), he said he was convinced that Rhee and his government would carry them out. He added a "fifth point": that the government would reform the police.

Among the questions asked by the press was, "It is being said that the revolution was achieved one-half by the student demonstrations and one-half by the U.S. Embassy. The Ambassador answered,

> Our consistent intention has been not to interfere in any improper way. We have tried to show our affection for the Korean people. Our actions have been motivated by our closeness to the Korean people and to the Korean government. We feel we know what the people consider to be their justifiable grievances. We have also maintained close and friendly contact with President Rhee. I hope the President and his advisers, his cabinet, will have opportunity to carry through these reforms in an atmosphere of order and security.

Later the same eventful day, a bare quorum of the National Assembly (with "hard faction" Liberals absent) unanimously passed a resolution calling for Rhee's immediate resignation. The Assembly also resolved that the March 15 election was invalid; that a new election should be held; that the constitution should be amended to provide for a parliamentary system of government; and that this should be accomplished under an interim cabinet, with a new legislature to be elected thereafter.

In the next day or two, Rhee resigned; Lee Ki-Poong and his family committed suicide together; and Huh Chung (in whose previous appointment as senior cabinet minister the U.S. had heartily concurred) became Acting President, naming respected and relatively nonpolitical figures to his interim cabinet.[61]

The Aftermath

In view of the unprecedented extent of U.S. influence and support in Korea resulting from virtually universal acclamation of the role its representatives had played during the April crisis, the Department exchanged views with the Embassy on what role the United States should play in shaping the future government of Korea. In a June message, the Department indicated that an experiment with parliamentary government should be tried, both because the people wanted it (and the former opposition was committed to it) and because it might bring leaders to the fore. However, there were obvious handicaps and weaknesses, which might be minimized by having an assured moderately-oriented majority in the legislature; hence the United States should "discreetly support" the Democratic party in the election campaign. Optimally, Chang Myon should be elected titular President and a younger, more dynamic man of executive ability should become Prime Minister. The present Defense Minister should preferably be retained for at least a few months, to ensure stability in the armed forces; this would be "most effective way of meeting rumors of coup d'état, whether or not they have any validity."[62]

The U.S. "discreet support" was provided, and was perhaps a factor in returning a crushing Democratic majority--so large, in fact, that the Democrats split among themselves. The weaknesses foreseen by the Department quickly appeared: Chang Myon became Prime Minister; the interim Defense Minister (Lee Chong-Chan) was an early casualty. Thus, although the interim government under Huh Chung, with American backing, did a creditable job of holding Korea together, the Democratic administration which succeeded it was unable to provide the necessary strong leadership and forward movement, despite massive American support. The 1961 military coup d'état resulted.

In May 1960, the State Department summarized for all diplomatic posts the U.S. policy in Korea, and the reasons for what had happened there. It noted that President Rhee "was not brought down by U.S. initiative," but the United States "could not have saved him had we wanted to," and any attempt to do so would have made matters worse for both the ROK and the United States. "Department and Embassy public and private statements and actions were not designed to stem tide brought on by Korean people, and doubtless augmented it." However, the U.S. role in Korea was unusual in view of the American obligations there. Moreover, every attempt had been made, and would be made, to minimize interfering with "internal dynamism of Korean national life." The

Department did not intend to draw parallels with other countries, although it would keep its options open, and did not foreclose the possibility that the "lessons" of Korea might be partially applicable to such situations as Turkey and Vietnam.

Among the many expressions of approbation both in Korea and abroad for the policies and actions of the United States and its Ambassador in Korea, one is particularly touching. The Embassy reported on April 27, 1960:

> At height of demonstration yesterday a large floral wreath with message of tribute was placed on statue of General MacArthur in Seoul. It hangs from his hand holding binoculars.
>   This spontaneous unadvertised action by Seoul citizens symbolizes attitude of Korea toward Americans.[63]

The "Military Revolution"

The brief and confused Korean experiment in parliamentary democracy was abruptly ended on May 16, 1961. Moving swiftly and with a degree of secrecy unusual in Korean politics, Major General Park Chung Hee and a small group of field-grade Army and Marine Corps officers seized control of key government and communication centers in Seoul within a few pre-dawn hours. The government of Chang Myon offered little significant opposition; Chang himself at first went into hiding. In a week, the junta's hold on the country was secure. The Chang Cabinet, after being cornered into resignation, was placed under house arrest; the National Assembly was dissolved; a series of emergency decrees and actions placed military men in control of government and instituted a Spartan regime for the country, designed to secure public compliance in the new order and to root out corruption and malfeasance.

U.S. Policies and Actions: Initial Stages

At 3:32 a.m. on May 16, 1961 (Korean time), American intelligence reported that a coup d'état attempt had commenced at about 1 a.m. During the early morning hours, the ROK Army Chief of Staff, General Chang Do-Young, asked the Commander-in-Chief, United Nations Command (General Carter Magruder) for commitment of U.S. forces to help put the coup down. General Magruder refused, pointing out that his authority related solely to the external security of Korea. He made it clear, however, that he supported General Chang's intention to support the legal government. Reporting to Washington at 5 a.m., the Chargé d'Affaires *ad interim* (Marshall Green) said he agreed with this decision, "although we of course support duly constituted authorities here, and will make this clear.[64]

General Chang called senior Army commanders to Seoul to sound out opinion. In accordance with American advice, however, he did not call the commander of the key front-line First Army, General Lee Han-Lim, who would thereby risk capture. Chang's soundings apparently led him to conclude that the Army's loyalty to the government was not assured.[65] Accordingly, faced with combined appeals and threats from representatives of the coup group, General Chang joined it and was named titular head of the military government.

General Magruder issued a public statement on the advice of the Korean Army commander: calling for support by the Korean armed forces of the duly established government:

> General Magruder, in his capacity as commander in chief of the United Nations command, calls upon all military personnel in his command to support the newly recognized government of the Republic of Korea headed by primin Chang Myon. General Magruder expects that the Chiefs of the Korean armed forces will use their authority and influence to see that control is immediately turned back to the lawful governmental authorities and that order is restored in the armed forces.

This statement was publicly supported by the Chargé d'Affaires as follows:

> The position taken by the commander in chief of the United Nations command in supporting the freely elected and constitutionally established government of the Republic of Korea is one in which I fully concur. I wish to make it emphatically clear that the United States supports the constitutional government of the Republic of Korea as elected by the people of the Republic last July and as constituted last August with the election of a Prime Minister.

Both statements were carried on the U.S. Armed Forces radio, but were reported (due to censorship) in only one Korean newspaper close to Prime Minister Chang.

The American representatives faced two serious problems in supporting the Chang Myon administration. First was the general lack of public enthusiasm for the government. Although in the previous five months it had begun to attack basic economic and social problems, its real accomplishments were overshadowed in the public mind by the endless political bickering and maneuvering in the National Assembly, the mounting corruption, and the continuing economic difficulties of the country (always worst at this time of year). Second, Prime Minister Chang Myon himself had disappeared from his suite in the Bando Hotel (across the street from the U.S. Embassy) an hour after the coup began, and his whereabouts, as well as those of many of the Cabinet, were unknown. Thus, in the critical hours when the coup leaders were consolidating their control, there was not alternative leadership to support.

Additionally, the principle of non-intervention greatly restricted the freedom of American action, even though the American role in the revolution of 1960 was both generally known and generally applauded. Yet the United States could not remain wholly passive. Like all previous political aspirants, the coup leaders were conveying the impression that they had American support.

The Prime Minister telephoned the Chargé on the morning of May 16. Without divulging his whereabouts, he expressed his appreciation for the American statements issued, and "urged that CINCUNC 'take charge' of situation." At the initiative of President Yun Bo-Sun, the Chargé went to call on the President at 11 a.m., conferring with him for three hours and a half. CINCUNC was also present.

The President received General Magruder's evaluation of the situation--which was that the coup was actively supported only by a small group within the Army, and that General Chang remained loyal to the government. CINCUNC emphasized "that [seizure] of governmental authority by a small insurgent group at gunpoint would be disastrous for future of Korea." The Chargé, supporting this point and the risk that one coup would lead to others, also pointed out the damage to Korea's international standing. He added that despite popular dissatisfaction and disillusionment with the Chang government, it had made real progress in attacking the country's problems. President Yun was unimpressed. He said that "Korea needed a strong government and that Chang Myon had proved himself incapable of providing such leadership." The President said he had refrained from giving any commitment to the coup group when Generals Chang Do-Young and Park Chung Hee, together with Chang Myon's Defense Minister and the chiefs of the military services, had called on him that morning; but if the coup should expand, he would resign the presidency. It was his opinion that a suprapartisan national cabinet should be formed, including leaders from within and outside the National Assembly.[66]

The Chargé emphasized that from the U.S. standpoint the essential element was that constitutional processes, from which the President himself derived his position, should be respected; if necessary, the problem of national leadership should be referred to the people in a constitutional manner. General Magruder asked whether the President would approve calling upon loyal ROK Army units to

take up positions surrounding Seoul in number overwhelming in comparison with coup group so that negotiations with insurgents could be conducted from position of secure government strength.

The President said he was not prepared to give his approval, in view of the possibility of bloodshed. He preferred trying to persuade the insurgents to withdraw voluntarily. However, the President's position was apparently somewhat influenced by American firmness, and he professed agreement that a change of government should be accomplished through constitutional means. Yet the Prime Minister and his Cabinet were nowhere in evidence; and some senior Army commanders had apparently conveyed to the President their acquiescence in the coup. Meanwhile, as time passed, the coup forces' position was solidifying.[67]

Careful, minute-to-minute reporting from the U.S. Embassy reached the State Department in a steady stream during the night of May 15-16 (Washington time), and during the following day. In the late evening of May 16, Assistant Secretary Walter McConaughy despatched a cable to the Embassy in response. The cable recognized

> the desirability of restoring authority of lawful government against reckless challenge of military clique invoking force to upset government freely chosen by Korean people under their own constitutional system. Even though no ideological issue apparently involved, our assessment is that coup attempt undermines stability and reputation of ROK and therefore is contrary to our joint interests.

However, the message continued, the Department had adopted a "cautious attitude of wait-and-see . . . pending clarification of situation." Considerations were the unwillingness of the President and other leaders to move, the disappearance of the Prime Minister and other Cabinet members, and the indifference of the general public.

> We will continue to hope Government can reestablish itself and we will avoid any action which would adversely affect its prospects. On the other hand, in absence some indication government able and willing put forth some effective effort save itself, we will refrain from public identification of U.S. with fate of what may be a lost cabinet."

The message added that the public statements made by the Chargé and CINCUNC were approved, and that the Department's press statement the previous noon was not a repudiation of them.[68]

In reaching its assessment that the coup was not Communist-inspired, and probably could not be controlled by the Chang Myon government, the Department had the fortuitous benefit of Korean advice as well as Embassy reporting. The highly respected Speaker of the ROK House of Representatives, Kwak Sang-hoon, had arrived a few days before on an official visit. On May 16, he called on Assistant Secretary McConaughy, whom he had known as Ambassador to Korea. Although opposing the coup, which he believed to represent only a small part of the Korean armed forces, the Speaker was confident that it was not Communist-inspired. On the other hand, the Speaker implied that CINCUNC "should not tolerate a situation which might endanger the nation's fate." The ROK Ambassador (Chang Lee-Wook) and Minister-Counselor (Koh Kwang-Lim) both urged American intervention in support of their government, but argued on the basis that instability would invite Communist intervention, rather than that Communists were involved. General Song Yo-Chan, former Army Chief of Staff and currently a student at The American University, as well as other high-ranking Korean military officers in the United States, called at the State Department to discuss the coup both at the time and subsequently. Among them, only General Choe Kyong-Nok (who arrived in the United States some time after the coup) argued that the coup was Communist-connected.[69]

On the morning of May 17, CINCUNC telegraphed his estimate of the situation to the Chairman of the U.S. Joint Chiefs of Staff. Noting that Prime Minister Chang "does not have a reputation for personal courage," and that there was little general support for him in any quarter, General Magruder observed,

> In summary all the powerful men in and around the Seoul government appear to have had knowledge of the plan for the coup and at least have not opposed it. The people appear to be divided for and against but they do not appear to be sufficiently concerned at this time to take an active part.[70]

He went on to conclude that the uprising did not appear to be Communist-inspired, although its leader, Park Chung Hee, had been at one time tainted with Communism. The ROK First Army, under his (Magruder's) operational control, would probably at the moment follow CINCUNC orders to suppress the uprising; but such orders, in the continued absence of Chang Myon, would restore a leaderless government, and the possibility that such action would be successful was diminishing with time. Moreover, General Magruder noted, his mission was the external security of Korea. For this purpose, "the Korean forces appear to be steadfast." His mission also included protection of Korea from Communist subversion; but the uprising did not appear to be Communist-inspired. "Accordingly I do not propose to direct FROKA [First ROK Army] to suppress the uprising on my own authority only."

Responding to a message from the Chairman of the U.S. Joint Chiefs of Staff (General Lyman Lemnitzer), CINCUNC commented that support he envisaged for the Prime Minister "if he comes out of hiding" would be "personally urging Lee Han-lim [First ROK Army Commander] and all other officers of the ROK military forces to comply with the orders of the Prime Minister if the prospects of success are favorable." This eventuality never materialized, since Chang came out of hiding only to resign his office.[71]

By the evening of May 17 (Washington time), the State Department reached, and cabled to the Embassy in Seoul, an interim policy position to work with the Military Revolutionary Committee to the extent necessary to "encourage early emergence of broadly based, responsible non-partisan government of national unity and of predominantly civilian composition." The importance was noted of "conferring to maximum attainable extent an aura of legality, continuity and legitimate constitutional succession" on a successor government --an objective best achieved by keeping President Yun Bo-Sun in office. President Yun did remain in office, despite one attempt to resign; the United States was thus relieved of the necessity to make a decision on recognizing the military regime as a new government.[72]

In Seoul, during the evening of May 17, Reconstruction Minister Chu Yo-Han telephoned the Embassy to report that a group of Cabinet ministers had decided to resign in order to "save the face of many people" and avoid bloodshed, but wanted the Embassy to arrange for them to consult with the Prime Minister before doing so. Other Cabinet officers also called the Embassy for advice as to whether they should resign, and were advised to follow the lead of the still-missing Prime Minister. Finally around noon the following day (May 18), Prime Minister Chang arrived at a State Council meeting in his office, his surfacing arranged by his American assistant, Donald Whitaker. He signed a resignation substantially as worked out during the all-night meeting of ministers in his office. All the ministers signed the statement; then, driven by Whitaker, they went to the President's residence to present it, and went to be confined under guard in their own homes.[73]

When the Commanding General of the First ROK Army, General Lee Han-Lim, issued a statement on May 17 (apparently under duress), throwing his support behind the revolutionary coup, the success of the coup was assured. The Chargé (Green) assessed the development as follows:

> Coup d'état succeeded partly because of dissatisfaction over economic hardships and stringencies, with Chang Myon government commanding little positive support, and partly because Koreans sat tight uncommitted or double-faced, trying to play it both ways. Meanwhile, a determined group of generals and colonels took over city of Seoul, commandeered radio and press, and with these facilities created impression that they had universal support in Korea. (At beginning, before CINCUNC and my statements, they spread the word that US was behind·coup.) These factors, plus understandable desire outside units not to force armed showdown with fellow-Koreans, left coup group in power which it rapidly consolidated.
>
> Bleak economic facts of life in Korea remain, and there seems to be good prospect that those who today prefer any change to existing order and who may be animated by new hopes, may tomorrow be disillusioned and resentful. Meanwhile, democratic institutions have suffered a serious setback, some recovery from which can only come as result of measures as soon as possible to reinstitute government by and of the Korean people.[74]

U.S. Acquiescence in the New Regime

Following General Lee Han-Lim's statement and his subsequent (or concurrent) arrest--along with other high-ranking military officers--the coup leaders ordered two divisions of the First Army into the Seoul area without consulting CINCUNC, thus challenging his operational control of the Korean armed forces. Responding to a message from CINCUNC, the U.S. Chairman of the Joint Chiefs of Staff agreed that CINCUNC should "contact General Chang Do-Young and General Park Chung Hee soonest and emphasize in strongest terms necessity of reestablishing command relationships as soon as possible and the vital importance of maintaining ROK armed forces at a high state of combat readiness responsive to the Commander-in-Chief, United Nations Command." Chargé

Green counselled patience rather than hasty action on the part of U.S. Army authorities as the best way of regaining normal command relationships. After considerable negotiation, General Park Chung Hee and General Magruder had reached agreement on the issue, and by June 9, CINCUNC believed he exercised 60 to 70 percent of the control he had prior to the coup. Much of the controversy revolved around Magruder's desire to stipulate in a public statement that CINCUNC would approve the appointment of general officers to commands in the Korean armed forces. As the Korean Foreign Minister explained to the Chargé, the fact of such approval was not at issue, but its public announcement offended Korean nationalist sensitivities. The final agreement left a Capital Security Command outside CINCUNC jurisdiction.[75]

A few days after the coup, without prior warning, General Chang Do-Young announced that he would visit the United States and call on President Kennedy. The announcement aroused annoyance and concern both in Washington and in the U.S. Embassy in Seoul. Eventually General Chang was brought to realize the irregularity of his proposal, and the Foreign Minister apologized for it. With this and the issue of CINCUNC operational control taken care of, and with an apparent willingness on the part of the military leaders to take positive steps to improve relations, the State Department authorized the Chargé to reciprocate. He could inform the Foreign Minister that a later visit by General Chang to Washington would be welcomed, and that a working visit would be arranged. He could also say that the Korean request for *agrément* for General Chung Il-Kwon (who had been ROK Army Chief of Staff during the Korean war and was well known to Americans) as Ambassador in Washington was under active consideration.[76]

By mid-June 1961, it was apparent that the United States would not be able for some time to bring about the "broadly based, responsible government of national unity and of predominantly civilian composition" postulated in early policy messages, or to achieve restoration of democratic civil rights. Chargé Green, in an appraisal on June 13, concluded that the military junta had "no intention of relinquishing power to civilian authority for a long time--perhaps years," nor would it move very far toward civilianization, despite pressures from both the United States and Korean public opinion. The new government's ultimate purposes were still unclear, and its political wisdom seemed doubtful. The Chargé correctly prophesied that "divisions among junta members and within ROK military may become accentuated in months ahead."[77]

Regarding U.S. policies, the Chargé noted that the junta was pressuring the United States for increased support on the basis that the resultant government strength would facilitate broadening its base and modifying its repression. On the other hand, the junta was capable of trying to intimidate the United States by noting the alternative of a Communist takeover. The Chargé concluded that the best U.S. policy for the short term was to capitalize upon the military government's uncertainty regarding U.S. support, pushing the junta in constructive directions through a position of "friendly reserve." He concluded:

US friendship and prestige in Korea should not stand or fall with this present regime. Our time-tested friends in Korea are still the Korean people, not necessarily those few who arrogate power to speak for them, who may be corrupted by the power they too long wield, and who may fail to hold this nation's confidence and support.

Aside from the obvious means of U.S. pressure--granting or withholding military and economic aid--the United States also had some power through the press and foreign opinion. The Chargé noted that world reaction to reports on Korean developments by foreign correspondents was fed back to Korea via the U.S. Information Service and passed to selected ROK leaders. ". . . I am convinced that knowledge of world attitude obtained through this USIA [U.S. Information Agency] service has had impact upon key leaders." On June 9, when the Foreign Minister expressed concern at unfavorable foreign press reactions, the Chargé took the opportunity to point out the advisability of bringing civilians into senior positions, respecting civil rights, and releasing non-subversive political detainees.[78]

Legitimacy and Normalization of Relations

The legitimization of the military regime was an early concern of both Koreans and Americans (and of the Japanese government as well). Continuity of government was provided by the continuance of President Yun in office, thus avoiding the necessity of a U.S. decision to extend or withhold recognition, and avoiding also the question of continuing relations with the United Nations. The President resigned his office on one occasion, but under both American and Korean pressure he reconsidered the following day, and remained as a figleaf of legitimacy until the following year. Legalization of the new domestic government structure was more difficult. Initially, the Koreans gave some thought to a provisional constitution which would be legitimated through referendum, but the Chargé, with Washington approval, discouraged this idea, suggesting instead that plans be made for a constitution which would be the basis for restored civilian rule after a three-month interim period. In the end, the junta on June 6 proclaimed an "Extraordinary Measures Law," somewhat tenuously within a constitutional context, which suspended most provisions of the 1960 Constitution. Pending reestablishment of normal government, the Extraordinary Measures Law established a Supreme Council of National Reconstruction (SCNR) with both legislative and executive powers, whose thirty-two members were all coup leaders or general-grade military officers.[79]

Up to this point, senior U.S. representatives had treated the coup leaders with reserve, maintaining contact with the civilian President and the junta-appointed Foreign Minister (Kim Hong-Il, a Chinese-trained army general). As the

Chargé had told foreign correspondents in a background press conference on May 20, the United States "expected to cooperate with the new regime in same measure which it truly manifested its desire to cooperate with us." On July 7, the Secretary of State (Rusk) spoke to the British and French ambassadors of U.S. puzzlement and concern about Korean developments. "We feel we must move in with advice and guidance, because much is at stake, but we have not yet been able to identify accurately the sources of power. . . ." The British expressed concern that the south Koreans might undertake a military adventure against the north; the U.S. sought to reassure them.[80]

Nevertheless, by June 9 it had been decided that the Chargé should meet Park Chung Hee, the coup leader. The ground for such a move had been prepared through intermediaries such as ex-Defense Minister Kim Chung-Yul. The first meeting took place on June 9, followed by a similar call on the titular Chairman of the SCNR, Gen. Chang Do-Young. To both men, the Chargé made the points suggested in the Department's instruction of the previous day: the United States (a) saw the SCNR "as an established government, with which it is prepared to work in good faith on friendly and cooperative basis"; (b) welcomed the six objectives of the May 16 message and accepted them in good faith; (c) hoped for a fruitful relationship serving "Korean people and our common interests and objectives." Also, (d) the newly designated Ambassador, Samuel Berger, on his arrival would discuss ways of U.S. cooperation, including economic reforms; and (e) the U.S. Government welcomed the joint statement reaffirming CINCUNC operational control of the ROK armed forces. At the same time, the Chargé cited American concerns regarding the "nature, purpose, and methods" of the SCNR. When General Park expressed concern regarding the effect in the United States of allegations of former Communist connections, Chargé Green reassured him, and said there was no need for repressive measures to prove his anti-Communism.

Following these calls, Green commented to Washington that the military leaders were often disregarding American advice, but were somewhat influenced by it. He suggested that it was premature to move too close to them, since some reserve would offer greater bargaining leverage.[81]

Several SCNR moves underlined the Chargé's observations. On June 13, a Central Intelligence Agency was established, with sweeping domestic powers, under the control of Colonel Kim Jong-Pil, generally referred to as the "brains" of the coup d'état. In early July, Chang Do-Young, the titular Chairman of the SCNR and one of the few coup leaders who had been favorably known to Americans in the past, resigned after an apparent bid for power. (His resignation followed by three days a conversation in which it became clear that Chang's gamble to win concessions from the United States by a visit to Washington had failed.) He and a number of supporters were arrested and charged with a plot on the life of Park Chung Hee. This and other personnel shakeups (amid feelers and explanations to the Americans) consolidated Park's leadership position, and he became Chairman of the SCNR. SCNR statements were made indicating that the former Chang Myon government had been paving the way for communism. Meanwhile, thousands of people were arrested on charges ranging from curfew violations to treason, and many of them were held without trial.[82]

In mid-July, during his second call on Park Chung Hee, the new American Ambassador (Berger) stressed the importance of steps toward return to civilian control, such as announcement of a small civilian-military committee to study the problem. He said that U.S. authorities would like to support Park's government publicly "to give it strength and reassurance," but could not do so while arrests, purges, and recriminations continued. Constructive moves from the ROK side would be quickly met with statements by the Ambassador helpful to the ROK government. Park seemed impressed; it appeared likely that he would tell the SCNR of the advantages of cooperation with the United States. The next day, the ROK Government responded with a general amnesty for 1,293 individuals held without charge for left-wing activities, plus other commutations of sentence. The Ambassador made a statement the following day.[83]

The political climate rapidly improved, and at the end of the month Park Chung Hee publicly pledged a return to civilian rule. The Secretary of State at his press conference on July 27 welcomed the "prompt and vigorous steps" of the new Korean government, especially the commitment for restoration of civilian rule, and said, "We feel that a new basis is being established for close cooperation between our nations." On August 15, Park pledged a civilian government by the Summer of 1963, and in November 1961 he came to Washington for a "working visit" at U.S. invitation.[84]

A Year of Trauma; the Ascendancy of Kim Jong-Pil

It took two and a half years of steady American pressure (described below, pages 217-223) to bring about fulfillment of the pledge for re-establishment of civilian government. The period was characterized by struggles within the military junta over power and policy, with younger officers pitted against older ones, and various leaders and factions struggling for position. Nationalist enthusiasm sometimes came through as hostility toward Americans and disinclination to accept American advice. Distrust of civilian politicians, on the part of the military, ran very deep and was in fact justified to a considerable extent by post-war Korean history; thus some of the younger officers were not at all responsive to American pressures for civilianization. Working relationships between Americans and Koreans became fairly effective in economic and technical matters, and the quality and energy of Korean government personnel, as well as their ability to act decisively, were much superior to the levels of previous Korean regimes. However, a number of rash moves by the Koreans--often without consulting or even notifying the United States--continued to keep relations uneasy.

Examples of such Korean moves were the Revolutionary Court trials of 1961 and 1962; the involvement of the ROK CIA in highly questionable commercial operations and in a blatant rigging of the Seoul stock exchange to acquire operating funds; the law for purification of political activities, promulgated by the SCNR in March 1962 to prevent return to political activity of 4,369 individuals in seven specified categories judged by a special SCNR screening committee (a measure that precipitated the resignation of the holdover civilian President, despite American pressure); the arrest of General Kim Ung-Soo on charges which included obedience to CINCUNC orders (see Chapter 3, page 72); the ROK commitment to an ambitious industrial center at Ulsan, without consulting the U.S.; a currency conversion and attempted capital levy in June 1962, also without consultation; and the trial and conviction of ex-Prime Minister Chang Myon and forty other civilian politicians on flimsy charges. (Chang's subsequent release was due in some measure to U.S. influence.)[85]

The currency conversion was viewed so seriously that Deputy Assistant Secretary of State Edward Rice called in the ROK Ambassador (Chung) to express concern at the trend of affairs, after Ambassador Berger had been unable to see Park in Seoul. Rice told Chung that the United States "fully respect ROK sovereignty but in joint undertakings U.S. must make own decisions in exercise of own sovereignty"--for example, in the expenditure of $500 million yearly in American taxpayers' money in Korea. He noted that the ROK Government unfortunately seemed to have taken the path of non-consultation. If the United States was to be helpful, it must know what was being planned. "If U.S. efforts are to be nullified, we must reassess assistance policy." U.S. representatives in Seoul talked to senior ROK leaders along similarly tough lines. In the end, the blocking provisions of the currency conversion were largely rescinded as a result of U.S. pressure.[86]

It became increasingly evident that Kim Jong-Pil as Director of the ROK CIA, and as a close associate and adviser of Park Chung Hee, was behind many of the moves that worried the United States, and that he and the Prime Minister (General Song Yo-chan) were locked in a power struggle. The United States weighed in on Song's side, endeavoring to get Park to force Kim out of the questionable business ventures he had launched to raise money for his political activities. Song resigned his office, and Park assumed the function in addition to his other positions. However, the Ambassador reported, on the basis of a two-hour conversation with Park on June 21, that the top leadership crisis was on the way toward a new balance. Park was still in command, although shaken; and Kim's influence might be on the wane. Park, the Ambassador said, "reluctantly has begun to recognize that KCP [Kim Jong-Pil] is liability and told me he is now considering how to cut down his power. . . ." In the light of Park's commitment to consult with U.S. representatives in advance in future, the

Ambassador recommended that the United States ease its pressure on the Koreans, and "give Park a breathing spell to work out his problems and test his sincerity and ability to deliver on his assurances." Kim was no longer to be a communication channel to the Ambassador or CINCUNC. Subsequently, the Ambassador assisted in downgrading Kim's power by appraising Park confidentially of some of Kim's overambitious activities.[87]

In September 1962, Kim Jong-Pil was invited by the U.S. Director of Central Intelligence to visit the United States. The Ambassador noted the tension between Kim and U.S. representatives in Seoul. The U.S. Embassy reported that Kim's visit would be complicated by his conviction that the American Ambassador was bitterly opposed to him--and therefore, in his eyes, to the military government as well. Kim saw this opposition, in the Embassy view, as lack of U.S. official sympathy, especially regarding Korean economic needs. Noting Kim's charm, complexity, fanatical zeal, and gift for intrigue, as well as the blame publicly attached to him for the shortcomings of the military government, the Ambassador observed,

> As result of his personality and his image, Kim represents a dangerous potential. His visit to the U.S. in some respects represents a liability to us, but we favored it in order expose him directly to Washington views and influence. More than anything we believe he should be impressed with limits within which military government must remain if our support to be maintained.

The ROK Ambassador also confidentially and privately urged that the visit be utilized to educate Kim (who had never before been in the United States) in Western ways of doing things, as well as to convince him of the necessity for an election in 1963.[88]

Kim endeavored to utilize the visit as a demonstration of U.S. support for himself personally and for the military government. After an interview with U.S. Attorney General Robert Kennedy, Kim reportedly quoted him as saying, "The U.S. President and Executive Branch understand the current situation and completely trust Korea's military government." Such reports were played up in the Korean press. Although considerable effort was made by both American and Korean officials in the United States to broaden Kim's viewpoint, there were no immediate indications of change in his position or attitude.[89]

Problems of Return to Civilian Control, 1962-1963

In mid-Summer 1962, a major political struggle developed that cast doubt on the direction of Korea's development and even raised suspicion (never substantiated) that subversive elements might be seeking to wreck the Korean economy and polity. The Koreans communicated less and less with U.S. representatives as they undertook a series of rash economic policies, largely the work of the young radical nationalists around Kim Jong-Pil. Various political groups in and out of the SCNR maneuvered for position. Chairman Park was sorely pressed to maintain balance among them, and Kim appeared to be gaining control. The Prime Minister (Song Yo-Chan) resigned. A government-inspired campaign against U.S. delay in negotiating a status of forces agreement backfired as civilian politicians encouraged student demonstrations, seeking to take advantage of the intra-junta struggle. American influence was reduced by an apparent conviction among junta officers that the United States would support any anti-Communist government, and American criticism of Korean economic policies caused strain in the Embassy's relations with the government.[90]

By late July, the struggle had subsided; some personnel changes were made, and the monetary reform had been significantly modified; but no major changes in underlying political differences resulted. The net result of the crisis was to weaken confidence in the military government on the part of both the Korean public and the United States. Nevertheless, progress began in earnest toward representative government. Professors Rupert Emerson of Harvard University (author of the landmark book on nationalism, *From Empire to Nation*) and Gilbert Flanz of New York University spent some weeks in Korea, as private consultants to the ROK Government at its invitation, to advise on constitutional reform. Drafting of a constitution was undertaken under the aegis of the ROK Central Intelligence Agency. It was completed, overwhelmingly approved by a popular referendum, and promulgated in December 1962. The Embassy, which had been kept informed during the drafting process, considered it an acceptable basis for the future government, and counselled critical civilian political leaders to be patient. The Ambassador implicitly acquiesced in Park's presidential candidacy, and promised him American neutrality, while asking for a broad political base for the new regime.[91]

Although the U.S. Embassy had been kept informed about the progress of constitutional revision, the same was not true of planning for party organization and election organization. While CIA Director Kim Jong-pil proceeded, largely in secret, with the organization of a disciplined and well-financed mass party that would maintain control of the future government, the military government attempted to claim blanket American endorsement of its political plans--a policy the Ambassador criticized in a conversation with Park. However, in a news conference on December 26, 1962, Assistant Secretary of State Harriman supported the moves toward civil government; and on December 27, Park Chung Hee announced that presidential elections would be held in April 1963 and Assembly elections in May. "Guidelines" for the Political Party Law and Election Law were announced in mid-December 1962, and the Political Party Law was promulgated on December 31.

Political activity was permitted to resume on January 1, 1963, but it provoked a renewed crisis within the junta, chiefly because of Kim Jong-Pil's bid for political supremacy as head of a new government party. The ensuing power struggle again imperiled the entire move toward civil government, and raised the possibility of a seizure of power by the Korean CIA. Ex-Prime Minister Song Yo-Chan (who had become a vocal critic of the regime) sent word to the U.S. Embassy, through an American "trader," that he was being threatened with assassination. Marine General Kim Tong-Ha and four other SCNR members submitted their resignations. Meanwhile, civilian and ex-military opposition figures were active, but were unable to combine their strength.[92]

In this critical situation, Chairman Park (who had been privately assured of U.S. support) asked the Ambassador and CINCUNC to visit him unobtrusively. He discussed with them his plan for resolving the crisis within the junta, including the detachment of additional forces from the UN Command to maintain security. The Ambassador and CINCUNC reiterated their neutrality, apart from their concern for stability during the transitional period. They did observe, however, that overcentralization of the prospective government party as a "government within a government" and arrests of SCNR members should be avoided. They did not comment directly on Park's decision that Kim Jong-Pil should resign from the new party and go abroad until after the elections.[93]

Subsequently, Kim rallied his forces and maintained his position by means of an uneasy truce with the anti-Kim factions. He also endeavored to reopen correspondence with the American Attorney General (Robert Kennedy), whom he had previously tried to use for political advantage, and spread rumors and criticism of U.S. influence.[94]

By early February 1963, word reached the Embassy of Chairman Park's discouragement with the worsening political situation, and his growing determination to withdraw as a presidential candidate. At the same time the public attitude toward the political and economic situation was deteriorating, and the public was apprehensive that the military government was losing American confidence. Student political activity seemed likely when universities reopened in March. The government faced the possibility of losing a fair election. At Embassy request, U.S. processing and announcement of development loans were suspended on February 7; and the Ambassador accepted a luncheon invitation from ex-President Yun Bo-Sun. In these circumstances, aggravated by the continued display of factionalism and posturing in the civilian opposition, the more radical military leaders wanted to call off the election and continue military rule.[95]

Chairman Park again in mid-February discussed his problems with the Ambassador, who advised him by the device of recalling the Chairman's own views previously expressed to him. On February 17, the Defense Minister and the four armed forces chiefs of staff delivered an ultimatum to Park: Kim Jong-Pil must withdraw from the new Democratic Republican Party and leave the country at once. This confrontation finally decided Park to proceed along lines similar to those the Ambassador had discussed with him.

The following day, in a dramatic press conference, Park announced a revised policy for return to civil government, involving his own pledge not to participate in the future civilian administration, conditioned upon public acceptance of his program by all political parties. Park confidentially asked the Ambassador to appeal to key civilian politicians for support for the program; in response, the Ambassador "sent word to them that we believed statement provides basis for smooth transition to civilian government in atmosphere of national unity and stability."[96]

The new policy was at first well received. Kim Jong-Pil resigned, and four anti-Kim SCNR members also resigned, to be replaced by seven more neutral appointees. Kim left the country for extended travel and observation abroad. Later in the month, over 2,300 former politicians were released from restrictions on political activity, leaving only 268 still proscribed (although these included some of the most able and outspoken opposition leaders).[97]

Proposed Extension of Military Rule and U.S. Reaction

Political pressures on the SCNR Chairman continued. He and his supporters were embarrassed by widespread rumors of American interference, including rumors that Park's offer to withdraw from politics had been caused by American pressure. There were reports of several plots to assassinate him and overthrow his government (resulting in 21 arrests, including a cabinet minister). U.S. Embassy observers surmised that much of this was the work of Kim Jong-Pil's supporters--who remained in influential governmental and political positions--and indicated as much to the Prime Minister and Defense Minister. Park at first proposed imposing martial law and postponing elections; then on March 16, with virtually no consultation with U.S. representatives or his own colleagues, and with little advance warning, he publicly proposed a national referendum on the extension of military government for four more years, in view of the unreadiness of the country for representative government. Political activity was suspended, assemblies restricted, demonstrations prohibited.[98]

The new program drew a strongly negative reaction in Korean circles. The U.S. Embassy reported that Park's new course of action had "brought him into head-on collision with opposing political forces"; and that "current forces in motion are serious and will probably lead to major clash between government and its opponents, unless new solution found." The solution would lie in some rapprochement between them.[99]

American reaction to this new setback in progress toward democracy was of course negative, among both officialdom and the general public. Recognizing this fact, Park wrote a justification of his policies to President Kennedy in a letter of March 19, which apparently was not conveyed to the U.S. Embassy until a week later. Many Korean observers took it for granted that Park's new policy could not have been adopted without U.S. approval, while in fact, as the

Embassy evaluated it, Park had sought to present the United States with a fait accompli. One SCNR member told the press the record showed that the "U.S. always accepts an accomplished fact."[100]

While the Embassy, responding to Washington's request, was formulating a program designed to "influence events in constructive way," six Korean civilian leaders seized the initiative by calling on Chairman Park on March 19. All but one were willing to consider Park's suggestion that if all "old politicians" would withdraw from the political scene by March 31, he would revert to his February 18 policy. (The holdout, ex-President Yun, could not be brought around, and the military leaders rejected the proposal; some SCNR members also opposed it.) As Ambassador Berger pointed out to the Prime Minister, this represented the fourth proposed solution to Korea's problems in five days; he "suggested that the destiny of a country required somewhat greater deliberation." The Ambassador in his report saw "scant hope that . . . stable situation is likely to emerge from the efforts of the Koreans themselves," and proposed within a few days to "begin, judiciously and selectively, to guide a few people in direction that may offer hope of stability."[101]

The guidance process began, amid rising Korean tensions, with a call by Ambassador Berger on Chairman Park on March 21. Acting on instruction, the Ambassador said that the United States "cannot possibly approve, and might be compelled openly to oppose, continuation of military government for four more years," and that a solution to the political situation "should be based on national unity and be acceptable to different power groups in nation. I am, therefore, under instructions from my government to urge that key members of your government, civilian leaders, and chiefs of staff be called together to sit in joint session and find agreement on pan-national solution." It was recognized that this process might be difficult and time-consuming; the United States was ready to help.[102]

For the next three weeks, the United States maintained a low public profile, while applying increasing pressure in private consultations and keeping active the threat of a negative public position if the referendum proposal was reaffirmed. The State Department made a low-key statement on March 25, calling for transition to civilian government, the mildness of which somewhat disappointed opponents of the military government. President Kennedy's response of March 31 to Chairman Park's letter was firm but moderate in tone.

Korean civilian opposition meanwhile grew. After three demonstrations on March 22, ex-President Yun and over 100 other political figures were taken into custody in Seoul and other cities. The Ambassador warned the Prime Minister that the United States would be forced to comment on such arrests, and most detainees were soon released. After attempts at compromise, Park announced on April 8 that the referendum would be postponed until September, and a final decision made then; meantime, political activity would resume.[103]

Park's statement was viewed by the Embassy as a "face-saving compromise" too vague for the U.S. to support it; nevertheless, it represented a substantial concession to the Korean opposition and to the U.S. view. Tension in Korea subsided, and both American and Korean attention turned to alleviating economic problems.[104]

Further political roadblocks had to be surmounted, in addition to the economic ones. In May, the Embassy learned of a struggle between the new CIA Director, Kim Chae-Chun (a leading junta moderate) and Kim Jong-Pil, involving as proximate cause the CIA Director's arrest of two Kim Jong-Pil advisers (Kim Yong-Tae and Chang Tae-Hwa). These two and others of the group around Chairman Park and Kim Jong-Pil had been regarded by the Embassy as "undesirable, generally anti-American, and with suspicious leftist backgrounds," and Washington suggested that the Ambassador might want to remind Park or others of previously-expressed concerns regarding the use of advisers with past Communist records. This struggle resulted in Kim Chae-chun's removal from the CIA, and the strengthening of the Kim Jong-Pil forces. The latter's supporters pushed for his immediate return to Korea (to which the United States was opposed) and to gain support for him abroad. At this time, the U.S. Ambassador privately expressed to Washington his concern that the U.S. Government apparently wanted to see Park defeated in an election (as indicated in some newspaper reports), although such an outcome would be no assurance of Korean political stability. In July, Chairman Park, in a "crude attempt to put pressure on the U.S.," broadly hinted that an announcement of elections in the Fall could not be made until the food problem was solved--i.e., until Korean demands for U.S. foodstuffs were met. They were met, in large part (although not purely for political reasons); and the Foreign Minister, expressing Korea's gratitude to the Secretary of State on July 16, said that an announcement of the elections would be made.[105]

Campaign and Presidential Election, 1963

On July 27, 1963, a statement in Chairman Park's name set the presidential election for mid-October and the Assembly election for November. Yet American concern remained, since Kim Jong-Pil's forces were again in the ascendancy. The arrest of ex-Prime Minister Song Yo-Chan on August 12, on charges that were far-fetched if not false, after he published a critical letter in a leading Korean newspaper, highlighted this concern; and Assistant Secretary of State Roger Hilsman expressed the negative U.S. appraisal to the ROK Ambassador. Anti-American posters appeared, apparently at ROK government instigation, protesting U.S. interference in the Song case. Nevertheless, U.S. influence was in part responsible for preventing sweeping government personnel changes, for lessening the danger of political repression by eventually bringing about Song's release, and for postponing Kim Jong-Pil's return.[106]

Chairman Park retired from the Army in a ceremony on August 30, and became the presidential candidate of the government (Democratic Republican) party. The election campaign finally began in September. The civilian opposition proved unable to unite against him: six candidates ran--some with probable government encouragement. The U.S. Embassy commented that the

> pulling and hauling, shifting of sides,back-biting and reversals, and all the rest that we are witnessing in both government and opposition camps are illustrative of the weakness of the political fabric in Korea, and the lack of inherent political cohesion and durable loyalties. . . ."

In the middle of the turmoil, some Korean observers saw in Washington statements a parallel between U.S. attitudes toward Park and those which had resulted in the overthrow of Ngo Dinh Diem in Vietnam. Explicit anti-Americanism became a dominant theme in the government party's campaign. Park himself, in one speech, attacked the opposition for their "flunkyism" before "foreign powers."[107]
Toward the end of the campaign, despite the lack of opposition unity, an opposition victory for ex-President Yun Bo-sun began to appear possible. The excruciating dilemmas that such an outcome would have posed for U.S. policy are evident from Embassy-Washington exchanges. Rumors began to circulate, on the eve of the election, of large-scale arrests, which elicited an expression of U.S. concern to the Prime Minister. The arrests did not materialize. In the event, Park narrowly won election over Yun Bo-sun, with the other five candidates trailing. (A combined opposition would have won.) UNCURK made a statement on October 18 that "the voting was properly organized and held in an orderly and regular manner." The Department also issued a statement which was intended to be guardedly positive in tone, although the Embassy found it less than satisfactory. In general, the result was not unacceptable from the standpoint of U.S. policy.[108]

Assembly Campaign and Election

The narrowness of Park Chung Hee's victory appeared to show the need for Kim Jong-Pil's political abilities. Despite the previous understanding with the Ambassador, Kim accordingly returned to Korea to be on hand for the Assembly elections, passing up a long-sought opportunity for high-level contact in Washington (with Assistant Secretary of State Hilsman). Seeking to consolidate his power, he campaigned for election as an Assemblyman, appealing for public support "with the most emotional and chauvinistic issues available." He emphasized nationalism and independence of foreign control, and in a speech at Seoul National University he delivered a "thorough indictment of U.S. policy and presence in Korea" since 1910. The Embassy commented, "none of the factors which led us to desire his departure eight months ago appear to have been mitigated."[109]

Nevertheless, Kim paid a conciliatory call on the Ambassador soon after his return, with the apparent purpose of re-establishing his primacy with the Americans in the Korean political picture. The Ambassador commented, "I intend to hold him at some distance, not to use him as a substitute for Chairman Park, but to be appropriately available to him at such times as I think useful."[110]

During the Assembly election campaign, in late October and November, the economic stabilization program became a major political issue. The United States had insisted in May 1963 upon Korean commitments to stay within specified quantitative limits of money supply, budgetary deficit, and foreign exchange holdings, so as to control inflation. Fifteen million dollars of scheduled Fiscal Year 1964 U.S. aid were withheld to ensure Korean compliance. The opposition discovered this fact, and used it to accuse Park's government of incompetence and diplomatic failure. Government officials pressured the Ambassador to release the money, both for economic reasons and to evidence U.S. Government support in the face of rumors that Washington was unhappy with Park's election. The Ambassador concluded that since the U.S. "attitude and withholding aid had become a major issue in campaign," it was essential that the United States defuse the issue by releasing some supporting assistance; otherwise the government party might not gain a majority in the Assembly. Ten million dollars were accordingly released from 1963 supplemental funds in November, although the $15 million was still withheld. The impact of the release was clouded by conflicting accounts of its source and significance, but the rumors of U.S. non-support were countered.[111]

The Assembly election itself produced a "smashing and surprising victory" for the government party, which won 110 out of 175 seats, although it received only a third of the popular vote. U.S. policies were not a major issue. However, the assassination of President Kennedy just before the election overshadowed local issues and was considered partially responsible for the unusually light turnout (72 percent). Despite some irregularities, the vote was considered essentially valid, and accepted by the press and by UNCURK.

As for U.S. policy toward the new Korean government, the Embassy commented:

> Although we need to redefine our working relationship with Park administration and try to exercise beneficial and helpful influence we believe we should continue avoid over-identification. We believe it will also be necessary establish overt and close liaison with Opposition, although on different basis than with administration, and try to guide it toward unity and constructive rather than destructive policies.[112]

Problems of the New Civil Regime

The new civilian government was formally inaugurated in December 1963, with the Governor of Hawaii (John A. Burns) and the U.S. Ambassador (Berger) as personal representatives of the U.S. President. The Embassy was confidentially informed of the new Prime Minister and Cabinet before public announcement, "in accordance with previous agreement." The State Department had suggested certain guidelines for Park in choosing his Prime Minister, but the record does not indicate whether these were actually communicated. The actual designee, Choi Doo-Sun, was essentially an interim choice--an elderly newspaper publisher who was respected but not considered particularly strong or capable.[113]

Within a very few months, the new governmental system was put to a severe test by the opposition's attempt to bring down the government on the issue of normalizing relations with Japan. Ex-President Yun was the leader in this campaign, which by Spring involved student demonstrations (egged on by the politicians), and Summer to the declaration of martial law and a second exile for Kim Jong-Pil, who had assumed a leading role in working out a settlement with the Japanese. The challenge to the government was aggravated by new financial scandals involving government and political leaders and the usual Spring economic problems.

As the crisis worsened, the Ambassador sent word to President Park in May through the Prime Minister that "if martial law become necessary, and any attempt is made in process to abolish Assembly, or any attempt made by extreme elements to stage a coup, President Park must not assume U.S. will go along." Anti-Kim elements in the Democratic Republican Party demanded Kim's resignation. In June, the Ambassador and CINCUNC acquiesced in the release of two combat divisions from UN Command operational control to meet the internal emergency, while cautioning the President about their use and counseling against repressive measures.

On June 3, the Ambassador told President Park that in the view of at least a dozen of the President's supporters, the government would be endangered unless Kim Jong-Pil was removed. A week later, the Embassy was approached for an American "leader grant" for Kim, and eventually it was arranged for him to attend the international seminar at Harvard University. Park, aware of the lack of popular support for his government, made some reforms; U.S. representatives assisted in bringing about negotiations between the government and opposition parties, and by late July 1964, as Ambassador Berger's Korean tour terminated, the crisis was largely resolved.[114]

Kim Jong-Pil's forces went promptly to work to bring about his return, despite previous assurances to the Embassy that he would be gone for a year. (Among Kim's supporters was retired U.S. General James Van Fleet.) Despite American efforts, Kim returned to Korea in January 1965. However, the intensity of political struggle of 1964 was not repeated, and the government was able to gain ratification of a treaty with Japan (see Chapter 4, page 135).

The process was not without its trauma. Student demonstrations against normalization began in April 1965, and continued to erupt on a sizeable scale until August; Christian congregations and leaders held prayer services in protest; opposition politicians marched and fulminated. In May, contingency plans were being made in Washington for CINCUNC action in case there should be another coup d'état in Korea. But the summer passed without a coup, and without a declaration of martial law as in 1964, although troops had to be used on occasion to contain demonstrations.

Amid the turmoil, there were positive developments. President Lyndon Johnson's visit to Korea in May 1965 was enthusiastically welcomed. This period also saw the merger of most opposition political groups into a single Civil Rule party, an action welcomed by the United States. In the final confrontation in the National Assembly between government and opposition forces on ratification of the treaty with Japan, the United States quietly supported the moderate opposition against the extremists in the Civil Rule party. Kim Jong-Pil remained behind the scenes until after the treaty with Japan was ratified, but then once more sought center stage. It appeared, however, that President Park was more firmly in control of political forces himself, and less willing than before to see Kim and the Democratic Republican party monopolize political power.[115]

7

Korean Economic Development: Years of Restoration, 1945-1957

When U.S. forces assumed control over Korea in 1945, they found a basically agricultural society, aspiring to industrialization according to the model of the hated Japanese, but without the skills, raw materials, or capital to operate and manage the industrial plant the Japanese had left behind.

The modern sector of Korea's dual economy had been almost wholly owned by the Japanese, and designed to serve Japanese rather than Korean needs. It was further unbalanced by the division of the country, since most heavy industry was in the north. Still another problem was that the Japanese had let their factories depreciate because of wartime demands and shortages.

Initially, the Americans had no plan to deal with the Korean economic situation, nor any resources for meeting critical rehabilitation needs; only the prevention of disease and unrest was authorized. Moreover, very few Americans in Korea had the necessary qualifications to replace the departed Japanese in directing the economy.

Attempts to formulate plans, both in the field and in Washington, were frustrated by four factors: the American desire to avoid any action which would jeopardize prospects for unification of the country under international auspices; the legal problems of dealing with the former Japanese properties; American reluctance to make basic decisions about Korea that would preempt the Koreans' right to make their own decisions; and the lack of priority and attention given to Korean problems, in comparison to the demands of the situations in Europe, in China, and in Japan.

Available U.S. funds for Korea under the GARIOA program (Government Aid and Relief in Occupied Areas--intended primarily for occupied enemy territory) for the period 1945 to 1949 totalled about $650 million; but this money was spent primarily for food and consumer goods, plus minimal requirements for industrial raw materials and maintenance parts. During the three-year occupation period, the only capital improvement, apart from the bootstrap operations of energetic individual American supervisors or Korean businessmen, was the import of war-surplus trucks and certain other items through a $25 million loan that the U.S. Military Governor negotiated on behalf of a Korean regime yet unborn.

Apart from their lack of plans and resources, the Americans had little comprehension of the requirements for rapid economic development. It was fully a decade after 1945 that a body of expertise and literature on the subject emerged in the United States. Prior to that time, a number of American preconceptions hampered a rational approach to Korean problems. These preconceptions included unconditional support of free private enterprise, dislike of government controls on business and the economy, antipathy toward comprehensive economic planning as akin to communism, and a firm commitment to the sanctity of private property rights.

Some Koreans shared the American economic viewpoint--notably those conservatives who had amassed large property holdings under the Japanese, and who therefore were regarded as collaborators as well as exploiters by many of their countrymen. It was such men with whom the Americans found it easy to deal.

The confused and inflation-ridden economy of the south stood in contrast to the tightly-regulated economy of the Soviet-controlled north. There, acting through Korean front men, the Soviets imposed their own brand of economic controls and set promptly to work to build up the former Japanese industrial plant to serve their own needs as well as those of the Koreans. Despite Soviet crudity and political repression, which sent a million or more people to the south as refugees, the firmly-directed and purposeful economic policies of the northern regime, the suppression of corruption, and the leveling-down of living standards impressed many people in the south.

Early opinion surveys by the American Military Government established that a majority of the Korean people favored a socialist economy; but at that stage in history, no official American agency could have put itself in the position of supporting socialism. Against this backdrop, it is hardly to be wondered at that the American Military Government was perceived as a somewhat malaprop economic administration, despite general belief in its basic good intentions on the part of most Koreans except the radical Left.

Korean dissatisfaction with economic policies (or non-policies) of the American Military Government period probably set the keynote for the many tensions and differences of succeeding years. But the Koreans--beginning with President Syngman Rhee--generally were far more deficient in economic understanding than the Americans. They had little theoretical comprehension of economics or industrial organization. They lacked any conception of the separation of politics and economics which is traditional in the United States; they tended to subor-

dinate all economic considerations to political ones and above all to the maintenance of the position of the group in power.

For many years after 1945, there was little long-range economic planning.
Available resources were concentrated on the immediately obvious requirements
of restoring pre-World War II consumption levels and maintaining security
against the threat of invasion from the north, with programs formulated from
year to year.

After the Korean War, national security resource requirements reached near-
astronomical proportions, while at the same time the Korean people were coming to expect an ever-higher standard of living. For the Koreans leaders, in the
absence of any more specific long-range economic goals, there was no political
basis on which they could effectively appeal to their own people to save for
investment and for economic stability. The American insistence on individual
freedom and democratic process inhibited them, in any case, in the use of many
of the coercive techniques of economic mobilization freely used in the north.

Accordingly, Rhee and his successors turned to U.S. economic aid as the
solution to their problems, and for a long time the effectiveness of the Korean
government, in the eyes of the Korean public, was based in large measure on
its success in getting as much or more American aid in any one year as in the
previous one.

In the face of all these problems, which recurred throughout the history of
U.S.-Korean economic relations from 1945 to 1965, the Republic of Korea
nonetheless attained and passed the point of economic takeoff. Viewed in a
larger perspective, a twenty-year period is not a long time for laying the
groundwork for the remarkable progress of succeeding years.

Pre-Independence Problems and Policies

North-South Division; the Electric Power Problem

Early U.S.-Soviet Negotiations. When representatives of the U.S. and
Soviet military commands met in January 1946, pursuant to the Moscow agreement of December 1945, it became apparent that the artificial economic as well
as political division of Korea would not soon be removed. The United States
wanted to move immediately toward economic integration, whereas the Soviets
would not go beyond limited agreements for the exchange of specified materials
and services in advance of a political settlement.

Within this framework, the confused economic position in the south, and the
lack of U.S. resources, gave the U.S. negotiators a poor hand. The south badly
needed coal and electric power from the north, whence they had traditionally
come. Yet the south could not supply metallic zinc, lead, and copper wanted
by the north; it would have to substitute concentrates, and these could not be

delivered until the second quarter of 1946. Moreover, the traditional bread-basket of Korea could supply no rice to the hungry north, because the farmers of south Korea were eating much of the surplus themselves, and holding the rest off the market because of inflation.[1]

Agreements were nonetheless worked out for the supply of electric power in exchange for specified electrical hardware and other materials; postal exchanges were provided for; and in the years prior to the Korean war, there was limited and quasi-clandestine private barter trade between the two zones. To a limited and decreasing extent, Korean citizens were allowed to cross the 38th parallel in both directions. Attempts to stimulate barter trade, encouraged by the United States after establishment of the Republic of Korea, were totally frustrated by the north and had to be abandoned after ships were confiscated (see page 247-248, below).

Cut-off of Electricity. The most serious short-term economic effect of the north-south division was the interruption of electric power in May 1948. Over half of the total electric supply of the south (60,000 of a total 100,000 kilowatts) had been received over long-distance high-tension lines from the north's hydro-electric generators; but even this total was inadequate for industrial rehabilitation and for meeting rising consumer needs. The cutoff forced drastic curtailment of industry, and a number of years passed before the loss was fully compensated. However, the United States, which had anticipated the cutoff, provided two military power barges (the *Electra* and *Jacona*) as stopgap suppliers; and through vigorous American efforts total south Korean power generation, including the barges, had doubled (to 80,000 kilowatts) by July of 1948.[2]

Although the interruption of electric power supply by the north was politically motivated, as a device to frustrate movement in the south toward independence through UN-observed elections, the failure of the U.S. command to live up to its bargain with the Soviet command for payment under the 1946 and 1947 agreements may also have been a factor. To the suspicious Soviets, the U.S. excuse that it couldn't procure the agreed electrical equipment or find shipping for it must have seemed strange. Eventually the Republic of Korea assumed liability for the remaining indebtedness of over $8 million for electricity received from the north, and acquired $11 million in assets from the United States, of which $9.5 million represented goods that had been collected for delivery to north Korea.[3]

Monetary and Fiscal Policies of the U.S. Military Government

Early Measures. Initially, the Supreme Commander, Allied Forces Pacific (SCAP) was authorized to import goods into Korea only to the extent necessary to prevent disease and unrest which would endanger the occupation forces (the GARIOA program). Obviously this was a wholly inadequate basis for carrying out U.S. policies for the revival of the Korean economy, and efforts began in State to prepare a suitable rehabilitation and development policy.[4]

These efforts moved slowly, however, and bore little fruit until after the occupation ended. Meantime, through 1945 and 1946, the Military Government "largely financed its operations through the printing of money," thus accelerating the inflation that had begun with a large Japanese release of currency just before the surrender. Moreover, in the view of State and Treasury observers, "the budget and fiscal operations of Military Government were not subject to an adequate system of checks and audits." Prices of most essential consumer goods increased twenty times between August 15, 1945 and the end of 1946; some prices were a hundred times greater. Currency circulation increased from 8 to 32 billion *won* from August 1945 to early 1948. The official exchange rate became a mockery; it was changed from 15 won to 50 won per dollar in mid-1947, but Treasury opposed further modification to a realistic level. A currency conversion was considered in 1948 but was put aside for lack of time and uncertainty of result. A won-for-won conversion was carried out, but only to avoid possible north Korean manipulations.[5]

Fiscal Improvement Efforts. In the Spring of 1947, the State Department initiated action to obtain funds from Congress for a larger scale relief and economic program than the "disease and unrest" levels previously maintained, and proposed a three-year total of $540 million for the fiscal years 1948-1950. Of this amount, $215 million was needed for 1948. However, it was judged politically infeasible to obtain Congressional action that year, and no rehabilitation funds were voted until after the Military Government had terminated, despite deterioration of the Korean economy and political embarrassment to the United States.[6]

In the absence of such appropriations, attempts were made to do something for the Korean economy in other ways. One of these was a loan of $25 million in 1946 from the Reconstruction Finance Corporation; it became a source of constant irritation and friction between the U.S. Government and the Republic of Korea, which was obliged to assume responsibility for it. Another was the institution of better fiscal controls in Korea and the establishment of a "pay-as-you-go" policy, under which the South Korean Interim Government was reimbursed in dollars for expenses of the occupation forces, retroactive to the date that U.S. forces entered Korea (September 9, 1945). For the fiscal years 1946 to 1948, the settlement totalled $35 million.

Commenting on the Interim Government's fiscal 1948 budget (April 1, 1947 to March 31, 1948, the fiscal period inherited from the Japanese), the Economic Adviser in Seoul (Bunce) noted that the deficit, in large part explained by unusual expenses for the national elections, power barges, refugees, and other factors, was nonetheless better than the previous year--31.1 percent of expenditures, compared to 1947's 64.7 percent. Of the fiscal 1948 revenues, 22.2 percent (6,300,000,000 *won*) were derived from the Civilian Supply Program of aid goods brought in by the United States.[7]

In April 1948, in a briefing for the Under Secretary of the Army (Draper), a senior American SKIG adviser said that inflation had been due to subsidized prices for utilities and industries (i.e., not increased in proportion to inflation) and to expansion of bank credit for rice purchase and other purposes, as well as deficit spending and occupation costs. He said the progress was being made in the fight against inflation through increased government revenue, income from sale of U.S.-imported civilian goods and of vested properties, and declining occupation expenses; but that the projected fiscal 1949 budget would probably not be in balance.[8]

Agricultural Policy

One of the first actions of the American Military Government was to remove the Japanese controls on rice marketing and distribution, creating a completely free market. At the same time there were rapid inflation, population growth from refugees and repatriates, lack of fertilizer, and adverse weather conditions. These conditions led to confusion, hoarding, and urban food shortages, and aggravated an already explosive political situation. Government rice collection programs were therefore reimposed, at first on a "voluntary" basis and eventually through a rice collection law passed by the Interim Legislative Assembly (KILA) in October 1947. By that time "the inevitability of a rice collection program" seemed to be "accepted without question." The rice collection procedure "suffered because of the conflict between the interests of the city dwellers and farmers and the desires of the leftists to favor small landholders and tenants and [of] the rightists to favor the large landowners." By 1948, the agricultural situation looked brighter, and American authorities could project south Korean self-sufficiency in food by 1949, or even a small exportable surplus. For 1948, however, continued imports of food were required.[9]

Land Reform

In 1945, almost three-quarters of the agricultural land was farmed by tenants. As of December 31, 1946, 43 percent of farm households rented all the land they tilled, while 38 percent were part-owners, and only 16 percent owned all their land. A Military Government reform of October 1945, limiting rent to one-third the annual yield of major crops, and the landlords' anticipation of eventual land reform, had reduced the tenancy ratio by 8 percent in comparison with the 51 percent tenancy of 1943.[10]

The State Department's economic mission in Korea drew up and submitted a land reform proposal in February 1946, limited to the disposal of ex-Japanese land. No action was taken on it at the time for various reasons, including a feeling (supported by Military Government surveys of Korean opinion) that disposition of land was a matter to be left to the Koreans themselves. Among Koreans, the conservatives opposed any kind of land reform, while the radicals favored confiscation of all land and free distribution to small farmers. Meantime, the north Korean authorities promulgated a land reform measure in March 1946, confiscating all holdings of over five to seven *chongbo* (twelve to seventeen acres, approximately) and distributing them gratis to farmers--who, however, were barred from reselling or renting it or using it as collateral, and were taxed 25 percent of their yield.[11]

In the Fall of 1947, the land reform issue came into prominence as a means of maximizing Korean public support for the non-Communist alternative in the elections to be held under United Nations observation. Up to that time, land reform had been discussed in committees of the Interim Legislative Assembly (KILA), but the conservatives had prevented any significant action. In September, KILA decided to consider a proposal involving Japanese land, although conservative pressure still barred attention to Korean landlords' holdings. In the end, however, the Military Governor (under direction from Washington) had to issue an ordinance on his own authority in March 1948, providing for the sale of 683,000 acres of Japanese land to the 588,000 tenants and part-tenants who farmed it. Another ordinance dissolved the hated New Korea Company, the Military Government successor to the Japanese Oriental Development Company that had been partially responsible for agricultural development in Korea.[12]

After the Republic of Korea received its independence in October 1948, it took control of the land distribution program, which up to that time had "turned over more than 15 percent total arable land South Korea to half million Korean tenant farmers. . . . As result . . . 34 percent Korean farmers now own land they till. . . ." The United States then sought to influence the Korean government to enact and carry out a reform program for Korean-owned lands. A bill for this purpose came to the floor of the National Assembly in March 1949, and was passed in April; conservative forces brought about its return from the Executive on "technical grounds," and, after its repassage and promulgation, managed to postpone its implementation on budgetary grounds.

In December 1949, the Under Secretary of State (Sumner Welles) expressed the view that the United States should "do everything possible to see that the Korean Government places the provisions of this legislation into effect." Americans in Seoul reported that they had "repeatedly made representations to the President of Korea," but that compensation for landlords was difficult to accomplish in an inflationary period. American pressure continued, but it was only after the fighting of the Korean war subsided in 1951 that the land reform program was completed, essentially following the model set in the economic mission's February 1946 proposal and the Military Government's 1948 distribution.[13]

Vested (Ex-Japanese) Properties

Under the Japanese surrender agreement and SCAP (MacArthur's) General Order No. 1, the American Military Government in Korea took title to all property, not only of the Japanese Government General, but of all private Japanese property that the repatriating Japanese were unable to carry with them. The office of Vested Property Custodian was established to look after all former private Japanese property.

The Custodian's holdings ranged from the biggest factories and public utilities in Korea down to miscellaneous household goods and art objects (which were mostly distributed to souvenir-hungry American soldiers). In December 1947, these holdings included the farmlands mentioned above, plus 100,000 residences, 13,461 business enterprises or stores, and 12,649 industrial enterprises. The latter were placed under the supervision of various national and provincial government agencies. A disposal program was undertaken for the smaller properties, but it moved very slowly. Koreans indicated a desire for nationalization of "major industries, mines, railroads, and utilities" in submissions to the U.S.-USSR Joint Commission; hence the U.S. authorities held them for transfer to the successor Korean government.[14]

The legal justification for U.S. vesting of private Japanese property under international law was somewhat murky at best. The problem was partially resolved by the terms of Article 13 of the 1951 peace treaty with Japan, but it remained an issue in negotiations for normalization of relations between Japan and the Republic of Korea (see Chapter 4, pages 120-122). The arrangements for supervision and use of the vested properties were frequently poor, resulting in extensive losses of property, inefficient operation, and reinforcement of already grave south Korean economic difficulties. However, those industries that served Japanese requirements, or were related to the economy of the north, had relatively little to contribute to current Korean needs in any case.

In the Spring of 1947, a special U.S. interdepartmental committee on Korea recommended that an industrial survey of south Korea be made to "provide a factual basis for the operation and ultimate disposition of vested property, for the determination of levels of industrial activity, for reparations claims by the United States on Japan on behalf of Korea, and for the subsequent integration of North and South Korea's industry." But two representatives of the Military Government in Washington made "no real progress" in getting such a program started, largely for lack of funds.

The Assistant Secretary of State for Occupied Areas (General Hilldring), noting this development, observed that the proposed survey was interrelated with another of the interdepartmental committee's recommendations: to civilianize the south Korean administration, which would require 2,500 American civilians, compared with 580 civilians and 3,000 military personnel then in the Military Government. But neither objective could be carried out without "trained and capable personnel," and recruiting of such people would be impossible in the absence of proper housing. Nothing was done until the decision for early termination of the occupation altered the situation. However, recognition of the need for a survey may have facilitated approval of the later mission of Day & Zimmerman (see page 241, below).[15]

The ROK government, after assuming jurisdiction over vested properties under terms of the Initial Financial and Property Settlement, maintained some of the largest properties as national enterprises, and disposed of others to Korean interests, usually those that had supported President Rhee. Many of the properties, by the time of turnover, had been reduced by mismanagement and vandalism to valueless shells.

Education

U.S. policy stressed education from the beginning of the occupation, but the difficulties were immense and the human and material resources were few. An Educational Commission of prominent Koreans was appointed by the Military Governor in 1945 to consider what should be done to reconstitute the educational system, which had been thoroughly Japanized in the course of the previous forty years. In January 1946, the Military Government's Bureau of Education submitted a program to re-establish the educational system of Korea "on a sound basis along American lines." In April and May 1946, the U.S. Office of Education arranged a series of conferences for members of the Korean Educational Commission, in which one of the basic assumptions, in contrast to the USAMGIK Bureau of Education recommendation, was that "projects concerned with Korean education should be developed with an acute awareness that Korean rather than U.S. needs be met."[16]

Action to implement these recommendations was slow, and it was not until June 1947 that an Educational and Informational Survey Mission to Korea made its report. This mission, a considerably less ambitious undertaking than the Military Government had earlier recommended, consisted of three educators and two government "experts," who spent from one to three months in Korea.[17]

The Mission's list of problems in educational development is revealing. First, the "Koreanization" program had encountered such problems as shortage of good text material in Korean and the unfamiliarity of a large part of the literate population with its own national script (*han'gul*). The centralized Japanese administrative system was difficult to decentralize because of shortage of competent personnel. Moreover, "the Mission found some evidence that certain aspects of the American system have been imposed upon Korea without necessary adaptations to Korean conditions."

Next, there was political turmoil in the educational system (due only in part to Communist agitation), and there were major administrative and operational problems, complicated with student and faculty strikes. Third, although

American personnel were "generally competent," their morale was low and turnover was high because of bad working conditions, short contracts, and the "apparent subordination of the needs of Korea to those of other occupied areas." Fourth, supply problems were almost insurmountable, with Japan getting priority on everything available.

Fifth, there was an acute youth problem, with nothing for young people to do and various "irresponsible radical and reactionary political groups" to stir them up. The Mission noted that Military Government had sought to meet this last problem by organizing the Korean National Youth for men 18 to 30, despite the obvious risks; establishing a 4-H movement (patterned on the program of the U.S. Department of Agriculture); and "reviving" the Boy and Girl Scouts.

The survey mission made various recommendations to alleviate these problems, and in particular proposed establishment of an Education Institute staffed with eight to twenty specialists to give short, intensive study courses, rather than bringing Korean students to the United States.

The last fling of the American Military Government in the educational field was a set of three ordinances (216, 217, 218) issued three days before Korean independence on August 12, 1948. The Political Adviser described them as "among the most important issued by the South Korean Interim Government in the area of education . . . the culmination of many surveys, studies, consultations . . . by the Department of Education, USAMGIK." The ordinances attempted among other things to solve the chaotic conditions of educational financing and to establish elective school boards at local levels. "The enactment of these ordinances immediately before the dissolution of USAMGIK represents apprehension over the slowness with which such ordinances would probably be enacted under a Korean administration." The Adviser to the Military Government's Director of Education submitted a final report in October 1948, chronicling Military Government's accomplishments in the educational field; the report provides much detail on the subject that cannot be included here.[18]

U.S. Assistance to the Republic of Korea Before the Korean War

Pre-Independence Planning

As noted above (page 233), the State Department in the Spring of 1947 prepared a three-year relief and rehabilitation program of $540 million--still assuming that the occupation would continue for several years. The program emphasized raw materials and such basic capital construction as fertilizer and electrical generation plants and additional mining facilities. It was expected that the assistance would taper off to $25 million per year after the fifth year. The proposal was approved by the Budget Bureau, but it was never presented to Congress because prevailing sentiment was believed to be against it.[19]

Subsequently, when early termination of the U.S. occupation was envisaged, a drastically watered-down "rehabilitation" program of $60 million for purchase of raw materials and repair parts was prepared for the Fiscal Year 1949 U.S. budget (and eventually included in the FY 1950 budget); capital construction was omitted. The appropriation for Occupied Areas for FY 1949 was considered to include $20 million for Korean rehabilitation, in addition to $95 million in relief, with the way left open for supplementary appropriations.[20]

Economic Assistance to the ROK: Policies and Programs

The basic decision to foster an independent state in south Korea, with a continuing hope for eventual reunification with the north, was expressed by a National Security Council document of April 2, 1948 (NSC8--see Chapter 1, page 5). As summarized in the Marshall-Hoffman letter of September 17 (see below), U.S. policy was now

> to assist the Korean people in establishing a sound economy and educational system as essential bases of an independent and democratic state . . . [which would] require substantial economic aid to the newly established Republic. It is therefore the policy of the United States to provide Korea with the aid which in the long run will be most effective for the fulfillment of these purposes and which will require the least drain on the economy of the United States."[21]

After considerable interagency debate, in which no government agency was really enthusiastic about shouldering the Korean burden, the Economic Coordination Administrator (Hoffman) reluctantly accepted responsibility for preparing a three-year aid program beginning in Fiscal Year 1950, along general lines arrived at in a State Department study, with the understanding that State would be responsible for justifying the need for it to Congress. The study and recommendations were sent to the ECA Administrator by the Secretary of State (Marshall) in a letter of September 17, 1948. They proposed a multi-year capital investment and assistance program totalling $410 million through Fiscal Year 1952 and tapering off thereafter. For the first year, $180 million would be required, of which $50 million was for capital expenditures. "The completion of such a program would reduce the future cost of maintaining Korea at the same level to about $45 million annually," as contrasted with the then-current estimated annual shortfall of $180 million) but "it is not believed . . . that South Korea alone can ever become fully self-supporting."[22]

The pervasive defeatism in the American approach to Korea is evident in the previous quotation. It appeared also in a meeting among the ECA Administrator (Hoffman), the Army Under Secretary (Draper), and the Assistant Secretary of State for Occupied Areas (Saltzman) on August 30, 1948. "Mr. Hoffman said that Korean aid is quite a different matter from the European Recovery Program. The whole problem is one of State Department foreign policy. It has no economic justification. He would not hold out hope that Korea would offer any kind of economic bulwark. He gathers that it has no strategic importance from a military point of view. ECA will look to the State Department for leadership in the program to be carried out. He regards the operation as a holding one-- making good on pledges to Korea. It is up to State to determine what should be done. . . .[23]

Such an approach seemed realistic and reasonable at the time, but hindsight shows that it failed to recognize either the threat or the promise of the Korean situation. Similar pessimism continued in basic U.S. appraisals after the Korean war--for example, in the National Intelligence Estimate of February 28, 1956; in a study of the Korean economy on May 1, 1956, by the Interdepartmental Committee on Certain U.S. Aid Programs (Prochnow Committee); and in policy papers of subsequent years.[24]

ECA began its operations in Korea on January 1, 1949, taking over both responsibility and remaining GARIOA funds from the Army, under a Presidential directive of August 25, 1948. By June 30, 1949, aid funds for Korea as computed by ECA had totalled $356 million, rising from $6 million in Fiscal Year 1946 to $144 million in 1949. An additional $60 million had been provided for the first half of fiscal 1950 (see page 239, above); meanwhile, ECA drew up the promised program for the entire fiscal year, totalling $125 million (as ordered by the Budget Director, in place of the original $184 million), for submission to Congress as a supplemental appropriation request. Assuming Korean government efforts to control the economy, balance the budget, and control inflation, the program aimed to support basic U.S. objectives by providing necessary raw materials, developing transportation facilities, increasing coal and electric production, working toward an export surplus of rice and marine products, developing exports of tungsten and other strategic minerals, training Korean technicians, and assisting the Korean government in its planning and administration.[25]

This program was already one-third less than originally planned, and aimed at lamentably modest goals--the idea of industrial expansion, for instance, was absent except for infrastructure--but the original skepticism of ECA and Defense over the prospects of legislative approval proved well-founded when the House of Representatives failed by one vote to pass an appropriation of $100 million (not $125 million) in January 1950. This Congressional rebuff was due in large part to the poor beginnings of the Korean government in managing its economic affairs, and to a generally poor press for Korea in the United States, coupled with the low priority that has dogged U.S.-Korean relations since their inception. Congress subsequently appropriated $50 million, only to have the benefits of the program swept away by the outbreak of the Korean war.

While State and ECA were working on Korean development policy, the chief American Civil Affairs Officer (Coulter) in October 1948 proposed a survey by a group of "eminently qualified industrial engineers" from the United States to analyze the Korean industrial situation and make recommendations to both U.S. and Korean governments on requirements and goals, at a cost of $175,000 to $200,000. Such a survey, he suggested, would help in getting the forthcoming aid request through Congress. As a basis for such a survey, he pointed out that American experience during the past two and a half years had indicated five priority industrial production problems: fertilizer plans, fishing and fish processing, textile and rubber industries, mining (especially of tungsten, gold, and graphite), and coal and electric power generation and distribution.[26]

The Korean government agreed to accept such a mission, paid for out of American aid funds, and a group from the firm of Day & Zimmerman arrived in early 1949 to make the survey. The field work was completed in May, but the final report was not submitted until November 28, 1949. Nevertheless, the ECA submission to Congress was largely based on its recommendations.[27]

The chief of the U.S. diplomatic mission (Ambassador Muccio), referring to the work on an industrial rehabilitation program for Korea, suggested in December 1948 that a program for stabilizing the Korean national economy was also needed. He noted three major problems in the financial field: monetary reform, strengthening of the central bank, and reorganization of Korean financial institutions. Although preliminary work had been done by American advisers in the field, "No program of action . . . has yet been formulated in terms of the present situation in Korea, the organization of the Government of the ROK, or the proposed ECA program. . . ." Noting that the time might be ripe because of President Rhee's then-current concern over currency expansion, he proposed that a highly qualified expert make a two- to three-week survey, prior to the sending of a team. The groundwork was thus laid for the Tamagna report of May 1949, and for the mission of Arthur Bloomfield of the Federal Reserve Bank, who drafted basic Korean financial legislation, including the statute for the Bank of Korea.[28]

The Korean government undertook its own economic planning: its Office of Planning prepared a confidential "Five Year Economic Recovery Program, 1949-1953," which was reported by the U.S. Embassy in October 1949. This effort was coldly viewed by U.S. agencies as intended mainly to maximize U.S. assistance, without the qualities of a really viable program.   Americans continued to view Korean economic development plans with great skepticism for a dozen more years--partly, of course, because of technical shortcomings, but also in part perhaps because of a basic disinclination to accept foreign planning-- or indeed any comprehensive planning of a kind that had any socialist flavor--for the use of American money. Such American feelings appear, for example, in the U.S. Mission's appraisal of the economic provisions of the new Korean Constitution of 1948 as "a presidential dictatorship rooted in an economic oligarchy." Subsequent experience tended to demonstrate that in comparison to other developing countries, the Korean constitution was quite mild in its economic centralization.[29]

The Aid Agreement and
Organizational Arrangements

After the Initial Financial and Property Settlement had been signed, the head of the U.S. Mission in Seoul (Muccio) wrote President Rhee, proposing negotiation of an agreement governing the aid program. (The draft for this agreement had been developed in Washington the previous Summer.) Rhee agreed, and negotiations began on October 4, 1948. There were relatively few real difficulties. The agreement, patterned after agreements with European countries, was signed by both sides at the 17th negotiating session on December 10. The Korean National Assembly was asked to ratify the agreement (which required no legislative action on the U.S. side), reflecting Rhee's need for political support at this early time. It did so on December 13. Two days later the ECA Administrator (Hoffman) made a three-day personal visit to Korea, which drew enthusiastic comment.[30]

The United States in the Fall of 1948 established an American Mission in Korea (AMIK), headed by the Ambassador (who was not accredited as such to the Korean government until U.S. *de jure* recognition in January 1949). Subordinate to him were four major agencies: the Embassy proper; the far larger ECA Mission, headed by the former economic adviser to USAMGIK (Bunce); the Korea Military Advisory Group (described in Chapter 3); and Joint Administrative Services (JAS), which under Korean conditions had to operate a complex plant rivaling that of a small American city. The ECA Mission Director reported to ECA in Washington, but was also subordinate to the Ambassador. The Director of JAS was not in theory a policy officer, but the nature of his responsibilities and the scope of his program made him an important element in the Mission's entire operation. These arrangements were authorized in a confidential Executive Order of the President on January 5, 1949, which also provided for the takeover by ECA of former Army relief and rehabilitation responsibilities and funds, with the exception of petroleum supply (see page 247, below). The former USAMGIK became USAFIK (U.S. Army Forces in Korea), which was deactivated upon withdrawal of the last American combat forces in 1949.[31]

On the Korean side, the ROK government established an Office of Planning (which included a shadowy continuation of the Military Government's National Economic Board) and an Office of Procurement, directly under the Prime Minister. The latter was subsequently moved directly under the President, at his own insistence and despite objections from the United States. These and some other ROK government agencies were to "develop and administer the program relating to requirements, procurement, allocation, distribution, pricing and accounting for supplies obtained" under the aid agreement. Full diplomatic immunities were extended to personnel of the ECA Mission.[32]

Agricultural Policies

Among various last-minute steps taken by the Military Government to assure an orderly transition to the Republic of Korea was Ordinance 212 of July 29, 1948, providing for collection of rice and fall grains, pending legislative action by the new government. The ordinance represented the accumulated Military Government experience. Reporting on it, the Economic Adviser noted, "The present administrative agencies designated to conduct the cereals collection program are relatively well organized and efficient, as indicated by the general success of the collection programs during the past two years." Prices and quotas, however, were left for the new government to determine.[33]

ROK officials conferred with SKIG authorities in August and September 1948, then submitted a draft /grain purchase law to the National Assembly. The draft endeavored to please various Korean pressure groups by concessions, while retaining essential features of previous legislation. However, the National Assembly wrote amendments into the bill, exempting "small quantities," which made it virtually useless. President Rhee and his Cabinet, their resolve stiffened by a telegraphic rocket from Washington regarding Korea's "international responsibilities vis-a-vis its food situation," continued the Military Government ordinance in effect until a better law was passed; but the delay and the surviving exemptions cut down the effectiveness of the 1948 grain collection. (The fact that the first agriculture minister was a former Communist did not make matters any easier.) In February 1949, actual collections were 43 percent of the goal.

Nevertheless, performance improved thereafter; Korea attained self-sufficiency in food in fiscal 1950, and had a small exportable surplus for sale to Japan, as a result not only of better government performance but of U.S. fertilizer and technical assistance, plus the psychological effects of the land reform program which began to be implemented in 1950. All these gains, including the exportable surplus, were of course wiped out by the Korean war.[34]

Economic Stabilization

The inexperienced new ROK government soon ran into difficulties in controlling the national economy, as had the American Military Government before it. Few Koreans understood economics, least of all President Rhee. Many of the more knowledgeable Koreans who had served the Military Government were discharged, and the men who took their places were not inclined to take official American advice. Friends of men in power were given key management positions, regardless of qualifications; Rhee especially favored his own coterie of private American "advisers." Conservatives who had supported Rhee's cause demanded preferential treatment, and opposed measures for more equitable sharing of national product. Given the danger from north Korea, which the Koreans took more seriously than the Americans, and constant guerrilla activity in many areas of south Korea, defense requirements had priority over economic stabilization.

The budget was virtually disregarded in government operations, and fiscal controls and audits were wholly inadequate. Tax collections were low--running at 24 percent of assessments in July 1949--and were exceeded by miscellaneous "voluntary contributions" to quasi-governmental organizations. The government was unable to raise the prices of utilities to a realistic level. Nor could the government collect the proceeds from sales of U.S. aid goods. Severe instability, inflation, unemployment, hoarding, speculation, widespread usurious private lending, an insignificant savings rate, a falling value of the Korean *won* in terms of the dollar, and widespread black market operations in foreign currency were the result.[35]

By the end of 1949, the situation was approaching crisis proportions. Responding to criticism both by the United States and by his own National Assembly, President Rhee convened a special committee to formulate counter-measures, some of which were implemented; but they were far from sufficient. The ECA Mission "advised the [Korean] Government that only drastic action by the Government at this time can properly justify the continuance of U.S. economic assistance." The Mission reported that it was taking "all possible steps . . . to dispel the complacency existing in some circles which have heretofore been led to believe that U.S. economic assistance would be forthcoming in spite of non-implementation of the Aid Agreement undertakings." These undertakings included balancing the ROK budget and maintaining control over currency issue and use of credit.[36]

Highlighting the extreme seriousness of the situation, the Assistant Secretary of State (Walton Butterworth) wrote to the Ambassador in December 1949 that a Department staff analysis of Korean economic trends "reads like China in 1948." He recalled his experience in China, where he

> used to be amazed at observers taking the view that 'anything can happen' whereas the trend to disaster was so clearly inevitable if really forceful steps were not taken to change it. . . . It seems to me that a thorough-going reformation has to be instituted. . . . What is needed is not simply good technical advice but firm, continuing and effective pressure by you to get the Korean Government to take determined measures to solve the problem which only it can solve. . . .

In the same month, the ECA Mission Director sent a memorandum to various ROK government leaders "at their request," outlining an eight-point program of reforms. By the end of the year, some improvements could be reported -- notably the very good results of the 1949 grain collection program, doubling of electric power rates, some rationalization of the understated *won*-dollar exchange rate, and programs for better controls and tax collection.[37]

Washington was not satisfied, however. On December 30, 1949, it instructed the Ambassador,

> in close cooperation with the Economic Cooperation Administration's representative, to present a detailed set of proposals to the President of the Republic of Korea. . . . Assurances should be sought that the advice and assistance which the ECA Mission in Korea stands ready to extend . . . will be fully utilized. . . .

The instruction noted that Korean self-help obligations under the Aid Agreement had not been met.

> Unless President Rhee and his Government show the willingness and the ability to inaugurate measures designed to stabilize the internal economy of Korea, the U.S. Government will be forced to re-examine the character and extent of economic assistance which can be made available. The U.S. Government therefore desires that the President make regular reports to the Embassy of progress being made by the Korean Government in this regard.[38]

Following up these instructions, Assistant Secretary Butterworth suggested to Ambassador Muccio that proposed ECA investment projects be held up until President Rhee had implemented the financial controls desired by the United States. He also said that, on the one hand, ECA recommendations should be made directly to the President rather than to lower authority; but, on the other hand, there should be a reversal of the trend toward growing centralization of authority in the ROK Government, with a better working relationship between Ministers and their ECA counterparts.

> Although the Department is traditionally reluctant to interfere in the internal affairs of a sovereign state, it should be borne in mind that, while Korea is sovereign politically, its reliance on ECA assistance is so vital as to justify our interest in these matters. You need, therefore, have no hesitation in pressing for the needed economic reforms.[39]

On January 15, 1950, following a near rice panic in Seoul, the Ambassador and ECA Mission Director called on Rhee to make representations as instructed, drawing a parallel with China in 1947-1948, and submitting detailed recommendations for economic controls. The message was underlined a few days later by the failure of the Korean assistance appropriation bill in the U.S. House of Representatives. Rhee's reaction to this shock was constructive, however, and the Secretary of State sent assurances that "everything possible will be done to obtain Congressional reconsideration."[40]

As a result of these representations, a Joint Korean-American Economic Stabilization Committee was established in January, with several high-level members of sub-cabinet rank on both sides, to develop concrete measures to control inflation. It received good cooperation from ROK Government agencies, except the military and police forces. Yet the following month it appeared that "despite strongest representations all components American mission, Republic of Korea does not recognize grave consequences continued deficit spending," and in March the Prime Minister in a letter to the ECA Mission Director "in effect undertook to deny the existence of an inflationary threat in Korea and therefore the necessity of any corrective measures."[41]

In a Washington conference of ECA and State officers in mid-March 1950, Bunce observed that "Rhee might be more compliant with our wishes if he were made to feel a little more uncertain about continuing U.S. support." Following the conference (which discussed political as well as economic problems) a State-ECA working group was established. It agreed on a reply by ECA Director Hoffman to the Prime Minister's letter; recall of the Ambassador for consultation; and an aide-memoire.

With a paragraph added as suggested by the Ambassador, opposing the postponement of National Assembly elections (see Chapter 5, page 165), the aide-memoire was delivered to the ROK Ambassador in Washington (Chang Myon) by the Assistant Secretary of State (Rusk) on April 3, and by Ambassador Muccio to President Rhee the next day. The Ambassador also noted antidemocratic developments such as "retention authoritarian education minister [An Ho-Sang], constant improper police arrests, use torture, threats by high officials against National Assembly." He said it would be "impossible to explain election postponement by [Korean] government." Rhee had the aide-memoire translated and circulated to members of the National Assembly. The gist of it was subsequently carried by the Korean press on the basis of wire-service despatches from Washington. (On June 9, 1952, Senator William Knowland inserted the full text of the note in the Congressional Record.)[42]

The strong American measures had the desired effect. The jolted Koreans began to accept and implement every recommendation of the joint Korean-American committee; the budget was balanced, taxes were raised, and foreign exchange regulated. The economic outlook for Korea took a favorable turn. Trade with Japan, including rice exports and import of badly needed spare parts, was getting underway despite Korean fears of Japanese economic engulfment, when the Korean war intervened.[43]

Electric Power

The North Korean cut-off of electric power in May 1948 was a severe economic blow to south Korea at a sensitive political time, partially alleviated by American rehabilitation efforts and the stationing of two power barges (see page 232 above). After the U.S. Army forces withdrew in June 1949, operation of the barges was turned over to Gilbert Associates under terms of a Korean-American agreement signed in September.[44]

Meanwhile the ECA Mission was endeavoring, with uncertain success, to pressure the Korean government into increasing power generation. In October

1949, reporting efforts to persuade the Minister of Commerce and Industry (Yun Bo-Sun) to step up mining and generation goals, the ECA Mission noted that industrial production in 1949 had been brought up to 50 percent above the same period in 1948, but that continuation of this trend depended upon increase in power output, which was "considered the top priority project by the ECA Mission in Korea. . . ." Not only was generation insufficient: only 55 to 60 percent of it was reaching destination, owing to unauthorized diversion and to the poor condition of transmission facilities. An intergovernmental agreement to implement "Operations 38" (turning over to the ROK the electrical equipment originally intended for north Korea) was signed in June 1949, but it was still before the National Assembly for ratification in October. The Korean War broke out before major improvements could be made.[45]

Petroleum Supply

The U.S. Army supplied Korea's petroleum needs during the American occupation, but the withdrawal of American forces called for new arrangements. In October 1948, representatives of the three non-Japanese oil companies that had operated in Korea before World War II--Standard-Vacuum Oil Company, Texas Company China, Ltd. (Cal-Tex Oil Company), and Shell Oil Company-- arrived in Korea with representatives of ECA and the Army Quartermaster General. The three firms, acting through a Delaware corporation they had established called Korea Oil Storage Company (KOSCO), entered into two contracts: an operating agreement covering January 1 to June 30, 1949 (the projected completion of American withdrawal), among the U.S. government, the ROK government, and KOSCO; and a lease agreement covering July 1, 1949 to June 30, 1950, with a renewal option for two additional one-year periods, between the ROK government and KOSCO. However, marketing of petroleum products within Korea was to be done by the three firms separately.[46]

Although the operating agreement involved no significant problems, the lease agreement was delayed by the concern of the Korean National Assembly that petroleum be under national control, and by the related question of who had title to oil landed in Korea. The operating agreement was extended for three additional months, until a lease agreement between the ROK and KOSCO was eventually reached on September 13, 1949, together with agreements between the ROK government and each of the three parent firms.[47]

Trade with North Korea

The Cold War dampened American enthusiasm for north-south economic relations after ROK independence, and in December 1948, Washington asked for a report on ROK trade with north Korea as a possible violation of restrictions on trade with Communist nations. The U.S. Embassy in Seoul reported that "more war potential was extracted from north Korea than contributed by South." South Korean exports were non-strategic (rubber, rope, and certain petroleum products, mostly imported for re-export) plus items remaining in the stockpile originally imported by USAFIK to pay for north Korean electric power. North Korea was committed to supply chemical fertilizer, chemicals, and wood pulp. The report also noted that the ROK was very sensitive regarding exports to north Korea, "as demonstrated by recent six-weeks ban by Minister Commerce on North Korean barter trade, lifted only after sustained USAFIK" representations.[48]

The United Nations Commission on Korea interested itself in trade with north Korea as one means of promoting contacts which might facilitate unification. In June 1949, the ROK Foreign Minister reported to the Secretary of UNCOK's Subcommittee I (Lucas) on the status of trade and exchange with north Korea. The ROK government, however, found no advantage in such trade. At one of his regular press conferences for foreign journalists, on October 7, 1949, President Rhee remarked that the ROK should not try to conduct barter trade with the north. "We tried it and the result was that we gave but received nothing. We lost ships, crews and goods time and again and we are tired of it. So, if the UN wants us to carry on barter trade with North Korea, we will object."[49]

After the Korean war there was of course no officially sanctioned north-south trade, but smuggling continued, much of it by the ROK Army Higher Intelligence Detachment (HID) through a trading corporation in Seoul, as well as by the ROK Army Counter-Intelligence Corps (CIC). Such operations, both overland and by sea, were estimated in April 1955 by Americans in Seoul to total $3 to $5 million annually. The north Koreans received auto parts, tires, electric motors, hand tools; in return they furnished kolinsky furs, hog bristles, ginseng, and narcotics, but their exports were less than imports and some of the latter were paid for in greenbacks. There was also some trade in luxury items-- radios, nylons, watches--from the south Korean black market. Movement across the demilitarized zone was largely handled by "Mongolians" who had been smuggling for years.[50]

Economic Problems of the Korean War
and Reconstruction

The north Korean attack of June 25, 1950 and the ensuing hostilities effectively destroyed the economic recovery that had begun to make real progress the previous Spring. During the early months of the war, emphasis again was upon prevention of disease and unrest; the Korean economy was subordinated to military requirements. With the stabilization of the battle lines in the Spring of 1951, attention once more turned to the rehabilitation of the Korean economy and industrial plant, but the problems of a vastly increased military force, plus the problems of the American military presence, continued to dominate the Korean economic scene. Additionally, as a result of Korean-American differences concerning the conclusion of an armistice (see Chapter 2, pages 49-50), President Rhee became more recalcitrant than ever in his disregard of American economic advice, and the old problem of inflation and deficit spending, aggravated by the spending of American forces, re-emerged in a more virulent form than ever.

Financial stability, and prewar production and consumption levels, were essentially re-established by the end of 1955; this date can be taken as the end of the war and reconstruction period. Given the magnitude of wartime destruction, and the political problems involved, it is perhaps a triumph rather than a failure that inflation, though serious, never reached runaway proportions, and that stability was substantially re-established within less than six years from the outbreak of the war.

During this period, the principal problems in U.S.-Korean economic relations were

--structure and organization,
--relief,
--expenditures of United Nations forces
    (discussed in Chapter 3),
--control of inflation and stabilization of the economy,
--foreign exchange rates and control,
--reconstruction and development planning, and
--funding and programming of U.S. aid.

These problems (except for UN forces' expenditures) are discussed in succeeding sections.

Structure, Organization, and Relationships

Military Assumption of Economic Responsibilities; Establishment of UNKRA. The relatively neat organizational pattern of the American Mission in Korea dissolved as the brigadier general commanding the Korea Military Advisory Group under the Ambassador was replaced by a galaxy of generals under a five-star United Nations commander. After a brief and confused period in which everyone did what little he or she could, a Presidential letter of September 29, 1950, relieved ECA and its Korean mission of all responsibility for direct civilian relief, and for supplies meeting both civil and military requirements. The UN Command established a UN Civil Assistance Command, Korea (UNCACK) to handle the disease-unrest requirements of the civil population.[51]

By April 1951, despite the Ambassador's objections, the ECA Mission was abolished. Some of its remaining functions were assumed by the United Nations Korea Reconstruction Agency (UNKRA), established pursuant to a UN General Assembly resolution in October 1950; the remainder were taken over by UNCACK (which later was renamed Korea Civil Assistance Command, KCAC), except that custody of the U.S. interest in the counterpart fund (depository for monies received from the sale of U.S. aid goods) was transferred to the Ambassador. The consequence was to transfer to the military command the implicit weapon of economic sanctions, leaving the Ambassador with no real power beyond persuasion and personal influence. UNCACK set up provincial offices throughout Korea, and performed some of the functions which would normally have belonged to the Korean government--a partial recreation of American Military Government, regarded by the Koreans with mixed emotions.[52]

From this time on, there were organizational difficulties not only between the Americans and the Koreans, but between the Koreans and UNKRA, between the Americans and UNKRA, between American military and American civilian representatives in the country, between the field and Washington and among Washington agencies, with the Koreans cannily exploiting all differences.

One of the first reported problems was between the UN (essentially U.S.) military command and UNKRA. The UN Command wanted a UN resolution making it responsible for all aid and assistance to Korea during hostilities. A State Department representative (Carwell) urged Sir Arthur Rucker, the UNKRA representative in Korea, to fight this move and make its own bilateral agreement with the Koreans. At the same time, Rucker was irritating the UN representative in Korea (Stavropoulos) by refusing to consult with the United Nations Commission for the Unification and Rehabilitation of Korea (UNCURK), which had replaced UNCOK after the invasion. This conflict was eventually solved by making the retired deputy commander of the prewar U.S. forces in Korea (General John Coulter) the Director-General of UNKRA.[53]

The Meyer Mission. In March 1952, the Ambassador (Muccio) reported that "relations between the ROK and CINCUNC [Commander-in-Chief, United Nations Command] representatives has become so acerbated that any further attempts at negotiations [for an agreement on coordination of economic aid] by same officers from Tokyo would be most inadvisable." (Negotiations had been in fitful progress for several months.) The Ambassador suggested the immediate establishment of a high-level joint Korean-U.S. economic committee "here in Pusan [the wartime Korean capital] empowered to take such steps as are necessary to stabilize local economic and financial situation."

As an alternative, he cited his previous suggestion of a "Dodge mission," parallelling the highly successful mission of Joseph Dodge to Japan in 1949; but he preferred the joint committee because immediate action was essential. He noted that the time was not propitious; the 1952 political crisis (Chapter 6, pages 187-189) was about to erupt.[54]

To solve this situation, in response to recommendations by both the Ambassador and CINCUNC (Ridgeway), Clarence E. ("Chief") Meyer was designated to head a special Presidential mission, which was to negotiate an economic agreement with the Republic of Korea as a basis for joint action for economic stabilization. The Mission was set up by the Pentagon. However, Meyer's terms of reference were provided by the Secretary of State, and the State Department (rather belatedly involving itself) assumed "primary responsibility for monitoring negotiations with the Korean government and for coordinating the views of the interested agencies of the UN Command."[55]

In a little over a month, Meyer and his staff succeeded in overcoming extreme Korean reluctance to negotiate. By threatening to depart without agreement, and actually packing to leave, he brought the ROK and UNC representatives together in an agreement on the coordination of Korean economic affairs, which was signed on May 24, 1952. He recommended against a civil affairs agreement, which was then desired by the U.S. military, on the grounds that it might provoke a request from the Koreans for a mutual defense treaty. Meyer made a final report to the Secretary of State on July 21, 1952, with recommendations for a multi-year program of Korean economic stabilization.[56]

Combined Economic Board. As provided by the May 1952 agreement, a Combined Economic Board was organized in July, after a delay "apparently occasioned by a political judgment on the part of CINCUNC and the Department of the Army" without reference to the Ambassador. The chief American representative on the Board was the commanding general (Herren) of the Korea Communications Zone (KComZ), a component of the UN Command, who took charge of all the Command's civil functions in Korea. The delay by CINCUNC and Herren also postponed agreed U.S. payments to Korea for past UN advances, by postponing the exchange of supplementary notes envisaged by the May 24 agreement, until Herren could be satisfied regarding the related issue of Korean foreign exchange, even though this interpretation went beyond the terms of the agreement.[57]

Commenting on the problems among the UNC, the new Combined Economic Board, and UNKRA at this point, a State economic officer (Strong) noted the disposition of the military to distrust the Koreans, to refuse to compromise, and to insist on black-and-white simplistic approaches, as well as to monopolize control of all activities which concerned the military command. He thought "the military authorities regard the Koreans as an unfortunate impediment in the path of their program." He concluded,

I am not objecting to firmness in relation to the ROK on the part of US officials, and it is possible that, by contrast, the UNKRA line is too soft or conciliatory. What we need is a certain evenness and moderation in attitudes and procedures. The exigencies of the situation in Korea seem to have engendered a tendency to extremes. Uncompromising attitudes on all sides are alternated with empathy and softness.[58]

Over three months later, an internal State memorandum noted the continuing lack of vigorous action on Korean economic problems. UNKRA, according to Ambassador Muccio, had so far "been able to bring the Koreans only hatching eggs, goats, and some little pigs"; many more things were needed, if only to boost lagging Korean morale. The Combined Economic Board, though now fully organized, had accomplished little basic planning, and the principal U.S. representative was now a newly-appointed Navy admiral with no background in the area, who (according to Ambassador Briggs, who succeeded Muccio, in another report) spent 90 percent of his time in Tokyo. The UN Command military staff in Tokyo "bitterly opposes UNKRA, dislikes the Koreans, and distrusts the State Department." The UN Command was limited by law to preventing disease and unrest; yet "Tokyo requires something like half a dozen kinds of approval for every UNKRA project." The drafter of the memorandum (Kenneth Young) commented:

> . . . It is hard to fathom what has saved the ROK from economic and financial collapse. It has certainly not been US relief plans and programs. Their inadequacy and tardiness, far from stopping inflation, are still partly contributing to it. . . . Relations between UNKRA and the United States military agencies in the field have nearly reached a breaking point. . . . The State Department must either act to save UNKRA as the economic action agency in Korea, or must propose an entirely new approach to reconstruction.

The Tasca Mission. Both organizational and substantive problems of the Korean economy, as an aspect of the deteriorating relations between the ROK and the United States, led the new Republican administration in April 1953 to despatch a new special mission to Korea. Headed by Henry J. Tasca as "Special Representative of the President for Korean Economic Affairs: but responsible to CINCUNC, its task was to investigate the Korean economy and recommend the forms and amounts of aid in a report through CINCUNC to the President. Tasca's report became a major point of reference for subsequent economic aid planning. Although he had to operate in the highly-charged political atmosphere of mid-1953, when the ROK and the United States were at loggerheads over the armistice negotiations, he nonetheless won the admiration of both Koreans and Americans.[59]

Establishment of Economic Coordinator. Pursuant to the Tasca mission, a subcommittee of the U.S. National Security Council developed recommendations for a new organizational framework for economic assistance, which were incorporated in a Bureau of the Budget memorandum. In a Washington conference with the Director (Harold Stassen) of the Mutual

Security Agency, successor to the ECA, and the Budget Director (Dodge) on July 29, two days after the Armistice Agreement was signed, the Secretary of State (Dulles) approved the memorandum for submission to the President. The Secretary pointed out that U.S.-ROK relations would be difficult in coming months:

> President Rhee continued to hold good cards. . . by reason of his power to disrupt the Armistice. . . . We must do everything we can both of a military . . . and an economic character to gain and hold control of as many aspects of the situation as possible. . . .

It was agreed that it was essential for a representative of the United States to go soon to Korea as economic coordinator. Tasca could not return permanently to Korea in this capacity, despite his qualifications, and C. Tyler Wood was selected for the job.[60]

On August 6, in his post-Armistice conference in Korea, Secretary Dulles informed President Rhee of general Presidential approval of the Tasca report, and they agreed in principle on the need for effective U.S.-ROK coordination of the aid program through the Combined Economic Board, as the Tasca report contemplated. Rhee made a strong plea for a "supreme planning body" such as the Board to coordinate all economic programs, but the details on the American side still remained to be worked out because "President Eisenhower presently discussing this question with his advisers and General Clark [the new CINCUNC]."[61]

Soon afterward, Wood assumed his functions as

> United Nations Command Economic Coordinator and representative of the Commander-in-Chief, United Nations Command, on the joint US-ROK Combined Economic Board [CINCREP]. The principal task set for him was to coordinate all US and UN aid programs, including those of the United Nations Korea Reconstruction Agency and of the Korea Civil Assistance Command. Although not given formal control over UNKRA, Wood worked out with General John B. Coulter, the new Agent General, an arrangement to assure effective coordination and avoidance of overlapping.

Although this arrangement still effectively separated the Ambassador, nominally the senior U.S. representative in Korea, from the chief sources of power, it functioned reasonably well until 1959 (when perennial military opposition was overcome and a normal country team under the Ambassador's over-all control was established). The effectiveness of the arrangement rested upon the ability of the three men principally involved--the Ambassador, CINCUNC, and CINCREP--to concert their policies and actions. In general, this concert was realized.[62]

Korean Attitudes. Korean officials, largely taking their cue from the economically naive but politically astute President Rhee, grew increasingly impatient and critical of U.S. aid efforts. They focused on the seeming lack of meaningful progress, in contrast with the billion dollars of aid that the Secretary of State had promised (albeit hedged with conditions) to Rhee in the 1953 conference. Throughout 1954, Rhee's English-language newspaper, the *Korean Republic*, criticized the aid program and the UNC Economic Coordinator personally, culminating with a vitriolic editorial on December 20 that Ambassador Briggs felt obliged to rebut. Although the editorial and previous stories twisted the facts almost out of recognition, there was an underlying message: that aid was too little, too late, and insufficiently aimed at reconstruction; and that the attitude of American aid officials was wrong. The administrators, said the *Korean Republic* editorial, had rationalized their own shortcomings by placing the blame on Korea or on "directives from Washington," and were

> . . . afflicted with a kind of aid paranoia that rapidly is leading toward a neo-colonial feeling of superiority not unlike that which led to the downfall of the British, the French and the Dutch in the Far East. It is an attitude of "we know best because we are great ones, and if you oppose us in anything you are persecuting your masters and your betters."[63]

Although Ambassador Briggs eloquently rebutted this and other critical comments, it is unquestionably true that the failure of each side to understand the other greatly aggravated the difficulties of planning and administering the aid program.

Another example of Korean criticism was a statement by Rhee's spokesman (Karl Hong-Kee), reported in The New York Times of September 3, 1954, and subsequent comments by Wood's Korean counterpart on the CEB (Paik Too-Chin). Addressing a rebuttal by Wood of the New York Times story, Paik commented that

> dismissing the Korean Government's criticisms with the sweeping assertion that they are 'groundless and without foundation of fact' is an unfortunate, summary method of attempting to dispose of a legitimate, basic position of the ROK Government.

Paik endorsed Karl's charges: excessive, free-spending and high-living American personnel to administer the aid program; poor coordination of effort; veto of CEB decisions in Washington; bureaucratic delays; a minimum ROK role; and partiality toward Japan. Paik's comments were incorporated in an aide-memoire, but it was decided in Washington not to reply to them unless they were submitted through the usual diplomatic channels.[64]

Such criticism of U.S. economic policies was accompanied from 1952 to 1955 by the same Korean negotiating intransigence on economic matters as in the political and military areas. Rhee seemed to believe, as he had in 1949 and 1950, that the United States would have to support him willy-nilly, and that obstinacy paid off. In fact, it did in many cases.

For example, the U.S. Embassy in Seoul, reporting on Tasca's May 4, 1953 conversation with the ROK Finance Minister (Paik), commented: "ROK Government apparently calculates that by firmly refusing to carry out [February 25] agreement [regarding the counterpart rate] it will force us to give in as we have done on several minor issues." Tasca was then endeavoring to get the Koreans to revise the counterpart rate upward, and the Embassy supported his position; but in the end the ROK won its point, and the rate was not revised for another year. The nadir of ROK-U.S. economic relations was reached in late 1954, when the United States cut off the supply of petroleum (which it then totally controlled) to Korea in order to force Rhee's agreement to the Minute of Understanding that was then pending (see page 258).[65]

The critical Korean attitude surfaced again in 1955, both in the economic negotiations of that year and in public. At the end of his tour as CINCUNC in June, General Maxwell Taylor made a farewell summary of U.S.-UN reconstruction work since the Armistice, and referred among other things to Korean "unjust criticism." An article in the Korean Republic took exception to this comment, which "asserted only [that] ROK persistent insistence forced aid administrators [to] include industrial projects in aid program, and concluded that criticism brings results."

In July 1955, the new U.S. Ambassador (Lacy) called for "shock treatment" for the recalcitrant Koreans to make them more amenable, but the State Department disagreed with him:

> We understand and appreciate frustrations which arise from dealing with complexities of Korean situation with added difficulty of President Rhee's fixed ideas about exchange rate and other economic subjects but there is no simple way cut through all problems which arise in dealing with another sovereign country. This is especially true of ROK which is on front line in Far East and where our position is vital to our general strategic and security interests. ROK leaders motivated in part by ignorance economic factors, honest doubts and fears arising from their history and their position between Communists and Japan, and their own knowledge some of peculiarities of Korean economic and social conditions. These factors must be taken into account in our dealings with them.
>
> It seems to us that prestige Ambassador, CINCUNC and OEC [Economic Coordinator's office] suffer to extent ROK is allowed to appeal over their heads to Washington. Only way we see to make progress is patiently meet ROK on individual issues as they arise in the field being firm where we are convinced we are right. . . .
>
> . . . There is no way in which we can punish ROK without also injuring larger US and free-world objectives in area.[66]

The U.S. Embassy, in a wide-ranging despatch of February 1954 on "Policies and Actions of the ROK Government in the Economic Field," summarized Korean attitudes. The Embassy acknowledged that Korean economic performance "appears to be about in line with what would be expected of a vigorous but undeveloped Far Eastern country," but was not sufficient to fulfill the "extremely ambitious goals set for it":

The Government has exerted itself strenuously to obtain the largest possible amount of foreign aid, . . . but has failed to call forth the internal effort of which the country is capable. The Koreans are a nation with remarkable resources of energy, ingenuity, and endurance. They are also a people who need direction and constructive discipline by responsible leaders. Yet the conditions and incentives necessary in order to put the people's energy fully to work have not been established, and the existing discipline and leadership have not been used for economically constructive purposes. . . . [67]

The despatch noted Rhee's economically uninformed one-man leadership as a major cause of difficulty, and chronicled his faults (no economic knowledge, no delegation of authority, poor judgment of men's character and ability, insistence on personal loyalty above everything, attraction of "foreign admirers and advisers of dubious ability or character"). It noted the "upside-down" Korean relationship, in which Rhee had more than once assumed the position of threatening to reject American aid, and Rhee's campaigns of criticism.

"The U.S. representatives here have long been on the defensive," the despatch continued, because Rhee capitalized on his estimation that the United States could not abandon Korea in the contest with the Communists, bluffed "fantastically," and took advantage of intensely anti-Communist but uninformed American public opinion to cultivate support for his position. Nonetheless, when the United States exerted real pressure, the Koreans yielded. Such pressure was applied by the UNC Economic Coordinator (Wood) during the 1953 negotiations, through withholding approval of procurement requests, and resulted in the dropping of extreme Korean demands. [68]

Accordingly, the Embassy recommended that although there would be no complete change so long as Rhee was head of the Republic of Korea, there should be an "application of pressure at selected individual points . . . starting with those where the ROK position is most vulnerable" to avoid dissipation of American aid. "At the same time a continuous effort should be made to bring about gradually the desired fundamental change of relationship." This effort involved an information program for influential Koreans and the general public, and pushing to completion a few conspicuous rehabilitation "showpieces," despite the risk of inflation. The Embassy also recommended that Washington agencies inform Congress and selected journalists on the Korean situation; that they provide information to known supporters of Rhee, "as was done with good effect at the time of the armistice crisis" of 1953, and to important visitors to Korea; and that Washington publicly support the UNC Economic Coordinator's position in Korea. To some extent, the State Department supported and carried out these recommendations. [69]

As the war receded into history and politics in Korea became more overt, opposition leaders also began to criticize American aid policies. One sample of their litany was voiced by a Democratic party member in the National Assembly in the winter of 1955-1956, as the presidential election campaign approached: the effect (though not the intention) of the U.S. aid program had been "to maintain a dictator in power and strengthen his political movement; aid was benefiting a privileged minority, while the masses continued at subsistence levels; Korean officials were making huge profits because agricultural shipments did not come at proper times; U.S. agricultural surplus imports were (paradoxically) hurting the Korean farmers; and the United States refused to use its power to promote democracy in Korea, even though the aid program itself was negative interference in Korean affairs because it enabled "persons and groups to maintain power that would otherwise have been eliminated by other forces."[70]

An added problem in U.S.-Korean relations during this period was the basic distrust of private enterprise among many Koreans. As already noted (page a majority of Koreans polled by the American Military Government preferred socialism to capitalism; and the Constitution of 1948 reflected such views to some extent, to the dismay of some Americans. The behavior of foreign businessmen in Korea did not always appear to put Korean development and Korean sovereignty very high among their operating priorities, thus reinforcing Korean suspicions, and it was very natural for Rhee to move against foreign businessmen as a means of embarrassing Ambassador Lacy to force his removal in 1955.[71] Moreover, the Koreans feared the possibility of Japanese economic domination.

However, Rhee was sensitive to American criticism in this area. The 1954 amendments to the Constitution, though primarily intended to give him a third term, also liberalized somewhat the "socialistic" economic provisions. In December 1955, Rhee called for the disposal of government-owned salterns to private owners; Korean officials believed that he did so in an effort to counteract charges by a U.S. Senator concerning "quasi-Socialistic economies."[72]

Basic Bilateral Economic Agreements

As soon as American military forces entered Korea in 1950, the United Nations Command negotiated an agreement with the Republic, dated July 28, under which it could draw Korean currency for its local expenditures, leaving the question of reimbursement for subsequent negotiation. This agreement, which led to extremely serious complications in subsequent Korean-American relations, was the only formal addition to the prewar economic agreements until 1952 (see Chapter 3 and page 263 below).

In late 1951, CINCUNC representatives began negotiating with the ROK government for an agreement on coordination of the aid program in Korea. The agreement was ultimately reached on May 24, 1952, as a result of the Meyer mission. Its most important provision was the establishment of the Combined Economic Board.

On February 25, 1953, following the Korean currency conversion, agreement was reached for the deposit of proceeds from the sales of U.S. aid goods into the U.S. counterpart account at a rate of 180 *hwan* (replacing *won*) per dollar, subject to quarterly review and revision. Revisions soon became justified under the terms of the agreement, but for political reasons (Rhee's intransigence on the subject, and the American desire not to cloud the climate for the new UNC Economic Coordinator) no revisions were made.

Following the Tasca mission and the arrival of the UNC Economic Coordinator, a new "Agreement for a Program of Economic Reconstruction and Financial Stabilization" was signed by the Korean and U.S. representatives on the Combined Economic Board (Paik and Wood) on December 14, 1953, after prolonged and difficult negotiations. This was the first postwar document that aimed at over-all coordination of Korean economic stabilization and reconstruction. As with previous agreements, it supplemented, rather than superseded, the basic economic assistance agreement of December 1948.

When President Rhee made a state visit to Washington in July 1954, efforts were made to incorporate agreements concerning the economic and military assistance programs in a "Minute of Understanding" to accompany the new Mutual Defense Treaty. Several more months of negotiation were required, however, before the Minute was initialled by both sides on November 17, 1954. A revision of the counterpart rate to 500 to 1 was agreed on August 12, 1955.

No further basic agreements concerning economic assistance were reached until the 1948 aid agreement was replaced by a new one in 1961. However, a Treaty of Friendship, Commerce, and Navigation was ratified in 1956, with some implications for economic aid in that it was intended to facilitate private U.S. trade and investment in Korea.

Relief and Non-Governmental Contributions

Military Relief Program. A 1953 State Department memorandum characterized the U.S. record for administration of relief in Korea as "on the whole good," in contrast to the poor record for attack on over-all economic problems. As already noted, the UN Command established UNCACK to handle Korean civilian requirements. Aid goods necessary to prevent disease and unrest were imported through military channels and financed by Defense Department appropriations for Civil Relief in Korea (CRIC), a latter-day equivalent of GARIOA. Some international contributions of money and goods were also received. Additionally, beginning in 1952, dollars paid to the Korean government for UN Command purchases of local currency were used to finance imports of consumer goods.

In Fiscal Year 1952, according to a U.S. Embassy report,

> . . . the method of determining requirements of Korea for procurement under the CRIK program was . . . each section chief (e.g., Social Affairs, Commerce and Industry, etc.) in UNCACK would prepare a series of projects, which he thought would represent worthwhile activities and would meet the needs of the relief program. In preparing these

projects, he might consult informally with officials of the Korean government, but no regularized procedure for such consultation was provided for, nor was such consultation always carried out. The various projects . . . were submitted to the UNCACK planning group, which reviewed and "coordinated" these projects as an integrated program. Further review might then be made by the Commanding General, UNCACK. . . . The program was carefully studied in Tokyo and thoroughly revised before submission to the Department of Army, which in turn presented it to the Bureau of the Budget and to Congress for final approval.

However, the report stated that the program for Fiscal Year 1954 would be drawn up in consultation with the Koreans and coordinated by the Combined Economic Board. "This change in procedure should permit closer coordination with the Korean Government. . . . Until now, the ROK has complained that it did not know what was being brought in under the CRIK program until the supplies arrived." Nevertheless, an *ad hoc*, impromptu "Central Relief Committee" of Korean Cabinet ministers and UNCACK section chiefs or their representatives allocated aid goods for sale or free distribution (chiefly the latter) from 1950 until the CEB was established in 1952.[73]

The consequence of the large and imperfectly coordinated influx of aid goods was that the Korean economy was kept alive, but it was also made dependent. The above-cited report commented,

It is possible that [aid goods] have damaged reserves of recuperative energy Korean industry may have possessed within itself. . . . Activating stagnant manufacturing capacity at the grass-roots level has been disregarded. Energy has been frittered away in planning long-range industrial projects that cannot be implemented until inflation is brought under control.

While the foregoing comment would seem to advocate backyard furnaces like those of the Chinese Communist Great Leap Forward, it nonetheless highlights one of the basic dilemmas of the relief program. Another dilemma was the problem of sale versus giveaways: the latter caused inflation and inflated popular expectations, while the former appeared heartless. In operation, what often actually happened was a combination of the two: theoretical sale, followed by non-collection. At the end of 1951, only 10 percent of imported goods had been sold, and collections were lagging even for the 10 percent. Still a third problem was that with the CRIK program and deep American involvement in Korean affairs (688 foreigners in UNCACK in mid-1952, up from 329 a year previously, with field teams of 27 to 28 people each in all provincial capitals), the ROK Government could balance its budget simply by withdrawing from many fields of its normal responsibility, while the UN Command extended its operations through inflationary overdrafts on the Bank of Korea. The American presence, in the 1950s as in the 1940s, appeared to encourage the "mendicant mentality" among Koreans that Hahm Pyong Choon (appointed ROK

Ambassador to the United States in 1973) referred to in a 1964 *Foreign Affairs* article.[74]

Gradually the relief operation was converted to a consumer-goods program aimed at controlling inflation through sopping up the money in circulation. As Korean industry gradually revived, the focus turned more and more to raw materials and other industrial essentials. The UN Command's relief responsibilities were transferred to the Economic Coordinator, and the KCAC organization abolished, in 1956.

Private Agencies. Aside from governmental programs, a host of private charitable agencies (chiefly American) sent relief food, clothing, medicines, and other goods to Korea, with transportation at U.S. Government expense, as well as providing medical and other personnel for relief work and even for reconstruction. Foremost among these agencies were the International Red Cross, American-Korean Foundation, Church World Service, National Catholic Welfare Conference, and CARE. Their activities from about 1953 were loosely coordinated in a Korean Association of Voluntary Agencies (KAVA), the formation of which was encouraged by U.S. Government representatives. In the calendar year 1956, voluntary assistance to Korea by 66 private agencies, not including individual U.S. donors, totalled over $15 million. In 1957, at the third annual conference of KAVA, the UNC Economic Coordinator (William Warne) said U.S. foreign aid policy was that

> assistance of universities and colleges, foundations, voluntary agencies, as well as private enterprise, should be enlisted to the greatest extent possible. Furthermore, voluntary agencies are peculiarly well equipped to assist a host country to develop community organizations and institutions. . . . The US has, with intent and forethought, left large fields of assistance almost wholly to voluntary agencies and their activities. Particularly there is the whole field of welfare.

Warne noted that the Government contribution to voluntary agencies for ocean freight on donated relief supplies in Fiscal Year 1958 was $800,000, plus an additional $3 million for internal distribution within Korea. He also said that the 67 agencies registered with this program had contributed 115,261 long tons of welfare goods, chiefly food, with an estimated value of $57 million, plus cash contributions of $1 million per year.[75]

The importance of foreign voluntary aid to supplement government programs was not only in its magnitude, but in the fact that it served people whom Korean government agencies could not or would not help. The basic Korean welfare agencies were the extended family and the community, which continued to operate during and after the war (else conditions would have been much worse than they were); but these institutions were increasingly inadequate to meet the challenges of both war and modernization. The government, however, was slow in moving into the resultant vacuum.

An example of this problem was the condition in one area of southwest Korea (Namwon County, North Cholla province) in November 1956, following a near-total crop failure. As a result of Ambassador Dowling's suggestion, based on Embassy reporting, the CARE representative in Korea investigated, and found that some 18,700 farm families were in desperate need. CARE provided one 25-pound package of grain per family per month until the following June, although the distribution was delayed by rail-car shortages. At the same time, the Ambassador spoke to President Rhee, who spoke to his welfare ministry, but nothing happened from November to February. The ministry said it had no resources. Finally, in March 1957, the Finance Minister agreed in a CEB meeting to release funds for relief in areas stricken by the crop failure.

This decision was hailed by U.S. observers as "a reassumption by the ROK Government of full responsibility for its normal relief requirements--something long sought by U.S. officials." But action to implement the decision was less than prompt. In June an Embassy officer reported that 80 percent of the agricultural population was "subsisting on wheat chaff, . . . wild grasses, and pine bark. . . . Only a small amount of the grains delivered to Korea to alleviate the food shortage has reached the rural population. . . ."[76]

AFAK. Another small, but highly visible, component of American aid to Korea was the so-called Armed Forces Aid to Korea (AFAK) program, involving small-scale projects at the community level (schools, youth centers, bridges, etc.) supported and in some cases supervised and carried out by personnel of the UN Command. The program sprang from two sources: the desire of many American soldiers to do something constructive for Korea, and the official U.S. desire to utilize the capacities of the armed forces in community projects that would build goodwill and counteract the adverse image that rambunctious troops on leave and trigger-happy guards had created among the Korean population. The idea of using U.S. troops for rehabilitation purposes originated with President Eisenhower personally in 1951. Modest amounts of money to pay dollar costs of construction materials were included in Defense Department budgets for a number of years, and were supplemented (although to a diminishing extent) by voluntary contributions of money, time, and talent of American personnel.[77]

Control of Inflation and Stabilization of the Economy

In May 1951, a visiting State Department economist (Carwell) noted the extreme difficulty of implementing deflationary policies in Korea because of President Rhee's lack of economic understanding and monopoly of decision-making power. However, even if John Maynard Keynes had been President of Korea, he would have had trouble. As Carwell put it:

. . . inflation is partly due to the Government's overdraft and partly due to the scarcity of commodities. With almost 500 billion *won* in the hands of consumers and with Korean industry operating at about 30 percent prewar, it is natural for consumers to bid for goods regardless of price. . . . The drawings of the UN Forces is [sic] responsible for at least 30 percent of the expansion in the *won* issue. The Korean Government regarding economic stabilization will depend, in large measure, on how successful UNCACK will be in devising plans to cover the expenditures by UN forces by releasing CRIK supplies. . . . Shipping has been so slow and procurement so poor that it is difficult to get a commitment from the military regarding the release of available aid supplies for revenue purposes. . . .[78]

Three of the basic elements in Korean inflation are manifest in the above observation: drawings by UN forces; deficit financing by the ROK government; and consumer-goods shortages (due both to insufficient goods availabilities and to poor distribution). Two other basic elements were the ineffective collection by the ROK government of money for the sale of the goods turned over to its Office of Procurement for distribution; and difficulties in determination of the *won* prices to be charged for American-supplied imports. Of all these problems, it was the fifth--the so-called "counterpart rate"--which most excited President Rhee.[79]

Rhee and his government understandably focused their attention on the UN Command drawings, and saw in American repayment for them a solution for all Korea's problems. American military men, as indicated in Chapter 3, were unwilling to make such repayment until after hostilities had terminated, in accordance with long-standing precedent. This issue plagued the stabilization negotiations for over two years, from the Spring of 1951 until a retroactive settlement and a pay-as-you-go plan settled it in 1954. The Koreans argued that they could use the money to purchase aid goods for sale on the Korean market; the Americans at first argued that with existing military priorities, no additional facilities would be available to import and distribute the goods even if they were purchased, but by late 1951 had shifted ground as the military situation stabilized.[80]

The question of Korean collections for sales of U.S. aid goods came up in negotiations between the ROK and the UN Command for an aid coordination agreement in late 1951. The talks reached an impasse and were suspended because of two issues: ROK refusal to deposit *won* proceeds into the counterpart fund until after the goods were sold; and ROK resentment, on grounds of national sovereignty, of UNC insistence that it control the Korean government's use of its own foreign exchange so long as the ROK government deficit was financed by the United States. By this time, the United States was endeavoring to encourage a Korean consumer-goods import program, using foreign exchange for essential consumer-goods imports and scarce items to soak up money in circulation. The Ambassador (Muccio), in a reply to one of President Rhee's letters on the subject of foreign exchange, noted that the restriction desired by the UN Command was not aimed at control of Korean foreign exchange *per se*, but at the proposition that "the entire resources of the country, including its foreign exchange, would have to be marshalled and organized to secure the utmost value of the pledged aid."[81]

The consumer-goods attack on inflation made economic sense, but it led to a serious paradox: in the long run, the only way to end the foreign-financed Korean deficit would be to substitute domestic production for the imports; yet the capital development needed for such production was inflationary, and until inflation was brought under control, economic development was not feasible. In late 1951, in an appraisal of the Korean economy, Arthur Bloomfield (author of the Korean central banking act) noted that ". . . given existing conditions, . . . long-term reconstruction projects and even rehabilitation work will have to be kept down to approximately their present levels unless the present inflation is to be accentuated. . . ." The same problem was involved in boosting exports.[82]

The compelling reason for the Meyer mission of 1952, aside from the organizational and negotiating difficulties in the field (see page 250 above), was the desire to avoid runaway inflation and the damage to the Korean economy and U.S. objectives that would result from it. But in September, some months after Meyer had brought about an aid coordination agreement, inflation was proceeding at 10 percent a month. A State memorandum chronicled the familiar list of causal factors: *won* advances to the UN forces, bank credit expansion, failure to distribute aid goods, and lack of effective ROK government controls over credit, foreign exchange, the exchange rate, or aid goods distribution. An additional problem was that "a significant portion of the total transactions of the economy [were] carried out wholly or partly without the use of money, resulting in escape from tax and inefficient allocation of resources."[83]

By November 1952 the State Department was in effect siding with the ROK government against the Army and CINCUNC in trying to bring about a settlement for *won* advances, as a means of stepping up imports of consumer goods. However, State officials feared that a settlement might jeopardize appropriations for CRIK and UNKRA aid 'unless it can be demonstrated there is agreed program for use of dollar proceeds which makes sense." The Koreans meanwhile threatened to stop *won* advances, and asked for a $300 million loan or credit as an interim measure to finance consumer-goods imports. The advances were cut off in December, as noted in Chapter 3, forcing the UN Command to resort to stopgap financing of its local expenses.[84]

By August 1953, the inflationary spiral had finally been slowed as a result of several factors. First was a program of currency conversion (at 100 to 1) and partial blocking of about 10 percent of deposits and of notes in circulation, which "appears to have had a contributing although minor part in the recent easing of prices of goods and commodities in Korea." Other factors, considered by the U.S. Embassy to be more important, were (1) large planned imports of grain through Korean foreign exchange and UN aid funds, (2) payment of $85.8 million by the United States on account against past *won* drawings, (3) the ROK government program of allocating its dollar exchange for the use of importers and industrialists; (4) improved ROK fiscal controls. In addition, the improved psychological climate resulting from the Tasca mission mentioned above (page 252) can perhaps be listed as a major anti-inflationary element.[85]

The inflation problem continued, however. After almost a year of relative stability, the wholesale price index again surged upward by 35 percent in the third quarter of 1954, as a result of public anxiety over U.S. troop redeployment, the cessation of U.S. Government tungsten purchases, and increases in the money supply. In one of his early conversations with the ROK Economic Coordinator (Paik), in May 1955, Ambassador Lacy discussed inflation. Rebutting Paik's point that nine years of American management had not brought inflation under control, Lacy replied that inflation had indeed been under control in Korea in 1950. He also noted the parallel with Greece, where four years after the fighting stopped, joint U.S.-Greek efforts had brought inflation under control. Paik nonetheless commented that his doubt of U.S. advice was based on sad experience. This encounter came at one of the low points in Korean-U.S. relations (partly because of Rhee's distrust of Lacy), but it was representative of the confrontation between the two sides.[86]

In the summer of 1955 there were high-level U.S.-ROK economic discussions in Washington, relating primarily to revision of the dollar-*hwan* conversion rate from 180:1 to 500:1, improved fiscal controls, and program revisions. Subsequently, inflation again slowed. It picked up in 1956, with year-end prices 50 percent above those of December 1955, due to a poor rice harvest on top of the usual list of deficiencies. However, real stability did materialize in 1957, and held fairly well thereafter. This development reflected better monetary and fiscal controls that resulted from improved Korean economic sophistication, American pressure (including the "carrot" of an extra $25 million in economic aid for Fiscal Year 1956), and gradually improving ROK-U.S. working relations. In early 1957, the Korean government began utilizing an annual financial program, which in the first year called for zero increase in money supply. In 1958, about five years after the Armistice (although renewed inflation was then feared), the Ambassador (Dowling), CINCUNC (Meloy), and the Economic Coordinator (Warne) could say in a joint memorandum to the ROK government: "The success of our cooperative efforts to maintain price stability . . . after years of rampant inflation, is the most significant single economic achievement in this country since it regained its independence."[87]

Foreign Exchange and Related Problems

The foreign exchange problem in Korea had two main aspects: the international valuation of Korean money, and the utilization of Korean foreign exchange holdings. International valuation was somewhat, but not wholly, related to domestic valuation; U.S. aid goods were priced into the Korean market at an agreed arbitrary rate; the same was true of dollar equivalents for local currency drawings of the UN forces. Domestic rice supply was a major determinant of purchasing power, while normal international commerce until the 1960s was very small. Korean economic dependence on the United States produced a psychological, even more than an economic, correlation among these factors.

Rhee's own psychology--influenced, perhaps, by that of his Austrian wife as well as by his own nationalism and economic naivete--also greatly influenced both the exchange rate problem and the use of Korean foreign exchange. Rhee (1) firmly believed that if the exchange rate were held constant, economic stabilization would follow, irrespective of the laws of supply and demand, and (2) was determined that the *won*-dollar (or *hwan*-dollar) rate should be lower than the Japanese yen-dollar rate (then 360:1), or at least no higher.

Rhee husbanded Korean hard-currency holdings as a French peasant his gold, exercising personal control over their disbursement. He vigorously opposed American efforts to make the ROK government disgorge these holdings in the interests of stabilization. Ambassador Muccio's 1952 statement regarding use of Korea's "entire resources, . . . including foreign exchange" for economic stabilization (see page 263 above) apparently bothered Rhee for this reason. The phrase, "entire resources," turned up in public Korean criticism of Korean policies two years later as evidence that the United States was seeking to assert total control over the affairs of a friendly independent state.[88]

Rate for Won *Drawings by UN Forces.* The problem of reimbursement for local expenditures of UN forces (discussed in Chapter 3) involved, first, agreement on the principle of reimbursement, and second, agreement on the dollar equivalent of the Korean currency drawn. In the settlement of February 1953, the conversion rate was set at 180 *hwan* (equivalent to 18,000 *won* before the conversion in that month) per U.S. dollar. Despite rapid subsequent inflation, the Koreans resisted revision as provided in the agreement. The issue was postponed until the new Economic Coordinator, C. Tyler Wood, arrived. In September 1953, Rhee was angered at Wood's refusal to agree to a permanent rate--"like the Japanese rate," in Rhee's words--but he eventually consented to permit negotiation of an agreed stabilization plan that would provide for fixing the conversion rate for a reasonable time. A stabilization agreement was worked out in the Combined Economic Board in December. Wood used his authority from Washington to allow the 180:1 rate to stand until the following June. The Koreans attempted to interpret this action as a permanent rate.[89]

In May 1954, in anticipation of the June review, the battle was joined once more. Wood wanted a 300:1 rate, based on retail prices, but the Koreans clung to their 180:1 demand. This issue was central in the discussions during and after Rhee's visit to Washington in the summer of 1954. In the end there was a compromise, drafted by the Director of the Foreign Operations Administration (Gov. Stassen), following up a hint by the Koreans: the formal rate remained at 180:1, but the UN forces obtained their local currency needs through periodic dollar auctions. This arrangement was incorporated in the Agreed Minute of Understanding of November 1954, accompanying the Mutual Defense Treaty.[90]

The final act in the exchange rate drama was to bring all the dollar-*hwan* rates (force expenditure conversion, counterpart, and dollar sales) together at a realistic level. Rhee continued his stubborn opposition to change, and his Economic Coordinator (Paik) even wrote a rudely-worded letter in early 1955 calling for cessation of the dollar auctions. This matter came up during Gov. Stassen's visit to Korea in March 1955; in briefing him, Wood's staff noted that ROK economic performance failures related primarily to Rhee's fixation on the 180:1 exchange rate and his psychopathic opposition to trade with Japan.

Gov. Stassen persuaded Rhee to withdraw Paik's letter, and reached other agreements, such as revision in the *hwan* price of petroleum products. But subsequent Korean reporting was again distorted. The Koreans refused to honor the agreement to change the petroleum price, and the Economic Coordinator's office reluctantly acquiesced. A brief war of public statements between the U.S. and Korean side as to what had been agreed. Protracted negotiations ensued in Washington, primarily on the exchange rate, resulting in an agreement on August 12, 1955, to establish a 500:1 rate which would remain in effect until September 30, 1956, thereafter being subject to quarterly review. However, the same basic rate remained until after Rhee resigned in 1960, although various expedients were required to live with it.[91]

Control of Hard-Currency Resources. The issues involved in Korean hard-currency resources were, first, the degree of U.S. control over Korean use of its dollar holdings, and second, the controls against improper diversion of hard currency earned or held by the Republic of Korea.

Rhee, as noted above, was personally concerned with the use of foreign-exchange holdings. The United States was also preoccupied with the use of these holdings. For many years, their principal source was the agreed reimbursements for UN force expenditures, which exceeded Korean commercial export earnings. The UN Command was reluctant in any case to make such reimbursements, partly on the basis that Korean contribution of local expenditures was the least the ROK could do in view of the heavy sacrifices made by other countries on its behalf. Thus in a sense the United States looked on the reimbursements as another kind of aid, in which it had a proprietary interest. Additionally, the American disposition to grant economic assistance was affected by what the Koreans did with their own dollars.

Both these attitudes clashed head-on with Rhee's nationalism and his desire to maximize his few levers of power. For example, in May or June of 1952, the ROK paid over $3 million for the purchase of two cargo ships and fertilizer, without consultation with the United States--an act which in the U.S. view was a violation of the 1948 aid agreement. Asked for an explanation, Asked for an explanation, the Koreans' representative in the deal (S.M. Vinocur, a private American) said that Rhee had ordered them because of "too much delay" in American aid. The UNC representative, partly as a result of this incident, held up the dollar payments for UN force advances, despite the May 1952 agreement, pending development of closer control over Korean foreign exchange. The Ambassador (Muccio), who at that time had little direct control over economic affairs, recommended to Washington that the payments be made nonetheless, observing that payment for the two ships was "not controllable," and it would be better to make a fresh start on coordination rather than prejudice a favorable prospect by recrimination.[92]

As the U.S. aid program began to deliver more goods, as the Combined Economic Board began functioning as an effective coordinating agency, and as the ratio of UN force expenditures to Korean exports decreased, the problem of U.S. jurisdiction over Korean hard-currency holdings receded into the background. Provisions for appropriate consultation, while respecting Korea's sovereignty, were worked out in various economic agreements.

The related issues of foreign exchange controls involved the use of dollars earned by private exports to finance imports, and the control of the black market. The black market flourished on Korean uncertainty as to the country's future; on the difference--as great as four to one in 1952--between Rhee's cherished low exchange rate and the market value of the dollar; and on the Koreans' desire for dollars to finance travel and education abroad and forbidden luxury imports. The exchange controls were required not only to conserve dollar holdings, but to encourage export growth while at the same time preventing imports not related to reconstruction and development. The story of these controls is an enormously complicated one, not further discussed in this study, except to note that manipulation of the controls was a fertile source of graft and political fundraising.

Reconstruction and Development Planning

Early Efforts. The Korean war largely invalidated previous economic planning for Korea, and for nearly three years virtually all attention was devoted to the prevention of disease, unrest, and economic collapse. The UN Korea Reconstruction Agency, from its establishment in 1950, was supposed to deal with rehabilitation and development, while the UN Command dealt with the current situation; but UNKRA's efforts were hampered for a long time by poor relations with the UN Command and by lack of resources.

American authorities were not unmindful of the need for reconstruction planning. A memorandum from the Assistant Secretary of State for International Security Affairs (Cabot) to Defense, ECA, White House, and Treasury representatives in July 1951 pointed out that the possibility of a Korean armistice brought forward "for immediate, co-ordinated solution" the problem of determining the need, purpose, composition and sources of a mutual security program for Korea, and suggested establishing an *ad hoc* working group. The ROK Office of Planning drew up a procurement plan for development projects in August 1951, but it was not highly rated by the U.S. Embassy. In 1952, Ambassador Muccio repeatedly expressed his concern over inaction on the rehabilitation of the Korean economy, which was having adverse effects on Korean psychology, and recommended that at the very least the United States should assist in the rehabilitation of Korean education.[93]

It was not until early 1953 that the need for planning became apparent at decision-making levels,

> that the relief assistance which the United States was at that time making available to Korea was inadequate to help the ROK support its rapidly growing military establishment, let alone rehabilitate the economy. . . . The huge military budget was leading to ever-increasing budgetary deficits which increased the money supply and threatened to provoke rampant inflation. Furthermore, it appeared to be the course of wisdom to begin to rehabilitate the economy despite the fact that a war was still in progress.[94]

Tasca and Nathan Reports. Accordingly, Dr. Henry Tasca was sent on his mission to Korea (see page 252 above), and prepared a plan that became the basis of Secretary Dulles's pledge of $1 billion in U.S. aid. In addition, a study was commissioned by UNKRA and performed by Nathan Associates, published as the "Nathan Report" in 1954. These two reports were the first major postwar efforts at development planning. The Tasca report, less detailed than the Nathan report, was concerned with establishing the over-all level of U.S. aid. It concluded (in the words of one State Department summary) that "United States assistance in the order of $1 billion over a 3- to 5-year period would enable the ROK to become self-supporting, except for military end-item assistance, assuming certain reduced force levels." The Tasca recommendations became the basis of a three-year assistance plan, aimed at ROK self-support. The Nathan report advocated specific projects and programs in various sectors of the Korean economy, and served as a guide for subsequent program planning both by UNKRA and by the United States.[95]

In mid-1955, the then-incoming Ambassador Lacy requested an assessment of the ROK economy, which was submitted to him by three senior officers: Lt.Col. A.A. Jordan of the UN Command; James A. Carey of the Economic Coordinator's staff; and Horace H. Smith, the Embassy economic counselor. Its summary was as follows:

The United States is beginning the third year of its large-scale rehabilitation effort in Korea. According to previous authoritative estimates the process of rehabilitation should be now be well under way with viability for the Korean economy approximately two years away, yet any realistic appraisal of progress to date will show that our goals are virtually as far away as they were in 1953. Although from the sheer magnitude of our effort the Korean economy is making some gains, the process of economic development is simply not "taking". Inadequate fiscal and credit policies--combined with unwise and politically motivated controls on foreign trade, domestic business and foreign investment--have produced disastrous inflation, stifled initiative, disrupted normal price relationships, prevented capital formation and so paralyzed the productive process in general that massive U.S. aid is producing little net progress in the economy.

Unless there is a marked change in the psychological attitude and the legal framework on which the economy rests, further aid, or even bigger aid, cannot provide the breakthrough to viability in anything short of decades. The process of improving this framework will be slow and painful, but must be accomplished before the termination of the aid program if unacceptable consequences are not to follow. An expanding population will make the attainment of viability even more difficult if the start is delayed. A forceful U.S. policy to secure the type of cooperation and action necessary from the ROKs will generate political difficulties in the present but can prevent even greater difficulties in the future.[96]

This pessimistic appraisal reflected two years of difficulty and misunderstanding between the Korean and American partners in the "reconstruction" effort, not to speak of the orphan role of the UN Korea Reconstruction Agency, which in theory had the primary responsibility for much of the rehabilitation effort. It reflected, also, the massive appetite of the military establishment, which gobbled up all available funds and asked for more (the principal reason for the reduction in Korean military forces in 1958), and the continuing instability of the resource-short Korean economy.

Supplementing the appraisal, the counselor for economic affairs at the U.S. Embassy (Smith) submitted a paraphrased "frank statement" on "impediments to an effective aid program in Korea" by an unnamed top U.S. aid administrator, listing both Korean and American faults. The report concluded,

The same conditions which existed in 1950--ROK non-compliance with agreements, bull-headed obstinacy in refusing advice, resistance to straightening out the internal price structure, failure to balance the budget, etc., etc.--exist today. There is little justification in continuing to spend US tax dollars in Korea if the ROK will not take the actions necessary to help themselves. Without mutuality of purpose the US economic aid program makes no sense. The question is how do we get the conditions for a successful mutual aid program established.

I suggest the use of a big stick--in this case the withholding of aid funds until the ROK comes through.[97]

Meanwhile, the Koreans were clamoring for allocation of more resources to economic development projects that would build up Korea's industrial strength, and being turned down most of the time, on the grounds that such projects would worsen an already inflationary situation (see page 263 above). One exception to the general U.S. policy was FOA Director Stassen's agreement in conversation with Rhee in February 1954 to go ahead with financing of a fertilizer plant, power facilities, and cement and glass factories, even though production costs in Korea might exceed the cost of imports.[98]

The 1955 economic discussions in Washington were described in the final press release of August 12 as "focused on exchange rate problems and related subjects including discussion of the steps each government should take to speed up the reconstruction and rehabilitation program which is designed to enable Korea to become self-supporting with a stabilized economy as rapidly as possible." Thereafter, the Koreans did in fact improve their economic performance, even to the extent that Rhee consented to a reduction in investment program for fiscal 1956 in the interests of stability; the Assistant Secretary of State approved a recommendation by his staff in January 1956 that he congratulate the Korean Ambassador on his government's "earnest efforts" and "wise budgetary and pricing policies"; and an additional $25 million was allocated, as already noted.

The results of the improved atmosphere were perceived in meaningful development areas, as well as in stabilization. In the annual economic report for 1955, the U.S. Embassy reported that economic progress was spotty: industrial production was 55 percent higher than in 1949 (base year for U.S. rehabilitation goals, but itself a poor year in comparison with pre-World War II performance), while grain and pulse production was slightly less than in 1949 on a per-capita basis. The gain in real gross national product was only 2.9 percent above 1954.

> The most notable achievements were the near completion of three thermal power plants with a total capacity of 100,000 KWs, improvements in the field of transportation and a sharp increase in coal output. Measures have been taken to construct or rehabilitate communication facilities, salterns, the fishing fleet and cement, flat-glass, and fertilizer plants.

The ROK Five-Year Plan. Up to this point, there had been no true long range development planning for Korea, nor any development goals beyond the desirable but rather vague ones of stability and self-support (with the partial exception of the Nathan report). However, Americans had begun to encourage the Koreans to think of their own long-range future. In March 1956, when Secretary of State Dulles visited Korea, the Finance Minister told him in the course of a conference that "in order to make planning easier the ROK government wanted very much to have a long-range U.S. aid program. . . . It would be very useful to have some sort of hint of the amounts of aid which the ROKs could expect over the next several years." The ROK Economic Coordinator added that "the ROK government had been working very seriously on a five-year plan of economic reconstruction" that "would involve the expenditure of approximately 2.4 billion dollars: $1.0 billion on reconstruction and $1.5 billion to sustain the economy during the period of the plan." The Secretary said only that he would study the problems raised in the conference. However, the growing American recognition of the need for a plan was implicit in an appraisal of the Korean situation by the U.S. budget director (Macy) later that year.[99]

Following the conference referred to above, the Koreans announced a five-year plan based on $2.3 billion in external aid, subsequently revised to $1.7 billion. An official of the Reconstruction Ministry privately told Embassy officers that the first step in preparing the plan had been to estimate the maximum amount of aid that the ROK could "reasonably" expect from the United States. Then the goals of the plan and an industry-by-industry allocation of investment funds was computed. The U.S. Embassy commented, "the creation of dynamic conditions depends upon more than the mere injection of more capital." Moreover, the "plan" appeared to be more of a shopping list than an integrated strategy. Nevertheless, it signalled a Korean awareness of long-range planning that bore fruit several years later.[100]

The Prochnow Committee. In the same general time frame, an Interdepartmental Committee on Certain Aid Programs (the Prochnow committee) studied the Korean situation in Washington, and in June 1956 reported to the National Security Council. In the view of State's Office of Northeast Asian Affairs, the report "was not able to contribute any significant new thoughts on posture in the Republic of Korea." In addition to noting the usual economic problems, it emphasized the economic burden imposed by the necessity (recently reaffirmed by the Joint Chiefs of Staff) to maintain the large Korean military establishment at the level then established. It concluded that "large scale aid is required to maintain present levels of production and consumption," and that "even in the absence of the military program, a Korean posture of self-support is nowhere in sight." However, the report made one innovation (seemingly disregarded at the time): it suggested that "the total cost and number of years required for [self-support in non-military fields] will be less under a program which *achieves an annual increase in per capita GNP of 3%,* than would be the case if no such increase were undertaken" (emphasis added). This was the first reference to such a planning goal.[101]

A new constraint on the aid program developed in the Spring of 1955, when it appeared that American aid was reaching Korea faster than it could be utilized--the problem called "absorptive capacity." U.S. Embassy reporting attributed it to difficulties in the exchange rate and pricing policy, shortage of transportation, insufficient budgetary arrangements for official supplies and commercial funds for civilian goods, and delay in the payment of wages for loading and handling goods. Resultant reductions in revenue from counterpart sales began to hamper operations under the special military and rehabilitation accounts (established to hold counterpart funds generated from aid goods sales until obligated by action of the Combined Economic Board). Korean officials attributed these difficulties to poor U.S. performance. Such charges were not wholly unfounded; but in any event the factors cited were largely institutional, and were eventually rectified.[102]

In making its annual appraisal of the Korean economy for 1956, the U.S. Embassy could say that although no progress--or negative progress--was recorded on inflation, the foreign trade gap, and agricultural production, yet manufacturing and minerals production advanced considerably, to a point appreciably above pre-Korean war levels.

> As a generalization, it can be said that 1956 witnessed the completion of the relief and rehabilitation phase of the economic program in Korea and the beginning of the phase of economic development. With this new phase emerged new and complex problems of long-range economic development planning, resource analysis, balance of payments and industrial and managerial training.[103]

U.S. Funding of Korean Economic Assistance

Defense and UNKRA Funding. During the Korean war, U.S. Government economic assistance to Korea was furnished in two principal ways: through Defense Department appropriations for Civil Relief in Korea (CRIK), limited to those measures necessary to avoid disease and unrest; and appropriations for the United Nations Korea Reconstruction Agency (UNKRA), which were restricted by the proviso that American contributions should be no more than 65 percent of the total. (At one point, the activities of UNKRA were in danger of suspension because of the insufficient contributions of other nations, which made additional U.S. contributions impossible because of the ceiling.)

FOA/ICA and PL 480 Funding. For reasons discussed above, the United States in August 1953 pledged $1 billion over a three- to four-year period for Korean economic rehabilitation. The initial $200 million of this amount was transferred by President Eisenhower from the Defense Department budget, as the equivalent of savings realized by the cessation of hostilities.

In subsequent years, Congress appropriated funds through the successors to the Economic Cooperation Administration--the Mutual Security Agency (MSA), the Foreign Operations Administration (FOA), and International Cooperation Administration (ICA). The billion-dollar target was surpassed by the end of Fiscal Year 1956, if non-military aid through the Defense Department was included, or by fiscal 1957, if these sums were not included.[104]

Beginning in fiscal 1955, aid was also supplied to Korea under Public Law 480, providing for the distribution of surplus American agricultural commodities. Contracts under PL 480 in fiscal 1955 and 1956 had reached nearly $60 million.

U.S. Constraints. In 1956, the current and future impact of American military and economic aid commitments abroad on the U.S. economy was a subject of growing concern among U.S. policy-makers. Thus, Secretary Dulles, in his meeting with ROK Cabinet ministers during his March 1956 visit to Korea, responded to Korean requests for economic aid by saying that during his trip he had received from various countries

> a total of requests for economic aid which, if met, would destroy the soundness of the U.S. economy. . . . American aid like ammunition must be rationed to those who need it most in fighting the cold war. . . . American economic aid was not accorded on the basis of friendship but as a contribution to winning the cold war. . . . The U.S. would weigh ROK needs in the light of overall requirements and then allocate available aid where it would best achieve our worldwide objectives. . . . The Korean aid program had been the U.S.'s largest one and . . . the amount of U.S. assistance to Korea should be taken as a measure of the importance [we] have felt Korea has had in the cold war.[105]

The Secretary's comments demonstrate the essentially military motivation of American aid during the mid-1950s. The money was intended to buy security against world communism, with national economic development a useful by-product rather than a principal goal. Coupled with this objective was, of course, the desire to make Korea increasingly self-supporting so as to reduce the drain on U.S. resources--a drain seen at the time as virtually endless.

In its June 1956 report to the National Security Council on the Korean economy, the Prochnow committee noted that the Korean economy, "as a result of the tremendous infusion of foreign economic aid," had "reached or exceeded pre-hostilities per capita levels of production in most fields" and had returned to a consumption level about the same as before the Korean war. But large-scale aid was required to maintain these levels: "the vast military establishment" was "responsible for a large part of the overwhelming dependence on outside aid," not only in direct costs but by "increasing the consumption level and making it politically difficult to control." These factors, added to other Korean economic and human problems, seriously hampered development prospects.

The committee projected aid requirements for both military and economic assistance on the basis of four alternative policies, ranging between $3 and $4.5 billion for the period 1957-1961, at the end of which Korea would have an annual deficit between $546 million (with annual economic growth at 3 percent per capita) to $898 million (with no economic growth but a 10 percent per capita increase in consumption over the period). Implicit in the committee's report, which made no recommendations, was that a high level of U.S. aid for 1957-1961 was justified to maintain Korean military strength in the cold war and to reduce the aid burden on the U.S. Subsequent policy decisions essentially reflected this view (see Chapter I).[106]

8

Korean Economic Development:
The March to Self-Reliance, 1957-1965

The emphasis in U.S.-Korean economic relations shifted from relief and rehabilitation to development after 1956, as noted above. By the end of 1965, it finally became clear that south Korea did, after all, have potential economic viability and had entered the stage of sustained rapid economic growth.

The intervening nine years can be divided into four quite distinct periods. First of these was the three years from 1957 to early 1960, during which increased Korean economic sophistication and efficiency contended with Rhee's senescence and the cynical drive for power by some of his supporters. The second period was the confused year of parliamentary democracy from the "student revolution" of April 1960 until the military coup d'état of May 1961, when a great deal of useful economic planning and institutional reform was undertaken, but without the political unity to reap the benefits.

Third came the two-and-a-half-year military government period from 1961 until establishment of a civilianized regime in December 1963--a period that saw concentrated political power and administrative efficiency often misused for dubious and even mischievous purposes while the young military leaders learned the iron laws of economics. Finally, in the years 1964 and 1965, President Park's will and ability, the efficiency of his administration, the years of American tutelage and support, and preparatory Korean-American planning from 1956, finally bore fruit. The "new look" in Korean economic development was as much psychological as economic: the Koreans had finally developed optimism and self-confidence about their own future and their own capability.

The economic problems of past years were present during the 1957-1965 time span also: the heavy military burden; inflation; poor or misconceived monetary and fiscal policies; unrealistic and inflationary development projects, motivated more by national prestige than by sound economics; shrinking U.S. aid; misuse of aid funds; corruption. In addition, new problems came to the fore as a result

275

of the new development emphasis: the development of economic and social infrastructure; local-currency working capital to accompany aid-financed industrial projects; justification and negotiation of foreign development loans as a replacement for grant aid; problems of promoting exports, including American resistance to trade competition; and maximization of domestic savings for investment. From 1960 on, once Rhee and his anti-Japanese prejudice had passed from the scene, the Koreans responded to American prodding and entered into serious negotiations with Japan (see Chapter 4). An agreement resulted in 1965, yielding several hundred million dollars to boost the Korean economy and (to a limited degree) opening the Japanese market for Korean exports.

American economic policy toward Korea altered considerably between 1956 and 1965. The departure of Rhee and the end of the U.S. Republican adminis-tration, both in 1960, put an end to the policy of placating and shoring up a wilful but heavily dependent regime, while waiting for a better day, that had characterized U.S. policy since 1950. When hard-eyed and somewhat anti-American military leaders took over in 1961, the old patron-client relationship rapidly shifted to one of eyeball-to-eyeball confrontation, with firmer goals and tighter administration on both sides.

In addition, the Kennedy administration brought a new understanding of the problems of economic growth, based on the governmental experience and aca-demic research of the 1950s. Economic development performance, as well as support of cold-war objectives, became a primary criterion for justifying U.S. economic assistance, and national economic planning was no longer suspected as socialist ideology. Thus, far greater emphasis was put on formulation of joint comprehensive multi-year plans and programs and insisting on their fulfillment, although the Congress could never be persuaded to make appropriations on a multi-year basis.

The following sections briefly summarize the highlights of Korean economic development, with emphasis on their political implications. For a sophisticated analysis of Korean economic and political development during this period, see the book by David C. Cole and Princeton N. Lyman (both formerly connected with the Korean aid program), *Korean Development; the Interplay of Politics and Economics* (Harvard University Press, 1971).

The Twilight of the Rhee Regime, 1957-1960

Institutional Problems

From mid-1956 until the end of 1958, Korean economic conditions and U.S.-Korean economic relations improved considerably over previous years, despite setbacks such as the poor rice crop of 1956 and Typhoon Agnes in 1957.

The difficulties of Rhee's reelection in 1956 acquainted him with the extent of public opposition. He responded to it by shaking up his Cabinet and bringing in capable economic administrators. These men in turn (especially Song In-Sang, the new Reconstruction Minister and Economic Coordinator, later Finance Minister) drew upon the talents of young, American-educated bureaucrats and scholars, who had previously been barred from meaningful positions by the opposition of the entrenched, ex-Japanese bureaucrats.

Some of the new men had been the targets of a low-key U.S. Embassy campaign to increase Korean economic understanding through regular, unpublicized informal seminars at the home of the economic minister (Edwin M. Cronk), the political counselor (William G. Jones), and other participants. There were four Korean participants and four Americans in these sessions, who jestingly called themselves "the thinkers." As Koreans were transferred to other responsibilities, the remaining Korean participants selected their replacements, thus assuring a group that could trust one another. As the political arena became more critical, the "thinkers" delved deeply into political problems as well as economic ones.

In May 1958, urging favorable consideration of a proposal to extend loan-type development financing to Korea, the U.S. Embassy could say that "ROK cooperation on economic policies and operations improving constantly during past two years, especially 1957," and the UNC Economic Coordinator (Warne), at a 1958 conference with the Assistant Secretary of State for Economic Affairs (Mann) and the ROK Economic Coordinator (Song) could note the "high capacity displayed by the Combined Economic Board and its function of coordinating all economic agencies of the Korean Government." Annual "stabilization agreements" reached in the CEB were generally enforced, and served their purpose, although the black-market value of the *hwan* nearly doubled.[1]

Institutional arrangements continued to cause problems, however. On the U.S. side, it was not until March 20, 1959, that a normal country team was established in Korea, over vigorous military opposition, and the Ambassador was given direction of the economic assistance program. (CINCUNC retained control of military programs and of U.S. funding for them.) In 1957, when the State Department made one of its many attempts to have the economic coordination role transferred from the UN Command to the Embassy, it argued that the relief and rehabilitation phase was over; but in a conference with the Under Secretary of State (Herter) and Defense Department officials, the outgoing Commander-in-Chief, UN Command (Lemnitzer) did not agree. He said that such a move would transfer to Washington decisions that should be resolved in Korea by one individual (i.e., CINCUNC). This position was not without merit, because of the continuing military threat from the north, and the very large military share in the economy. However, it posed the fundamental question of whether defense or economic development should have priority--expressed in the conference in terms of whether the transfer would involve upgrading the Ambassador or downgrading CINCUNC. Moreover, it led to constant Korean questioning as to which official--the Ambassador, CINCUNC, or the UNC Economic Coordinator--was the main locus of American responsibility, and encouraged Korean attempts to play one U.S. agency against another.[2]

On the Korean side, institutional problems were interrelated with over-all economic problems because of the presumed correlation between the morale and efficiency of the bureaucracy and their rates of pay, which had been ridiculously low since 1945. Failure to increase the pay rates led to corruption and poor performance; but to increase the rates for a quarter-million employees to realistic levels (estimated in 1958 to require a 100 percent increase) would have a tremendous inflationary impact. The military pay scales (affecting over 600,000 individuals) also required revision. The United States was in the unenviable position of opposing pay raises because they would unbalance the budget, at a time when U.S. aid levels were declining.[3]

The shortcomings of the ROK bureaucracy were highlighted by the food crisis of 1957. A U.S. Embassy survey in August noted the failure of Korean agencies to distribute relief food to "3.5 million people on starvation rations" the previous Spring (highlighted by an Embassy officer's visit to an impoverished farm district--see page 261 above), and the belief of farmers, dissatisfied with fertilizer distribution, that the "government and commercial interests" were "profiteering at their expense" by diverting low-priced government fertilizer into higher-priced commercial channels. The Embassy commented that in its belief,

> ROK Government and [Liberal] Party either not sufficiently aware situation or incapable rectifying it. Attitude of ROKG last spring . . . not one of a government responsive to needs of people. . . . At same time Embassy has noted growing awareness over past year among younger government officials that positive action must be taken meet popular needs. . . . Seems probable that dissatisfaction evidenced in farmers' conversations with Embassy officers has long been existent but is now becoming articulate to increasing degree and is encouraged by organized opposition and independent press.[4]

Yet in August 1957, the price of rice had fallen to a level below that of the previous year--the first time this had happened in many years--largely because of the large importation of U.S. surplus grains. By October, a good Korean harvest had sent rice prices to the lowest level in eighteen months, and their continued decline had Korean officials worried because of the impact on the farmers. It later became apparent that the government estimate of the 1957 rice crop was badly understated--partly because farmers and local officials colluded to avoid taxes by under-reporting. American grain had thus hurt the Korean farmer on the basis of inadequate Korean government information. However, it must be noted that the Koreans were under heavy U.S. pressure to accept 50,000 tons of rice, while in the Finance Minister's view Korea "needed other grains more urgently." At the same time the United States, anxious to dispose of its agricultural surplus and sell it in Korea to raise local currency for the military budget, also tried to ship tobacco to Korea which was then trying to export its own tobacco crop.[5]

The "era of good feeling" between Koreans and American receded during 1959 into disagreement, confrontation, and Korean obstinacy. This situation was a result of the growing political crisis (described in Chapter 6), which led the hard-line Rhee supporters to sacrifice economic stability and development to political expediency.

In April 1959, Washington was concerned with ROK deficit financing, inconsistent with the agreed stabilization program. By April 1960 (just prior to Rhee's downfall), the U.S. Embassy was recommending stringent actions to counter efforts to use economic aid funds for ROK political purposes. The Embassy listed examples of such practices: aid projects awarded to Liberal party favorites; allocation of aid funds on the basis of political rather than economic criteria; administration of fertilizer distribution and similar programs for political advantage in local communities; indirect manipulation of the aid program.

The State Department did not accept the Embassy's proposals--particularly those that would establish non-governmental Korean participation in review and investigation of the aid program--but the Department recognized the need for modification of existing machinery. However, the collapse of the Rhee regime within a week, and its replacement with a more reasonable caretaker government, restored an atmosphere of cooperation.[6]

Waste and Corruption

The twin issues of waste and corruption came into growing prominence from 1956 onward. In 1956, an ICA post-audit of ROK aid expenditures (a procedure followed since 1948) revealed improper expenditures by ROK government authorities totalling $6 million. These were very likely due to inefficiency or attempts to maximize ROK benefits, rather than simple corruption ($4.8 million was attributed to violations of the provision that the ROK pay 50 percent of shipping costs), but the ROK indicated its intention to refund $5 million. In 1957, the U.S. Comptroller General (Campbell) in Congressional testimony criticized waste and deficiencies in the American aid program and the lack of Korean cooperation, and a committee of the Korean National Assembly undertook its own investigation. In 1958 a fraud surfaced in connection with procurement of soap for the Korean Army under the U.S. offshore procurement program, recalling the "raw cotton scandal" of 1954 (cited on page 96).[7]

Aside from conspicuous particular instances such as those above, there was general awareness among both Koreans and Americans of endemic corruption in Korea. Its growth and seriousness provoked the resignation of a U.S. deputy aid mission (USOM) director, Hugh Farley, in early 1961, and his personal anti-corruption campaign, which resulted in inclusion of an anti-corruption goal in the task force policy recommendations of that year (see Chapter 1, page 29). Corruption was also one of the reasons given for the 1961 military coup d'état.[8]

Modern theorists on political corruption maintain that it sometimes serves functional purposes. In Korea, it did provide a crude form of redistributing wealth for penniless bureaucrats and their relatives, and to this extent it followed the age-old custom of "squeeze," although without the traditional relatively modest limits. Similarly, election payoffs of food, drink, entertainment, and expense money could be viewed as wealth redistribution.

However, there was at least one area in which the process was clearly dysfunctional: the governing Liberal party's practice of levying contributions on businessmen, either as a penalty of success or as a precondition to loans from the banks. The purpose was to ensure the continuation of the Liberal party in power, as well as the welfare of party members; but its effect was to dampen private initiative to a degree which, in one qualified observer's view, acted as a strong deterrent to Korean economic development. Two competent middle-sized businessmen told a U.S. Embassy officer (Jones) during this period that there was no point in developing their businesses further, since the massive political contributions they would be required to pay would negate the gains from larger-scale operations.[9]

Changing U.S. Aid Policies and Their Consequences

Over-all American aid policies were in gradual transition during the 1957-1960 period, reflecting a growing awareness of developmental requirements as well as a growing concern at the drain of foreign aid on U.S. resources. Some of the new American concerns were reflected in a speech made by the UN Command Economic Coordinator (Warne) at the third annual conference of the Korea Association of Voluntary Agencies (KAVA) in August 1957 (see page 260). Pointing out that the U.S. government and voluntary agency programs were "complementary, not competitive," he spoke of problems and dangers faced by both: impatience for results, leading to assumption of action responsibility by Americans, rather than training and equipping Koreans to achieve them; the temptation to continue relief services, rather than move toward rehabilitation channels ("it is easier and more appealing to raise money and give it out in this way"); the growing Korean rebellion against organized Western influence from any source, which called for training native leaders and giving them the leadership; and the need to evaluate and check on the use of aid funds.[10]

Reduction of U.S. Aid

The first major reduction of American economic aid was announced in November 1957, affecting Fiscal Year 1958--a reflection of the 20 percent reduction in global aid levels that year. (Through an unhappy sequence of events it reached President Rhee through the newspapers before the U.S. Embassy could tell him the final U.S. government decision). Despite Korean apprehensions, however, the effect of the announcement was viewed by the Embassy as constructive. Several officials hoped for subsequent reconsideration, and the Reconstruction Minister (Song) called for "at least $50 million" in development loans, plus $25-30 million in U.S.-financed offshore procurement of military requirements and a large PL 480 program. Nevertheless,

> Government officials and the press . . . have pressed the 'need for more careful use of the aid monies' and 'the urgency of building up the export capacity of Korea.' In discussing Korea's economic future with ROKG officials, Embassy officers for the first time receive the impression that the Korean economic leaders are facing up to the likelihood of a future which does not indefinitely include enormous grants from the United States. This may introduce a degree of realism into their forward 'planning' that heretofore seems not to have existed in sufficient amount.[11]

Rhee's own reaction, however, was caustic. Ever the anti-Communist warrior, he told Ambassador Dowling in a thirty-minute diatribe that he had concluded the United States was "incapable or unwilling to lead the free world"; was following a policy of "peace at any price"; and was ignoring Communist gains. In contrast with his more reasonable attitude of the previous year,

> He declared Korea could not exist on US aid and vain hopes and said early reunification was required if Korea is to survive. Instead . . . US was concentrating on co-existence with Communists and on assisting Japan to Asian dominance. Throughout his discourse there ran vein of resentment at Washington for what he obviously sees as neglect of Korea and disregard his own views.[12]

The shock of reduced aid was cushioned somewhat by the continuing PL 480 program of surplus agricultural commodities, some of which were distributed through voluntary agencies and the remaining (and much larger) part sold for Korean currency, most of which supported the military budget. In addition, the Department of Defense began offshore procurement for dollars in Korea. At first, goods like tires and batteries were purchased to supply the UN forces, with the added objective of promoting Korean industrial efficiency through enforcement of production standards. Subsequently the program was extended to the needs of Korean forces as well--a peculiar expedient under which Korean goods were bought for the Korean forces with U.S. dollars, reflecting the political fact that American appropriations were easier to get for military than for civilian purposes.

Development Loans

A third means of meeting the aid gap was the use of development loans under the newly-established Development Loan Fund. The State Department had suggested a loan component in the Fiscal Year 1956 aid program, but withdrew the suggestion after "strenuous objections by both the Economic Coordinator and the Korean Government"--the former because the Korean economy did not justify a loan, the latter because it viewed a loan as unfair. The Director of ICA suggested in October 1956 that a loan component of $25 million be included in the Fiscal Year 1957 program, but the Under Secretary of State opposed the idea as "unwise on both political and economic grounds." However, the reduction of grant aid and the improved Korean economic situation altered both U.S. and Korean perspective. In May 1958, the U.S. Embassy urged consideration of DLF loans for sound Korean investment proposals such as power and cement plants and telecommunications facilities, which could not be undertaken otherwise. Moreover, there were Korean sensitivities to be considered: the announcement of such loans to other Asian countries, especially the politically uncommitted ones, would have unfortunate repercussions unless the Koreans were somehow reassured of continuing American support.[13]

Although agreement in principle for the DLF loans was eventually forthcoming, it was not until nearly two years later that the first loan (for design of an electric power plant at Ch'ungju in central Korea) was actually approved. When action on it was completed in Washington, Korea was in the midst of the political crisis of December 1958 (see Chapter 6, pages 195 ff.), so that announcement of the loan was held up until the following Spring, and the Korean National Assembly did not ratify it until December 1959. The delay in U.S. approval was due partly to Korean ineptitude in the preparation of adequate project proposals, and partly perhaps to excessive American bureaucratic caution in venturing into a new field. (Similar delays, for similar reasons, continued in subsequent years.) The delay in ratification of the pioneering Ch'ungju loan after its approval was due, of course, to the political atmosphere in Korea, with the usual priority to politics over economics. The processing of development loans was a time-consuming one for several years, and became a focus of Korean complaints about American aid policies.[14]

Private Investment

Encouragement of foreign private investment was another possible response to declining aid levels. The United States had been promoting the idea for several years, with the Treaty of Friendship, Commerce, and Navigation of 1956 as a first step. The Ministry of Finance drafted a bill to promote foreign private investment in 1954, but nothing came of it. In 1956, the ROK Ministry of Reconstruction prepared a foreign capital induction bill, but it also ran into opposition. When U.S. representatives pushed for such a measure, the Koreans said it would be impossible to get it passed without provisions to keep out undesirable nationalities (i.e., Japanese) and to protect vested Korean interests. In August 1957, the ROK government accepted, with hopeful alacrity, an Embassy/OEC proposal to recruit an investment consultant under ICA auspices to advise on suitable draft legislation. Such a consultant arrived in early 1958, and made recommendations to the Korean government. At the same time, $2 million in local proceeds from surplus agricultural sales became available for loans to U.S. business in Korea under the Cooley amendment to PL 480, despite vigorous Korean objections. (A Korean official remarked privately, "Not only are you making us take your farm surpluses off your hands, but you also want us to finance the foreign traders.") But as of mid-1958, there was virtually no foreign private investment in Korea, no facilitating law, and no formal application for a Cooley loan.[15]

Export Promotion

A further means of meeting declining American aid levels was to increase Korean exports, which up until the mid-1950s had been minuscule. The U.S. Economic Coordinator's staff undertook an export promotion project, including the development of handicrafts and the establishment of a trade promotion center. Foreign exchange policies were adopted by the Korean government to encourage exporters. Progress, however, was slow; exports for the calendar year 1960 (admittedly a difficult year for Korea, because of the political upheaval) totalled only $30 million (not counting U.S. procurement) against imports of three quarters of a billion. There were a number of reasons for the difficulty, including Korean inexperience at conforming to production standards and delivery schedules. American problems also inhibited exports, notwithstanding the policy of export encouragement. For example, in 1957 the ROK Ambassador in Washington (Yang) asked for U.S. help in promoting the export of $2 million worth of Korean textiles to Hong Kong; but the Assistant Secretary of State said it would be very difficult because the cotton had been supplied by the United States under PL 480.[16]

Foreign Exchange Rate

Despite improved economic management, the Korean currency continued to depreciate after the 1955 agreement had established a 500:1 conversion rate (see page 264 above). By 1958, American officials were broadly hinting that the rate should be revised, possibly to 900:1; but in fact no change was made until after Rhee's resignation. Instead, a series of expedients were adopted that amounted to a multiple-rate system. In early 1957, the ROK Economic Coordinator (Kim Hyon-Chul) suggested a 2:1 currency conversion that would result in a 31 percent devaluation and put the Korean unit at the same dollar value as the

Japanese yen (360:1). The U.S. Economic Coordinator indicated that a 900:1 rate would be realistic, and the Governor of the Bank of Korea subsequently agreed with him, but no action was taken. There was talk--but no action--about a special tourist rate. In 1959, the ROK decided to utilize coins for the first time since 1945, and asked the United States to supply 100 million *hwan* in coins of 10- and 50-*hwan* denomination. The first shipment of 23 million *hwan*, received in October, disappeared from circulation overnight, presumably because of their souvenir value.

The "Brain Drain"

A problem of economic development involved the departure of Korean students. In 1959, the ROK Ministry of Education records indicated that 4,703 Korean students had gone abroad for study after 1951, but only 685 had returned. Of the returnees, "more than half" had found jobs. In 1957, ROK Ambassador Yang in Washington pointed out to Assistant Secretary of State Robertson that the recently-passed U.S. Immigration and Nationality Act, PL 85-316, aggravated the brain drain by allowing change in status (i.e., permanent residence) for certain technically qualified students. Yang said that too many Korean students wanted to stay in the United States, and cited the notorious case of medical doctor Yi Yong-T'ae and his wife, which was then pending before the U.S. immigration authorities (the Yis had greatly overstayed their visas).

The main reasons for the Korean students' attitude were, first, that they often encountered discrimination and opposition at home, particularly from bureaucrats with Japanese training; second, that salaries were higher and opportunities greater for trained people in the United States than in Korea. No bureaucratic solution for this problem was ever found, except that trainees at U.S. government expense were issued visas that required them to return to their homeland for two years on completion of their training.[17]

The Democratic Interlude, 1960-1961

The caretaker government of Huh Chung which held the Republic of Korea together after President Rhee's resignation in April 1960 brought competent men into Cabinet economic portfolios, but no major policy shifts were made in the interim period except to cooperate fully with the U.S. economic mission and to permit a change in the exchange rate. The parliamentary government of Chang Myon took over in August 1960, committed both to democracy and to rapid economic development. It had competent economic leadership and good ideas; but it faced enormous handicaps. The Democratic party split into two almost equal opposing groups, plus other smaller factions, as soon as it came to power, making both executive and legislative action difficult. The new administration, unlike the old one, was responsive to a two-house parliament which itself was largely composed of new, inexperienced, and power-hungry people. The bureaucracy, for many years staffed and organized to do Rhee's bidding, was distrusted by the new leaders. The police force was totally discredited. Prime Minister Chang was respected and honest, but timid. The students, who had toppled Rhee by their demonstrations, continued to demonstrate, and their example was followed by other groups with diverse and unrealistic demands.

The consequence of these factors was a confused and weak administration, heavy government personnel turnover (including dismissal of some competent and badly needed bureaucrats), and economic stagnation. A group of competent young economists was brought into key positions by the vigorous and imaginative Finance Minister (Kim Young-Sun), but they did not have the requisite time and firm executive support to develop and implement their programs. They were preempted by the military coup of May 1961, at a time when it seemed that their efforts were starting to bear fruit. Nevertheless, their work gave the new military regime a running start in its economic policies.

"Normalization" of U.S. Aid

The Chang administration also faced an external challenge: the United States was already committed to reduce its aid burden worldwide, and was less and less inclined to continue the massive levels and special treatment accorded Korea. Before Rhee's resignation, the U.S. Embassy and economic mission had made a study of future aid requirements for Korea pursuant to the new Mansfield amendment to the Mutual Security Act. It concluded that grant aid-- now termed "defense support"--could decline to around $45-70 million by calendar year 1970; and that the rest of Korea's annual deficit on foreign account, projected at $130-140 million per year, could be financed through PL 480 surplus agricultural commodities, loans, and foreign private investment.[18]

In March 1960, the decision had been reached in Washington to bring the Korean mutual security (i.e., economic and military aid) program into conformity with worldwide procedures--meaning an increase in the local-currency costs of aid to the Koreans retained in U.S. account, and increased U.S. control over counterpart funds. In deference to the political situation, U.S. announcement of the decision was postponed until July, but at that time the Koreans called for suspending such action, particularly during the interim government period. The State Department sympathized with this view, partly because the Korean press was in effect accusing the United States of taking advantage of the interim government's weakness to win various concessions. Normalization was eventually accomplished through a revised aid agreement (see page 287).

Despite his long record of cooperation with the United States, Prime Minister Chang could not politically afford to respond to all U.S. demands when he acceded to power, even though he and his associates accepted the validity of some of them. On the other hand, the United States was obliged, both because

of Congressional and public pressures and for the sake of Korean economic stability, to press for a number of basic reforms. In addition to normalization of
aid arrangements, these included primarily the revamping of the Korean foreign
exchange system and revision of the economic assistance agreement of 1948.

Expansion of Economic Assistance; the "Dillon Letter"

The Chang administration, for its part, needed an increase in economic
assistance--not only to finance development projects, but also to show the
Korean people that it could deal with the Americans as well as, or better than,
Rhee had done. In the face of declining American worldwide aid levels, even
to maintain existing levels of aid for Korea was a diplomatic challenge.

To meet this challenge, Chang sent an able, American-educated economist,
the Vice Minister of Reconstruction (Tchah Kyun-Hi) to Washington in October
1960 for discussions of Korean aid requirements with the Under Secretary of
State (Douglas Dillon) and other U.S. officials, while U.S. Embassy officials
at Washington direction were pressing the Prime Minister for exchange rate
reforms. At the same time, the Finance Minister stressed to the Deputy Chief
of Mission (Marshall Green) and other Embassy officers the urgency of keeping
the U.S. aid figure at the $180 million level of the previous year, rather than
lowering it to the $165 million in defense support proposed by the United States,
both to support a reconstruction budget and to meet the socialist opposition in
the National Assembly. The Americans rejected the contention that the lower
aid level would upset the proposed ROK budget; but Green in his report to
Washington confirmed the political delicacy of the situation, at a time when the
prospects of political and economic stability seemed to be improving.[19]

As a climax to the negotiations in both Seoul and Washington, the ROK
Finance Minister (Kim) went to Washington at the request of the United States.
In his conference with Under Secretary Dillon on October 25, 1960, it was
agreed that if the ROK carried out specified economic reforms, the United States
would provide a $25 million exchange stabilization fund and $15 million in
supplementary aid (a figure achieved largely through bookkeeping and seman-
tics), thus bringing the total aid for Fiscal Year 1961 above the magic $180
million figure. The undertakings of both sides were incorporated in a letter of
October 25 from the Under Secretary to the Finance Minister, thereafter
referred to as the "Dillon Letter."

During these conversations, responding to the Koreans' emphasis on their
problems of poverty and unemployment, the Under Secretary repeated previous
American suggestions that a works program be established, similar to that used
in the United States during the Depression of the 1930s, and financed by the
distribution of surplus American grain under new provisions of Title II of PL
480. This suggestion was translated into action the following Spring, when the
Finance Minister personally led a march in Seoul to mark the establishment of

a National Reconstruction Corps. The organization of this group was imaginative, not only putting unemployed rural and urban people on useful projects of social infrastructure (irrigation, street improvement, etc.), but also utilizing the skills and energy of restless college students. Difficulties were encountered in the distribution of surplus grain, and the experience did not serve as an endorsement of the Title II program. The Corps itself was continued for a time after the military coup d'état, but the military regime was unable to provide the elan or enthusiasm that Finance Minister Kim had given it, and it was eventually discontinued.[20]

The Republic of Korea was committed by the Dillon Letter to four basic reforms: modification of the foreign exchange system; renegotiation of the bilateral economic assistance agreement, including normalization of the administrative and fiscal arrangements of the aid program; rationalization of a group of small and medium industrial plants that had been constructed with U.S. aid funds but never brought fully into economic production (the notorious so-called "sick industries"); and increase of rates for transportation and electric power to realistic levels.

ROK Economic Reforms

In November 1960, the ROK State Council agreed on a task force plan to implement the provisions of the Dillon Letter, and set up seven subcommittees for the purpose. The Prime Minister then set to work to get opposition support for his reconstruction budget (the opposition being chiefly former members of his own party).[21]

Chang's government now found itself in a dilemma. It was committed not to reveal U.S. aid levels until it had met its undertakings under the Dillon Letter, which it was supposed to do by March 1, 1961; hence it could not make full use of its diplomatic triumph to gain legislative support. On the other hand, it discovered (contrary to its original assumption) that legislative approval would be required for action on two or more of the four specified reforms. The Ambassador (McConaughy), however, would not agree to the Prime Minister's request to extend the March 1 deadline.[22]

Disagreement between the ROK government and Washington developed over exchange reform actions in December, with the Embassy supporting the ROK. At issue was the Koreans' reluctance to go all the way to a realistic exchange rate level at once because of its political risk. They requested the International Monetary Fund to approve a 1,000:1 rate (which was used for budget projections) as of January 1, and proposed, following passage of the budget, to announce a realistic rate around 1,200:1. To resolve the dispute, the ROK requested the dispatch, "as silently as possible," of an American expert to help work out the exchange reforms. A State Department expert was sent, and eventually a single rate was agreed among the ROK, the United States, and the IMF.[23]

New Aid Agreement

Negotiations for a new bilateral aid agreement with the Executive Branch of the ROK government encountered relatively minor substantive difficulties. Koreans (as always) were concerned about granting tax exemptions to employees of contractors under U.S.-financed programs; and they wanted limits stipulated to the American use of counterpart funds. A number of small language changes reflected ROK national sensitivity. The Commander-in-Chief, UN Command (CINCUNC) wanted language included regarding the interrelationship of economic and military assistance programs, which would be effectively separated by the new agreement.

The main problem concerned prospects for National Assembly ratification of the agreement. The Koreans worried (rightly, as it turned out) over the political impact of the agreement, and wanted it to be confidential and without ratification, but U.S. requirements made publication necessary.[24]

Public criticism of the agreement began even before it was signed (on February 8) and presented to the National Assembly for ratification. Thereafter, protested mounted both inside and outside the legislature, directed at points that were construed to violate Korean sovereignty. Legislative criticism focused on provisions for U.S. observation and review of programs and operations. There was irony in such criticism, since the party in power, when in opposition, had been calling for better control over aid programs during the Rhee regime. Assemblymen also asked why parallel negotiations were not in progress for a status of forces agreement (see Chapter 3).[25]

To assist the government in supporting its case, the U.S. Embassy supplied copies of aid agreements with other countries to demonstrate that the criticized provisions were standard ones, and Ambassador McConaughy gave a public assurance that the provisions were not intended to infringe Korean sovereignty. Although the statement had a sobering effect on political leaders, public criticism continued, and broadened to include the whole field of ROK-U.S. relations, then, subsiding, focused on the status of forces issue. Finally, the aid agreement was ratified by both houses of the National Assembly on February 28, the day before the deadline set in the Dillon letter. Supplemental notes were exchanged regarding privileges, immunities, and facilities for individuals and agencies of the UN Command.[26]

Two of the four Dillon Letter reforms still remained for action, in a climate of mounting nationalist opposition to American pressure and Korean compliance, aggravated by a poor rice crop and rising prices. Prime Minister Chang had told the Ambassador, during the debate over the comprehensive aid agreement, that he feared his government had tried to go too far too fast. Announcement of the $25 million stabilization fund in mid-March came too late to have much political impact. The United States continued to apply pressure for completion of the reforms, although the U.S. Embassy called for American understanding that the ROK government might not be able to do everything it was trying hard to accomplish, and called attention to the political hazards of pushing a cooperative government too hard in the face of nationalist sentiment. On March 31, the State Department informed the U.S. Ambassador that unless he saw overriding political considerations to the contrary, the $15 million in additional aid would be withdrawn "for reallocation to other urgent problems." The Embassy, in response, pointed out that the Dillon Letter requirements had by then been substantially met, including lower-house passage of increased power rates on April 2. Additional steps toward compliance ensued, and in mid-April, the Chargé d'Affaires (Green) was authorized to inform the Prime Minister that the $15 million was available to Korea.

Korean Resentment at U.S. Policies

At the end of March 1961, the U.S. Embassy characterized Korean attitudes toward the United States in the following terms:

> During recent months there has been a growing questioning of the U.S. position in the ROK, focusing on the question of ROK sovereignty, US economic aid, and on demands for a Status of Forces Agreement. In this climate of criticism there has developed a public hypersensitivity regarding the effectiveness of US aid, *especially as concerns lack of long-range economic development* and of our involvement in the ROK economic decision-making process. The controversy over ratification of the economic aid agreement, the negative public reaction to press reports of Under Secretary Ball's speech March 7 in Chicago, and the disproportionately extravagant, favorable press treatment of the recently concluded ROK-West German Technical Aid Agreement, are illustrative of this public climate. [Emphasis added.][27]

Reflective of this climate, the ROK National Assembly on April 18, 1961, passed a resolution that (1) urged long-range economic planning by both the ROK and the United States to produce economic self-sufficiency and improved living standards; (2) asked the United States to "give the fullest consideration to the sovereign rights of the Korean Government in the administration of the economic aid plan," while Korea paid full respect to American advice; (3) called for a nationwide austerity drive, emphasizing rehabilitation of the rural economy and of basic industries, with U.S. policies to support this goal. (The resolution did not officially reach the U.S. Embassy until three days after the military coup.)[28]

Korean planners had in fact produced a five-year economic plan and discussed it with U.S. representatives, who found it unrealistic and inadequate (like all such plans before it). However, an American developmental economist

(Charles Wolf of the Rand Corporation) was retained with U.S. funds as a consultant to examine the plan and make recommendations for possible action. Action on his report was interrupted by the military coup, but both the Korean planning and Wolf's study were important elements in working up the subsequent five-year plan of the Korean military government (see page 290).

The Military and Post-Military Period, 1961-1965

The U.S. reaction to the military coup of May 16, 1961, after initial statements of rejection, was one of watchful acquiescence, pending a clearer understanding of the junta's intentions. After a few months, the United States resumed full economic support for Korea, but conditioned it more firmly than before upon ROK performance in accordance with mutually agreed goals and programs. In 1965, the United States finally agreed to provide $150 million in concessionary loans for Korean long-range economic development--the first specific commitments of this kind since Secretary Dulles's pledge of 1953. Moreover, reflecting the policies of the Kennedy administration, American emphasis was placed upon Korean economic development as an end in itself, rather than as a means of supporting an anti-Communist defense. However, pressure for reduction of the drain on American resources continued, and plans were made--causing considerable unhappiness among the Koreans--for rapid reduction and eventual phasing-out of grant economic assistance except for surplus agricultural commodities.

A new country team, a new Korean government, and a new U.S. policy all combined to change markedly the climate of U.S.-Korean relations in the economic field, as in all others. There was a new air of cold realism on both sides, but there was also a new optimism for the future. Hard bargains were driven on a strictly quid-pro-quo basis. American efforts were concentrated on selected priority objectives. The size of the U.S. economic mission was greatly reduced. The new Ambassador (Samuel Berger) now not only had all non-military operations under his control as a country team, but also had the over-all authority given him by the "Kennedy Letter" of May 1961 to all U.S. chiefs of mission, reconfirming their primacy in their countries of assignment, to help him cope with bureaucratic challenges in both Seoul and Washington. He was fully prepared to exercise this authority.

In some respects the economic issues of the 1961-1965 period were similar to those of previous years. As before, U.S. authorities had to restrain the Koreans from inflationary policies and from the misuse of resources for political purposes, making full use of the leverage provided by Korea's continued need of large-scale economic and military assistance. Also, as before, the Koreans wanted to undertake grandiose projects that the Americans viewed as economically unsound. The Koreans vigorously resisted American-imposed reductions in yearly allocations of grant assistance, and concessions to them sometimes were made for political as well as economic reasons. However, the military government had more economic sophistication and competence than its predecessors. It was more realistic in its understanding of the requirements for economic development; and it was better able than any previous regime to force the discipline and sacrifice necessary to mobilize the nation's resources for the development effort. Above all, the military leaders were prepared to make peace with Japan, because they wanted Japanese economic assistance and Japanese markets.

Beginning Relations with the Military Regime

Notwithstanding its nationalist enthusiasm, the military junta early recognized the necessity of continued (if not increased) American aid, and sent out signals designed to ensure it. The new Foreign Minister (Kim Hong-Il) on June 19, 1961, told the American Chargé d'affaires (Green) that his government would uphold the letter and spirit of the Dillon Letter and other recommendations made by the United States. In mid-June, one of the members of the Supreme Council for National Reconstruction (Yu Yang-Su) told an Embassy officer that two civilians would be named to economic ministries to bring in expertise and ability to get along with American agencies, as well as to give a civilian flavor to the new Cabinet. This step had been repeatedly recommended by the Chargé.[29]

In early June 1961, when the new leaders appeared to have secured their political power, the U.S. Embassy and U.S. Operations [economic aid] Mission formulated their post-coup policy regarding the release of aid funds. Noting that the intentions of the junta were still not clear, but that operational control of the UN Command (a major CINCUNC concern in the early days of the coup) had been restored, they concluded that the United States should not appear overly critical or harsh, while preserving some freedom of maneuver. Accordingly, approval for new obligations for Fiscal Year 1961 that had been held up when the coup occurred, would now be acted upon. Applications for DLF loans, however, would still be held in suspense. The Fiscal Year 1962 program, soon to be formulated, would offer additional leverage.

At the end of the same month, the new Ambassador (Berger) requested obligation of the remainder of fiscal 1961 non-project funds, to provide public evidence of the American decision to work with the new government, and to reduce encouragement for a second coup, as well as to recognize constructive steps already taken by the military regime. He had held a series of meetings with senior ROK officials to explain the new U.S. policy (formulated in the Presidential Task Force report--see Chapter 1, page 29). At the July 1 meeting, he told the economic ministers that he would obligate the remaining Fiscal Year 1961 aid funds, but that economic reforms must be completed before the United States would commit itself to the five-year economic development program that the regime was developing. He also noted persecution of the Korean business community and official criticism of the existing exchange rate as contributing causes to the economic stagnation then current. Reporting the conference to Washington, the Ambassador referred to a perennial problem of U.S. representatives in Korea:

> I want to underscore importance of Department and ICA [International Cooperation Administration, the name of the U.S. aid agency--soon thereafter changed to AID, or Agency for International Development] taking precisely the same position as we. If ROKs get idea they can make an end run around Embassy\USOM our efforts here will be nullified.[30]

By October 1961, the Ambassador could report, in a general political-economic appraisal of the new regime, that it had "taken hold with energy, earnestness, determination, and imagination," notwithstanding its unappealing military authoritarianism. It was

> a genuine revolution from the top trying to introduce sweeping reforms of a most fundamental kind. Projects of reform long talked about or under actual consideration by previous governments are becoming realities in banking and credit policy, foreign trade, increased public works for unemployed, tax evasion, agriculture, trade union organization, education, public administration, social welfare . . . and other fields. Many reforms are constructive and some long urged by American advisors. Others while well-intentioned have been too hastily developed or are poorly implemented. . . . Government, at least in some cases, prepared to admit and correct mistakes.

The Ambassador went on to note that one of the threats to government stability was the possibility of rapid price inflation in 1962, as a consequence of too many economic reforms at once (public works employment, farm price supports and fertilizer subsidies, higher government salaries, industrial and agricultural loan policy, and capital investment in the public sector). On the other hand, improved tax collection, financial administration, and the prospects of increased savings and greater industrial activity, were counterbalancing factors.[31]

The Era of Rash Initiatives, 1962

During 1962, the Koreans undertook a series of economic actions without consulting the United States. These actions were motivated by poor economic reasoning, or by the desire to mobilize resources for political purposes, compounded to some extent by prospects of personal gain. They included the undertaking of a large industrial complex at Ulsan, in southeast Korea; the establishment of an automobile "assembly plant," which actually thinly disguised the import of Japanese "Bluebird" automobiles for sale in Korea under the name "Saenara" ("new country"); the construction of an enormous tourist complex on the outskirts of Seoul, known as Walker Hill, to attract American soldiers to spend their leave dollars in Korea rather than going to Japan; a massive fraudulent rigging of the Seoul stock market; and a currency conversion and blocking scheme.[32]

Responsibility for these schemes was placed by the U.S. Embassy primarily upon Kim Jong-Pil, Director of the Korean Central Intelligence Agency, and a group of Marxist-oriented advisers. The Embassy saw these developments as interrelated with a struggle for power within the junta and a crisis in leadership, resulting, among other things, in the resignation of the Prime Minister (see Chapter 6, page 219).[33]

The Embassy commented that from the first of the year 1962 until May, the economy had been running well and the outlook was promising, but that such measures as the currency "reform" would have a serious adverse effect on it. The German postwar revival appeared to have been a model for certain Korean planners, who had studied it and "fondly hope produce a 'miracle on the Han'" (equivalent to the "miracle on the Rhine"). On the other hand, the schemes raised the possibility that some economic advisers were seeking deliberately to wreck the Korean economy for subversive reasons (although this hypothesis was not subsequently proven). Another explanation was the

> single-minded fanaticism of some revolutionaries seeking to retain power and make fundamental changes in economic and political institutional structure of Korea at great speed, regardless of cost or methods, in defiance of economic and political reality, and without substantial regard for legitimate opinion and interests of the United States.

In this connection, the Embassy noted that on both political and economic matters, "in contrast to last six months of 1961, in recent months there has been a deliberate and unnecessary secrecy in dealing with us."[34]

Once again, as in the Rhee regime, it appeared that

> running through the minds of some leaders in Korea is belief that US must support a Korean government willy-nilly, so long as they are anti-Communist. . . . We must demonstrate that this is not enough, but that a prime necessity is sound, responsible government. . . . If military government persists in refusing consult with us on key economic and political policies, and does not remove the barriers of secrecy, sooner or later we will clash with the regime and be forced to change our present policy.[35]

To underline the seriousness of the American view, the Deputy Assistant Secretary of State (Edward Rice) called in the Korean Ambassador (Chung Il-Kwon) in June 1962 to express U.S. concern at recent ROK behavior in both the military and economic fields. He noted that while the United States respected Korean sovereignty, "in joint undertakings US must make own decisions in exercise of own sovereignty." "If US efforts are to be nullified, we must reassess assistance policy." Subsequently, relationships improved somewhat.[36]

Economic Stabilization, 1962-1964

The military government remained expansionist-minded, even though its economic extremes were somewhat moderated. (It was persuaded, for instance, to suspend its heavy proposed investment in an iron and steel complex at Ulsan, and in fertilizer plants.) For the remainder of 1962 and into 1963, the Korean economy was unstable, with mixed indicators. Industrial production increased considerably in 1962, but the rice crop was poor. The government budget ran a dangerous deficit for 1962, and set out to run an even larger one (estimated by the U.S. Embassy at 15 percent of expenditure) in 1963, through "an enormous overestimation of revenue" to meet pressures for salaries, operating expenses, subsidies, higher defense spending, and a high investment level. Bank credit was growing, partly because of political activity in anticipation of forthcoming elections. There were public fears of hyperinflation.[37]

On his return from a Washington visit in November 1962, the USOM Director (James Killen) told ROK government leaders that additional U.S. aid would depend on "ROK government performance in crucial issues involving stabilization, improved resource use, and demonstrated need." From February to April 1963, a joint US/ROK task force discussed a stabilization program, including limitations on the budget deficit and on credit expansion.

> The basic reason for the discussion was the growing unwillingness of the U.S. to provide additional aid to Korea, particularly Supporting [i.e., economic] Assistance until it had received firm assurances that inflation would be brought under control, i.e., that additional aid would not be wasted in simply satisfying excess demand created by the Government's own budget and credit policies.

Agreement was reached on a new program with a lowered budget deficit, accomplished primarily by lowered investment levels (except for communications) and a decreased fertilizer subsidy. Compliance would result in an additional $15 million of U.S. supporting assistance. But expansionist pressures continued, as did efforts to centralize the economy in the service of political objectives. The resignation of the Governor of the Bank of Korea (Min Byung-Do) in June 1963 was a symptom of these pressures. American counter-pressure was a continuing requirement, if stabilization objectives were to be achieved.[38]

The agreement had already begun to come unstuck in July, and the U.S. Embassy requested (and received) authority to withhold the scheduled increments of the promised additional $15 million supporting assistance, as well as to suspend approval of new development assistance applications, if the anticipated August review indicated unsatisfactory performance. The increments were in fact withheld; the fact became public knowledge in October 1963, and embarrassed the government. The issue was fudged by release of $15 million in other money already allocated.[39]

Although performance on the stabilization program was not given high marks by the Embassy, it was credited with having "called halt to rapid growth of money supply of previous two years." By January 1964, the price rise was stemmed and the economy had adjusted to a lower level of imports. Rice and barley prices continued to rise for a time, but then started to fall. A statement by the Prime Minister of the new civilian government (Choe Doo-Sun) in January 1964 was encouraging in its reflection of the agreed objectives of the stabilization program.[40]

In the Spring of 1964, the program was revised, with the objectives of containing inflationary pressures, using Korean productive capacity to the maximum, curtailing non-essential imports, rapidly expanding exports, protecting Korean foreign exchange reserves, and strengthening the management of ROK budget and credit. Ceilings were set on budget expenditures, credit, and money supply; a floor was set under foreign exchange reserves. The policy of withholding U.S. aid as necessary to enforce compliance was continued despite some Washington reservations. The stabilization program had to deal with the effects of currency devaluation, as well as with the squeeze on farmers from reduction of fertilizer subsidies, at the same time as good 1963 crops and large PL 480 food grain imports were lowering domestic grain prices.[41]

Again in December 1964, the Ambassador told President Park that the Americans "were frankly worried. We had received many promises from ROKG but so far too little evidence of results." He commented that the American restraint on making specific suggestions did not mean lack of concern. Subsequently, the President reportedly addressed his Cabinet strongly on the subject of stabilization. Thereafter, Korean economic performance (as well as other non-economic factors such as normalization of relations with Japan and the Korean contribution to the U.S. military effort in Vietnam) justified an American commitment in the Spring of 1965 to support long-range economic development in Korea.[42]

The departure of James Killen as Director of the US Operations Mission in August 1964 brought out expressions in the press of the prevailing Korean unhappiness with the tightly controlled program that the Ambassador and he had carried out (and, in considerable measure, designed). The large daily *Hankook Ilbo*, probably expressing the views of the expansionist former publisher and current ROK Vice-Premier, Chang Key-Young, criticized Killen's administration as unresponsive to Korea's needs. Referring to a comment Killen had made in an earlier speech about the attainment of Korean self-support in five to eight years, the editorial said, in part:

> If the United States is not to repeat her mistake in Vietnam, it is hoped that the United States will not overlook the fact that many economic tasks remain in this land--problems which are more important than the financial stabilization program that US aid officials in Korea would

refer to so often. Unless this is solved, economic self-sufficiency can hardly be expected even in ten years.[43]

Nonetheless, the dramatic economic growth of Korea in succeeding years might be regarded as evidence of the soundness of economic foundations laid under American tutelage over the past two decades, and particularly in the years of the Korean military regime.

Revision of the Foreign Exchange Rate

After the economic stabilization plan had been adopted, the State Department initiated an exchange with the U.S. Embassy in June 1963, on the desirability of external stabilization through devaluing the Korean currency. Such a move was important to the United States not only in terms of Korean economic viability, but also for its impact on U.S. aid levels and the generation of counterpart funds for investment and military support. The exchange rate also affected individual Americans living in Korea, who were paying artificially high prices (or using the black market).

At first, Washington acquiesced in the Embassy's judgment that such a move was politically unwise for the time being. In October, however, the National Advisory Council on International Monetary and Fiscal Problems (NAC) was asked to establish an interagency working group to study the situation, and Irving B. Kravis was retained to head a technical study. Officials of the country team in Seoul informally discussed the problem with ROK officials.[44]

The exchange rate at this time was nominally 130:1--the rate established under the Chang government in February 1961, divided by 10 as a result of the unhappy currency conversion of 1962. But there were multiple rates in reality, involving export subsidies, an export-import link system, and barter trade, with an effective rate of 180:1 to 200:1. The ROK government had utilized its foreign exchange to stabilize prices, hasten investment, and satisfy the demand for prestige and luxury products; but in 1963 government controls began to tighten up. Adjustment of the exchange rate, in the Embassy's view, required interim measures such as an exchange tax on dollar sales and extension of import-export links, to cushion Korean exports and price levels against the shock before conversion to a lower unitary rate could be undertaken.[45]

In January 1964, the country team recommended an interim premium of 50 *won* per dollar (the name for the unit of Korean currency had reverted from *hwan* to the original *won* in the 1962 currency conversion), added to the existing 130:1 rate. The ROK partially accomplished this by extending an existing premium to firms supplying U.S. force requirements. Before additional interim measures could be agreed, however, the country team decided to propose moving directly to a unitary rate--partly because of the complications, and partly to end the prevailing uncertainty.

After NAC approval, negotiations for a new unitary exchange rate began. The International Monetary Fund was not included, but was to be consulted by the Koreans to get its approval. An additional $10 million in supporting assistance was authorized to help avoid a temporary price rise, as the country team had recommended, plus an advance of $10 million from scheduled 1964 aid. The possibility of additional surplus grains, as an additional safeguard against price rise, was left open, and an additional 175,000 tons were authorized in June. A new floating rate starting at 255:1 was agreed in secret negotiations in April, and announced on May 2, after approval by the IMF.[46]

US Economic Assistance Levels

ROK-U.S. economic relations were affected, during this period as in others, by Korean fears of reduced U.S. aid levels. Such fears were reinforced in 1963 by two factors. American encouragement of negotiations for normalization of relations with Japan led to Korean suspicions that Japanese economic assistance would result in U.S. assistance reductions. Additionally, the United States itself, faced with growing balance-of-payments difficulties, was under pressure to reduce its aid program worldwide, and a speech by the Director of AID (Bell) in early 1963 signalled a progressive cutback in grant aid, in favor of concessional development loans. Rumors reached the Koreans in 1963, and again in 1964, that grant aid to Korea would be phased out in two years.

The United States officially reassured the Koreans on both points: U.S. aid levels would not be affected by a Korea-Japan settlement, and there was no timetable for substituting development loans for supporting assistance. Nevertheless, when Ambassador Berger returned from a Washington visit in June 1963, he spoke to Chairman Park of the SCNR (military junta) about American political and economic problems in regard to the aid program, and said that the total grant aid for the following year would be less than the $90 million of 1963. (Later, it was set at $66 million, compared with $180 million in 1961.) Commenting on the conversation, the Ambassador wrote: "I sense that Koreans remain oriented inward to their own problems for which they see U.S. aid as panacea and we will have to continually impress upon them by word and action the limits of assistance and need for self-help."[47]

From this time on, grant assistance levels were steadily reduced, except for occasional additional allotments aimed at specific needs. The National Policy Paper of 1965 established the phasing-out of such assistance as an objective of U.S. policy, and the goal was in fact realized in Fiscal Year 1968. At the same time, development loans increased (reaching a public-relations climax with the announcement of the $150 million U.S. commitment in 1965). The Korean reaction was mixed. One newspaper editorialized in June 1963 that Korean dependence on American aid was like opium addiction; it and other newspapers (all, of course, under government censorship), while pointing out the many

Korean economic problems, nonetheless emphasized the need to develop self-help.[48]

The continuing reluctance of the Koreans to accept the prospect of an end to grant aid was clearly demonstrated in a conversation in October 1965 between the ROK Ambassador (Kim Hyun-Chul) and a Deputy Assistant Secretary of State (Robert Barnett). Kim called to convey the ROK apprehension that supporting assistance might be sharply cut. Barnett acknowledged the danger of a "brutal cut," and the continuing need of assistance for military support. But he pointed out that it was only one component of American aid; that PL 480 grains were a comparable form of assistance; that the United States had made a commitment of $150 million in loan resources; that there was rising European interest in Korean investment; and that Korea's exports were rising, with the strength of Korea's skilled labor force and management improvement. Kim acknowledged the merits of these arguments, but said "the Korean people had gotten into the habit of looking solely at the supporting assistance as aid. Development loans were all very well, but they had to be paid back." He pointed to the problem of debt service. Notwithstanding Barnett's observation that the reduction of supporting assistance was a testimonial to Korean economic progress, Kim remarked that opposition members in the National Assembly would interpret a cut as indicating the American intention to turn Korea over to Japan.[49]

These Korean feelings were turned to advantage, when the United States needed bargaining leverage, by arranging "carrots" in the form of one-time extra aid authorizations--e.g., in enforcing stabilization in 1963, and devaluing the Korean currency in 1964 (withholding of part of regular allocations was also used as a bargaining lever on occasion). In early 1964, the ROK Foreign Minister suggested that an extra $10 million might make a settlement with Japan more palatable. The Ambassador told him no such proposal could be considered. Nonetheless, the following year, the U.S. Embassy suggested exactly such an inducement to support the Korean government at a time when it was "facing possibly critical challenge on issue ROK-Japan settlement."[50]

The Food Crisis of 1963: U.S. Assistance under PL 480

The effects of the poor 1962 rice crop in Korea were greatly magnified by the failure of the Spring barley crop in 1963--the result of heavy unseasonable rains and a fungus disease. The problem had serious political as well as humanitarian and economic aspects, because the military government was then seeking to promote popular support for the coming elections. Moreover, farmers themselves were consuming more grain than before, as a consequence of higher living standards and the recent agricultural credit reforms. A further complicating factor was the heavy destruction and loss of life resulting from Typhoon Agnes. The food shortfall was estimated at from 250,000 to 560,000 metric tons; it became evident as time passed that the government was overestimating the shortage, but the need was nonetheless real.[51]

Anxious to avoid unsettling the political and economic situation, Washington in mid-June authorized the U.S. Embassy to announce U.S. concern at the loss of part of the barley crop and promise U.S. help. The Embassy meanwhile proposed that 400,000 metric tons of grain (barley or wheat) be provided under the Title II work-relief provisions of PL 480. Despite adverse recollection of the 1961 experiment with Title II work relief (see page 286), the United States on June 27 announced that it would furnish 100,000 tons of grain, of which 75,000 would be for Title II programs.[52]

ROK government leaders put strong pressure on the country team for 400,000 tons more grain, pleading the danger of food riots and of upheavals in the government, as well as alleging widespread public criticism of the United States. ("The country could not understand why US was allowing Korea 'to starve.'") Representatives of the Korean flour millers (an industry that had grown from virtually nothing in ten years on the strength of American surplus wheat) claimed in Washington that stocks were nearing exhaustion and mills were closing down.

The country team in Seoul confirmed their report, but commented, "We regard this as a planned crisis which if [the requests] were honored would result in continuous harassment through CY [calendar year] 1964." In mid-July, SCNR Chairman Park told the Ambassador he was prepared to make a statement on elections and transfer of political power, but considered it essential to wait until the food problem was solved--in the Ambassador's judgment, "a crude attempt to exert pressure on US" for prompt and large grain shipments. Even opposition leaders signed petitions to President Kennedy and to the U.S. Congress. The ROK unilaterally purchased 50,000 tons of Canadian wheat. In the end, an additional 175,000 tons of U.S. grain were authorized, subject to compensation for commercial purchases.[53]

As supporting assistance levels declined, PL 480 grain became steadily more important to the Korean economy as a basic source of money to support the military establishment. (The peculiarities of American politics permitted--even encouraged--PL 480 assistance to continue without the strictures applied to other forms of aid, although in 1964 there were plans to charge PL 480 shipping costs against aid allotments.) However, sales of imported grains in Korea had the effect of depressing domestic grain prices and discouraging growth toward agricultural self-support.

The USOM Director (Killen) in late 1963 proposed that the PL 480 policy should be aimed at helping attain Korean food self-sufficiency, while requiring Korea to buy its food imports in the United States so long as PL 480 aid continued. He also argued that if Korea exported rice, it should import an equivalent value of grain. The Ambassador differed with him on the last point, holding that the equivalence should be in caloric value so as to permit Korean export earnings in good rice years.[54]

After the poor crops of 1962 and 1963, Korean agricultural production improved, and in late 1964 the United States proposed a PL 480 food grain program of $52 million, compared with $88.2 million in the previous year. ROK officials argued vigorously against the proposal. They presented statistics purporting to show that the equivalent 200,000 metric tons of grain would be insufficient, but their main emphasis was on the psychological shock to Korea of such a large reduction, and the fuel it would give to the opposition in the National Assembly.

The country team implicitly accepted these arguments, particularly because of the various political problems facing Korea and the fact that the reduction might be taken by the Korean public as an indication of U.S. disapproval of the government in power. In addition, the steady availability of PL 480 grains had a stabilizing influence on rice price fluctuations, particularly in the politically explosive springtime (as had been demonstrated by the experience in early 1964). As an additional factor, Koreans had developed a taste for wheat over their years of exposure to American grain; thus an abrupt cutback would have a disruptive effect. (This new Korean taste was in part the result of missionary work by American agricultural attaches, responding to direction from Washington.)[55]

Department of Agriculture approval of PL 480 grain exports was usually conditioned on tight control of competitive agricultural exports by the recipient country. This problem came up in connection with the 1965 PL 480 program for Korea above discussed, since there were plans for export of Korean rice to Japan to earn foreign exchange. In December 1964, the AID Administrator (Bell) wrote the Secretary of Agriculture (Freeman), suggesting that no arbitrary U.S. limitations be imposed on Korean rice exports to Japan, although commensurate commercial food imports from the United States should be required. This policy was justified on the basis that export restrictions would be contrary to U.S. interests in both Korea and Japan, while Korea's rice export capacity was so limited that it would not become a major competitor of the United States there.[56]

Support for Korean Science and Technology

During President Johnson's visit to Korea in 1965, he expressed an interest in the promotion of Korean science and technology, which was referred to in the presidential communique. This took the ROK government by surprise, but it rose quickly to the opportunity thus afforded to stimulate lagging Korean research. In July of that year, the President's Science Adviser (Hornig) visited Korea for a week, and stimulated "a ferment of activity on the part of the Korean scientific community, universities, research institutes, and Government departments" in reviewing the situation and making development plans. Less than a year later (February 1966), the Korean Institute of Industrial Technology and Applied Sciences (KIST) was established with extensive U.S. assistance.[57]

*   *   *

From the beginning of Korea's sustained rapid economic growth, the publicity of the south Korean government gave full credit to the military leadership and to Park Chung Hee personally for the achievement. While they do deserve much of the credit, it must be recognized, first, that it was the American effort of the previous fifteen or more years--however inefficient and ill-informed at times--that prepared the material and social ground for Korea's economic take-off; and second, that many of the accomplishments for which the military took full credit, such as the five-year plan, had already been under development in previous regimes. Moreover, if it had not been for the guidance and restraining hand of the United States, its ambassadors during the 1961-1965 period (Samuel Berger and Winthrop Brown), its aid mission chiefs (James Killen and Joel Bernstein), and their staffs, the economic excesses of the military might well have jeopardized Korea's economic future. It nevertheless remains true that the economic transformation of Korea after 1961, psychologically as well as in material and monetary terms, was a dramatic and historic accomplishment.

List of Abbreviations

AFAK   Armed Forces Assistance to Korea (U.S.)
AMIK   American Mission in Korea (former umbrella agency for U.S. in Korea)
ANZUS   Australia, New Zealand, United States (mutual defense treaty)
APACL   Asian Peoples' Anti-Communist League
ASPAC   Asia and Pacific Council (former multinational group)
CEB   Combined Economic Board (U.S.-ROK)
CIC   Counter-Intelligence Corps (U.S. and ROK armies)
CINCREP   Economic Coordinator, United Nations Command
CINCUNC   Commander-in-Chief, United Nations Command
CNO   Chief of Naval Operations (principal Navy officer, U.S. and ROK)
CRIK   Civil Relief in Korea (U.S. military relief operations)
DAC   Development Assistance Committee (of OECD)
DLF   Development Loan Fund (U.S.)
DNP   Democratic Nationalist party (ROK opposition party, 1949-1955)
DPRK   Democratic People's Republic of Korea (north Korea)
ECA   Economic Cooperation Administration (U.S.)
ECAFE   Economic Commission for Asia and the Far East
              (former regional affiliate of UNESCO)
EPB   Economic Planning Board (ROK)
FOA   Foreign Operations Administration (U.S.)
FROKA   First Republic of Korea Army (majority of ROK Army combat units)
GARIOA   Government Aid and Relief in Occupied Areas (U.S.)
ICA   International Cooperation Administration (U.S.)
ILO   International Labour Organisation (UN specialized agency)
JAS   Joint Administrative Services (administrative agency for AMIK)
JCS   Joint Chiefs of Staff (armed forces, U.S., also ROK)
KATUSA   Korean Augmentation to U.S. Army (ROK soldiers in U.S. Army units)
KAVA   Korean Association of Voluntary Agencies
KCAC   Korea Civil Assistance Command (successor to UNCACK)
KCIA   Korean Central Intelligence Agency
KComZ   Korea Communications Zone (component of the United Nations
              Command, in charge of areas in rear of combat zone)
KCP   (abbreviation for Kim Jong-Pil, influential figure in 1961 coup d'état)
KFTU   Korea Federation of Trade Unions (ROK)
KILA   [South] Korean Interim Legislative Assembly (1946-1948)
KIST   Korea Institute of Industrial Technology and Applied Sciences

KMAG	Korea Military Advisory Group (U.S.)
KOSCO	Korea Oil Storage Company (former joint venture of U.S. oil firms)
MAP	Military Assistance Program (U.S.)
MDAP	Mutual Defense Assistance Program (U.S.)
MSA	Mutual Security Agency (U.S.)
NAC	National Advisory Council on International Monetary and Fiscal Problems (U.S.)
NSC	National Security Council (U.S.)
NNIT	Neutral Nations Inspection Team (former operational unit of NNSC)
NNSC	Neutral Nations Supervisory Commission (four-nation commission established by the Armistice Agreement)
OCB	Operations Coordination Board (former agency of the NSC)
OEC	Office of the Economic Coordinator (see CINCREP)
OECD	Organization for Economic Cooperation and Development
OSP	Offshore procurement (aspect of U.S. aid)
PROVMAAG/K	Provisional Military Assistance Advisory Group, Korea (U.S.)
PL 480	Public Law 480 (foreign distribution of U.S. agricultural commodities)
ROK	Republic of Korea (south Korea)
SCNR	Supreme Council for National Reconstruction (military group in charge of ROK government, 1961-1963)
SKIG	South Korean Interim Government (1946-1948)
SOFA	Status of Forces Agreement
SNIE	Special National Intelligence Estimate (U.S.)
SWNCC	State-War-Navy Coordinating Committee (U.S.)
UK	United Kingdom (Great Britain)
UNC	United Nations Command
UNCACK	United Nations Civil Assistance Command, Korea (unit of UNC)
UNESCO	United Nations Economic, Social, and Cultural Organisation
UNCOK	United Nations Commission on Korea (1948-1950)
UNCURK	United Nations Commission for the Unification and Rehabilitation of Korea (1950-1973)
UNGA	United Nations General Assembly
UNKRA	United Nations Korea Reconstruction Agency (1950-1957)
UNTCOK	United Nations Temporary Commission on Korea (1947-1948)
USAMGIK	United States Army Military Government in Korea
USAFIK	United States Army Forces Korea
USIA	United States Information Agency
USIS	United States Information Service (field offices of USIA)
USOM	United States Operations Mission (field office of U.S. aid agencies)
USSR	Union of Soviet Socialist Republics (Soviet Union)
WFTU	World Federation of Trade Unions (socialist-oriented international labor organization)

Notes

As explained in the preface to this edition, only the notes for the preface and Chapters 2 and part of 4 (Chapters 3 and 5 of the original manuscript) were released by the Department of State. For the other chapters, only a few notes added in the course of revision are shown. The note numbers in this edition do not always correspond to those in the original classified manuscript because of some rearrangement and abridgement of text.

Preface to Original Study

1. The Historical Office has prepared several very useful documents that provide detailed information on the historical background of American-Korean relations. See particularly *United States Policy Regarding Korea*, Parts I (1834-1941, Research Project No. 29), II (1941-1945, Research Project No. 158), and III (1946-1950, Research Project No. 252). For a discussion of relations during the Korean War period, see the nine-part study, *American Policy and Diplomacy in the Korean Conflict*, covering the period June 25, 1950 to December 1951. All the foregoing studies are Top Secret except the first part (1834-1941) of *United States Policy Regarding Korea*, which is Official Use Only. For a listing of other studies on Korea by the Historical Office, see its pamphlet, *Historical Office Research Projects on Foreign Policy and Diplomatic History*, August 1959 (Limited Official Use), pp. 81-84.

Chapter 1. Evolution of U.S. Policy on Korea, 1961-1965

1-69. Notes not released.

Chapter 2. Korean Unification and North-South Relations

1. One small indication of State's role at this time is a memorandum in the files from the War Department General Staff (Lt.Col. C.H. Bonesteel III, who over 20 years later became Commander of UN forces in Korea). [Portion of note excised.] State also contributed [to policy] through the State-War-Navy Coordinating Committee, a precursor of the National Security Council. [For an indication of State Department thinking, see "Inter-Allied Consultation Regarding Korea," prepared for the briefing book at the Yalta

Conference. *Foreign Relations of the United States. Diplomatic Papers. The Conferences at Malta and Yalta* (Washington, D.C.: U.S. Government Printing Office, 1961), p. 359.

2. See the remarks made by the Soviet Chief Delegate to the opening session of the U.S.-USSR Joint Commission in Seoul, March 1946.

3. For the political background of Korean nationalist movements and their divisions, see the study by Chong-Sik Lee, *The Politics of Korean Nationalism* (Berkeley: University of California Pres, 1967). As for Korean attitudes of this period, POLAD Seoul despatch 142, Nov. 6, 1947, "Interview with Two Koreans from Hamheung, North Korea," 895.00/11-647, reflects the usual criticisms of Russian control but acknowledges that many of the ordinary people supported communism. For example, "The upper half of the people know the truth and can think for themselves. The lower half do not think for themselves and are deluded by Kim Il Sung." The two informants suggested that in a free election, 70 percent would vote for the Democratic party (non-Communist), and 30 percent would vote for the Communists--a fairly substantial concession for anti-Communists to make. One of them quoted a Christian friend who thought the Communists would eventually win in Korea and was going along with them for self-preservation. See also Memorandum of Conversation, Gen. A.V. Arnold, Gen. Hilldring, J.C. Vincent, *et al*, Oct. 9, 1946, Top Secret.

4. The Moscow decision (also referred to as the Moscow Declaration), announced Dec. 27, 1945, was to establish a five-year four-power trusteeship of Korea, comprising China, the Union of Socialist Soviet Republics, the United Kingdom, and the United States. The military commands of the two occupying powers--the Soviet Union and the United States--were to confer immediately on cooperation between the two Korean zones of occupation, and then to establish a Joint Commission which, in consultation with the Koreans, would establish a transitional government for the whole of Korea under the general control of the trustee powers.

5. For a more detailed summary of the Joint Commission proceedings, see *U.S. Policy Regarding Korea*, Part III, pp. 3-14.

6. *U.S. Policy Regarding Korea*, Part III, pp. 2-3. Regarding interzonal mail and trade, see Embassy Seoul Despatch 341, June 9, 1949, "Transmittal of Letter re the Nature of Present Legal Trade between the Northern and Southern Zones of Korea and Frequency and Method of Mail Exchange," 895.50/6-949, Restricted. Trade was cut off by the ROK as of April 1, 1949 (Embassy Seoul Despatch 273, May 17, 1949, 895.00/5-1749, Confidential). Re U.S. soldiers going north, see POLAD Seoul Despatch 127, Oct. 24, 1947, 895.00/10-2447, transmitting an exchange of letters between the U.S. and Soviet commanders.

7. See POLAD Seoul Despatch 64, Nov. 19, 1946, 895.00/11-1946, "Report on Current Events in North Korea," Confidential. See also U.S. Department of State, Office of Intelligence and Research, *North Korea: A Case Study in Communist Takeover* (Washington, D.C.: U.S. Government Printing Office, 1960).

8. Telegram, Commanding General, USAFIK, to CINCFE, ZGCG 652, May 17, 1947, 895.01/5-1747, Secret.

9. [This note excised.]

10. Letter, A.A. Bunce (Economic Adviser) to Edwin M. Martin, Office of Far Eastern Affairs, July 12, 1947, 895.00/7-1247, Secret.

11. Letter, Bunce to Martin, July 12, 1947.

12. Seoul CONGENUSAFIK ZGBI 1281 to G-2 CINCFE, Oct. 17, 1947, 895.00/10-1747, Secret.

13. POLAD Seoul telegram 239, April 14, 1948, 895.00/4-1448, Secret.

14. POLAD Seoul telegram 242, April 15, 1948, 895.00/4-1548, Secret.

15. POLAD Seoul telegram 210, April 5, 1948, 895.00/4-548, Confidential.

16. For Hodge's public statements on the North-South Conference, see POLAD Seoul telegram 214, April 6, 1948, 895.00//4-648, and 311, May 3, 1948, 895.00/5-548, both Unclassified. For letter of April 20, see POLAD Seoul Despatch 108, May 3, 1948, 895.00/5-348, Restricted. See also POLAD Seoul Despatch 116, May 7, 1948, 895.00/5-748, Restricted.

17. United Nations. General Assembly. Resolution

18. Embassy Moscow telegram 1821, Aug. 31, 1948, 895.00/8-3148, Confidential.

19. Embassy Seoul Despatch 16, Jan. 10, 1949, 895.00/1-1049, Confidential; Embassy Seoul Despatch 788, Dec. 10, 1949, 895.00/11-1049, Confidential.

20. Embassy Seoul Despatch 427, July 11, 1949, 895.00/7-1149, Confidential. Gaillard's trip to the 38th parallel is a recollection of the author.

21. Embassy Seoul Airgram A-268, Aug. 25, 1949, 895.00/8-2549, Restricted.

22. For a sample ROK appraisal of the military threat, see Memorandum for President Rhee from Sihn Sung Mo, Minister of National Defense, Oct. 22, 1949, "Status of Korean Forces," 895.20/10-2249.

23. For an interesting discussion of the problem of the effect of the U.S. public posture on Korea in the months preceding the war, see Memorandum, Rusk (State/FE) to Webb (Under Secretary), May 2, 1950, "Statements by Senator Connolly Regarding U.S. Policy in Korea," 611.95/5-250, Confidential.

24. UN General Assembly Resolution No.   , Oct. 7, 1950. [The text of the Joint Chiefs of Staff memorandum can be found in *Foreign Relations of the United States*, 1950, pp., 707-708.]

25. [The full text of the occupation directive was included in the original State Department manuscript at Appendix A, Document 3, but the appendices were not released.]

26. Memorandum of Conversation, Greenhill (British Embassy)-Johnson (State/NA), Nov. 8, 1950, 795B.00/11-850, Secret.

27. Material in this section is drawn from the following Embassy Seoul despatches: 29, Nov. 14, 1950, 795A.00/11-1450, "Transmitting Reports of Civil Assistance Activities in North Korea," Confidential; 36, Nov. 18, 1950, 795A.00-11-1850, "Message of National Assembly to People of North Korea," Unclassified; 75, Dec. 8, 1950, 795A.00/12-850, "Transmitting Further Reports of Civil Assistance Activities in North Korea," Secret; 78, Dec. 9, 1950, 795A.00/12-950, Confidential; 30, Nov. 15, 1950, briefed in Memorandum, Emmons (State/NA)-Johnson (NA), Dec. 5, 1950, 795A.00/12-550, Restricted.

28. Embassy Pusan Despatch 137, Nov. 9, 1951, 795B.00/11-951; Memorandum, Johnson (FE)-McClurkin (NA), Feb. 3, 1953, 795B.0221/1-353; Memorandum, McClurkin (NA)-Johnson (FE), Feb. 4, 1953, 795B.0221/2-353; Memorandum of Conversation, McNicol (Australian Embassy)-Johnson (State), Feb. 5, 1953, 795B.022/2-353. All documents Confidential.

29. Letter, Dulles to Wiley, July 3, 1954, Confidential. Department telegrams 38 to Seoul, July 2, 1954, 795B.00/7-254, and 17 to Seoul, July 7, 1954, 795B.00/7-754, both Confidential. Department telegram 88 to Seoul, July 30, 1954, 795B.5/7-3054; Embassy Seoul telegram 167, Aug. 6, 1954, 795B.5/8-654; Department telegram 112 to Seoul, Aug. 8, 1954, 795B.5/8-854; Embassy Seoul telegram 130, Aug. 9, 1954, 795B.5/8-954; all foregoing Secret. Department telegram 126 to Seoul, Aug. 11, 1954, 795B.00/8-1154, Confidential. Embassy Seoul telegram 207, Aug. 19, 1954, 795B.5/8-1954, Secret.

30. Embassy Pusan despatches 199, June 5, 1951, 795B.00/6-551, and 204, June 9, 1951, 795B.00/6-951, both Confidential.

31. Embassy Pusan Despatch 222, June 24, 1951, 795B.00/6-2451, Confidential.

32. Embassy Pusan Despatch 9, July 9, 1951, 795B.00/7-851, and 39, July 30, 1951, 795B.00/7-3051 [classification blurred in original manuscript].

33. [The text of the letter was included in the original manuscript as Appendix A, Document 8, but the appendices were not released.]

34. Embassy Pusan telegram 91, July 28, 1951, 795B.11/7-2851, Secret; Embassy Pusan Despatch 64, Aug. 6, 1951, 795B.00/8-651, Confidential.

35. Embassy Seoul telegram 91, July 28, 1951, 795B.11/7-2851, Secret; Embassy Pusan Despatch 46, Aug. 6, 1951, 795B.00/8-651, Confidential.

36. [Text of Truman's letter was included in the original manuscript as Appendix A, Document 9; appendices were not released.]

37. [Text of Rhee's letter responding to President Truman was included in the original manuscript as Appendix A, Document 10; appendices were not released.]

38. [Text of Eisenhower's letter was included in the original manuscript as Appendix A, Document 11; appendices were not released.]

39. Embassy Pusan telegram 1194, April 3, 1953, 795B.5/4-353, Secret. See also Department telegram 649 to Pusan, April 23, 1953, 611.95B/4-2353, Confidential, Eyes Only Briggs, and Embassy Pusan telegram 1292, May 3, 1953, 795B.00/5-353, Secret.

40. Memorandum, K.T. Young (State/NA)-Robertson (FE), April 23, 1953, 795B.5/4-2353, "Draft Instructions to Ambassador Briggs Regarding the Security of the ROK," Secret.

41. Embassy Tokyo telegram 49, July 6, 1953, 795B.00/7-653, Secret-Nodis [no distribution], Personal for Acting Secretary, Eyes Only.

42. Letter, Rhee to Eisenhower, July 11, 1953, 795B.00/7-653, Secret. See also the exchange of correspondence between Rhee and Robertson between July 1 and 11, attached to file 795B.00/7-2453.

43. [The Secretary's letter was included in the original document as Appendix A, Document 13; the appendices were not released.]

44. Memoranda for the Record, First [Second, Third, etc. . . . .] Meeting Between President Rhee and Secretary Dulles. Cited in Department airgram A-382 to Paris, Sept. 8, 1953, 611.95B/9-853, "Meetings Between Secretary and President Rhee," Secret.

45. Memorandum, Secretary of State to Under Secretary, Aug. 14, 1953, Secret. In FE Office files.

46. Embassy Seoul telegram 350, Oct. 21, 1953, Top Secret. In FE Office files.

47. Memorandum of Conversation, Yang (ROK Ambassador)-Robertson (State/FE), Feb. 15, 1954, 795B.11/2-1554, "President Rhee's Letter of Feb. 4 to President

Eisenhower," Secret. Text of revised letter is in Embassy Seoul telegram 896, March 16, 1954, Top Secret. In FE Office files.

48. Embassy Seoul telegrams 1110, May 4, 1954, 795B.00/5-454; 1140, May 10, 1954, 795B.00/5-1954; 1226, May 21, 1954, 795B.00/5-2154; 1248, May 26, 1954, 795B.5/5-2654 (text of Dean letter to Rhee); Department telegrams 932 and 934 to Seoul, May 20, 1954, 795B.00/5-1954. All Secret.

49. Department telegram 322 to Seoul, Nov. 10, 1954, 795B.00/11-1054, Confidential. See also Embassy Seoul telegrams 282, Sept. 10, 1954, 795B.00/9-1054; 295, Sept. 13, 1954, 795B.00/9-1354; 317, Sept. 18, 1954, 795B.00/9-1854; and Department telegrams to Seoul 200, Sept., 17, 1954, 795B.00/9-1754, and 217, Sept. 22, 1954, 795B.00/9-1654. All Confidential. The quotation is from Department telegram 200.

50. For Ambassador Briggs's evaluation of Rhee's posture and motivation, see Embassy Seoul telegram 384, Nov. 11, 1953, Top Secret (cited in Note 42, Chapter II [of original manuscript, not released]. See also the Department's response, telegram 324 to Seoul, Nov. 5, 1953, Top Secret.

51. Embassy Seoul telegram 1126, May 6, 1954, 795B.00/5/654, and 1127, May 7, 1954, 795B.00/5-754, both Secret.

52. Embassy Seoul telegram 389, Nov. 3, 1953, 795B.00/11-353, Confidential.

53. U.S. Department of State, *The Korean Question at the Geneva Conference*. Washington, D.C.: U.S. Government Printing Office, 1954. Unclassified.

54. *The Korean Question*.

55. *The Korean Question*.

56. For the subsequent evolution of the visit, see Embassy Seoul telegrams 1376, June 21, 1954, 795B.11/6-2154; 1383, June 23, 1954, 795B.11/6-2354; 1404, June 29, 1954, 795B.11/6-2954; 6, July 3, 1954, 795B.11/7-354; 37, July 13, 1954, 795B.11/7-1354, and Department telegram 18 to Seoul, July 7, 1954, 795B.11/7-354, all Secret; also Seoul telegrams 27, July 10, 1954, 795B.11/7-1054; 170, July 16, 1954, 795B.11/7-1654; 111, July 22, 1954, 795B.11/7-2254; and Department telegram 6, July 3, 1954, 795B.11/7-354, all Confidential. For Rhee's letter to Dulles of July 1, with his "price" for making a visit, [the original manuscript footnote here referred to an appendix which was not released]. For the aftermath of the visit, see Embassy Seoul telegram 362, Sept. 27, 1954, 795B.5/9-2754, and Department telegram 226 to Seoul, Sept. 25, 1954, 795B.5/9-2754, both Secret. See also Department of State, Bureau of Intelligence and Research, Intelligence Note, Aug. 16, 1954, 795B.11/8-1654, "Probable Impact on ROK Policies of President Rhee's Visit to the U.S.," Secret.

57. Embassy Seoul telegrams 1088, April 1, 1955, 795.00/4-155, Official Use Only, and 1450, June 29, 1955, 795.00/6-2955, Secret.

58. Memorandum, Parsons (State/NA)-Robertson (FE), Nov. 6, 1956, 795.00/11-666, Secret; Embassy Seoul telegram 455, Nov. 10, 1955, 795.00/11-1056, Secret.

59. Department telegram 496 to Seoul, Jan. 11, 1957, 795.00/1-1157; Embassy Seoul Despatch 280, Jan. 22, 1957, 795.00/1-2257; Department airgram A-130 to Seoul, March 7, 1957, 795.00/10-2257. All Confidential.

60. Memorandum, Jones (State/FE)-Herter (Acting Secretary), July 3, 1957, 795A.00/7-357; Department telegram 43 to Canberra, July 23, 1957, 795A.00/7-1057; Department telegram 44 to Seoul, July 12, 1957, 795.00/7-1257. All Confidential.

61. Telegram, U.S. Delegation to UN (USUN), DELGA 171, to Department, Oct. 15, 1957, 795.00/10-1557, Official Use Only; Embassy Seoul telegrams 397, Nov. 13, 1957, 795B.00/11-1357, Official Use Only, and 400, Nov. 15, 1957, 795B.00/11-1557, Confidential.

62. Memorandum, Parsons (State/NA)-Jones (FE), Feb. 8, 1958, 795.00/2-858, Confidential; Memorandum of Conversation, Pyman (Australian Embassy)-Parsons (State/NA), Feb. 18, 1958, 795.00/2-1858, Confidential.

63. British Embassy Note 1091/9/58, No. 60, to the Department, Feb. 10, 1958, 795.00/2-1058, Confidential, transmits the Chinese note. For details of subsequent notes and consultations, see Memorandum of Conversation, Greek Embassy [name illegible]-Parsons (State/NA), Feb. 12, 1958, 795.00/2-1258; Memorandum of Conversation, Lough (New Zealand Embassy)-Henderson (State/NA), Feb. 14, 1958, 795.00/2-1458, both Confidential; Embassy Seoul telegram 676, March 4, 1958, 795.00/3-458, Secret; Embassy Seoul telegram 872, May 6, 1958, 795.00/5-2658, Secret; British Embassy Note 1091/200/58, No. 183, to Department, May 7, 1958, 795.00/5-758, Confidential; Department telegram 764 to Seoul, June 2, 1958, 795.00/6-258, Confidential; Embassy Seoul telegram 886, June 4, 1958, 795.00/6-458, Confidential; Record of Meeting, March 4, 1958, "Reply by the Sixteen to the Chinese Communist Statement of February 7, 1958," Confidential; Memorandum, Robinson (State/FE) to Secretary of State, Nov. 18, 1958, 795.00/11-1458, Confidential; Memorandum of Conversation, DelaMare (British Embassy)-Parsons (State/NA), March 9, 1959, 795.00/3-959, Confidential; Memorandum, Robertson (State/FE) to Acting Secretary of State (Herter), March 12, 1959, 795.00/3-1259 [classification not shown]; Department telegram 405 to Seoul, March 19, 1959, 795.00/3-1959, Confidential. The last three documents concern the British recommendation and U.S. decision, with concurrence of the Sixteen, not to reply to the last Chinese Communist note of March 4, 1959, since it had nothing new in it and ignored the crucial issue of free elections. Regarding the news leaks, see Department telegram 966 to Seoul, cited above; Seoul telegram 705, March 13, 1958, 795.00/3-1358; Department telegram to Seoul, March 13, 1958, 795.00/3-1358. All Secret.

64. Embassy Seoul telegram 676, March 4, 1958, 795.00/3-458, Secret; Embassy Seoul Despatch 574, March 5, 1958, 795.00/3-558, Secret; Memorandum, Parsons (State/NA)-Robertson (FE), March 31, 1958, 795.00/3-3158, Confidential; Embassy Seoul Despatch 666, April 18, 1958, 795.00/4-1858, Confidential; Embassy Seoul airgram G-91, June 13, 1958, 795.00/6-1358, Official Use Only; Embassy Seoul Despatch 167, Sept. 24, 1958, 795A.00/9-2458, Confidential; Embassy Bangkok Despatch 229, Oct. 6, 1958, 795.00/10-658, Confidential; Memorandum, Parsons (State/NA)-Robertson (FE), Dec. 12, 1958, 795.00/12-1258, Confidential; Embassy Seoul telegram 517 to Department, April 14, 1959, 795B.00/4-1459, Confidential; Department telegram 458 to Seoul, April 16, 1958, 795B.00/4-1459, Confidential.

65. [An analysis of the north Korean campaign was included as Appendix A, Document 17 of the original manuscript; but the appendices were not released.]

66. Embassy Seoul airgram G-39 to Department, Nov. 9, 1959, 795.00/11-959; Embassy Tokyo telegram 1276, Oct. 25, 1959, 795.00/10-2559; Memorandum of Conversation, Van Muyden (Swiss Embassy)-Lane (State/NA), March 24, 1960, 795B.00/3-2460. All Confidential.

67. Cf. Marshall Green's conversation with Yun Suk Heun of the ROK Foreign Ministry, reported in Embassy Seoul Despatch 432, Feb. 23, 1960, 795.00/2-2360, "Korean Reunification," Confidential.

68. Department telegram 1230 to Seoul, June 18, 1960, 795B.21/6-1660, and Embassy Seoul telegram 1399, June 23, 1960, 795.00/9-2360, both Confidential.

69. Embassy Seoul telegram 1436, June 30, 1960, 795.00/6-3060, Confidential; Department telegram 1286 to Seoul, June 24, 1960 [file no. not shown], Unclassified.

70. Embassy Seoul telegram 380, Sept. 23, 1960, 795.00/9-2360, and airgram G-94, Dec. 30, 1960, 795.00/9-2360 [sic], both Confidential.

71. Memorandum of Conversation, Rettie (Canadian Embassy)-Macdonald (State/NA), Nov. 7, 1960, 795.00/12-1460; Embassy New Delhi airgram G-327, Nov. 23, 1960, 795.00/12-1460. Both Confidential. For a useful review of Korean problems, see Memorandum of Conversation, McDermot (United Kingdom Foreign Office)-Steeves (State/FE), Dec. 8, 1960, 795.00/12-860, Secret. For the Indonesian proposal, see Department telegram 1338 to USUN, New York, Dec. 12, 1961, 795.00/12-1261, and USUN telegram 942 to Department, Sept. 27, 1962, 325.95/9-2762, both Confidential.

72. Embassy Seoul airgram G-43, Aug. 22, 1960, 795.00/8-2260, Confidential.

73. Record of Meeting, March 1, 1961: Commonwealth representatives, State/IO (Jones), FE (Sullivan), 795.00-3161; Department telegram 968 to Seoul, March 4, 1961, 795.00/3-461; Memorandum of Conversation, Chang (ROK Ambassador)-Steeves (State/FE), March 7, 1961, 795.00/3-761; Embassy Seoul telegram 1145, March 13, 1961, 795.00/3-1361; all Confidential. Korean press comment in Embassy Seoul telegram 1152, March 14, 1961, 795.00/3-1461, Official Use Only. See also an earlier Canadian feeler in Memorandum of Conversation, Rae (Canadian Ambassador)-Parsons (State/NA), Feb. 26, 1958, Confidential [no file number given].

74. CINCUNC telegram UK 3022 AS, to JCS, 090700Z, March 9, 1961, 795.00/3-961, Unclassified (belligerent statement in Military Armistice Commission); Embassy Tokyo telegram 3049, April 18, 1961, 694.95B/4-1861; Embassy Seoul telegrams 1424, April 21, 1961, 795.00/4-2161, and 1430, April 24, 1961, 795.00/4-2461. All Confidential.

75. Embassy Seoul telegram 1499, May 8, 1961, 795.00/5-861, Confidential.

76. Department telegram 1424 to Seoul, June 2, 1961, 795.00/6-261; Embassy Seoul telegrams 1751, June 8, 1961, 795.00/6-861, and 1898, June 25, 1961, 795.00/6-2561; Department telegram 1230 to Seoul, June 18, 1961, 795B.21/6-1060 [sic]; Embassy Seoul telegram 619, Oct. 24, 1961, 895B.424/10-2461. All Confidential.

77. USUN telegrams to Department, 2048, March 13, 1962, 325.95/3-1362, and 3879, May 31, 1962, 795.00/5-3162; Embassy Seoul telegram 339, Oct. 8, 1962, 320.10/10-862; USUN telegram 1705 to Department, Nov. 9, 1962, 325.95/11-962. All Confidential. Memorandum, Cleveland (State/IO)-Secretary of State, Dec. 12, 1962, 795.00/12-1262, Unclassified; Department circular airgram 7531, Jan. 17, 1963, 795.00/1-1763, Confidential. For a statement of the ROK government position on the Korean question in 1962, see Embassy Seoul airgram A-309, Nov. 8, 1962, 795.00/11-862, Confidential. See also USUN telegram 943 to Department, Sept. 27, 1962, 795.00/9-2762, Confidential.

78. Embassy Seoul airgram 231, Dec. 23, 1965, POL 2-1 KOR S (Joint Weeka 51), Confidential; Embassy Seoul telegram 1430, April 24, 1961, above cited.

Chapter 3. Politico-Military and Security Issues

1-80. Notes not released.

81. [The following statement was part of the text of the original study: There was not complete unanimity among U.S. military authorities. In October 1955, a State Department memorandum reported "unofficially" on a letter of September 6, 1955 from General Lyman Lemnitzer (who had replaced General Taylor as CINCUNC), proposing a phased cutback of ROK forces over an 18-month period by moving 11 of the 20 active divisions into the reserve. State's Director of Northeast Asian Affairs (Hemmendinger) commented that although this proposal was moderate and in accord with the Agreed Minute, it would stir up a furor in Korea. No such reduction was ever made.]

82-91. Notes not released.

Chapter 4. Korean International Relations

1-10. Notes not released.

11. Note, Chief ROK Delegate (Yang) to Secretary of State (Acheson), March 25, 1952, 694.95/3-2552; Note, Assistant Secretary (Allison) to ROK Ambassador (Yang), April 29, 1952, 694.95/3-2552); Aide-Memoire, State to Japanese Embassy, May 15, 1952, 694.95/5-2552, no classification. Memorandum of Conversation, Han (ROK Chargé)-McClurkin (State/NA), April 8, 1952 (694.951/4-852); Embassy Tokyo telegram 2180, April 12, 1952, 694.95B/4-1252; Memorandum of Conversation, Johnson (State/FE)-Takeuchi (Japanese Embassy), May 15, 1952, 694.95/5-1552; Memorandum, Hemmendinger (State/NA)-Robertson (FE), Aug. 28, 1956, 694.95B/8-2866. All Confidential.

12. [Blank in original].

13. Tokyo telegram 1462, Dec. 13, 1953, 694.95B/12-1353, Secret; Embassy Seoul telegram 558, Dec. 18, 1953, 694.95/12-1853, Secret; Embassy Tokyo telegram 2037, Feb. 19, 1954, 694.95B/2-1954, Confidential; Embassy Tokyo telegram 2981, June 2, 1954, 694.95B/6-254, Secret; Memorandum of Conversation, Young (State/NA)-Shima (Japanese Embassy), July 30, 1954, 694.95B/7-3054, Confidential.

14. Memorandum, Hemmendinger (State/EA)-Robertson (FE), Sept. 7, 1956, 694.95B/9-756, Confidential; Memorandum, Jones (State/FE)-Secretary of State, Feb. 10, 1958, 694.95B/2-1058, Confidential; Embassy Seoul telegram 397, Dec. 3, 1959, 694.95B/12-359, Confidential; Embassy Tokyo telegram 1702, Dec. 30, 1957, 694.95B/12-3057, Confidential.

15. Embassy Tokyo telegram 1829, Dec. 23, 1960, 694.95B/12-2360; Department telegram 1021 to Tokyo, Dec. 1, 1960, 294.9541/12-160; Embassy Tokyo Despatch 1329, May 29, 1961, 694.95B/5-2961; Embassy Seoul telegram 234, Aug. 4, 1961, 795b.00/8-461. All Confidential.

16. Embassy Tokyo telegram 786, Sept. 7, 1961, 694.95B/9-661; Embassy Seoul telegram 456, Sept. 8, 1961, 694.95B/9-861; Embassy Seoul airgram A-222, Jan. 9, 1962, 694.95B/1-962; Embassy Seoul telegram 1097, April 11, 1962, 374.800/4-1162; Embassy Tokyo telegram 295, Aug. 1, 1962, 694.95B/8-162; all Confidential. Embassy

Tokyo telegram 621, Aug. 31, 1962, 694.95B/8-3162, and Embassy Seoul telegram 218, Sept. 3, 1962, 694.95B/9-362, 694.95B/9-362,m both Secret-Limit Distribution; Department telegram 795 to Seoul, Sept. 19, 1964 (POL JAPAN-KOR S), Confidential.

17. US Mission Tokyo telegram 1281, Dec. 29, 1950, 694.95/12-2950, Unclassified.

18. Embassy Seoul telegram 21, July 16, 1958, 694.95B/7-1658; Embassy Tokyo telegram 3020, March 19, 1960, 694.95B46/3-1960. Both Confidential. Embassy Tokyo telegram 1577, Feb. 7, 1959, 694.95B/2-759; Memorandum of Conversation, Yang (ROK Ambassador)-Robertson (State/FE), June 17, 1959, 694.95B/6-1759; Embassy Seoul Joint Weekas 30, July 24, 1959, 795B.00(W)/7-2459, and 53, Dec. 31, 1959, 795B.00(W)/12-3159; Embassy Tokyo telegram 304, July 27, 1959, 794.95B/7-2759, and 1071 to Seoul, June 2, 1960, 694.95B/5-2760. All Confidential. Department telegram 919 to Seoul, April 30, 1963 (611.95B/4-2860, and 1002 to Seoul, May 18, 1960, 694.95B/5-1860; Embassy Seoul telegram 1182, May 20, 1960, 694.95B/5-2060; Embassy Tokyo telegram 3801, May 23, 1960, 694.95B/5-2360; all Confidential, Limit Distribution. Embassy Seoul telegram 1063, May 4, 1960, 694.95B/5-460, Confidential. Embassy Tokyo telegram 309, July 27, 1960, 694.95B/7-2760; Embassy Seoul telegram 510, Oct. 25, 1960, 694.95B/10-2560, and 535, Oct. 31, 1960; all Confidential. Embassy Tokyo airgram A-480, Nov. 21, 1961, 694.95B/11-2161, Limited Official Use. [Note: This includes notes numbered 17, 18, 19, 20, and 21 of Chapter 5 in the original manuscript.]

19. US Mission Tokyo telegram 1522, Jan. 23, 1952, 694.95B/1-2352, and Embassy Tokyo telegram 115, July 10, 1952, 694.95B/7-1052, both Confidential.

20. US Mission Seoul telegram 460, June 15, 1948, 895.00/6-1548; Embassy Tokyo Despatch 79, Nov. 14, 1952, 694.9513/11-1452; Department telegram 365 to Pusan, Nov. 26, 1952, 694.9513/11-1452. All Confidential.

21. Memorandum, Dunning (State/EA)-McClurkin (NA), July 22, 1953, 694.9513/7-2253, and Embassy Tokyo despatch 427, Sept. 1, 1953, 694.95B/9-153, both Confidential. Embassy Tokyo telegram 1306, Nov. 23, 1953, 694.95B/11-2353, and Department telegram 1387 to Tokyo, Nov. 23, 1953, 694.95B/11-2353, both Secret. Embassy Seoul telegram 215, Aug. 20, 1954, 694.95B/8-2054, Limited Official Use. Tokyo (?) telegram 753 (?), Sept. 27, 1954, 694.95B/9-2754, Confidential; Embassy Seoul telegram 383, Sep. 30, 1954, 694.95B/9-3054, Limited Official Use; Embassy Seoul telegram 1316, June 15, 1965 (?), POL JAPAN-KOR 5, Secret, Limit Distribution. [Original partially illegible.]

22. Embassy Tokyo telegram 2271, March 3, 1958, 795B.5 NSP/3-358, Official Use Only.

23. US Mission Tokyo Despatch 1298, March 21, 1952, 694.95B/3-2152; Embassy Tokyo Despatch 66, May 15, 1952, 694.95B/5-1552. Both Confidential. Embassy Seoul telegram 1322 (?), June 2, 1955, 694.95B/6-255, Secret.

24. Department telegram 678 to Seoul, Jan. 3, 1961, 694.95B/1-361; Embassy Tokyo telegram 1893, Jan. 4, 1961, 694.95B/1-461. Both Secret.

25. Embassy Tokyo telegram 3227, May 16, 1962, 694.95B/5-1662, Confidential.

26. Memorandum, Snow (State/Le/P)-Baker (OE), Oct. 20, 1947, 895.85/10-2047, issued Oct. 29 as SANAC 387, no classification; Embassy Seoul telegram 348, Apr. 7, 1949, 895.85/4-749, Unclassified.

27. US Mission Tokyo telegram 119, Apr. 14, 1949, 895.85/4-1449, Unclassified; Embassy Seoul Despatch 395, June 28, 1949, 895.85/6-2849, Restricted; US Mission Tokyo Despatch 464, July 18, 1949, 895.85/7-1849, Restricted.

28. WAR message 94022, Sept. 8, 1949, 895.85/9-649, Confidential; Department airgram A-175 to Seoul, Sept. 13, 1949, 895.85/8-2949, Confidential; Note, ROK Ambassador (Chang) to Secretary of State (Acheson), Oct. 21, 1949, 895.85/10-2149, no classification. Embassy Seoul airgram A-285, Sept. 24, 1949, 895.85/9-2449; Embassy Pusan Despatch 98, Sept. 28, 1951, 795B.00/9-2851; both Confidential.

29. Department telegram 743 to Seoul, March 25, 1960, 694.95B/3-2560, Unclassified.

30. Embassy Seoul telegram 209, Feb. 16, 1950, 694.95B/2-1660, Confidential; Embassy Tokyo telegram 170, Feb. 18, 1950, 694.95B/2-1860. Unclassified.

31. Embassy Pusan telegrams 245, Sept. 11, 1951, 695.95/9-1151, Secret, and 273, Sept. 21, 1951, 694.95B/9-2151, Confidential; US POLAD Tokyo telegrams 812, Oct. 20, 1951, 694.95B/10-2151, Confidential, and 856, Oct. 26, 1951, 694.95B/10-2651, Restricted; Embassy Pusan despatches 98, Sept. 28, 1951, 795b.00/9-2651, and 159, Nov. 27, 1951, 694.95/11-2751, both Confidential; US POLAD Tokyo Despatch 613, Oct. 18, 1951, 694.95B/10-1851, Confidential.

32. Embassy Pusan telegram 230(?), Sep. 22, 1951, 694.95B/9-2251; Department telegram 552 to SCAP, Tokyo, Oct. 1951, 694.95B; Department airgram A-357 to Tokyo, Feb. 15, 1952, 694.95B/1-1452. All Confidential. Embassy Pusan telegrams 1042, April 25, 1952, 694.95B/4-2552, and 162, Aug. 1, 1952, 694.95B/8-152, both Restricted; Embassy Seoul telegrams 538, Dec. 7, 1951, 694.95B/12-751, and 537, Dec. Dec. 11, 1951, 694.95B/12-1151, both Confidential; US POLAD Tokyo telegrams 750, Oct. 13, 1951, 694.95B/10-1351, Confidential; 796, Nov. 19, 1951, 654.95B/11-951, Confidential; 1117, Nov. 16, 1951, 694.95/11-2051, Secret; 1701, Feb. 16, 1952, 694.95B/2-1652, Restricted; 1255, April 22, 1952, 694.95B/4-2252, Restricted; Embassy Tokyo telegram 155 (?), May 28, 1952, 694.95B1/5-2852, Confidential; Embassy Pusan despatches 167 (?), Oct. 5, 1951, 694.95/10-551, Confidential; 167, Dec. 31, 1951, 694.95/(?), Restricted. Embassy Pusan telegram 647, Jan. 9, 1953, 795b.11/1-953; Embassy Seoul telegram, unnumbered, Feb. 6, 1952, 694.95B/2-353; Embassy "Tokyo telegrams 2054, Dec. 29, 1952, 694.95B/12-2952; 2164, Jan. 7, 1953, 795B.11/1-753; 222?, Jan. 21, 1953, 694.95B/1-2153; [no. illegible], March 4, 1953, 694.95B/3-453. Department telegram 281 to Pusan, Oct. 28, 1952, 694.95b/10-2852, No Distribution outside Department; Department telegram 1739 to Tokyo, Jan. 19, 1953, 694.95/1-1953. All Confidential. Embassy Tokyo telegrams 2998, March 17, 1953, 694.95B/3-1753; 3226, April 7, 1953, 694.95B/4-753; 3312, April 16, 1953, 694.95B/4-1653; 789, Sept.2 25, 1953, 694.95B/9-2553; 852, Oct. 2, 1953, 694.95B/110-253. Embassy Tokyo despatches 1572, June 2, 1953, 694.95B/6-253; 713, Oct.2 28, 1953, 694.95B/10-2853. All Confidential. [This note comprises note numbers 36, 37, 38, and 39 of the original Chapter 5.]

33. Embassy Tokyo telegram 1441, Dec. 101, 1953, 694.95B/12-1053, 694.95B/12-953; Embassy Tokyo despatches 713, Oct. 28, 1953 (cited above, fn. 32), and 899, Dec. 9, 1953, 694.95B/12-953. All Confidential.

34. Embassy Seoul telegram 261, Sep. 228, 1953, 694.95B/9-2853, Confidential; Embassy Tokyo telegrams 634, Sep. 30, 1953, 694.95B/9-3053, Confidential; 1039, Oct.

23, 1953, 694.95B/10-2353, Secret; 1082, Oct. 27, 1953, 694.95B/10-2753, Secret; 1122, Oct. 30, 1953, 694.95B/10-3053, Secret; 1275, Nov. 18, 1953, 694.95B/11-1853, Secret; 1338, Nov. 27, 1953, 694.95B/11-2753, Secret; 1587, Dec. 26, 1953, 694.95B/12-2853, Secret; Department telegram 275 to Seoul, Oct. 27, 1953, 694.95B/10-2753, Secret; Department telegram 1686 to Tokyo, Jan. 19, 1954, 694.95B/12-2853, Secret; Memorandum, Herrington (State/U/FW) to Bedell Smith (Under Secretary), Jan. 6, 1954, "Japanese-ROK Negotiations," 694.95B/1-854, Confidential.

35. [Corresponding note omitted in original.]

36. Embassy Seoul telegrams 458, Nov. 26, 1953, 694.95B/11-2653, Confidential; 560, Dec. 19, 1953, 694.95B/12-1953, Secret; 715, Jan. 26, 1954, 694.95B/8-1954, Secret; 726, Jan. 28, 1954, 694.95B/1-2854, Secret; 794, Feb. 17, 1954, 694.95B/2-1754, Confidential; 918, March 19, 1954, 694.95B/3-1954, Secret; Embassy Tokyo telegrams 1339, Nov. 27, 1953, 694.95B/11-2753, Secret; 1596, Dec. 28, 1953, 694.95B/12-2853, Secret; 1956, Feb. 9, 1954, 694.95B/2-954, Secret; Department telegrams to Seoul, 648, Feb. 4, 1954, 694.95B/1-2854, Secret; [one citation illegible]; Department telegram 1309 to Tokyo, Dec. 2, 1953, 694.95B/12-253, Secret; Letter, President Rhee to Dulles (Secretary of State), Nov. 10, 1953, 694.95B/11-1053 (no classification); reply, Dulles to Rhee, Dec. 3, 1953, 694.95B/11-1053, Confidential (transmitted to Seoul by Department airgram A-66 to Seoul, Dec. 4, 1953, same file number).

37. Embassy Tokyo telegram 2793, May 13, 1954, 694.95B/5-1354, Confidential; 2981, June 2, 1954, 694.95B/6-254, Secret; 131, July 18, 1954, 694.95B/7-1854, Secret; 796, Oct. 1, 1954, 694.95B/10-154, Secret.

38. Memorandum, Jones (State/FE) to Secretary of State, Feb. 10, 1958 (cited in fn. 14, above).

39. Embassy Tokyo telegrams 1466, Dec. 21, 1954, 694.95B/12-2154; 1785, Jan. 255, 1955, 694.95B/1-2555; 1863, Feb. 2, 1955, 694.95B/2-255; 1922, Feb. 9, 1955, 694.95B/2-955; 1923, Feb. 9, 1955, 694.95B/2-955; 2139, Mar. 6, 1955, 694.95B/3-655; all Secret. Embassy Tokyo Despatch 1061, Mar. 10, 1955, 694.95B/3-1055, Confidential; Department telegrams 1208 to Tokyo, Dec. 16, 1954, 694.95B/12-1654, Secret, and 1660, Feb. 10, 1955, 694.95B/2-955, Confidential.

40. Embassy Seoul telegrams 1100, April 4, 1955, 694.95B/4-455, Official Use Only; 1122, April 11, 1955, 694.95A/4-1155, Official Use Only; 1314, May 22, 1955, 694.95B/5-2255, Confidential; 1449, June 29, 1955, 694.95B/6-2955, Secret; 726, Jan. 6, 1956, 694.95B/1-656, Official Use Only; 1032, April 9, 1956, 694.95B/4-956, Official Use Only; Embassy Seoul Despatch 340, June 23, 1955, 694.95B/6-2355, Confidential; Department telegram 769 to Seoul, June 13, 1955, 795b.00/6-1355, Confidential; Memorandum of Conversation, Tanaka (Japanese Embassy)-Jones (State/NA), Feb. 15, 1956, 694.95B/2-1556 [no classification stated].

41. Embassy Seoul despatches 267, Jan. 17, 1957, 694.95B/1-1757, Confidential, and 313, Feb. 13, 1957, 694.95B/2-1357, Secret; Embassy Tokyo telegram 2899, June 7, 1957, 694.95/6-757, Confidential; Embassy Tokyo Despatch 382, Sep. 30, 1957, 694.95B/9-3057, Confidential.

42. Embassy Seoul telegram 500, Jan. 2, 1958, 694.95B/1-258; Embassy Tokyo telegrams 1379, Nov. 19, 1957, 694.95B/11-1957; 1706, Dec. 30, 1957, 694.95B/12-

3057, "For the Secretary"; 1708, Dec. 30, 1957, 694.95B/12-3057; 1761, Jan. 8, 1958, 694.956/1-858; Letter, Rhee to Dulles (Secretary of State), Jan. 23, 1958, 694.95B/1-2358 (cited above, fn. 14 and 38); reply, Dulles to Rhee, Feb. 1, 1958, same file number; Memorandum, H. Parsons (State/NA) to H. Jones (FE), Feb. 5, 1958, 694.95B/2-558; all Confidential.

43.   Embassy Seoul Despatch 84, Aug. 20, 1959, 795b.00/8-2059 (Sec. 4), Confidential; Embassy Tokyo telegrams 2672, April 11, 1958, 694.95B/4-1158, Confidential; 2788, April 23, 1958, 694.95B/4-2348, Official Use Only; 734, Oct. 3, 1958, 694.95B/110-358, Unclassified; 1163, Dec. 4, 1958, 694.95B6/12-458, Confidential; Embassy Tokyo despatch 293, Aug. 28, 1959, 694.95B/8-2859, Confidential; Embassy Tokyo airgram G-334, Jan. 25, 1960, 694.95B/1-2560, Confidential; Department telegrams to Seoul 640, Feb. 27, 1960, 694.95B/2-2760, Confidential, and 715, March 17, 1960, 694.95B/3-1760, Official Use Only.

44.   Embassy Seoul telegrams 1027, April 30, 1960, 694.95B/4-3060; 1107, May 11, 1960, 694.95B/5-1160; 1119, May 12, 1960, 694.95B/5-1260; Embassy Seoul Despatch 637, May 19, 1960, 795B.00/5-1960; Embassy Tokyo telegrams 3504, April 29, 1960, 694.95B/4-2960; Department telegram 1073 to Seoul, June 2, 1960, 694.95B/5-2360; all Confidential.

45.   Embassy Seoul telegram 260, Aug. 29, 1960, 694.95B/8-2960; Embassy Tokyo telegram 838, Sep. 9, 1960, 694.95B/9-960; both Confidential.

46.   Seoul telegram 189, July 30, 1961, 694.95B/7-3061, and 190, same date and file; 535, Oct. 31, 1960, 694.95B/10-3160; 1158, March 14, 1961, 611.95B/3-1461; 1510, May 11, 1961, 694.95B/5-1161; Embassy Seoul Despatch 281, Dec. 14, 1960, 611.95B/12-1460; Embassy Tokyo telegrams 1680, Dec. 10, 1960, 694.95B/12-1060; 2230, Feb. 7, 1961, 694.95B/2-761; Embassy Tokyo airgrams G-887, Jan. 30, 11961, 694.95B/1-3061; G-1312, April 13, 1961, 694.95B/4-1361; all Confidential. Department telegrams to Seoul 772, Jan. 24, 1961, 694.95B/1-2361, Confidential, and 204, Aug. 2, 1961, 694.95B/8-261, Secret. Embassy Seoul telegrams 223, Aug. 3, 1961, 694.95B/8-361, Secret, and 553, Oct. 6, 1961, 694.95B/10-641, Confidential; Embassy Seoul airgram G-181, July 4, 1961, 694.95/6-3061, Confidential; Embassy Tokyo telegrams 423, Aug. 3, 1961, 694.95B/8-361, Secret; 463, Aug. 9, 1961, 694.95B/8-961, Confidential; 764, Sept. 6, 1961, 694.95B/9-661, Confidential; Embassy Tokyo Despatch 1334, June 1, 1961, 694.95/5-2961, Confidential; Department telegrams to Seoul 1486, June 19, 1961,, 694.95B/6-961, Confidential; 247, Aug. 11, 1961, 694.95B/8-361, Secret; 325, Aug. 31, 1961, 694.95B/8-2961, Confidential.

47.   Embassy Seoul telegrams [no. illegible], Oct. 12, 1961, 694.95B/10-1261; 721, Nov. 16, 1961, 694.95B/11-1661; 785, Dec. 7, 1961, 694.95B/12-761; Embassy Seoul airgrams A-133, Oct. 26, 1961, 694.95B/10-2361; A-185, Dec. 6, 1961, 694.95B/12-661; all Secret. Embassy Tokyo telegrams 1216, Oct. 19, 1961, 772.56351/10-1961, Secret; 1235, Oct. 21, 1961, 694.95B/10-2161, Limited Official Use; 1272, Oct. 24, 1961, 033.95B94/10-2461, Secret; 1233, Oct. 28, 1961, 694.95B/10-2861, Secret; 1452, Nov. 12, 1961, 694.95B/11-1261, Confidential; Memorandum of Conversation, Ikeda (Japanese Prime Minister)-Rusk (Secretary of State), Nov. 2, 1961, 694.95B/11-261, Secret.

48.   Embassy Seoul telegrams 1109, April 14, 1962, 294.9541/4-1462; 1117, April 23, 1962, 2294.9541/4-2362; both Confidential. Embassy Tokyo telegrams 1960, Jan

16, 1962, "Geneva for Harriman," Confidential; 2017, Jan. 22, 1962, 294.9541/1-2262, Confidential; 2618, March 20, 1962, 110.15-A/3-2062, Confidential; 2901, April (?), 1962, 294.49541, Confidential; 1033, Oct. 10, 1962, 694.95/10-1062, Secret, Limit Distribution--Eyes Only Ambassador Berger (in Seoul); [citation illegible]; Embassy Tokyo airgram A-262, Aug. 24, 1962, Confidential; Department telegrams to Seoul 966, April 5, 1962, 294.9541/4-562, Confidential; 40, July 13, 1962, 694.95B/7-1562, Secret; 738, Jan. 11, 1962, 294.9541/1-962, Confidential; Department telegrams to Tokyo 1796, Jan. 19, 1962, 294.9541/1-1962, Confidential; 406, Aug. 23, 1962, 294.9541/8-1762, Secret, Limit Distribution--For Ambassador; Letter, President Kennedy to Prime Minister Ikeda, Aug. 23, 1962, 694.95B/8-2362, no classification; Letter, President Kennedy to General Park Chung Hee, Aug. 26, 1962, 694.95B/8-2662, no classification; Memorandum of Conversation, May 3, 1962, "Call of former Prime Minister Yoshida on the President," 611.94/5-362, Confidential.

49. Embassy Seoul telegrams 411, Nov. 15, 1962, 033.95B11/11-1562, Secret, Limit Distribution; 646, May 2, 1963, PS 8-4 KOR-JAP, Confidential; 230, Sept. 17, 1964, POL JAPAN-KOR S, Confidential; 260, Sept. 19, 1964, POL JAPAN KOR S, Confidential; 760, Feb. 18, 1965, POL 7 JAPAN, Limited Official Use; 779, Feb. 20, 1965, POL JAPAN-KOR S, Unclassified; Embassy Tokyo telegrams 224, July 24, 1962, 694.95B/7-2462, Secret; 1834, Feb. 6, 1963, POL JAP S KOR, Confidential; 1823, De.c. 18, 1963, POL 33-4 JAP S KOR, Confidential; 2581, March 3, 1964, POL JAPAN-KOR S, Confidential; 2034, March 9, 1964, POL 33-4 JAPAN S KOR, Confidential; 1523, Oct. 28, 1964, POL JAPAN-KOR S, Confidential; 1653, Dec. 3, 1964, POL JAPAN-KOR S, Secret; 3120, April 3, 1965, POL JAPAN-KOR S, Unclassified; Department telegrams to Seoul, [number illegible], Feb. 12, 1963, POL 33-4 JAP S KOR, Confidential; 480, Feb. 12, 1963, POL 33-4 JAP-S KOR, Confidential, Personal for Ambassador Berger from Harriman; 552, Dec. 21, 1963, POL JAP-S KOR, Confidential; 775, March 3, 1964, POL JAPAN-KOR S, Confidential; 798, March 6, 1964, POL 33-4 JAPAN-KOR S, Confidential; 407, Nov. 11, 1964, POL JAPAN-KOR S, Confidential; 407, Nov. 11, 1964, POL JAPAN-KOR S, Secret; 1029, May 12, 1964, POL JAPAN KOR S, Confidential, Limit Distribution; 894, April 2, 1964, POL JAPAN-KOR S, Confidential; Memorandum of Conversation, Rusk (Secretary of State)-Ohira (Japanese Foreign Minister), Jan. 28, 1964, ORG 7 S, Secret; Memorandum for the President from Secretary of State, July 28, 1964, "Proposed Oral Message on Korean-Japanese Negotiations . . .," POL JAPAN-KOR S, Confidential (approved by the President, July 31, 1964).

50. Embassy Seoul telegrams 1213, March 25, 1964, POL 23-6 KOR S, Confidential; 1277, April 10, 1964, POL JAPAN-KOR S, Confidential; 12, July 6, 1964, POL 15-1 KOR S, Confidential; 596, Jan. 5, 1965, POL JAPAN-KOR S, Limited Official Use; 774, Feb. 19, 1965, POL JAPAN-KOR S, Limited Official Use; 1009, April 15, 1965, POL JAPAN-KOR S, Confidential; 1025, April 17, 1965, POL JAPAN-KOR-S, Confidential; Embassy Tokyo telegram 44652, June 22, 1965, POL $ JAPAN-KOR S, Unclassified; USFK Message JK 51870 BJ UNC/USFK/EUSA Intelligence Summary No. 15-65, 16 April 65, [file reference not given], Confidential; CINCUNC Message to CJCS UK 60212 (Flash) DTG 260245 Z March 1964 for Taylor from Howze, POL 23-8 KOR S, Top Secret; Department telegrams to Seoul 856, March 24, 1964, POL 23-6 KOR S, Confidential; 925, April 13, 1964, POL JAPAN-KOR S,

Confidential. Embassy Seoul telegrams 1375, June 24, 1965, POL 4 JAPAN-S KOR, Limited Official Use; 23, July 7, 1965, POL 4 JAPAN-KOR S, Limited Official Use; 1380 (?), June 25, 1965, POL JAPAN-KOR S, Limited Official Use; 43, July 12, 1965, POL JAPAN-KOR S, Limited Official Use; 140, Aug. 12, 1965, POL 4 JAPAN-KOR S, Confidential; 157, Aug. 14, 1965, POL 4 JAPAN-KOR S, Limited Official Use; 176, Aug. 14, 1965, POL 4 JAPAN-KOR S, Limited Official Use; 612, Dec. 17, 1965, [file reference illegible]; Embassy Tokyo telegrams 4341, June 22, 1965, POL JAPAN-KOR S, Confidential; 4352, June 22, 1965, POL 4 JAPAN-KOR S, Unclassified; 4387, June 24, 1965, POL JAPAN-KOR S, Confidential; 1736, Nov. 12, 1965, POL JAPAN-KOR S, Limited Official Use; 2073, Dec. 11, 1965, POL 4 JAPAN-KOR S, Limited Official Use; Department telegrams to Seoul 1318, June 22, 1965, POL 4 JAPAN-KOR S, Unclassified; 1319, June 22, 1965, POL JAPAN-KOR S, Limited Official Use; 1320, June 22, 1965, POL JAPAN-KOR S, Limited Official Use; 586, Dec. 17, 1965, POL 4 JAPAN-KOR S, Unclassified; 591, Dec. 18, 1965, POL 4 JAPAN-KOR S, Unclassified; Memorandum, Hilliker (State)-McG. Bundy (White House), June 29, 1965, POL JAPAN-KOR S, Confidential.

51. Memorandum of Conversation, Bane (State/NA)-Koh (ROK Chargé), Jan. 31, 1961, 694.95B/1-3161, Confidential.

52. Embassy Seoul telegrams 52, July 14, 1965, AID 1 KOR S, and 244, Sept. 8, 1965, AID 9 KOR S, both Confidential; Embassy Seoul airgram A-561, May 20, 1965, AID 9 KOR S, Confidential; Embassy Tokyo telegram 1100, Sept. 28, 1964, AID 9 KOR S, Unclassified; Embassy London telegram 5546, May 19, 1965, AID 9 KOR S, Limited Official Use; Embassy Paris telegram CEDTO 89, July 24, 1964, AID 1 KOR S, Confidential; Department telegram 184 to Seoul, Aug. 26, 1964, POL JAPAN-KOR S, Confidential; Department circular telegram AIDTO CIRC XT 285, Sept. 9, 1965, AID 9 KOR S, Confidential; Department airgram AIDTO A-594 to Seoul, Jan. 11, 1964, AID 9 KOR S, Limited Official Use.

55. For background on Japanese nationals introduced into Korea during the war by the United Nations Command, see Department telegram 169 to Seoul, Sept. 24, 1952, 694.95B/9-2452 (a summary of CINCUNC message C55544) and Embassy Pusan telegram 392, Sept. 26, 1952, 694.95B/9-2652, both Secret. See also Letter, Murphy (Ambassador to Japan)-U.A. Johnson (State/NA), Sept. 22, 1952, 795B.00/9-2252, Secret.

56-60. Not released.

Chapter 5. Korean Political Development

1-19. Not released.

20. The purpose of this loan was to acquire trucks and other goods needed for the Korean economy that legally could not be obtained with so-called GARIOA funds that were restricted to the relief of disease and unrest.

21-74. Not released.

Chapter 6.   U.S. Involvement in Major Korean Political Crises

1-6. Not released.

7. Harold Noble, son of missionaries to Korea, was the main channel for liaison between the U.S. Embassy and President Rhee before the Korean war.

8-115. Not released.

Chapter 7.   Korean Economic Development: Years of Restoration, 1945-1957

1-5. Not released.

6. Detailed projections of the Korean economy in support of this proposal were supplied by the State Department's economic mission to Korea in its despatch 117 of April 25, 1947; see also the mission's "The Economic Potential of an Independent Korea," prepared in collaboration with the South Korean Interim Government in June 1947.

7-11. Not released.

12. [add to original note, not released]: It is an interesting commentary on American priorities at the time that when the political urgency of land reform was finally recognized, the economic mission's proposal of February 1946 could not be found in Washington, and a new proposal had to be requested from the field. A history of the New Korea Company is contained in the U.S. Mission's Despatch 265, Aug. 18, 1948.

13-26. Not released.

27. [add to original note, not released]: The files also record that Colonel M. Preston Goodfellow, former member of the Office of Strategic Services and adviser to President Rhee as well as publisher of the Pocatello Tribune-Journal, approached the Armour Research Foundation in February 1949 for a survey of Korean mineral and industrial capabilities.   The State Department, approached by Armour to verify Goodfellow's status, apparently gave the firm no encouragement. Goodfellow was prominent among the Americans identified as Rhee's "kitchen cabinet."

28-39. Not released.

40. [add to original note, not released]: The Ambassador's recommendations were under ten headings: control of government expenditures and establishment of budgetary accounting controls; control over extension of bank credit and creation of government debt; elimination of subsidies in prices and rates of government-produced goods and services; increase of counterpart deposit rate, etc.; improvement of tax assessments, enforcement of tax collection, and elimination of the "voluntary contribution" system; expansion of extraordinary and non-recurring government revenues (e.g., vested property sales, which had moved at a glacial rate); implementation of the land reform law; expansion of exports and facilitation of improved imports; unitary rate of foreign exchange; termination of the rice purchase program.

41-50. Not released.

51. [add to original note, not released]: ECA retained responsibility for supply and advice to agriculture, fisheries, and civil industrial facilities not utilized by the UN Command, as well as fiscal advisory assistance, certain training programs, requirements and plans for postwar rehabilitation, and information and analysis regarding Korean

economic problems. ECA was also responsible for assistance to the UN Command, at its request, in Korean distribution of supplies by the Koreans to prevent disease and unrest.

52-70. Not released.

71. In the original manuscript of this study, the final chapter dealt at some length with the problems of foreign businessmen in Korea; it had to be omitted for space reasons. Briefly, as foreign business interest in Korea increased after 1953 and U.S.-Korean problems also increased, the Korean government imposed new restrictions on the entry of foreign businessmen; it also enforce income-tax regulations more strictly. Following Ambassador Lacy's arrival, in June 1955, businessmen were told to pay a business tax, based on a new interpretation of a 1949 law, retroactive to 1954 or earlier. Businessmen were outraged, and the American Chamber of Commerce in Korea issued a sharp protest, which angered the Koreans. By August 29, eight businessmen had been denied exit visas because their taxes were not paid. Efforts of the U.S. Embassy on behalf of the businessmen were fruitless, despite the personal involvement of Ambassador Lacy. The Ambassador resigned his post and departed Korea on October 20, 1955. Within a week, the atmosphere surrounding the tax controversy had dramatically improved, and the issues were resolved soon thereafter.

72-106. Not released.

Chapter 8. Korean Economic Development: The March to Self-Reliance, 1957-1965

1-41. Not released.

42. [add to original footnote, not released]: (For a historical study of banking and financial policies in Korea, see a study prepared by the ROK Ministry of Finance in August 1966, "Outline of Banking System and Policy of Korea," transmitted by U.S. Embassy airgram in November 1966.)

43-45. Not released.

46. [add to original footnote, not released]: The American bureaucratic effort involved in these negotiations was enormous. One cable to Seoul was labelled, "Joint State/AID/Treasury/Defense/Agriculture message"!

47-57. Not released.

Index

Fulbright, J. William 178

Gaillard, John P. 43
General Order No. 1 (SCAP) 1
Geneva Conference 53, 54
Germany 113, 135, 141, 292
Gilbert Associates 246
Gilpatric, Roswell L. 69, 102
Girard case 87
Glass 270
  factory financed by U.S. 270
Gold bullion (ROK claim) 117
Good offices mission. *See* Normalization
Goodfellow, Preston 114
Government Aid and Relief in
  Occupied Areas (GARIOA)
  229, 232, 240, 258
Grain collection 243, 244
Gray, Gordon 96
Great Britain. *See* United Kingdom
Greater sanctions statement 50
Greece 67, 70, 264
Green, Marshall 72, 160, 285, 290
  appraisal of military coup 213,
  214
  meets coup leader 216
  supports legal government 208
Greenhill 46
Gross, Ernest 15
Guerrilla activity 44, 105. 244

Hahm, Pyong-Choon 114
Hahm, Tai-Yung 189
Hallstein doctrine 113
Han, Pyo-Wook 53, 58, 121
Han'guk Democratic party 154,
  160, 171, 184
Han'gul (Korean alphabet) 237
Hankook Ilbo 294
Harriman, W. Averill 69, 220
Harrington, Julian 129
Harvard University 227
Hemmendinger, Noel 83
Henderson, Gregory 181
Henderson, Loy W. 201

Herren, 251
Herter, Christian 59, 69, 127, 138,
  201
Hijacking
  of south Korean airplane 57
Hilldring, J.H. 149, 182, 236
Hilsman, Roger, Jr. 224
Hoarding 234, 244
Hodge, John R. 1, 4-6, 38, 39, 41,
  42, 104, 156, 163
Hoffman, Paul G. 165, 239, 242
Holt, Vivian 139
Hong, Chin-Ki 202, 204
Hornig, Donald 299
Howze, Hamilton H. 98, 102, 108
Huh, Chung 80, 120, 123, 132, 133,
  159, 160, 283
  acting president 207
  modifies "march north" policy 59
Hull, John E. 73, 100, 130
Human rights 41
Hungary 55
Hwan (Korean currency unit) 258,
  276
Hyangbodan 164

Ideology 37
Ikeda, Hayato 133, 134
Illegal Korean entrants in Japan
  124
Imports 262
  controls 294
  luxury products 295
  substitution problems 263
Inch'on 92
Independence 4, 6, 153
India 99
Individual liberties 141, 231. *See
  also* Politics
Indonesia 60
Industry
  activity 291
  production 247
  projects approved 270
  survey 236
Inflation 83, 183, 230, 233, 234,